OPEN ROAD TRAVEL GUIDES SHOW YOU
HOW TO BE A TRAVELER – NOT A TOURIST!

*Whether you're going abroad or planning a trip in the United States, take Open Road along on your journey. Our books have been praised by **Travel & Leisure, The Los Angeles Times, Newsday, Booklist, US News & World Report, Endless Vacation, American Bookseller, Coast to Coast,** and many other magazines and newspapers!*

Don't just see the world – experience it with Open Road!

ABOUT THE AUTHOR

Larry H. Ludmer is a professional travel writer whose Open Road travel guides include *Utah Guide, Arizona Guide, New Mexico Guide*, and *Colorado Guide*. Larry is also the updater and co-author of Open Road's *Las Vegas Guide*.

His other travel books include *Arizona, Colorado & Utah; The Northern Rockies; The Great American Wilderness: Touring America's National Parks*; and *Cruising Alaska*.

BE A TRAVELER, NOT A TOURIST - WITH OPEN ROAD TRAVEL GUIDES!

Open Road Publishing has guide books to exciting, fun destinations on four continents. As veteran travelers, our goal is to bring you the best travel guides available anywhere!

No small task, but here's what we offer:

• All Open Road travel guides are written by authors with a distinct, opinionated point of view – not some sterile committee or team of writers. Our authors are experts in the areas covered and are polished writers.

• Our guides are geared to people who want to make their own travel choices. We'll show you how to discover the real destination – not just see some place from a tour bus window.

• We're strong on the basics, but we also provide terrific choices for those looking to get off the beaten path and experience the country or city – not just see it or pass through it.

• We give you the best, but we also tell you about the worst and what to avoid. Nobody should waste their time and money on their hard-earned vacation because of bad or inadequate travel advice.

• Our guides assume nothing. We tell you everything you need to know to have the trip of a lifetime - presented in a fun, literate, no-nonsense style.

• And, above all, we welcome your input, ideas, and suggestions to help us put out the best travel guides possible.

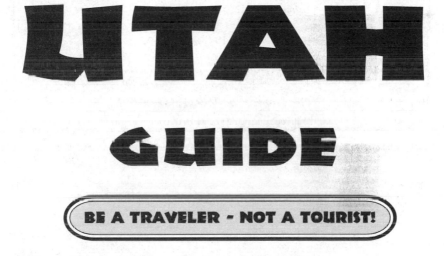

UTAH GUIDE

BE A TRAVELER - NOT A TOURIST!

Larry Ludmer

OPE ROAD PUBLISHI G

1st Edition

Front and back cover photos copyright©1999 by James Kay Photography (www.jameskay.com). Maps by James Ramage.

TABLE OF CONTENTS

SIDEBARS

1. INTRODUCTION

It is difficult to comprehend, let alone see, all of the beauty that nature has bestowed upon the world. How can one possibly even decide what is the most beautiful place of all? A most difficult task–but I don't feel that I'm going out on a limb by unequivocally stating that Utah has far more than its share of the most beautiful scenery in all the world, and certainly among the most unusual. Not just majestic snow-covered mountains (although the state has lots of that), but dazzling places where mother nature almost seems to have run amok and that almost defy description. They simply must be seen to be believed and even then you may be left rubbing your eyes to make certain you're seeing clearly.

Places like Arches, Bryce Canyon, Canyonlands, Capitol Reef and Zion. Five breathtaking national park treasures whose beauty is so overpowering that they can literally leave you on the verge of tears. My own experiences and those of many other seasoned travelers is that a visit to Bryce, for example, is a more profound experience than the Grand Canyon, even though the latter is a much more known destination. The national parks, monuments and recreation areas of Utah aren't the only splendid scenic wonders in this remarkable land of strange shapes and vivid colors. Kodachrome Basin, the Goosenecks and Goblin Valley, to name just a handful of dozens of equally fantastic state parks and reservations, will vie strongly for your attention and memories.

Utah is also the ideal destination for the outdoor enthusiast. Boating, fishing and hiking are just some of the many popular pursuits that attract travelers to Utah. Adventure travelers will find plenty of challenges, too. And don't forget the winter, because Utah has outstanding skiing. While the slopes and resorts may be fewer in number than in neighboring Colorado, the quality is first class all the way. In fact, the state's slogan–"the greatest snow on earth"–is supported by many avid skiers who come back again and again to Utah.

Even if mother nature isn't your prime interest, Utah still has much to offer. Salt Lake City is the largest community in the state and for a city of its size boasts a surprisingly sophisticated cultural life. It's also the home of the Mormon Church, one of the fastest growing religions in the world. Beautiful Temple Square is the location of the impressive Mormon Temple and the famous Tabernacle with its acoustic perfection.

This book contains everything you'll need to plan a trip to every corner of Utah, whether it's a short holiday weekend jaunt or a lengthy exploration. Hotels, restaurants, recreation, nightlife and entertainment are all covered, as are dozens of practical tips. Extensive sightseeing information will acquaint you with the well-known attractions, as well as scores of lesser known points of interest. With a little planning you'll be all ready to explore Utah and all of its wonders on your own. I'm confident that it will be more than just another vacation trip...it's an experience that you will never forget.

2. OVERVIEW

Strange natural wonders fill the state from one end to the other. Perhaps it is fitting because so many Americans are unfamiliar with Utah. Maybe the vast open spaces of the Great Salt Lake Desert and other remote regions make it seem as if Utah is somehow different than the rest of the United States. Perhaps the common belief that Utah is inhabited only by Mormons, long a misunderstood group to be sure, adds a little more to that impression of strangeness. Well, it isn't an exotic foreign locale, but Utah does have a degree of difference that makes a visit to this state so special. As the biggest city has only around 200,000 people, there's plenty of room for you to spread out and not much traffic or congestion to contend with.

Utah is unlike many other western states in several respects. First of all there are far fewer major Indian reservations as well as considerably less history associated with Native Americans. In fact, there's a whole lot less "cowboys and Indians" atmosphere. This is, in a way, a result of Utah's natural splendor. The land was inhospitable to settlement and Native American tribes never occupied the territory that now comprises Utah in great numbers. Certainly, the level of their civilization never matched what was achieved in some of the other southwestern states. The ghost towns of mining days so common in neighboring states are also relatively scarce, as Utah's history didn't include nearly the level of wild and rambunctious frontier settlements of Arizona, Colorado or even New Mexico. Some of this can be attributed to the Mormon influence on the state's nineteenth century development. All of this is good news for the visitor, because it helps to make Utah quite a bit different than the states that surround it.

Outdoor activities in Utah are, however, just as abundant as in other western states. Activities range from the mildest to the wildest. There is something for every interest and level of expertise.

Because Utah is such a large state you have to possess a plan in order to take in as many of the sights and activities as possible. This book will

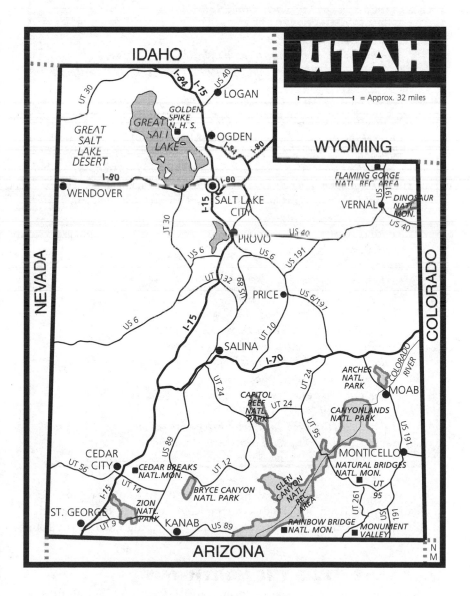

UTAH PROFILE

Entered the Union: January 4, 1896, becoming the 45th state
Area: 84,904 square miles, ranks 12th
Number of counties: 29
Number of state parks: 45
Number of areas administered by National Park Service: 14
Population: 2,000,494 (official 1996 Census Bureau estimate),
ranks 34th.
Population growth (1990-1996): 16.1%
Population density: 21 (United States average is 73)
Largest localities: Salt Lake City, 159,9278; West Valley City, 86,
969; Provo, 86,835; Sandy, 75,240; Orem, 67,561; Ogden, 63,943;
Taylorsville-Bennion, 52,351; West Jordan, 42,915; Layton, 41,784;
Logan, 32,771. (All of the above communities except Provo, Orem, Ogden,
Layton and Logan are part of the Salt Lake City metropolitan area.)
Nickname: Beehive State
Motto: Industry
State flower: Sego lily
State bird: Sea Gull
State tree: Blue spruce
State song: Utah, We Love Thee
Highest point: King's Peak, 13,528 feet
Lowest point: Beaver Wash Dam, 2,200 feet
Tourism industry: Almost $4 billion a year.
Major agricultural products: Hay, corn, wheat, barley, apples,
potatoes, cherries, onions, peaches, pears
Major natural resources: Copper, potash, gold, molybdenum, iron
ore, magnesium, salt
Major manufactured products: Electronic components, food prod-
ucts, medical instruments, steel, transportation equipment

help you do that by dividing Utah into four different touring regions that you can identify from our "Utah Touring Regions" map. The remainder of this chapter is mainly devoted to briefly describing each of the four regions.

SALT LAKE CITY & THE NORTHWEST

Salt Lake City is the state's capital and largest city. Set along the foothills of the magnificent **Wasatch Mountains**, it provides a beautiful urban landscape with outstanding architecture, spacious streets, parks, and an unusual amount of cultural activity for a city of its size. As headquarters of the worldwide **Mormon Church**, Salt Lake City boasts a lot of interesting facilities that document the history of Mormonism. In fact, **Temple Square** is literally the heart of the city, an impressive collection of buildings and monuments. The area around Salt Lake City provides natural beauty with a host of recreational possibilities. Several canyons to the east of the city are the focal points for outdoor recreation. World class ski resorts in **Park City** and other communities are within an easy short drive of downtown Salt Lake City.

The **Great Salt Lake** itself is also high on the list of attractions that visitors to this area want to see. A day of swimming on the lake can literally be a buoyant experience! The contrast between lake and the desert to the west is quite stunning. Other attractions nearby include the Kennecott Copper open pit mine in **Bingham Canyon** and the place where the nation's transcontinental railroads first linked together.

Among the other communities of interest in this region are **Ogden**, **Logan** and **Provo**. The latter, especially, has many things to see and do. These include recreation on **Utah Lake**, a visit to **Timpanogos Cave National Monument** and **Brigham Young University** with its many museums.

SOUTHWEST UTAH: COLOR COUNTRY

Few places in the world can match the unusual beauty of southwestern Utah (except perhaps for southeastern Utah). **Color Country** aptly describes the never ending panorama of vividly shaded rocks that fill this region from end to end. And the nature of the rock formations is often stunning, at times even overpowering. Sometimes fanciful, sometimes bordering on the bizarre, but always beautiful, the national parks and monuments, state scenic reserves, as well as simply driving along miles of lonely stretches of highway, nature is at its most unusual and constantly on display. Well known places like **Zion** and **Bryce** may be the star attractions, but **Cedar Breaks**, **Kodachrome Basin**, **Snow Canyon** and many others are all awaiting their chance to dazzle you with their own special beauty.

You can see it the easy way, from your car or by many easy walks, or you can choose to do it the adventurous way, by rock climbing, four-wheel adventures on back roads or hiking in remote areas. Either way the outdoor nature of a trip to the southwest will dominate. But there are also some interesting towns as well, like **St. George** and **Cedar City**. The latter, for instance, is well known for its outstanding Shakespearean festival held each summer. While the southwest is quite arid in general, there is enough snowfall in the mountains during the winter to provide for some first class skiing as well. The **Brian Head** area is just one outstanding area ski resort.

SOUTHEAST UTAH: CANYON LANDS

The break between the attractions of Color Country and **Canyon Lands** isn't a sharp one. Nature has chosen to instead slowly blend one into the other. But a book isn't like mother nature and the line has to be drawn somewhere. Although the landscape of southeastern Utah has more than its share of colorful and unusual rock formations, it is best known for the amazing beautiful gorges that have been carved out by the Colorado and other rivers.

It is these river forces that have created **Canyonlands National Park** and the superb **Dead Horse Point State Park**. Other types of erosion contributed to the splendid scenery that awaits you at **Arches National Park, Capitol Reef National Park**, the **Goblin Valley**, the **Goosenecks and Natural Bridges National Monument**. While even the names are often unusual they serve as fitting introductions to sights that have to be seen to be believed and fully appreciated. Words and pictures can only begin to tell the story of the delights of canyon country.

PROTECTING NATURE'S HANDIWORK

The sights of Utah are for all to see and enjoy. Protecting this often fragile landscape for future visitors is everyone's business. The rules for doing so are simple and represent the state of Utah's official "tread lightly" policy.

• Tread lightly when traveling, and leave no trace of your camping area.

• Help keep the forests and canyons clean. Pick up and pack out trash and dispose of human waste properly.

• Protect and conserve water sources. Carry your own water for drinking and washing to protect scarce desert water sources and forest watershed areas.

• Allow space for wildlife. Maintain your distance and remain quiet. Don't chase or pick up wild animals and keep pets under control.

• Leave historic sites, rock art, ruins and artifacts untouched for the future. Admire remnants from a distance and report violations.

It isn't too often that I can wholeheartedly concur with the pronouncements of government, but these five policy statements are good advice indeed.

Not all of the sights in this region are natural either. **Lake Powell** is one of North America's largest man-made lakes. Its brilliant blue waters contrast with the blazing red rocks that tower above the shoreline. The lake shares space with the southwest touring region although the biggest part is in the southeast. In general, when speaking of man-made sights they're much harder to come by in sparsely populated southeast Utah. **Moab**, with a population of fewer than 5,000 people, is the region's largest community. On the other hand, it is one of the oldest inhabited parts of the state. Of the few remains of ancient Indian civilizations that do exist in Utah, most are located in this corner of the state. **The Navajo Indian Reservation**, mostly associated with Arizona, extends into this area as well.

The opportunities for outdoor recreation in the southeast are similar to those in the southwest except that there isn't any skiing. One thing that there is more of, though, is river rafting. The Colorado, San Juan and other rivers offer some of the best white water to be found anywhere. Adventurers and visitors looking to get away from the maddening crowd will both surely love the solitude of Canyon Lands.

NORTHEAST UTAH: DINOSAUR COUNTRY

More remains of **dinosaurs** have been found in this part of Utah than anywhere else in the world. Although lots of them have found their way to museums throughout America and elsewhere, there's still plenty of evidence of dinosaurs to make a trip to the northwest a most interesting and educational experience. You'll see not only dinosaur quarries and fossilized remains in place where they've been for millions of years, but excellent museums that explain what is known to science about these creatures in understandable terms.

But dinosaur remains aren't the only thing on tap in Dinosaur Country. The region is part of the Rocky Mountains and contains some of the most impressive mountain scenery in all of Utah. Much of it is in designated primitive and wilderness areas that are accessible only to the true adventurer, but some can be easily reached as well. Some of the wild areas along the **Green River** in **Gray Canyon** and **Desolation Canyon** can only be seen by a river rafting expedition. For drivers, gorgeous scenery awaits you along the **Drive Through the Ages** and in the **Flaming Gorge National Recreation Area**.

Although portions of the northeast aren't far from Salt Lake City, this is a region of sparse population and many small towns. All of its communities have fewer than 10,000 people. A simple, outdoor life style prevails both for residents and visitors. While most of the region isn't quite as spectacular as southern Utah is, it is ideal for those who want to hunt, fish, hike or just desire to get away from it all. Finally, in keeping with the rural character, many of Utah's guest ranches can be found in the northeast.

THE BEST OF UTAH

You're going to encounter several lists of "bests" as you read on. This not only satisfies my compulsion to compile lists of different things but has a more practical side for you as well. Since you almost certainly won't have the time to do every attraction and activity in this book, even if you had the inclination to do so, "best" lists are a good way to make sure that you do the things that are most important to you. The places I've selected would probably appear on almost every experienced Utah visitor's list of must-sees. It should come as no surprise that the Best of Utah is dominated by natural splendors. And the winners are, in alphabetical order:

• ***Arches National Park****: The world's greatest concentration of natural rock arches amid an artist's palate of rich colors and unusual formations.*

*•****Bryce Canyon National Park****: Expert travelers will gladly tell you that few places in the entire world can compare with Bryce!*

• ***Canyonlands National Park/Deadhorse Point State Park****: Geographic and geologic neighbors, one large and one small, will both delight you with awe-inspiring vistas of endless, deep and winding gorges as well as other natural wonders.*

• ***Capitol Reef National Park****: A massive colorful rock wall stretching for miles and miles is just the beginning of this vast park that is unknown to so many travelers. Maybe that makes it even more enjoyable–it's our private secret.*

• ***Lake Powell boating****: whether it's via a guided boat tour, a sailboat or just floating serenely around on a rented houseboat, Lake Powell's deep blue waters, colorful mountains and side channels filled with wonders (like Rainbow Bridge National Monument) will relax and astound.*

• ***Monument Valley Navajo Tribal Park****: So what if this attraction is shared with Arizona–beauty knows no borders and the famous sights of towering rock formations above a desert floor are out of this world.*

• ***Panguitch-Escalante-Boulder Scenic Highway****: Commonly known by the more mundane name of Utah State Highway 12, this is 120 miles of sheer joy! There are beautiful sights at every turn and plenty of turns in this road that can be enjoyed by adventurer and casual motorist alike.*

• ***Temple Square****: If there's one thing that Utah is known for besides natural beauty, it's the Mormons, and what better place to exemplify that aspect of the state than this impressive square that lies at the heart of Salt Lake City.*

• ***Utah Shakespearean Festival****: Plays in a Globe-style theater, merry making a la medieval England on the green and much more highlight this most enjoyable summer long event.*

• ***Zion National Park****: It's back to nature for my final selection and what a way to end the list. Gigantic rock formations with fanciful names, narrow canyons and sprawling vistas abound.*

3. SUGGESTED ITINERARIES

As a travel writer, I am frequently asked by people how much time to allocate for a visit to various destinations. Unfortunately, that's an impossible question to answer in a simple manner. It depends upon your level of interest in the sights and activities of a particular area as well as, of course, your available time and budget.

These considerations certainly apply to Utah, which is a big state with so much to see and do. While you can see many of the highlights in a few days, it would take at least a month to cover everything that is in this book. Utah is the type of place that visitors return to again and again so that they can explore things that are of special interest to them in greater depth. Therefore, the itineraries in this chapter will range from only a few days to more than two weeks. One or more should coincide with the approximate amount of time you have for a vacation. The itineraries don't have a step-by-step, attraction-by-attraction detail: instead, the idea is to provide you with a framework for each day that allows you a degree of flexibility. You can add another sight or two or take some time off to relax.

The itineraries are by type. The first one is primarily for those people who are interested in visiting Utah's largest city, while itineraries two through five closely correspond with the regional destination chapters. Another concentrates on Utah's national parks since they are among the top attractions in bringing visitors to the state. Two other tours pretty well cover the entire state, one in greater detail than the other. There is also a tour that is ideally suited to visitors who will be traveling through Utah rather than concentrating on it as their main destination.

Most of the itineraries do involve moving from one place to another each night, but a few also stay put for several days at a time. In fact, many of the attractions are especially well suited to being seen via a series of day trips from one location. If this type of travel has appeal to you, look at the sidebar later in this chapter. Any trip in this chapter can be extended for as long as you want should you decide to relax at the pool or partake in sports. This is important to remember because the itineraries allow for sightseeing time but not for recreational pursuits.

Because Utah is not a heavily populated state the level of public transportation is rather slim. Only in the Salt Lake City-Ogden-Provo corridor is there good bus transportation. Therefore, the first itinerary and most attractions in the second can be easily managed using local or regional bus service, but it's not a good way to get around most of Utah. A final important point to keep in mind is that these itineraries assume that you will be arriving in Salt Lake City because that is the only major airport with service to all parts of the country. Where other starting points are logical, it will be so noted.

Remember, too, that these itineraries are merely suggestions. After you've read through the regional destination chapters and have a better idea of what you want to see, you can start to play around with the itineraries–adding things, dropping others and combining portions of two or more trips. Chances are you'll come up with something ideally suited to your tastes and the amount of time you have available.

ITINERARY 1: SALT LAKE CITY PLUS

(5 Days/4 Nights)

While the majority of visitors to Utah come to explore the wonders of nature there is plenty to see in the state's capital and largest city. This trip is for the city lover but there's also enough time to get around to some of the scenic sights that lie within close proximity to Salt Lake City.

Day 1

Settle into town and use the afternoon to see the many sights in and around Temple Square as well as the State Capitol. Perhaps you can see a show or attend a concert in the evening.

Day 2

The rest of the city also has plenty to see. Visit the impressive Pioneer Monument in Emigration Canyon, the zoo, University of Utah and much more. Shoppers can find plenty of interest in the historic and unique Trolley Square.

Day 3

A lovely drive is afforded by following a loop consisting of Interstates 80, 84 and 15. The route is on excellent roads through the beautiful Wasatch Mountains and passes beautiful Park City, one of Utah's premier ski centers, as well as many interesting sights in Ogden.

Day 4

Today you head south along I-15 to visit Provo, home to the many museums and other sights of Brigham Young University. Return via a

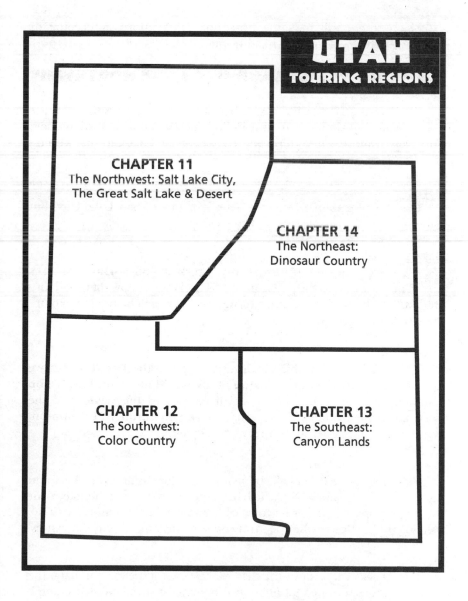

UTAH
TOURING REGIONS

CHAPTER 11
The Northwest: Salt Lake City,
The Great Salt Lake & Desert

CHAPTER 14
The Northeast:
Dinosaur Country

CHAPTER 12
The Southwest:
Color Country

CHAPTER 13
The Southeast:
Canyon Lands

scenic mountain route that passes pretty Bridal Veil Falls and allows time for a visit to Timpanogos Cave National Monument.

Day 5

Maybe there will be some time for a little more sightseeing or shopping before you have to head home.

ITINERARY 2: SALT LAKE CITY & THE NORTHWEST
(7 Days/6 Nights)

This trip is an extension of the first itinerary. It covers much of the same ground but allows more time in outlying areas than in the city itself. You'll also explore some interesting areas near Salt Lake City that weren't part of the previous trip.

Day 1

Use the afternoon to explore the highlights of Salt Lake City, but especially the impressive sights of the Temple Square area.

Day 2

After stopping at Emigration Canyon pick up I-80 east and visit Park City. Continue east to the junction of I-84 and then follow that road into Ogden, your home for the next two nights. There will be time to explore the city this afternoon.

Day 3

North from Ogden this morning to explore Brigham City before moving onto the Golden Spike National Historic Monument. Then a loop route through some interesting small towns and the scenery of the Wasatch-Cache National Forest that takes you through Tremonton, Logan and Mantua before returning to Ogden.

Day 4

Explore the Great Salt Lake by visiting Antelope Island State Park and then proceed west along I-80, which hugs the south shore of the lake. Your overnight stop is in the border town of Wendover but you should visit the Salt Flats of the Bonneville Speedway before finishing the day's activities.

Day 5

Head back now towards the east. Make a stop at the vast pit that is the Kennecott Copper open pit mine in Bingham canyon. Upon reaching I-15 head south to Provo. You'll have time this afternoon to explore BYU and its many museums.

Day 6

North from Provo this morning through the canyon of the same name. See Bridal Veil Falls and Timpanogos Cave National Monument. Then its through Heber City to Park City and the several ski resort areas (beautiful and busy year round) that lie to the east of Salt Lake City which you'll reach late in the day.

Day 7

There should be some time to hit a few more sights in town before you depart for home.

ITINERARY 3: THE SOUTHWEST (COLOR COUNTRY)
(8 Days/7 Nights)

The name of this region hardly does justice to the many wonderful sights you're going to see on this fascinating adventure. If your Utah trip is going to be limited to the sights of the southwest you might consider using Las Vegas as your gateway city if flying in from another part of the country. It's actually closer than Salt Lake City. If you do, arrange the itinerary as a loop from St. George rather than Salt Lake. St. George is less than three hours drive from Las Vegas.

Day 1

Travel from Salt Lake City south on I-15. Visit the historic territorial state house in Fillmore. Then its on to the first scenic wonder–Cedar Breaks National Monument, a fitting preview to what is to come later on. Then check into your accommodations in nearby Cedar City. If you visit during the famous Shakespeare Festival then you're in for a special treat this evening.

Day 2

The beautiful Kolob Canyons section of Zion National Park is not far from Cedar City, just off the Interstate, physically separated from the main portion of the park and not heavily visited. From here it's on to St. George, a growing and bustling community in Utah's mild "Dixie." There are a number of interesting attractions in and around town, including the beautiful Snow Canyon State Park.

Day 3

Leave St. George this morning and travel through the increasingly beautiful scenery until you arrive at Zion National Park. Visit Zion Canyon and then travel through the fantastic Zion-Mount Carmel Highway. Then it's on to Kanab, an attractive community set amid colorful mountains and cliffs not far from the Arizona border.

Day 4

Skirt the border before going a couple of miles into Arizona and the town of Page. Take a boat ride on vividly blue Lake Powell in the Glen Canyon National Recreation Area (which is almost entirely within Utah). See incredible Rainbow Bridge National Monument. You'll return to Kanab for the night.

Day 5

From Kanab it is under a two hour drive to one of the world's greatest sights–Bryce Canyon National Park. You'll have almost the whole day to explore this natural wonder as accommodations are available inside or immediately adjacent to the park.

Day 6

The scenery doesn't end with Bryce. Today you'll be amazed by the sights along Utah Highway 12, also known as the Panguitch-Escalante-Boulder Scenic Highway. See Kodachrome Basin and numerous other wonders before ending the day in the small town of Torrey. (Time permitting you can take a brief detour into the southeast region and take a peek at Capitol Reef National Park.)

Day 7

This morning will be devoted to the pleasant drive back to Salt Lake City. You should have a few hours upon your arrival to at least see the highlights of Utah's capital city.

Day 8

Today you travel home with fond memories of so many outstanding sights.

ITINERARY 4: THE SOUTHEAST (CANYON LANDS)

(8 Days/7 Nights)

As you'll soon see, the southwestern quarter of Utah certainly doesn't have a monopoly on outstanding scenery. The natural wonders of Utah's canyon country are among the most remarkable places on earth.

Day 1

It's a long haul from Salt Lake City to Moab, your temporary base for the first two nights of this trip. You should have some time to explore this small town, which has been home to many famous motion picture productions.

Day 2

The entire morning will be devoted to the scenic splendors of nearby Arches National Park. More beauty is on tap in the afternoon as you take a short loop trip through the Manti-La Sal National Forest.

Day 3

Nothing can quite prepare you for the awesome sight that is Canyonlands National Park and the much smaller but equally gorgeous vistas from adjacent Dead Horse Point State Park. These two attractions will take up almost the entire day, allowing the later afternoon for the ride to the town of Monticello.

Day 4

A pleasant two-hour jaunt south brings you to famous Monument Valley with its towering and colorful rock formations. Located on the Navajo Indian Reservation, Monument Valley straddles the Arizona-Utah border. Drive through the valley yourself or take a guided four wheel jeep tour for an even better experience. Spend the night in the tiny community of Gouldings that is just outside of Monument Valley.

Day 5

After making brief stops at three close by scenic attractions–the Goosenecks, Valley of the Gods, and Muley Point Overlook, you'll spend some more time at the Natural Bridges National Monument before heading out on Utah state route 95–one of the more desolate yet beautiful roads in the nation. Overnight will be in Hanksville, population about 100 hardy souls.

Day 6

The last of the southwest's star attractions is unforgettable Capitol Reef National Park. Then you'll head northwest, finally reaching Interstate 15 and checking in for the evening in Nephi.

Day 7

It is under two hours from Nephi back to Salt Lake City. You can choose between doing some of the attractions in the Provo area or concentrate on the bigger capital city. Maybe a combination of both will be more to your liking.

Day 8

It's time to return home to the real world.

ITINERARY 5: THE NORTHEAST
(DINOSAUR COUNTRY)

(7 Days/6 Nights)

The northeast part of Utah is more isolated and less visited than most of the areas we've quickly taken a look at so far, but it doesn't have a lack of things to do and see. But because it is smaller there will be time to combine this section with a more thorough visit to the Salt Lake City area.

Day 1

Heading south for a short while on I-15, we'll first take a loop around the Provo area before proceeding through Nephi and Manti and the Wasatch Plateau on the way to Price, your first night's stop.

Day 2

In the vicinity of Price are a museum and dinosaur quarry that will serve as an excellent introduction to Dinosaur Country. After that it's on to Vernal, where you will stay for three nights. The Utah Field House of Natural History highlight's the town's attractions.

Day 3

You'll be taking an all day excursion to nearby Dinosaur National Monument, which spills over the Utah state line into a remote corner of northwestern Colorado. You'll explore both parts and learn much about the many dinosaurs that roamed these parts millions of years ago. The Monument also contains some wonderful scenery.

Day 4

US Highway 191 north of Vernal is highly scenic and important from a geological standpoint because the rocks in this area are a lesson in earth's history. The beautiful journey is known as the Drive through the Ages and ends at the spectacular Flaming Gorge National Recreation Area, which you can take all afternoon to explore before returning to Vernal.

Day 5

It's about 3-1/2 hours from Vernal back to Salt Lake City but add some time near the end of this jaunt to visit Park City. The afternoon can be used to begin your exploration of Salt Lake City. It will also be your home for tonight and tomorrow night.

Day 6

You'll have a full day to finish seeing all the city's sights. Or perhaps you will want to spend some time taking a look at the Great Salt Lake or open pit mine in Bingham Canyon. They are all nearby so the possibilities are almost endless.

Day 7

Perhaps some last minute sightseeing, shopping or just relaxing before it's time to bring this trip to a close.

ITINERARY 6: NATIONAL PARKS OF SOUTHERN UTAH

(7 Days/6 Nights)

It would be hard to argue with the fact that Utah's national parks are the true highlights of the state. If you love nature, and especially unusual scenery, then this week-long trip will be hard to beat.

Day 1

Journey from Salt Lake City to Moab where you'll be staying for two nights.

Day 2

What could be a more fulfilling day than to explore the wonders of Arches National Park in the morning and Canyonlands National Park in the afternoon. It will be a long and busy day but one that you'll be sure to cherish forever.

Day 3

The drive from Moab to Bryce covers 270 miles, almost all of it highly scenic. That's especially true of the afternoon along Utah Highway 12, the state's best known scenic byway. But that's only after you've spent a few hours in the middle of the day exploring lightly visited Capitol Reef National Park, a gem that is unknown to most travelers.

Day 4

A first time visitor to Bryce should allocate an entire day for this remarkable place and that's exactly what we're going to do.

Day 5

Leaving Bryce this morning we'll travel to Zion National Park. On the way in you will traverse the famous Zion-Mount Carmel Highway, an engineering wonder that will take you through rugged and beautiful country in surprising ease. Zion may well be Utah's best known national park. It's wonderful, as they all are. Picking out which one you like best may be an impossible task. From Zion it's a short ride to your overnight stop in St. George.

Day 6

Just a little north of St. George and immediately off of Interstate 15 is the Kolob Canyons section of Zion National Park. This won't quite be the last of the great scenery because a short loop off of I-15 from Cedar City to Parowan will bring you through Cedar Breaks National Monument which some people describe as a miniature Bryce. You'll reach Salt Lake City late in the day.

Day 7

Depending upon your connections home you may well have several hours to take in the highlights of the city. What a contrast that will be to the events of the last six days!

ITINERARY 7: THE INTERSTATE TRAVELER
(5 Days/4 Nights)

No doubt there are many travelers swinging through the western states who will want to take advantage of the time they spend driving through Utah by seeing some important attractions. This trip will let you do just that. It can, of course, be reversed to be done in the opposite direction.

Day 1

Crossing into Utah along I-15 in the extreme southwestern corner of the state at St. George you'll divert from the highway for the short ride east to Zion National Park before returning to St. George for the evening.

Day 2

Explore some of the sights in and around St. George before your next Interstate detour at Cedar City for Cedar Breaks National Monument. Then it's north on the highway until Provo, where you will spend the night.

Day 3

In the morning you can visit Brigham Young University and take the Alpine scenic loop road past Timpanogos Cave National Monument and then back to the highway. Another detour to Bingham Canyon to visit the Kennecott Copper open pit mine before finally reaching Salt Lake City in the late afternoon.

Day 4

You'll have a full day to explore the many attractions of Salt Lake City and the nearby mountain resorts.

Day 5

Two options present themselves for the final day in Utah depending upon your next destination. If you're headed north stay on I-15 and visit Ogden and Logan before heading into Idaho. Or if the east is on the agenda follow I-80 through a scenic portion of the Wasatch Mountains before you cross the border into Wyoming at Evanston.

ITINERARY 8: UTAH HIGHLIGHTS

(11 Days/10 Nights)

Because Utah has so many large and time consuming sights, even the short highlight tour has to involve well over a week! But you will have hit all of the high points and be a veteran explorer of scenic wonders.

Day 1

After arriving in Salt Lake City you'll utilize the afternoon to visit downtown, including Temple Square and the state capitol as well as Emigration Canyon.

Day 2

North to Ogden before looping around on Interstates 84 and 80 to Heber City and Provo. Brigham Young University and Bridal Veil Falls highlight the Provo area.

Day 3

Head south on I-15 from Provo stopping to visit the old territorial capital in Fillmore before making a call at Cedar Breaks National Monument. Overnight is in Cedar City, a pleasant college town that is home to a famous Shakespeare festival during the summer.

Day 4

It's a short drive south to St. George and the scenic state parks that surround the town. But the highlight of the day is a visit to Zion National Park. The day ends with the scenic ride to Bryce.

Day 5

All morning and the early afternoon will be used to discover Bryce Canyon National Park. Then it's an incredible scenic byway–Utah 12, the Panguitch-Escalante-Boulder Scenic Highway–which will bring you to your overnight destination, the town of Torrey.

Day 6

This morning you'll visit amazing Capitol Reef National Park and then head south on Utah 95, another highly scenic route. Stop at the

Natural Bridges National Monument before arriving in Mexican Hat for the evening.

Day 7

This morning you will visit unforgettable Monument Valley before heading north to Moab, your home for the next two nights.

Day 8

A spectacular day is on tap: Arches National Park in the morning and Canyonlands National Park in the afternoon. Also be sure to stop at Dead Horse Point State Park on the way out of Canyonlands.

Day 9

It will take the entire morning to drive from Moab to Vernal. Two nights will be spent in this tidy community. Visit the Utah Field House of Natural History and other in-town sights as a prelude to tomorrow.

Day 10

This morning you will visit the Utah section of Dinosaur National Monument. This is the short highlight tour, so there won't be time to go into the Colorado portion of the monument. Don't fret: you will use the afternoon, instead, to take a quick jaunt along the Drive Through the Ages and briefly visit Flaming Gorge National Recreation Area.

Day 11

An early drive back to Salt Lake City this morning to make connections for the return home.

ITINERARY 9: UTAH IN DEPTH

(16 Days/15 Nights)

This comprehensive trip covers everything that was included in the shorter highlight tour but allows some more time at the most important attractions as well as adding several places that weren't reached on the previous trip.

Day 1

Your first two nights will be spent in Salt Lake City. You should use the first afternoon to see the major sights of Utah's capital city.

Day 2

A drive westward along I-80 will take you past the Great Salt Lake and through the Great Salt Lake Desert to Wendover where you can visit the Salt Flats and the Bonneville Speedway. Then return to Salt Lake City.

Day 3

Before leaving the Salt Lake City area take the short detour to Bingham Canyon and visit the Kennecott Copper open pit mine. Then it's on to Provo to see the sights at Brigham Young University and the scenic loop north of town that includes Bridal Veil Falls and Timpanogos Cave National Monument. Overnight is in Provo.

Day 4

Heading south along I-15 from Provo this morning to Cedar Breaks National Monument and then on to Cedar City itself with its historic attractions like Iron Mission State Park and the Utah Shakespeare Festival.

Day 5

St. George and Zion National Park will take up almost the entire day. The last part of the day is the ninety minute drive through colorful country to Kanab, your home for the next two nights.

Day 6

An excursion to the Arizona border town of Page where you'll head back into Utah by boat to see the Glen Canyon National Recreation Area's beautiful Lake Powell and incredible Rainbow Bridge National Monument before returning to Kanab.

Day 7

In a couple of hours you'll reach Bryce Canyon National Park, thus enabling you to spend virtually the entire day taking in the marvels before you check in overnight in the park or just outside of it.

Day 8

An in-depth journey along the Panguitch-Escalante-Boulder Scenic Highway. Beginning with Kodachrome Basin the sights are almost continuous. The last attraction of the day is the equally fascinating Capitol Reef National Park. Then back-track a few miles to the town of Torrey where you can spend the night.

Day 9

At Hanksville you'll embark on the scenic drive along Utah 95 through one of the most remote portions of the state. In the afternoon visit Natural Bridges National Monument, Valley of the Gods and the Goosenecks State Park before arriving overnight in Gouldings, which is located just outside of Monument Valley.

Day 10

Beautiful Monument Valley covers an area along the Utah-Arizona border and is home to some of the most gorgeous and famous scenery in the southwest. In the afternoon you'll drive to Moab where you'll set up base camp for the next three evenings.

Day 11

You will have all day today to explore Canyonlands National Park. Adjacent and tiny (by comparison) Dead Horse Point State Park is geologically similar and equally spectacular.

Day 12

Most of the day will bring you face to face with the indescribable shapes of Arches National Park but before returning to Moab a drive on the Manti-La Sal National Forest scenic loop road is a worthwhile experience.

Day 13

The day will be mostly devoted to the long drive from Moab to Vernal. Along the way there are several interesting dinosaur related sights in the town of Price and more once you get to Vernal. Tonight and tomorrow night will be spent in Vernal.

Day 14

A full exploration of Dinosaur National Monument, including both the Utah and adjacent Colorado sections, requires just about a full day.

Day 15

Along the scenic Drive Through the Ages north into Flaming Gorge National Recreation Area. The last few hours of the day will be for the return drive through the rugged northwest to the town of Heber City, your last overnight stopping place.

Day 16

Park City and Ogden are on the agenda for your last morning before you return to Salt Lake City and connections home. It's been a long trip but one that has been packed with adventure.

SEEING UTAH FROM A HOME BASE

Some travelers don't mind living out of a suitcase, spending a night or two in one place and then moving on to the next destination. Certainly this allows you to see the most. But, for those of you who feel more comfortable being settled into a nice hotel and staying there, Utah offers the opportunity for seeing a great deal through a series of day trips. This is more so than in most of the neighboring southwestern states. The regional tour concept is especially well suited to this approach.

You can also combine the home base method with the more flexible point to point method. After several days at one base, go on to another and perhaps another, depending upon the total length of your trip.

TOURING AREA BASE(S)

Northwest: The northwest touring chapter already utilizes a home base approach from Salt Lake City. You could also stay in Provo, Ogden or the mountain resorts but the amount of driving would be more.

Southwest: Panguitch or Cedar City. Bryce is also a possibility.

Southeast: The southeast chapter makes use of Moab as a home base for a significant part of the trip. Blanding can be an alternative.

Northeast: Much of the region's attractions can be explored from a base in Vernal.

4. LAND & PEOPLE

LAND

While Utah covers a vast territory it is not as large as most of the other western inter-mountain states. In fact, of the five states that surround it only Idaho is a bit smaller. When thinking of Utah, the Great Salt Lake and the adjacent desert usually first come to mind. While both of those features are important aspects of the state's landscape, the variety of land forms within Utah is absolutely mind boggling. Mountains, plateaus, gorges and rock formations of limitless shape and form are everywhere. The southern half of the state is an especially scenic wonderland.

Utah occupies nearly 85,000 square miles of land, much of it remote and forbidding. The state is rectangular (with the north-south axis being longer) except for a block that is cut out of the northeast to form kind of a strange looking letter L. To the north is Idaho, while Wyoming fits into the "L" in part of the northern and eastern borders. Colorado is the neighbor along most of the eastern edge. Arizona lies to the south and Nevada to the west. Utah is one of the so-called **Four Corners** states because it shares the only point in the United States where four states converge. Besides Colorado and Arizona, New Mexico is diagonally across the Four Corners. Utah stretches approximately 350 miles from north to south and about 280 miles from east to west.

A geologist's description of Utah hardly begins to do it justice but it does help to understand the reasons for the unusual terrain. Utah can be divided into three distinct geological regions. The first and smallest is the **Rocky Mountains**. Occupying a relatively small area of the northeast in the L-shaped corner of the state, this extension of the Colorado and Wyoming Rockies includes the **Wasatch Range** that runs from north to south and the **Uinta Mountains**, the only major mountain chain in the United States that runs east to west. The latter are glacial in origin, while the upward thrusting of the earth's crust created the Wasatch.

The western third of the state (roughly encompassing the area located to the west of I-15) is a part of the **Great Basin**. This arid and mostly flat high country also contains scattered small mountains. A valley between the Great Basin and the Wasatch Range is the home of the overwhelming portion of Utah's population.

The Great Basin encompasses the **Great Salt Lake**, by far the state's largest body of water. While Great Salt Lake has one of the highest salt concentrations of any body of water in the world, nearby **Utah Lake** (the second largest) is fresh water. Both of them are remnants of a much larger body of water that existed in prehistoric times and is now known as Lake Bonneville. Great Salt Lake and Lake Utah as well as all of the rivers of the Great Basin region are interesting in that they do not flow into the sea. Rather, they drain into portions of this large natural basin–thus the origin of the name Great Basin.

THE GRAND CIRCLE

*It's almost certain that at some time during your journey through the southern half of Utah you will see or hear the term **Grand Circle**. This refers to a vast area of the southwest that is centered approximately at the Bullfrog Marina in the Glen Canyon National Recreation Area and covers everything within a radius of approximately 160 miles. It encompasses most of the Colorado Plateau and contains the greatest concentration of breathtaking scenery in all the world. All of southern Utah is part of it, as are a big chunk of northern Arizona (including the Grand Canyon), the southwest corner of Colorado (including Mesa Verde National Park) and a small corner of New Mexico including Shiprock and the Four Corners area.*

*The Grand Circle contains eight national parks and many more national monuments and other scenic areas. About two-thirds of it is in Utah, so if you explore southern Utah in detail you will be able to claim to be a Grand Circle veteran. A vacation (and it could be a lengthy one) comprised solely of the Grand Circle is a wonderful idea. All you have to do to complete preparations for it is to read this book and my **Colorado Guide**, **Arizona Guide** and **New Mexico Guide**–all published by Open Road Publishing. I hope that plug wasn't too subtle! But, all kidding aside, the Grand Circle is nature at its most glorious and amazing best.*

The biggest region of the state is the **Colorado Plateau**. Covering about half of Utah's land area, it is home to the greatest number of Utah's scenic wonders. Created by the carving action of rivers in the geologically soft sedimentary rock, the plateau is a high region of deep gorges. The state's largest rivers run through this region. These are the **Colorado River** and its two major tributaries, the **Green** and **San Juan Rivers**. While the action of rivers over millions of years is the chief architect of the many canyons for which the southeastern portion of the state is famous, the effects of wind and rain cannot be overlooked. The hundreds of natural arches, bridges and other unusual formations can be attributed at least partly to the latter forces of erosion. The splendid colors of southern Utah's rocky lands are mainly a result of iron and other minerals in the various rock strata. Abundant sunshine also helps to increase the dazzle of the colors that is so vivid that a portion of the state is officially known as Color Country.

Besides the aforementioned lakes and rivers there are few other significant natural bodies of water. However, the southern part of the state contains **Lake Powell**, the largest man-made body of water in Utah and one of the biggest in the United States. It extends into Arizona.

PEOPLE

With a population of just a little more than two million people Utah is, indeed, a lightly populated region. The overwhelming majority of those people live in a relatively small section of the state–a valley that extends from the Wasatch Mountain foothills on the east to the desert on the west. From north to south the urban corridor extends on both sides of I-15 for approximately a hundred miles, covering the area from Tremonton and Logan in the north to a little below Provo in the south. The state's ten largest cities as well as many of the next ten biggest all lie within this area.

Utah's population growth is one of the fastest in the nation. This results not only from a relatively high birth rate among the Mormon population but immigration from other parts of the nation. A favorable business climate has attracted an increasingly large number of companies to relocate to Utah, further accelerating the population growth.

Despite the recent influx of people from all over the country, the people of Utah remain relatively homogeneous compared to most other parts of the nation. Almost 90 percent of the population are of white European ancestry (Anglo-Saxon and Greek being the two largest subgroups within the main group). The most significant minority is the Hispanics, mostly Mexican, who comprise a little more than seven percent of the population. Utah has a surprisingly small Native American population–only about one percent. These are mostly the Ute Tribe who live on the Uintah & Ouray Indian Reservation in the northeast. Some Navajo reside on a portion of the huge Navajo lands that spill over into the southeast corner of Utah from Arizona and New Mexico. There are also about five other small Indian reservations in various parts of the state.

During Utah's earlier days, people of the Mormon faith comprised the vast majority of the state's population. The wider economic base of

THE MORMONS

Probably few groups in the United States are as misunderstood as the **Mormons** are. To many people they seem "different" than the rest of us based on what we've heard about their past (polygamy stands out in the minds of a lot of people) and limited contacts with them. Most of those contacts probably have been with Mormon missionaries trying to convert you. It is, for sure, a highly evangelical religion. But let's lay one thing to rest right off the bat—polygamy was never common in Mormon society. Even in the old days fewer than five percent of Mormon men practiced polygamy. Those who do today are excommunicated from the church. There are now more than eight million Mormons in over 130 countries, but Utah is their stronghold, representing home to one in every eight Mormons worldwide.

The Mormon religion, officially known as the Church of Jesus Christ of Latter-day Saints (they refer to themselves as "Saints" and all non-Mormons are called "Gentiles") is based upon the belief of revelations from God that Christianity must return to its pure form—that other churches are corrupt. That accounts for its evangelical "true" church program, but it is highly tolerant of other religions. Beliefs are set down in, besides the Bible, the **Book of Mormon** and two other documents known as **Doctrine & Convenants** and the **Pearl of Great Price**. The **Book of Mormon** is claimed to have been discovered by church founder **Joseph Smith**—the location given to him by the **Angel Moroni** and divine inspiration helping him to translate the gold plates which contained inscriptions in an unknown ancient tongue.

The church has no professional clergy but uses lay members on a rotating basis, although the church organization is hierarchical and authoritarian. On a local level there are wards presided over by a bishop. Wards are grouped into stakes headed by a presidency of three and a council of twelve. On top of that are the church's general authorities. The main policy making body in that authority is the First Quorum of the Seventy. Above that is the Quorum of the Twelve Apostles and the church President. Mormons believe that their President is a prophet of God.

Mormon worship consists of a simple ceremony in simple churches (there are no crosses on their plain church steeples). More elaborate temples are used for consecration of marriages and other important functions. Only members of the church in good standing may enter a Mormon temple. Mormons are known for their active missionary programs throughout the world and for a belief in helping themselves. The latter accounts for the extensive welfare program run by the church and partly financed by a required tithe of ten percent from all members.

Despite their strict and devout religious beliefs Mormons have always been a practical and industrious people as well. They place a strong emphasis on traditional family values, excellent education, a healthy life style (no alcohol or caffeine, for instance), and a solid tradition of patriotism and American work ethic.

present-day Utah, however, has resulted in a shrinkage of that majority. The Mormon population now represents slightly less than one half of the state's residents. How the Mormons wound up in Utah is detailed in a sidebar in the history chapter that follows. For some greater insight into contemporary Mormon society, refer to the preceding sidebar.

5. A SHORT HISTORY

THE EARLY YEARS

Utah prior to the 16th century was a sparsely inhabited region that was home to the **Ute** tribe in the east, the **Gosiute** in the northwest, the southern **Paiute** in the southwest and the **Navajo** in the southeast. The first three groups were somewhat akin, all sharing a language based on the Shoshonean branch of Native American languages. The name of the state is taken from the word Ute. It is estimated that at no time prior to the arrival of white settlers did the native population of what is now Utah ever exceed more than 10,000 people.

The native groups were generally characterized by a simple hunting-gathering society. This was especially true of the Utes who often came into conflict with the other tribes. The more advanced civilizations of northern Arizona, New Mexico and southwest Colorado barely extended into a small corner of southeastern Utah. It never reached the size, complexity or level of development of its neighbors. The reasons for this are not known with any certainty, but a hostile environment seems likely to have played an important role.

The earliest European explorers may have reached what is present day Utah by the 1540s, but the first definite evidence is the visit of Spanish missionaries in the 1770s. They reached an area as far north as Utah Lake near present day Provo. An American trapper named **James Bridger** discovered the Great Salt Lake in 1824. The land was jointly claimed by Spain and Mexico but by that time Spanish influence in North America was waning and Mexico assumed control. However, the Mexican government never did get a real handle on governing the vast Utah territory because American influence became greater and greater with the arrival of more trappers and immigrants on their way to California and Oregon.

By the early 1840s Utah was still largely unexplored, which is in sharp contrast to the conditions prevailing in most of the surrounding territories. The arrival of the Mormons in 1847 was to change all of that.

THE MORMON ERA

The Mormons, persecuted elsewhere, were looking for a home in the late 1840s. Under the leadership of church president **Brigham Young**, they reached the location of present day Salt Lake in 1847. Tradition tells us that when Brigham Young looked out on the Salt Lake Valley he said to his followers, "This is the place..." With those words the Mormons set out to make this strange land their home.

The Mormons quickly set about building a community and developing agriculture. By 1852 the population was around 15,000 people. The area had technically remained a part of Mexico until the 1848 signing of the Treaty of Guadalupe Hidalgo, which ended the Mexican War. However, the United States hadn't thought about providing for a government in the newly acquired land. So the Mormons did it themselves, including the establishment of their own militia.

An increasing number of non-Mormons began to arrive and these people wanted the area to become a state to go under the name of the State of Deseret. Admission to the union was denied because of hostility to the Mormons and their polygamous practices. However, Congress did decide to establish the Utah Territory in 1850. Brigham Young was designated as the first territorial governor. Two other attempts at statehood were to follow and end in failure.

Conflict between Mormons and non-Mormons became increasingly frequent and turned ugly and violent on several occasions. The most important event was the massacre of a group of non-Mormons. This aroused anger in Washington and the dispatch of troops. The Mormon leader of the attacking band was arrested, tried, and executed. But that didn't settle things quite yet. More resentment among Mormons was aroused when Colorado and Nevada were carved out of the Utah Territory. This period of time is often referred to in Utah as the "Mormon War" although actual conflict between American troops and the Mormon militia never did materialize.

The 1860s saw an increase in Indian warfare, especially after the end of the Civil War and a continuing increase in non-Mormon immigration. In 1882 Congress disenfranchised polygamists. Although polygamy was never that important in Mormon society the church leaders had always upheld the right to practice it. Finally, however, in 1893 the church officially disavowed the practice of polygamy. With that sticking point gone statehood wasn't long in coming and Utah entered the union in January of 1896.

THE ROAD TO UTAH

Joseph Smith, son of a New York farmer, is said to have been visited by an angel who disclosed the location of the Book of Mormon to him. He published the book in 1830 and organized the Church of Jesus Christ of Latter-day Saints in Fayette, New York. A year later he moved to Kirtland, Ohio with his followers and then on to Missouri. The majority of people in the communities where the Mormons settled were never happy with their new neighbors.

Persecution, often of a violent nature, continued and the group moved again, settling in an Illinois community they named Nauvoo. It grew to more than 11,000 residents by 1844. Opposition to the Mormons grew commensurate with their increase in numbers and Mormon leaders and followers alike were accused of numerous crimes. Some, like polygamy, were true in some cases but many were trumped-up charges. Joseph Smith and his brother were arrested for treason and conspiracy in Carthage, Illinois. The governor of Illinois promised that they would be safe but a huge mob broke into the jail and killed both men.

The persecution and the execution of their leaders caused a deep splintering among the Mormon people. Many of the spin-off groups would soon fade away. One large group was to become the Reorganized Church of Jesus Christ of Latter Day Saints (a much smaller religion still headquartered in Missouri) while the single biggest group of Mormons continued to follow the new church president. Brigham Young headed that group. Although authoritarian and often uncompromising, Young was intelligent and had driving energy as well as excellent foresight.

He led his people westward and decided that the Salt Lake Valley was a good place to settle. Within a few years the Mormons had not only begun the development of Salt Lake City but they had established, despite continued hostility, more than three hundred other communities, mostly in Utah. As they say, the rest is history.

Mormon history is not only of interest to theologians and members of the faith. Their struggle is inseparably linked in many ways to the American westward exploration and expansion. The 1,300 mile long **Mormon Pioneer Trail** traces the 1846-47 journey of the Mormons from Nauvoo, Illinois on the Mississippi River all the way to Trail's End in Salt Lake City. Dozens of sites along the way are of interest and the entire route has been designated as a National Historic Trail. Some of the original wagon ruts are visible in places along the route (mostly in neighboring Wyoming). In Utah the trail roughly parallels modern I-80 and Utah Highway 65.

20TH-CENTURY UTAH

True growth in Utah did not began until after the irrigation successes of the Mormons had turned arid land into productive agricultural land. Mining operations started in 1906. Although mining quickly became an important industry and remains so today, Utah never did see the wild boom and bust gold and silver rushes that surrounding states did. That was mostly because the mineral finds in Utah (such as iron ore) lent themselves to a more stable economic process. Mormon influence was also a factor in holding down the degree of lawlessness often found in other western states, although Utah certainly wasn't gunfighter-free.

Despite excellent growth in the first quarter of the century, Utah was severely hit by the Great Depression. Economic weakness elsewhere nearly shut down the mining industry and agriculture was also severely affected by lack of new investment. It was not until World War II that the economic recovery of Utah began to take hold.

The postwar era has seen impressive growth. The federal government now owns almost two-thirds of all the land in Utah and is a major employer, especially the military. Defense-related industries have become an important sector of the economy as well. New mineral discoveries have kept the mining industry as a major employer and the agricultural legacy of the Mormons is still active as well.

Contemporary Utah is a modern society that is increasingly popular with non-Mormons because of the traditional values associated with picking a good place to raise a family. The Mormons may not quite dominate politics in Utah as they did earlier in this century but they still are a powerful force and voice in many aspects of life in Utah. And finally, tourism has become one of the most important businesses in the state.

6. PLANNING YOUR TRIP

WHEN TO VISIT

Every area of Utah has four distinct seasons. Most of the state is quite hot during the summer months, although it's considerably cooler in the higher altitudes. The high temperatures are somewhat mitigated by the fact that the humidity is generally on the low side. The winter, on the other hand, is cold and sometimes even bitter. The one exception to that is the extreme southwest corner of the state around St. George, known as "Utah's Dixie." But even there it's definitely not swimming weather in mid-winter. That becomes especially so if you go into the higher elevations that surround St. George. Spring and fall may be the most pleasant times temperature-wise but the drawback is that some roads (and attractions) may be closed. Also a late spring or early fall cold-snap could leave you chilled out.

As you can see from the weather chart below, Utah is a semi-arid state. There is more precipitation in the winter months (including heavy snowfalls in the higher elevations). Summer rain is mostly confined to late afternoon thunderstorms. Sometimes these can be severe.

Add up all of the weather conditions and it comes out like this—for a sightseeing vacation, especially one that involves lots of outdoor recreation, you're best off coming between late May and early September. The heat isn't nearly as oppressive as it can be in Arizona, for example. However, if you really have trouble tolerating hot weather then you can opt for the fall. The weather is less likely to be troublesome than it can sometimes be in the spring and you have the added attraction of viewing the fall foliage.

The winter is the only time to visit if you want to ski. Those obvious observations aside, however, the cold months do have certain advantages besides the fact that you'll have many attractions virtually to yourself. The amazing sights of Color Country, for example, take on a completely different but equally gorgeous appearance when they are snow-covered. I suggest that such a visit wait until after you've seen them in summer because there is the possibility that heavy snow (even a month or more before your visit) could make what you've come to see unreachable.

AVERAGE TEMPERATURE & PRECIPITATION
Highs/Lows & Precipitation

	Jan.	April	July	October	Annual Precip.
Bryce	39/8	56/25	83/47	63/29	16.3"
Cedar City	43/20	60/35	86/60	64/38	10.6"
Duchesne	31/6	62/32	88/54	64/33	9.6"
Fillmore	40/17	64/36	92/60	68/34	14.9"
Kanab	48/23	68/36	93/59	73/40	13.5"
Logan	32/16	59/36	87/59	62/39	16.4"
Moab	41/16	72/39	96/61	71/38	7.7"
Monument Valley	42/17	69/40	98/65	73/42	5.7"
Price	36/6	62/31	89/55	67/33	9.7"
St. George	54/27	77/44	102/69	81/63	7.8"
Salt Lake City	37/20	62/37	92/61	66/39	16.1"
Vernal	29/5	62/32	88/52	62/30	8.4"
Wendover	36/18	62/41	92/67	64/42	4.9"

WHAT TO PACK

The key to proper packing on any vacation is to take only what you are going to need and use. Excess baggage only weighs you down and makes packing and unpacking more of a chore. This is especially true if your vacation is going to involve switching from one location to another each night or even every few nights. But an even more important consideration is to pack appropriate to the climate you can expect to encounter and appropriate for the types of activities you're going to be participating in.

Utah, like most western and mountain states, is a casual and informal sort of place. Comfortable clothing is the rule, especially during the hotter months. There is the possibility of a dress code in some of the finer restaurants in Salt Lake City and a few resort areas. If you do plan to frequent those kinds of establishments then you should bring along some fancier dinner attire. The same is true if you are going to be visiting some of the theaters in Salt Lake City.

For the summer you should dress in lightweight clothing that breathes, such as cotton. Lighter colors are best. A light sweater or jacket may also come in handy during the evening. Although it's normal to think that the less you're covered the cooler you're going to be, this isn't necessarily the case. Exposed skin just soaks up the sun. While shorts or sleeveless tops are alright for sightseeing activities, intensive outdoor activity requires more protection. Long pants and long sleeve shirts are better. Sturdy boots with good traction are essential. Your clothing should also provide some protection against rocks or sharp vegetation that you might unexpectedly encounter. Waterproof clothing is a must if you're going rafting or fishing and a light raincoat can come in handy at all times just in case of a sudden shower.

In the higher elevations (and much of Utah is at 7,500 feet or more) the temperature will be much cooler. Being prepared for the sudden changes in weather in the mountains is of critical importance. The best way to handle the situation is to dress in layers. Have a sweater and an outer jacket with you for when it's colder and peel off one layer at a time as it warms up–or vice versa.

Regardless of the type of activity you're going to be participating in, sunglasses and a hat are recommended at all times. Utah is sunny and the higher elevation makes the rays of the sun stronger than you might think, even if the temperature is relatively low. Fair skinned individuals should always use a sun screen.

It's very important to make sure that you not only bring a sufficient supply of any prescription medication that you're taking, but to have a copy of the prescription as well. An extra pair of glasses (or, again, a copy of your prescription) also makes sense. At the risk of overstating the obvious, make sure that before you leave that your tickets and any other documents are in your possession and that you have plenty of film and tapes for your cameras or video recorders. I have always found that the best way to make sure that you have everything you need is to make a packing list in advance of your trip and check things off as you pack them. Getaway day is always hectic and even confusing so it's easy to forget something if it isn't written down.

UTAH TOURISM INFORMATION

The objective of this book is to give you all of the information that you need to plan a successful trip to Utah. However, I've never limited my own trip planning to a single source, so I won't find fault if you wanted to look elsewhere too. One good source is go straight to the source–in this case

A FEW TIPS FOR FOREIGN VISITORS

Utah is an increasingly popular destination for visitors from all over the world. It sometimes seems that Europeans, especially, have more advance knowledge of Utah's wonders than many eastern Americans.

American customs regulations and formalities are generally quick and easy. The American embassy or consulate in your home country can familiarize you with the exact requirements, which vary from one country of origin to another. Passports are always required except for visitors from Canada or Mexico; visas are only needed in a small number of cases unless you're going to be staying for an extend period of time. Also find out what the limitations are on what you can bring in or take out of the United States. If you plan to rent a car be sure to have an International Drivers License, since the only foreign licenses recognized in the United States are those from Canada or Mexico.

A common annoyance to overseas visitors is the fact that America doesn't use the metric system that almost the entire world has adopted. Formulas for conversions vary so much from one type of measurement to another that you shouldn't count on memory. It's best to have quick reference conversion charts, especially if you're going to be buying clothing. The most important item that should be committed to memory, however, is the relationship of kilometers to miles. One kilometer is equal to about 6/10 of a mile. So, that 65 miles per hour speed limit isn't as slow as you think–it's almost the same as 100 kph!

Some other common conversions that you might find handy are:
• Temperature: Celsius to Fahrenheit: Multiply by 1.8 and add 32;
   Fahrenheit to Celsius: Subtract 32 and divide by 1.8
• Gasoline:1 US gallon = .83 British Imperial gallon;
   1 US gallon = 3.785 liters

the **Utah Travel Council**, *Council Hall/Capitol Hill, Salt Lake City, UT 84114, Tel. 800/200-1160, fax 801/538-1399.* They can supply you with a general state visitor's guide as well as numerous other brochures, publications and maps. More specific information about cities, towns and even regions is available from local chambers of commerce or visitor bureaus. Information on where to contact these offices is given in the Practical Information section of each regional destination chapter.

Good maps are an essential ingredient for any driving trip. While the city and area maps in this guide are sufficient to get you to the major sights, a statewide road map showing all highways is beyond the scope of what can be included here. Therefore, make sure you procure one before you begin your trip (or at least no later than your arrival in the state). Members of the AAA can get an excellent Utah map from their local office; other good maps are published by Rand McNally and other companies and can be found in the travel section of your favorite bookstore or department store. The map put out by the Utah Travel Council is also quite good. If you do await until your arrival in Utah you can purchase road maps at the Salt Lake City airport. However, if you're driving into the state then you should stop at the first welcome center to get the state-issued travel map. These offices are located at the following locations:

- I-15 south bound between Exit numbers 375 and 368 near Brigham City
- I-80 west bound near Echo Junction just before exit 169
- I-15 north bound just after the Arizona state line in the vicinity of St. George
- I-70 west bound between exits 185 and 190 near Thompson
- Along US 40 in the town of Jensen, about 13 miles before Vernal

VIRTUAL UTAH

OK, cyber travelers, here's what you've been waiting for–a list of web sites where you can get all sorts of goodies about Utah. One word of caution before I let you have it. As we all know the Internet has excellent information as well as rubbish. You should confine any search for information about Utah to official travel sources or respected private services. Don't rely on someone's e-mail! Also, many private tour operators, hotels, etc., have their own web sites. Of course, "http://" precedes each Internet address shown.

Utah Travel Council: *www.utah.com*
Bicycle Utah: *www.bicycleutah.com*
Bridgerland Travel Region: *www.bridgerland.com*
Dinosaurland Travel Region: *www.dinoland.com*
Great Salt Lake Travel Region: *www.saltlake.org*
Kane County (Color Country) : *www.kaneutah.com*
Odgen/Davis County: *www.ogdencvb.org*
Park City: *www.parkcityinfo.com*
Salt Lake City Convention & Visitors Bureau: *www.visitsaltlake.com*
Salt Lake Olympic Committee: *www.slc2002.org*
Ski Utah: *www.skiutah.com*
Utah Reservations Center: *www.rescenter.com*
Utah Valley (Provo area) : *www.utahvalley.org/cvb*

BOOKING YOUR VACATION

There are two basic ways of approaching any trip. Pick a destination, get there and then decide what you want to do and where you should stay. The other is to plan in detail beforehand and know exactly where you'll be each night and have room reservations in hand. Of course, there's a wide range in between if you want to combine methods. While there's definitely something positive to be said for the flexibility and spontaneity of the day-to-day or "ad hoc" approach, there are potential serious pitfalls. You can't always count on rooms being available when you show up. NO VACANCY signs are all too common in Utah during the peak summer season in the southern portion of the state near national parks and other scenic attractions, as well as during the ski season at the mountain resorts. Not having a place to stay, to say the least, can be a bummer. So unless you have a great deal of time and are willing to risk the consequences of not having reservations, I strongly suggest at least some degree of advance planning for any Utah trip.

Planning can be a lot of fun and the whole family can get involved. Reading about what you're going to do and see creates a greater sense of anticipation, at least it always does for me. More importantly, for most people it makes it possible to ensure the best use of the time you have available for your vacation. I know some travel books are written as if you're going to be spending six months traveling, but that isn't reality for too many people. Advance reservations are also often a good way to save money on transportation and hotels, although I won't deny that when space is available at the last minute it, too, can be had at a substantial discount.

In this section I'll offer advice on what to book in advance and how to go about doing it, first in a general sense and then on items specific to Utah. After you've come up with an itinerary that you like, be prepared to make advance reservations for (1) air transportation (or other form of common carrier) to and from Utah, almost certainly Salt Lake City; (2) lodging, and (3) car rental or escorted tours if you're not going to be driving within Utah. If you plan to drive to Utah from your home then, of course, hotel reservations are generally the only thing you have to worry about.

If your itinerary does include a tour or special activities like rafting, then be sure to ascertain whether advance reservations are required for these things. I'll mention them in the Seeing the Sights sections where appropriate. If reservations are "suggested" read that as being "required"–you might save yourself from some big disappointments.

DO YOU NEED A TRAVEL AGENT?

Once you're ready to book your trip, the first question that you need to address is whether to use a professional travel agent or do it on your own. Securing and reading airline schedules isn't at all difficult nor is getting information about hotels, car rentals and other things. Except for airline schedules, all of that is contained in this book. I strongly prefer self-booking (despite the hostility that I might engender with travel agents). However, many people simply feel uncomfortable about doing that–they figure why not let a travel agent do the work–they're professionals, know the travel world better and do it no cost to the consumer. I can't strongly argue with that. It's a matter of your level of confidence.

Even if you do use a travel agent don't always assume that he or she knows much more than you do about the place you want to go. An agent in Netcong, New Jersey isn't that likely to be an expert on Utah. Do your homework first. Then, when using a travel agent make sure that they're reliable. Go on references from friends and relatives who were happy with the services of a particular agent. A good indication of their reliability is if the agency is a member of the American Society of Travel Agents (ASTA). Membership in that group or other industry organizations should be considered as a minimum requirement when selecting a travel agent.

Regardless of which travel agent you choose, their services should be free of any charge to you. They get paid commission by the airlines and hotels. It is true that the airlines especially are trying to cut down the amount they pay to agents. As a result some travel agents are imposing fees, claiming they can only make money in that manner. Well, I don't know about the financial aspects of their business but most still do it free of charge, so I would be skeptical about one who does require that you pay a fee. The only exception is that you should expect to pay for special individual planning, which is commonly referred to as F.I.T. travel. Although travel agents are supposed to have access to the best rates I have always found that it's a good idea to check the rates on your own first. You may find that it's better than what the agent tells you. If so, advise him or her of what rate you got and from where. They should easily be able to get the same rate.

It is sometimes difficult if not impossible to book, as an individual, a reservation on completely escorted tours. These are often exclusively handled through travel agents. If this is the type of trip you're planning to take then you are probably best off going immediately to a travel agent. Organized tours usually include discounted air options.

INDIVIDUAL TRAVEL VS. ORGANIZED TOURS

I almost always opt for travel on my own instead of being herded into a group. Many travelers do like the group situation for its "people interaction" and the expertise of the guides. However, there are a lot of shortcomings. The first one is that you are on a schedule that someone else sets. And that schedule has a lot of built in down-time to accommodate what will be the slowest person in the group. Organized tours generally dictate where and when you will eat, which is not always to everyone's liking. Careful reading of an organized tour itinerary will show that you do not always spend a lot of time seeing what you want to see. In fact, finding an itinerary that suits your own interests can be the single biggest problem with an organized tour.

While you may feel uncomfortable about being on your own in some exotic foreign destination where the food is strange and people may not speak English, you won't have any such problem while in Utah. In short, organized tours in Utah aren't necessary or even advisable for most people, especially those who take the time to read a book like this and get all the information they need to do things on their own. Of course, one or more short guided tours during an independent vacation may be advisable in various types of adventurous situations where the special knowledge of an expert can be helpful or even of life-saving importance.

Otherwise, the main exceptions to my recommendation of individual travel are for people who do not drive and those who are traveling by themselves. Going on a group tour is certainly far better than not being able to see anything because you can't or won't drive. It's also better than trying to get around the vast expanse of Utah with a limited public transportation system. Likewise, while some people don't mind traveling alone, almost everyone would agree that it's better to share your experiences with someone else, even if that person sitting next to you on the bus was previously a stranger.

Many airlines offer individual travel packages that include hotel and car rental in addition to the airfare. Sometimes these plans can save money but often you can do even better still by arranging everything separately. You see, package "deals" are coordinated by a wholesale tour package company and that middleman has to make a profit too. So the savings that are gotten by bulk purchase of airline seats and hotel rooms aren't always passed on to you like they claim in the glossy travel brochures. Also, you need to be careful about how restrictive "fly-drive" packages are. Some are highly flexible but others have a lot of rules regarding which cities you can stay overnight in or require a minimum number of nights. If they fit into your plans, fine; if not, simply build the pieces of your trip block by block.

TOUR OPERATORS

Having said all of this, here are a few suggestions for those readers who are going to opt for organized tours. Travel agents, of course, will be able to provide you with brochures on lots of itineraries covering Utah. For a general escorted bus tour that covers the biggest amount of Utah the best bus tour operators in North America are **Tauck Tours**, *Tel. 800/468-2825*, and **Maupintours**, *Tel. 800/255-4266*.

There are also a host of tour operators within Utah. Among the better ones are:

- **Executours of Salt Lake City**, *Tel. 801/898-8561*. Custom and package tours in the Salt Lake City area and throughout the state.
- **Lewis Brothers Tours**, *Tel. 801/826-5844*. Statewide bus tours and specialty tours.
- **Passage to Utah**, *Tel. 800/677-0553*. Custom guide service. Individual travelers and small groups. Tours throughout Utah and surrounding states.
- **Sample Salt Lake, Inc.**, *Tel. 801/278-9212*. Despite the name, has guided tours covering the entire state.
- **Utah Escapades**. *Tel. 800/268-8824*. Custom tours for individuals and groups.

In addition to the above operators, visitors can see many attractions through **Gray Line Tours**, *Tel. 800/309-2352 or 801/521-7060*. They have many single and multi-day trips not only in the Greater Salt Lake region but also to all parts of the state. Their Salt Lake City terminal is located at *553 West 100 South*.

GETTING THE BEST AIRFARE

Even travel agents have trouble pinning down what the best airfare is on a given flight on a given day. It's like trying to hit a moving object. If you call one airline ten times and ask what it will cost to fly from New York to Salt Lake City on the morning of July 10th and return on the afternoon of July 20th you'll probably get several different answers. I wouldn't even rule out the possibility of ten different responses. Unfortunately, such is the state of the airline fare game. There are, however, a couple of things to keep in mind about getting a good rate.

Midweek travel (Tuesday through Thursday for sure, but may include Monday afternoon and Friday morning depending upon the route and airline) is lower priced than weekend travel. Holiday periods are usually the highest priced but entire travel seasons often mean higher rates. Night flights are considerably less expensive than daytime travel if you don't mind arriving on the "red-eye" special.

Advance confirmed reservations that are paid for prior to your flight are almost always the cheapest way to go. The restrictions on these low fares vary considerably. In general you must book and pay for your tickets at least seven to 30 days in advance. In most cases they require that you stay over a Saturday night. They usually are non-refundable or require payment of a large penalty to either cancel or even make a change in the flight itinerary. So be sure when and where you want to go before reserving.

You can sometimes find big bargains by doing the opposite strategy–waiting for the last minute. If the airline has empty seats on the flight you select they're often willing to fill it up for a ridiculously low price. After all, they figure that some money in their pocket is better than none at all. The problem with this is that you don't know if there will be an available seat at the time you want to go. If you have definite reservations for everything else during your trip this can be a very dangerous game to play. If you do get a ticket at the last minute it can also wind up being an expensive proposition.

In this era of deregulation, airfares from one airline to another can sometimes be radically different, although carriers flying the same routes will often adjust their fares to the competition more often than not. Some of the low cost carriers are as good as the major airlines. None of them have their hub in Salt Lake City, but among the cheaper airlines going there are **Frontier Airlines** and **Southwest Airlines**.

One thing you should always be on the lookout for regardless of who you plan to fly with is promotional fares. Scan the newspapers or just call the airlines. It's always best to phrase your inquiry something like "What is the lowest available fare between x and y on date z?" Another possibility is to purchase your tickets on-line via the Internet. There are reportedly good bargains to be found using this method. More and more airlines allow you to buy tickets in this manner.

Finally, I know that those accustomed to first class air are going to squirm in their seats at this, but the cost of first class is simply not worth it when flying to Utah. Regardless of where you live in the United States the time spent on the plane is likely to be four hours or less. This isn't a week long cruise where you need to be pampered every minute. Go coach, or whatever they're calling it these days, bring along a good book and enjoy the flight.

FLYING TO UTAH

The only airport in Utah with scheduled service via major carriers to other parts of the country is **Salt Lake City International Airport**. Nine airlines provide service and several have extensive choices of non-stop flights to all over the nation. Limited service is available into Cedar City and St. George from neighboring states.

Here's a more detailed look at all of the carriers serving Salt Lake City from destinations outside of Utah:

- **American Airlines**, *Tel. 800/433-7300; Web site: http://www.aa.com.* Non-stop service to American's hubs in Chicago and Dallas which provides connections to their entire system.
- **America West**, *Tel. 800/253-9292; Web site: http://www.americawest.com.* Non-stop service to their system hub in Phoenix as well as Las Vegas and Reno.
- **Continental Airlines**, *Tel. 800/523-3273/; Web site: http://www.flycontinental.com.* Non-stop service to their hubs in Houston and New York.
- **Delta Airlines**, *Tel. 800/221-1212; Web site: http://www.delta-air.com.* Non-stop service to Albuquerque, Anchorage, Atlanta, Boise, Boston, Chicago, Cincinnati, Colorado Springs, Dallas, Denver, Fresno, Houston, Idaho Falls, Kansas City, Las Vegas, Los Angeles, Minneapolis, New Orleans, New York, Oklahoma City, Omaha, Orlando, Philadelphia, Phoenix, Portland, Reno, Sacramento, San Antonio, San Diego, San Francisco, San Jose, Seattle, Spokane, Tucson, Tulsa and Washington as well as Calgary, Edmonton and Vancouver in Canada. Through **SkyWest**, Delta offers service to another 20 smaller cities throughout the western United States.
- **Frontier Airlines**, *Tel. 800/432-1FLY; Web site: http://www.frontierairlines.com.* Non-stop service to their Denver system hub.
- **Northwest Airlines**, *Tel. 800/225-2525; Web site: http://www.nwa.com.* Non-stop service to their Minneapolis system hub.
- **Southwest Airlines**, *Tel. 800/1FLY-SWA; Web site: http://www.southwest.com.* Non-stop service to Albuquerque, Boise, Kansas City, Las Vegas, Los Angeles, Oakland, Phoenix, Portland, Reno, Sacramento, San Diego, Seattle, Spokane and St. Louis.
- **TWA**, *Tel. 800/221-2000; Web site: http://www.twa.com.* Non-stop service to their St. Louis hub.
- **United Airlines**, *Tel. 800/241-6522. Web site: http://www.ual.com.* Non-stop service to Chicago, Denver, Las Vegas and San Francisco. The first two destinations are United hubs and transfer points to more than 200 different destinations.

BY AIR

Inter-city scheduled air travel within Utah is almost exclusively by **SkyWest Airlines**, *Tel. 800/453-9417 or 800/443-4952.* They operate from

Salt Lake City to several regional airports, including Cedar City and St. George. SkyWest is affiliated with a couple of major carriers as their commuter arm. They are Delta Airlines through the Delta Connection and United Airlines through United Express. If you are traveling into Utah via one of those airlines you can be ticketed directly onto SkyWest, including baggage transfers for the continuation of your trip to any SkyWest city.

Two other Utah flying options are **Alpine Air**, *Tel. 801/575-2839*, from Salt Lake City to Moab and **Eagle Canyon Airlines**, *Tel. 702/736-3333*, which flies from Las Vegas to Cedar City.

BY BUS

Greyhound *(Tel. 800/231-2222 for route information and reservations)*, provides most service between points in Utah. In addition, Salt Lake City's municipal bus system, the **Utah Transit Authority**, *Tel. 801/262-5626*, serves neighboring Davis and Weber counties as well as the mountain ski resorts to the east of the city. The Practical Information section of each regional destination chapter has a selected listing of bus locations. In cases where no telephone numbers are listed it is because the station is unstaffed. The same applies to train stations.

BY CAR

I've already indicated that a car, whether it's your own or a rental, is definitely the best way to get around in Utah. Besides being the most time- and cost-effective method, it also offers the traveler a degree of flexibility that cannot be matched by any form of public transportation. That's true almost everywhere you travel in this country (except if your trip is confined to one or more major cities with a good transit system) but is even more so in the western United States in general and Utah for sure.

Driving in Utah will not, for the most part, present any significant problem for the majority of visitors if you stay on paved highways. More information about unpaved and back country roads will be given a little later. Although you can encounter some traffic congestion in Salt Lake City and the surrounding areas, it is considerably less of a problem than in most big cities. Once you get away from the Wasatch Valley and it's 1-1/2 million people, the roads are almost always free and clear of heavy traffic. Of course, except for the interstate highway system, the majority of Utah's roads aren't designed for high speed travel. In many parts of the state you'll wonder where all of the cars are–it isn't that unusual not to see another car for several miles in some areas. Parking facilities at most attractions are adequate or even better. This is even true in the more populated areas although is not the case, of course, in central Salt Lake City.

Interstate highways in Utah are excellent. These and most major roads (either state or federally designated) are kept in good driving condition and don't present any unusual hazards. However, Utah has many mountainous areas where the roads are almost always narrow and twisting, often with steep grades and an absence of comforting guard rails. Roads into and within national parks are usually within this category but if you simply take it slow there shouldn't be a problem even for the relatively novice mountain driver.

On the other hand, Utah has dozens of dirt and gravel roads, especially in the southern part of the state. While the majority of the important attractions don't require that you negotiate such roads to get to them, there are literally dozens of places of unique worth that can only be reached by traveling on roads that provide some challenge. Slow up to avoid kicking up dust that can block your view or send gravel pellets flying toward your windshield. And never attempt to travel on an unpaved road during or after a heavy rain.

In fact, if you're going to be going for any significant distance on unimproved roads it will be necessary to check locally about the road conditions before proceeding. While many unpaved roads can be driven on in the family sedan, scores of others require high clearance and/or four wheel drive. Those features are always helpful in the back country but the regional destination chapters will always advise you when they are an absolute necessity. There are some roads that are definitely for the most experienced and adventurous of drivers. I'll also let you know which ones fall into that category.

If you are traveling during the winter, early spring or late fall, and plan to be in areas which are in excess of about 7,000 feet high then you have

UTAH'S SCENIC BYWAYS & BACKWAYS

*Some of the most spectacular scenery in Utah isn't at a particular destination at all, but is located along one of the state's designated **Scenic Byways** or **Scenic Backways**. The former are all paved roads and generally don't require any special vehicle or skills to drive except for paying careful attention to the road. The latter can often be another matter, though. While some aren't that difficult (they're backways only because they are really out of the way), others are dirt or gravel and involve the most demanding driving conditions imaginable. In all there are 27 Scenic Byways and 58 Scenic Backways. They can run from just a few miles to well over a hundred miles. Many of these scenic routes are detailed in the regional destination chapters. Then you can decide which ones are best suited to you.*

to be prepared for snow, even if the roads are kept open throughout the winter. Snow tires are a minimum requirement if you are going to be restricting your driving to the Interstate highways. Otherwise carrying snow chains is essential. Bring along blankets, flares, first-aid kit and some nonperishable food if you plan to travel extensively in the back country during winter.

Information on **highway road conditions** can be obtained by calling the state highway department, *Tel. 801/964-6000,* in the Salt Lake City area, and *Tel. 800/492-2400* in the remainder of the state. Utah driving laws are essentially the same as in most states although they do have strict DUI laws.

This book will use several prefixes to designate various types of roads. "I" before a number indicates an Interstate highway. "US" will precede a United States highway, while Utah state road numbers are indicated by "UT." Other types of roads such as county routes, forest roads and the like will be so indicated.

When it comes to familiarizing yourself with Utah's road system there is no better way than to carefully study a good road map. However, you should know a few major routes and that I can do you for here. It's even better if you read this section with a map in front of you.

The principle Interstate highway is **I-15**. It extends for 402 miles from the Arizona state line at St. George north to Idaho in the direction of Pocatello. **I-84** cuts off of I-15 at Tremonton and travels northwest to Idaho in the direction of Twin Falls. **I-80** cuts across the narrowest northern section of the state. It goes about 200 miles from the Nevada line at Wendover to the Wyoming line at Evanston. I-15 and I-80 intersect in Salt Lake City. The only other Interstate highway is **I-70**, which extends for some 225 miles from the Colorado state line and heads west until it ends at I-15 about midway between the towns of Beaver and Fillmore.

There are also several important US highways. Those running north to south include **US 89**, which roughly parallels I-15 and US 191 in the eastern portion of the state. It extends from the Navajo reservation in the south to the Flaming Gorge National Recreation area in the north. Major east-west routes are **US 50**, concurrent with I-70 until Salina and then continuing west to the Nevada line, and US 40 from the Colorado line near Vernal to I-80 near Salt Lake City.

Many state routes are also necessary in order to get to specific attractions but they'll be addressed in the regional destination chapters as we get to them.

UTAH DRIVING DISTANCES

	Bryce	Cedar City	Green River	Kanab	Moab	Price	St. George	Salt Lake City	Vernal	Wendover
Bryce	–	78	222	77	270	219	126	260	332	375
Cedar City	78	–	232	79	288	229	53	250	342	338
Green River	222	232	–	265	53	63	285	182	176	302
Kanab	77	79	265	–	321	262	83	303	375	418
Logan	341	331	263	384	319	176	384	81	256	201
Moab	270	288	53	321	–	119	341	238	232	358
Monticello	304	341	109	290	53	172	373	291	285	411
Ogden	295	285	217	338	273	154	338	35	207	155
Panguitch	24	62	198	67	254	195	115	236	308	343
Park City	261	251	183	304	239	120	304	31	146	151
Price	219	229	63	262	119	–	282	119	113	239
Provo	215	205	137	258	193	74	258	45	154	165
Richfield	101	111	121	144	177	118	164	159	231	274
St. George	126	53	285	83	341	382	–	303	395	391
Salt Lake City	260	250	182	303	238	119	303	–	175	129
Vernal	332	342	176	375	232	113	395	120	–	295
Wendover	375	338	302	418	358	239	391	120	295	–
Zion	84	59	272	41	328	269	43	309	382	397

Renting a Car

If you thought that trying to get a straight answer on airfares was difficult you'll be disappointed to learn that things won't be much easier when it comes to renting a car. Here, too, there is a jumble of rates depending upon a host of factors. However, a few basic rules apply at most rental companies that will put things into sharper focus. First of all, it is almost always less expensive to rent a car if you return it to the same location. In other words, a **loop trip** is more economical than renting in one place and returning the car somewhere else. There are exceptions to this rule. In many cases the major companies will allow you to return the car at a different location with no extra "drop-off" charge so long as it is within the same state. This won't, unfortunately, be common in Utah since Salt Lake City is the only big city where one-way charges might otherwise apply.

The second thing to look for in a rental is whether there's a **mileage charge** in addition to the basic rate. If there is, avoid it unless you plan to only use the car minimally. Utah is a big state and the miles will add up quickly. When you tack on what you're paying per mile to the rate you were quoted it won't be the great buy you thought it was. You should also inquire about weekly rentals because these are often less expensive than if you take a simple daily plan. Often you can wind up getting one or two days per week for free when you go weekly.

Other things to keep in mind are having the **proper insurance**. Every rental company will try to sell you coverage at significantly inflated rates. Check with your insurance agent at home if you can't determine whether your auto insurance covers a rental car. If it doesn't, then you have to decide whether or not to take a chance and waive the rental insurance coverage. One other way to often avoid having to purchase insurance is to charge the rental on a major credit card. The credit card companies frequently include rental insurance as a benefit when you do so. Be sure to check it out.

Turning to a couple of other considerations now, the rental car companies often impose an additional fee if more than one person will be driving. Tell them about additional drivers because their name has to appear on the rental agreement or else you could be in a lot of trouble if there's an accident. I can't figure out the justification for this extra fee except that they're trying to make a few more bucks. Finally, if you are going to be driving on unpaved roads with a rental car, be sure to find out if it is allowed. There are companies that will rent you four-wheel drive and high clearance vehicles for such circumstances.

All of the major car rental companies are located in Salt Lake City. If you plan to rent in other localities finding one or more rental agencies is usually not a problem if it is in a popular tourism area.

MAJOR CAR RENTAL COMPANY PHONE NUMBERS

	Nationwide Toll-Free	Salt Lake City Airport Local #
Alamo	800/327-9633	801/575-2211
Avis	800/331-1212	801/575-2847
Budget	800/237-7251	801/575-2222
Dollar	800/421-9849	801/575-2580
Enterprise	800/534-1888	801/575-5151
Hertz	800/654-3131	801/575-2683
National	800/227-7368	801/575-2277
Thrifty	800/355-RENT	801/265-6677

You can often beat the rates offered by the major companies by dealing with a local or regional firm. These almost always require that you return the car to the same location. Some local operations in Salt Lake City that you might want to consider are **Advantage Rent-a-Car**, *Tel. 800/777-5500* and **High Country Car & Truck Rental**, *Tel. 800/327-3631.*

By Train

Travelers who love to ride the rails will be disappointed when they hear what train service is available in Utah. **Amtrak**, *Tel. 800/USA-RAIL*, has limited service in the state. The California Zephyr (Chicago to San Francisco) has one daily trip in each direction. Besides Salt Lake City the train's Utah stops are Provo, Helper and Green River. There is connecting bus service from the Salt Lake City station to Ogden. Amtrak also offers package vacation plans that combine rail travel with other modes of transportation.

Although quite a few western states have a number of historic railroads that can be used to get around to a degree or just for sightseeing, Utah has only a single one. This is the **Heber Valley Railroad** in Heber City. The short excursion is described in the Northwest regional destination chapter.

ACCOMMODATIONS

Once you've decided where you're going in Utah and come up with an itinerary, the next biggest decision for most people is where to stay. An unpleasant hotel or motel experience can be a big downer while an unusually nice place will become part of your fond vacation memories. Giving advice on where to stay is difficult because different travelers are looking for very different things when it comes to lodging.

The cost of lodging, which has been increasing at a much faster rate than inflation for quite a few years, is only one factor to consider. Some people just want a clean and comfortable room to plop themselves down for the night while others want to be pampered in luxurious surroundings and take advantage of many of the amenities of either a first class hotel or resort. I have selected more than 110 hotels that run the gamut from simple budget motels to some of the most luxurious resorts in the world. There is an emphasis on the higher end of the scale because people looking for basic, "no surprises" accommodations will often opt for chain hotels (see below). Also, there's simply a whole lot more to be said about a fancy resort, for example, than a small roadside motel. Lodging prices in Utah are lower than in other southwestern states such as Arizona, Colorado and New Mexico, but they often don't come cheap either. That's especially true in the ski resorts.

This section will point out several things that should be kept in mind about lodging. Some are generic to travel anywhere but others are specifically geared towards Utah. The style of most accommodations in Utah is casual in almost all instances. A few places in and around Salt Lake City are more formal.

Regardless of what type of lodging you choose, it is important to have advance reservations in all popular resort and tourist areas. Even those places that are more off the beaten track often fill up fast during the summer months because there are relatively few lodging establishments in those locations. Finding a room in or near Utah's five national parks and some other better known scenic attractions can be especially difficult during the peak travel season. I strongly urge you to have advance reservations before arriving in Utah.

Most chain properties do not require that you pay in advance so long as you arrive before 6:00pm. However, it's a good idea to guarantee a late arrival with your credit card. Many times the reservations agent will ask you for this information. Small, independent establishments and many resort properties require that you do pay in advance, at least for the first nights' stay. Be sure you understand and comply with payment regulations and cancellation requirements at the time you make your booking.

Reservations can be made in a number of ways. All major chains and many independent hotels accept reservations made through travel agents. You can make reservations on your own by contacting the hotel directly or via a chain's central reservation system. It is also becoming increasingly common for independent establishments to belong to associations that handle reservations through a toll free-number. Internet booking of hotel rooms isn't quite as developed as airline ticket sales but is quickly becoming another option in many cases.

Reservations for many hotels throughout Utah can also be made free of charge by contacting any of the following organizations. They can also arrange package tours.
• **All Utah Free Reservation Center**, *Tel. 800/776-4685*
• **Bed & Breakfast Inns of Utah**, *Tel. 435/645-8068*
• **Resort Rentals of Utah**, *Tel. 800/333-1400*
• **Travel Council Super Hosts**, *Tel. 800/200-1160*
• **Utah Hotel & Lodging Association**, *Tel. 800/733-8824*
• **Utah Reservation Service**, *Tel. 800/554-2741*

Hotel prices for the same room can vary tremendously depending upon the time of the year, the day of the week, and whether or not you can qualify for any discounted rates. Don't be bashful when making reservations. Balk at what you believe to be too high a price and they may well do better by miraculously finding that they have one more room left at a special price!

The recommended lodging listings in this book are arranged by location. They are further broken down in each touring chapter alphabetically by city. In the case of Salt Lake City they're also divided by the area of town as well. Then they'll be broken down one last time by price category during the peak season. The rates shown are known as the rack rate. That means what the normal rate for the room is. Most places in Utah have higher rates during the summer months. The only exception, of course, is for the ski resorts. When only one rate is shown it means that the rate is the same all year or only varies slightly. Large price ranges within a time category can be attributable to two things. First, sometimes there are wide swings in price within a season due to local events or other factors. Second, the hotel may have many different types of accommodations including suites. The write-up on each establishment will indicate the latter.

Unless otherwise specified, the rate shown is the price charged for the room, not per person, although the room rate is based on double occupancy. Single rates are often the same or only slightly less than the double room rate. Hotel policies concerning additional charges, if any, for children in the same room vary considerably. If you plan to have your children stay in the same room with you inquire with the individual hotel as to the charge.

All prices listed in this book are for the room only (no meals) unless otherwise indicated. The majority of hotels (with the exception of some resorts) charge on this basis, which is often known as the **European Plan**. When another plan is involved it will be indicated. A **Continental Plan** is the next most common rate plan and it provides a small breakfast consisting primarily of pastry and beverage. Depending upon the hotel and your appetite this may or may not be sufficient to satisfy your morning hunger pangs. A **Breakfast Plan** includes a full breakfast. The **Modified American Plan** (MAP) includes a full breakfast and dinner and is rarely found these days outside of resort facilities. Some hotels, especially higher priced ones, do offer plans where you can add on meals for a fixed price.

On-premise restaurants will be indicated and also mentioned if there is a separate listing for it in the *Where to Eat* section. All hotels listed have private bath in every room except for a small number of properties where it is otherwise indicated.

Rates were accurate as of press time but, as mentioned earlier, hotel prices have been rising fast and most hotels don't guarantee their rates for very long, if at all. However, you still will have an idea based on the category. The majority of hotels do raise their prices each year. But a hotel in the moderate category will probably raise its rates in line with other hotels in the same category.

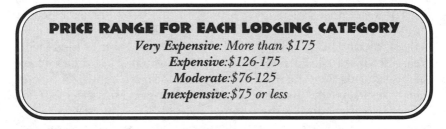

PRICE RANGE FOR EACH LODGING CATEGORY
Very Expensive: More than $175
Expensive:$126-175
Moderate:$76-125
Inexpensive:$75 or less

MAJOR HOTEL CHAINS

In each destination chapter there will be many suggested places to stay. Most of them are either independent hotels not affiliated with a major chain, or if they are affiliated, will belong to one of the more upscale chains. The main exception is that in a lot of the smaller towns, especially those along interstate highways, the best places to stay are often chain properties. Some people like the convenience of making reservations with nationwide hotel companies because they more or less know what they will be getting come check-in time. I myself make frequent use of them.

Therefore, for your convenience, the toll-free reservations number as well as the Utah locations of most of the larger chains are listed here. I've only included chains that have a significant presence in Utah. The listing shows the localities where the chain has a property. In many instances they may have multiple properties at a given location.

While some people like the recognizable standards of chain proper-ties there are also many travelers who are somewhat put off by the relative sameness of many chains. Therefore, where I have listed chain properties below the upscale chain level in the regional destination chapters, I have mainly chosen members of the Best Western family. This is not because they are inherently better than other similarly priced organizations but is due to the greater variation in the style and appearance of their properties.

BEST WESTERN, *Tel. 800/528-1234 or 800/241-7234. Web site: http://www.bestwestern.com.* Properties located in Beaver, Blanding, Cache Valley (Brigham City area), Bryce Canyon, Cedar City, Delta, Fillmore, Green River, Hurricane, Kanab, Lehi, Logan, Moab, Monticello, Mt. Carmel Junction, Nephi, Ogden, Panguitch, Park City, Parowan, Provo, Richfield, Roosevelt, St. George, Salina, Salt Lake City, Sandy, Springville, Tooele, Torrey, Vernal and Wendover.

CHOICE HOTELS: Quality Inn, *Tel. 800/228-5151. Web site: http://www.qualityinn.com.* American Fork, Beaver, Cedar City, Richfield, St. George, Salt Lake City and Sandy. **Comfort Inn**, *Tel. 800/228-5150. Web site: http://www.comfortinn.com.* Blanding, Cedar City, Green River, Hurricane, Logan, Moab, Ogden, Payson, Provo, St. George, Salt Lake City, Sandy and Tooele. **Sleep Inn**, *Tel. 800/753-3746. Web site: http://www.sleepinn.com.* Ephraim, Moab, Ogden, Provo, St. George, South Jordan and West Valley City. **Rodeway Inn**, *Tel. 800/228-2000.* Cedar City, Fillmore, Green River, Moab and Vernal. **Econolodge**, *Tel.800/55-ECONO.* St. George, Salt Lake City and Vernal. For all Choice hotel chains without their own separate web site you can make reservations at *http://www.hotelchoice.com.*

DAYS INN, *Tel. 800/329-7466. Web site: http://www.daysinn.com.* Beaver, Hurricane, Logan, Midvale, Moab, Monticello, Ogden, Parowan, Provo, Richfield, St. George, Salt Lake City, Torrey, Vernal and Wendover.

HAMPTON INN, *Tel. 800/HAMPTON. Web site: http://www.hamptoninn.com.* Murray, Orem, Provo, St. George, Salt Lake City and Sandy.

HOLIDAY INN, *Tel. 800/HOLIDAY (Includes Crowne Plaza & Holiday Inn Express). Web site: http://www.holidayinn.com,* Kanab, Layton, Park City, Provo, St. George and Salt Lake City.

MARRIOTT HOTELS: Courtyard, *Tel. 800/321-2211.* Provo, Salt Lake City and Sandy. **Fairfield Inn**, *Tel. 800/228-2800.* Layton, Moab, Provo, Salt Lake City and Woods Cross. **Marriott**, *Tel. 800/228-9290. Web site: http://www.marriott.com.* Salt Lake City. **Residence Inn**, *Tel. 800/331-3131.* Provo, Salt Lake City and Sandy.

MOTEL 6, *Tel. 800/466-8356. Web site: http://www.motel6.com.* Green River, Midvale, Ogden, Provo, St. George, Salt Lake City, Wendover and Woods Cross.

RAMADA INN, *Tel. 800/2-RAMADA. Web site: http://www.ramada.com.* Cedar City, Moab, St. George, Salt Lake City and South Jordan

SUPER 8, *Tel. 800/800-8000. Web site: http://www.super8.com.* Beaver, Blanding, Cedar City, Clearfield, Green River, Hurricane, Kanab, Lehi, Logan, Moab, Monticello, Nephi, Ogden, Price, Provo, Richfield, St. George, Salt Lake City, Sandy, South Jordan, Torrey and Vernal.

TRAVELODGE/THRIFTLODGE, *800/578-7878. Web site: http:// www.travelodge.com.* Cedar City, Logan, Moab, Ogden, Provo, St. George and Salt Lake City.

CAMPING & RECREATIONAL VEHICLES

Camping sites or places to hook up an RV are in as much demand these days as hotel rooms. So, once again, early advance planing is an absolute must. Reservations are not always accepted for camping on federal lands. Inquire as to whether they operate on a first come, first served or reservation basis. All campgrounds in Utah state parks are by reservation only. ICampsites and RV facilities range from back to nature "roughing it" to, in some commercially run establishments, facilities that have almost as many amenities as an average motel. Many campgrounds in Utah's higher elevations are closed during the winter months.

Aside from commercial RV parks that are often located near natural areas and in towns along Interstate highways, you'll find both camping and RV facilities in almost all national and state parks. National forests are extremely popular among campers. Often only a small fee is charged in these places. However, while you can generally just show up at sites within national forests, a permit is required for camping in national parks. The permits are free and can be obtained at the visitor center of the park you are planning to camp in.

Some important contacts for camping in Utah are:

•**Bureau of Land Management (BLM)**: Reservations can be made through the appropriate district BLM office. Cedar City District, *Tel. 435/ 586-2401;* Moab District, *Tel. 435/259-6111;* Richfield District, *Tel. 435/ 896-8221;* Salt Lake District, *Tel. 801/977-4300;* and Vernal District, *Tel. 435/789-1362.*

•**National Forests**: The centralized reservation number for camping in all national forests is *Tel. 800/280-2267.* However, if you want specific information about a particular location then it is best to contact the appropriate Forest Service supervisor's office.

•**National Parks & Monuments**: See the listing for each park in the regional destination chapters. Camping sites in national parks are in greater demand than at any other location so it is best to make arrangements as much in advance as possible, where allowed.

•**Utah State Parks**: The state of Utah has a centralized reservation system for all camping in state parks. Do not contact individual park offices for reservations although they will be able to provide general information. *Tel. 800/322-3770.*

For a sampling of commercially operated sites at major localities throughout the state, see the listings in each regional chapter. Major chain operators of campgrounds offer nationwide directories and reservation services.

7. BASIC INFORMATION

ADVENTURE TRAVEL

Adventure travel has become an increasingly popular and important force in the travel industry in recent years. Its growth has been fueled by the large number of tour operators specializing in out of the ordinary experiences as well as by the popularity of four-wheel and off-road vehicles. A lot of people simply are no longer satisfied with keeping their feet planted solidly on the ground and walking or riding by car from one sightseeing attraction to another. If you like to get involved in the action and aren't afraid of vigorous activity and sometimes highly unusual modes of transportation, then you're ready for adventure travel. Certainly, Utah is one of the best places in the country for adventure travelers. There are many beautiful parts of the state that can only be reached by activities that fall into the adventure travel category.

The possibilities for adventure travel are almost unlimited. Among the activities that can be included are rock and mountain climbing, river running, mountain biking, horseback trips, wilderness camping (and not in a comfortable RV) and much more. All of these can be easily found in Utah. General information on the most popular types of adventure travel in Utah will be found in the next chapter on Sports & Recreation. In addition, reputable operators can be found under specific categories in the various destination chapters. All regions of Utah have their fair share of adventure travel opportunities. Many are within a short drive of Salt Lake City.

ALCOHOLIC BEVERAGES

Drinking laws in Mormon-influenced Utah are somewhat restrictive compared to a lot of other places. Restaurants that choose to serve alcoholic beverages are allowed to do so after noon. You can ask for a liquor menu. If you want to drink earlier in the day then you have to go to private clubs that are allowed to serve at any time. Most such clubs will allow visitors to sign up for short-term memberships at a cost of $5. The temporary membership lasts for two weeks and allows the holder to bring along up to five guests.

Taverns and lounges are only allowed to offer beer for sale. You can buy alcohol in state-owned liquor stores. All state licensed stores are required by law to be closed on Sundays and holidays. Food markets and convenience stores are only allowed to sell 3.2% beer.

ALTERNATIVE TRAVEL

As if adventure travel wasn't enough of a choice for the traveling public, the last few years has also seen the growth of a new segment within the travel industry. Going under various different names, I'll categorize them all under the heading of alternative travel. It covers an enormously large range of possibilities–everything from special trips for gays, seniors, children traveling with grandparents, or any other of a number of groups. It also encompasses travel for people who are interested in specific aspects of an area or region, such as the environment, social history of various ethnic or national groups, and so forth.

I don't pretend to be an expert in the needs and interests of all these special groups and, frankly, in most cases don't even see a great need for "alternative travel" as such. A broad-based vacation experience provides more than enough opportunity for intellectual improvement and meeting people of like interests. However, at least a part of the traveling public is asking for this type of information and like the focus these types of vacations can bring. So, I would be remiss if I didn't at least direct you towards a few organizations that can help you with alternative travel in Utah:

- **Canyonlands Field Institute**, *Tel. 800/860-5262.* Specializes in eco-studies. Also has programs for women only.
- **Earthspirit Adventures**, *Tel. 435/644-5457.* Ecologically oriented tours with mild adventure.
- **Four Corners School of Outdoor Education**, *Tel. 800/525-4456.* Emphasis on archaeology and ecology as well as the fine arts.
- **White Mesa Institute**, *Tel. 435/678-2201.* Tours by and about Native Americans.

Finally, if you're interested in traveling with people that you "fit" in better with, it is best to contact organizations serving those common interests. For example, senior travelers might want to check with the AARP about trips that they sponsor.

CHILDREN

While many of Utah's most famous scenic wonders aren't especially well suited to small children, there is still much that will appeal to youngsters. A child may appreciate the fantastic forms and colors of Bryce Canyon, for example, in a different way than will adults. If you always bring your children along on vacation then there is certainly no reason why you shouldn't consider doing the same for Utah. There are several situations that have to be addressed when traveling with children. The first is what to do with the little tykes when you and your spouse (or whoever) decide that it's time for a night out on the town by yourselves. The second is what to do to keep the kids busy during long drives (also known as avoiding the "are we there yet?" syndrome). And last, but certainly not least, finding attractions and activities that the children will really enjoy. Hopefully, they'll be enjoyable for the grown-ups as well. Let's take a closer look at each situation.

How do you go about finding a good baby-sitter in a place you've never been before? One of the best sources is an obvious one but often overlooked–the staff at your hotel. They have definitely heard this question before and can usually direct you to a qualified care giver because they have had feedback from previous guests. Many hotels, especially the better ones or resorts, have supervised child care or children's programs. These services will be indicated in the hotel listings. One bonded and insured child care agency that specializes in hotel room care is **Guardian Angel Babysitting**, *Tel. 801/598-1229*. They serve Salt Lake City and vicinity including Park City and other nearby mountain resorts.

Road activities don't have to be elaborate and shouldn't present a major hurdle. You know best what will occupy your children while riding in the car. It may be a coloring book, a small hand-held computer game, a favorite doll or toy or even something that doesn't involve having something with you, such as a sing-along or word games. It's easy to get children involved in simple little games that make the time go faster. For example, keeping track of license plates from various states can be fun and an education in geography. Stores specializing in educational activities for children also sell "travel kits" that contain numerous activities to amuse your kids. Just don't let the driver get to close the kits–he or she is likely to get distracted!

The list of places to see in Utah and things to do that everyone can enjoy is quite long. Some of the very best will be listed here but each of the regional destination chapters will make special mention of what should appeal most to children. The list below doesn't include one of the most obvious diversions for children, which are amusement parks. The latter can be found listed under the Sports & Recreation section of some regional chapters.

My selections of the best activities for children are:

Dinosaurs are so popular with kids today but television and movies all too often portray them either as Barney or Godzilla. A little education along with the prehistoric creatures is a good way to entertain children. There are many dinosaur-related attractions in Utah. Among the best are the Utah Field House of Natural History and dinosaur gardens (Vernal), Eccles Dinosaur Park (Ogden), Utah Museum of Natural History (Salt Lake City), College of Eastern Utah Prehistoric Museum and Cleveland-Lloyd Dinosaur Quarry (Price), and the Dinosaur National Monument.

Hogle Zoological Gardens in Salt Lake City has more than 1,200 animals in natural settings along with a petting zoo and miniature railway.

The **Sundance Childrens' Theater** in Sundance Resort near Provo has an excellent program in a mountain amphitheater.

Greenshows held as a part of Cedar City's **Utah Shakespearean Festival** is a delight for all ages. Children will especially appreciate the puppet shows.

Golden Spike National Historic Site, with its old steam trains, is sure to hit a positive chord with most children, especially young boys.

The 18 mile corridor from Park City to Heber City contains a number of kid friendly attractions including the **Park City Silver Mine Adventure** (you can dig for gemstones), an alpine slide, and the **Heber Valley Railroad**.

Wheeler Historic Farm in Salt Lake City is a turn of the century dairy farm. Both educational and entertaining, children will be delighted by the opportunity to gather eggs or milk a cow!

Finally, the **great outdoors** that brings so many grown-ups to Utah should not be overlooked as a means of entertaining and educating children. Younger children are most apt to enjoy the unusual and colorful more than the beauty associated with alpine mountains or desert solitude. Among the former are Bryce Canyon National Park, Coral Pink Sand Dunes State Park, Goblin Valley State Park, Arches National Park and Monument Valley.

CREDIT CARDS

Each hotel and restaurant listed in the regional destination chapters indicates whether credit cards are accepted. Where four or less cards are accepted the names of the valid cards are shown. If five cards are taken the listing will indicate "most major credit cards accepted." That also means that, at a minimum, American Express, Discover, MasterCard and Visa are honored. When "major credit cards accepted" is shown it means that the establishment takes a minimum of six different cards.

Because of the high price of many admissions to visitor attractions more and more of these businesses are accepting credit cards for payment. However, acceptance of cards at these locations will only be mentioned if the admission price is greater than $15. If so, the listing will state "credit cards."

DINING & FOOD

If you're expecting a long treatise on the cuisine of Utah, forget it. The state doesn't have what can be described as a unique local style of food preparation. However, the types of cuisine that are among the most popular in Utah's restaurants include regional southwestern dishes (Mexican and/or Native American influences), western (beef and local game), and fresh fish from mountain streams and lakes. All are quite good and often outstanding but the recent growth in Utah's population has led to a dramatic increase in the range of ethnic and other type restaurants. While many of these are concentrated in metropolitan Salt Lake City, there is also surprising variety to be found in resort areas and other popular travel destinations.

The destination chapters contain descriptions of about a hundred different restaurants. The descriptions are geared towards dinner but if a place is especially notable for either breakfast or lunch I will certainly let you know. The inexpensive category usually encompasses what is termed "family" dining, but also is generally good for lunch. I have tried to provide a sampling of as many different cuisines as possible to reflect the variety that can be found throughout the state. That cross section also applies to price so you'll find that the restaurants, besides being divided up by area, are classified according to the price for dinner.

Fast food chains aren't mentioned but you can almost always find one for lunch in all the larger towns and especially along the major interstate highways. Likewise, popular nationwide restaurant chains aren't generally listed unless they're the best available choice in a given location. The chain restaurants are mostly concentrated in the Salt Lake City metropolitan area.

No one person can possibly sample all of the restaurants in a state and I don't pretend to have done so in Utah. So when traveling, especially in the smaller towns, don't hesitate to try a place simply because it may not look like what you expect a good restaurant to look like from the outside. More often than not these simple or rustic eateries will turn out to cook up some real good vittles served by a pleasant and eager-to-please staff. Then you can write me and tell me about it so I can include it in the next edition. Asking hotel employees about good places to eat is almost always an excellent way to find out about restaurants that are suited to your taste and budget.

THE BEST OF UTAH DINING

While dining preferences are, of course, an individual "thing," I highly recommend the following ten establishments as representing the best that Utah has to offer. They cover a variety of cuisines and price ranges. As indicated above, Utah doesn't have a particular recognizable cuisine that exemplifies the state but the locals heavily favor western and southwestern restaurants. The location and type of each restaurant is shown below:

- *Adriana's (Cedar City), Continental/American*
- *Cedars of Lebanon (Salt Lake City), Mediterranean*
- *The Garden Restaurant (Salt Lake City), American*
- *Glitretind (Park City), Continental*
- *La Caille Restaurant (Salt Lake City), French*
- *Log Haven (Salt Lake City), Continental*
- *The Roundhouse at Solitude (Solitude), American/Continental*
- *Santa Fe Restaurant (Salt Lake City), Southwestern*
- *Simon's (Midway), American*
- *The Tree Room (Provo/Sundance), Southwestern*

Prices listed in each entry are for dinner entree unless otherwise specified and are exclusive of tax, tip and beverages. Here are my restaurant price guidelines:
- **Very Expensive**: $31 or more
- **Expensive**: $21-30
- **Moderate**: $11-20
- **Inexpensive**: $10 or less

DISABLED TRAVELERS

If you are physically challenged you will be glad to hear that most hotels, restaurants and commercial tourist facilities in Utah have your ease of access in mind. On the other hand, the natural scenery of the state is often difficult to reach and may be almost impossible in some cases, depending upon the nature of your disability. The first priority is to recognize your own limitations and not attempt something that could be hazardous. I've tried to give some indication of the degree of physical abilities needed where appropriate in each of the destination chapters.

Information and assistance for travelers with disabilities is available from a number of sources. Two national organizations that can assist you are the **Information Center for Individuals With Disabilities**, *Tel. 800/462-5015*, or the **Society for the Advancement of Travel for the Handicapped**, *Tel. 212/447-7284*. The State of Utah and the Utah Travel Council will also be happy to provide you with information, *Tel. 800/333-UTAH or 800/200-1160*.

If you have any doubt as to whether you are capable of touring a particular area it is best to speak with someone at the attraction or area. National and State Park personnel will be especially frank and forthcoming on these issues. Likewise, when making hotel reservations it is good idea to inquire about the availability of handicapped rooms and other special facilities, both of which are increasingly common.

GAMING LAWS

Utah is one of the few states in the nation that does not have at least some form of legalized gaming. There isn't even a state lottery. Or Indian gaming. The small Indian reservations haven't actively sought to introduce gaming and the state isn't inclined to enter into a compact with them to do so even if they wanted to. Nevada, of course, is next door.

HEALTH CONCERNS

A trip to Utah won't involve any unusual health risks for the overwhelming majority of visitors. With a few simple precautions and situations to be aware of, it shouldn't present a threat to anyone. The availability and quality of health care in the more populated portions of the state is as good as anywhere else in the United States. Care in sparsely inhabited regions is also good but sometimes may take time to reach in the case of an emergency. Always dial 911 for any medical or other emergency throughout Utah.

If you are taking prescription medication be sure that you have an adequate supply for your entire trip with you. It's also a good idea to have a copy of the prescription. If you're going to be staying in one hotel for more than a day then leave your medicine in the room, only taking with you what you have to use during the course of the day. Otherwise, do what you can to keep all prescriptions out of excessive heat. In the hotter parts of the state you shouldn't leave them in a closed car for any length of time. It's far better to carry the medicine with you even if it is extremely hot outside because a parked car will be even hotter.

Most potential health problems are related either to the altitude, heat, cold, outdoor activity or a combination of these factors. Let's take a brief look at each one. If you live in low country, a sudden increase to great heights can sometimes cause serious consequences known as **Acute Mountain Sickness**. AMS rarely occurs below an altitude of 5,000 feet but becomes increasingly common above 8,000 feet. The latter level is frequently reached in Utah's mountains as well as parts of the high plateau country in the southern portion of the state. Symptoms include difficulty in breathing, dizziness and disorientation. It can be avoided by increasing altitude slowly, preferably over a period of a couple of days. Sometimes your schedule can't conform to that. In such instances it's a good idea to eat lightly and avoid alcoholic beverages for the first day or so that is spent at or above 8,000 feet. If you should start experiencing the symptoms of AMS then descend immediately–that will almost always effect a quick cure. Symptoms that persist, however, require medical attention.

While the higher locations in Utah don't generally get hot enough to cause problems, the summer can see extended periods of temperatures in the high 90's or low 100's. Coupled with strenuous outdoor physical activity, the possibility exists for **heat exhaustion** or more serious **heat stroke**. Both are medical emergencies and require prompt attention. Most of Utah is quite dry, not just the Great Salt Lake Desert area. Therefore, **dehydration** is always a potential problem. Again, chances of it occurring are greater for those expending a lot of energy in the sun. Always be sure to drink plenty of fluids. Have drinks frequently. Don't wait until you're thirsty. Be sure to carry enough water with you if you are going to be hiking. Water isn't readily available in many wilderness areas. A canteen for the car is also helpful as there will be long stretches without towns where you can stop and have a drink. As a rule of thumb you should drink four quarts of water per day if taking part in outdoor activity.

The summer sun is quite strong and the generally high elevation means that the ultra-violet levels can be extremely high. The result can often be a quick and severe **sunburn**. The best way to avoid it is to limit your exposure to the sun as much as possible, especially during the first couple of days. If you are going to be spending a lot of time outdoors, whether it's sitting at the pool or hiking in the back country, you should use a high quality sunscreen. Wearing a hat is also helpful.

The cold is a potential problem for fewer visitors. Most winter visitors will be spending their time at ski resorts and, as a group, are well prepared for dealing with it. Other winter touring, especially in the mountains, requires plenty of warm weather gear. The biggest cold problems often occur in warmer weather. **Hypothermia** can result from spending time in wet clothing. If you are going to be boating or partaking in other activities where you're likely to get soaked, always have a change of clothing handy. Hypothermia can also occur due to sudden drops in temperature. This is most likely to occur in mountainous terrain. Again, the best prevention is to be properly attired. Wear clothing in layers.

Another special hazard that is unique to visitors who will be spending time in the back country hiking or camping is **water contamination**. Even the cleanest looking mountain stream can contain dangerous microorganisms. Be sure to boil all water or use filtration or purification equipment.

Whenever you go hiking in remote areas it is always advisable to be with someone else. Hiking alone is often asking for trouble. Besides being with a partner you should **tell someone else about your hiking plans**–where you plan to go and when you expect to be back. In national and state park facilities you can leave this information with park rangers or officials. At other times you may want to tell someone at the hotel where you are staying or a campground operator. It may seem silly but an ounce of prevention can help to ensure that you won't have any problems. At a minimum it will make certain that someone else is aware of the fact that you may be in trouble when you don't return on time.

A final brief word of caution is in order concerning **hantavirus** and **plague**. The former has appeared from time to time in the southwest and early on imitates the symptoms of flu. It is caught by being exposed to waste from contaminated animals. If you are doing a lot of hiking in remote areas and suddenly come down with flu-like systems, see a doctor. Hantavirus can be fatal. Plague has occurred infrequently in the Four Corners region and shouldn't be a major concern. However, it is always wise to avoid contact with wild animals.

NEWSPAPERS & MAGAZINES

Since both newspapers and magazines are published frequently they offer the most up-to-the-minute information on special events and what's going on in a particular area. Popular magazines geared towards visitors are distributed in most hotels and motels, especially those located within larger metropolitan areas. The most common ones you're likely to encounter while in Utah are *Discover Utah* and *This Week*. Both can be useful for seeing who's in town and are distributed free of charge. Be careful to distinguish between what are paid advertisements versus editorial content. They tend to blur in these types of publications.

Salt Lake City has two newspapers. The largest is the morning daily, *The Salt Lake Tribune*. The *Deseret News* is an afternoon paper but has morning editions on Saturday and Sunday. The *Tribune* is sold throughout the state. *Salt Lake City Magazine* is directed at residents as much as visitors but it does have useful information for travelers. The performing arts are usually well covered. *Utah Highways Magazine* has some useful information for first time visitors but is geared more towards the more experienced back country explorer. The magazine also publishes some specialized brochures on various types of outdoor activity. You can reach them at *Tel. 801/571-1471*.

NIGHTLIFE & ENTERTAINMENT

A lot of people are under the impression that Utah shuts down at sunset and that there isn't much cultural life during the daytime either. In the case of Salt Lake City and the surrounding populated areas, nothing could be further from the truth. Salt Lake City has a rich cultural life and nightlife, and there is also a variety of entertainment available in the mountain ski resorts.

Once you get away from the Salt Lake area, however, things change fast. Although Utah doesn't have any particular type of entertainment that is unique to the state, some of the pageant like shows that have to do with Mormon and pioneer history are excellent. In addition, Cedar City's **Utah Shakespearean Festival** is outstanding. Beyond that the pickings are slim. If you are the type of person who considers nightlife to be an important part of your vacation, then you will be disappointed with most of Utah. The fact is that most visitors don't come to the remote parts of Utah (and that's about eighty percent of the state) to whoop it up come sundown.

The nightlife and entertainment options, both plentiful and hard to come by, will be detailed in each of the regional destination chapters.

SAFETY

Safety from crime should always be on your mind when traveling. The typical tourist, often preoccupied, sometimes appearing perplexed and usually carrying more than a little cash, is often a target for thieves. This is true whether you're in a big city, in a national park, or even in a small town in the proverbial middle of nowhere. In fact, the latter two are often places where visitors are robbed because they think that there isn't crime in such places.

Even though Utah has among the lowest crime rates in the United States you should always remember that there is no spot that is free of crime. Minimize possible crime situations by always having a firm plan as to what you're doing next. Plan your route in advance whether it's by foot or by car. Don't carry much cash. Use credit cards or travelers checks whenever possible. Record credit card and travelers check numbers and keep them in a separate place from the actual cards and checks. Don't leave valuables lying around exposed in your car, even for a short time. Cars with trunks that hide luggage completely are better than hatchbacks where you can see into the storage compartment. Don't wander around after dark in areas that you're unsure about. Again, high crime areas in Utah, even Salt Lake City, aren't as much of a problem as in most states but every city has a few areas that are more dangerous than others. Inquire at your hotel if you have any doubts.

Hotel security is also important. Keep your door locked and don't open it unless you are absolutely sure about the identity of the person seeking entry. Use the deadbolt where provided. If you must have expensive jewelry with you inquire as to the availability of safe deposit boxes in the hotel. While hotel safety is important in any location, it is especially worthy of consideration in larger metropolitan areas. Be sure to familiarize yourself with the location of fire exits. Also make certain that you memorize one or more fire escape routes from your room to the nearest exit and be sure your children understand them as well. This isn't as critical in motels where you have easy access to the street but is of paramount importance in hotels with interior corridors and especially in high rise structures.

In any emergency situation you should dial 911 for coordinated assistance. All of Utah is on this system and your call will be automatically routed to the nearest emergency service.

SHOPPING

Some people almost literally live to shop and make that activity one of the most important parts of any vacation trip. Even those who aren't quite in that category often still want to incorporate some shopping into their travels, especially if they can find unique or unusual items that are "part" of the area they are visiting. In that sense Utah isn't one of the great shopping destinations in the United States. Oh, for sure, you're going to find a decent selection of southwestern and Native American items for sale, especially in the southern portion of the state, but it isn't on the same level as in neighboring southwestern states. The same is true for fine arts.

Utah does have an excellent variety of shopping centers and villages and you won't have any trouble finding just about anything you're looking for. When I do get to places to shop in each of the regional destination chapters I will place special emphasis on things and places that are at least a little out of the ordinary.

TAXES

The statewide sales tax rate is a cumbersome 6.1%. Localities can impose additional taxes of up to 1.5%. Many resort areas are allowed to assess another percent on top of that. Of course, every place in the nation loves to soak the tourist for revenue and Utah is no exception. So, lodging can carry up to a 3% special tax in addition to the sales tax. All in all you can expect to average about 7.5% sales tax on most items and about 10% on lodging. That is lower than in many other states although I would hesitate to refer to Utah as a tax-free zone!

TELEPHONES

Utah used to be easy–just one area code. That ended in 1998. The 801 area code formerly used statewide is now limited to a small geographic area but it covers most of the state's people. Salt Lake City, Ogden, Provo and the corridor between the three localities all use the **801 code**. The remainder of the state lies in the **435 area code**. Calling from one Utah area code to another requires the use of the "1" prefix and the area code. Many calls within the same area code (if they are outside the local dialing area) also require the "1" prefix. Toll-free "800" and "888" numbers must also be preceded by "1."

With so many "800" numbers in use and the fact that part of Utah has "801" for an area code, it can sometimes be confusing as to whether a call to Utah is toll-free or not. So be careful when reading the numbers and when dialing.

TIME OF DAY

Telling what time it is in Utah is quite easy since the entire state is on a single time zone. That is, Mountain Time, two hours earlier than the east coast and an hour later than the west coast. Utah also observes Daylight Savings Time.

TIPPING

The general "rules" of tipping, if there is such a thing, are the same in Utah as anywhere else in the United States. Tipping is strictly a personal decision and, while I don't feel that it's appropriate to tell folks how to tip, for those of you looking for some generally accepted guidelines, it's standard to tip 15% on the total bill for meals (before tax), 10% for taxis, and $1-2 a day for maid service. And of course, if people provide exceptionally good service or go out of their way for you, a more generous tip is often given.

It is also considered the norm to offer a gratuity to tour bus drivers and guides. About $5-10 per day should be adequate. Many tour operators and guide services suggest an amount to give but don't feel obligated to comply exactly with their suggestions.

Keep in mind that most people who are employed in the tourism industry, specifically hotels and restaurants, don't get great salaries. They count on tips for a significant part of their income.

8. SPORTS & RECREATION

Few states in the nation are as outdoors-oriented as is Utah. Whether your recreational interests only involve an occasional easy walk or range all the way up to an adventure-filled expedition on raging rivers or climbing mountains, Utah has it all. Activities extend through all seasons and at all levels of expertise. General information on many of these activities is briefly outlined in this chapter while specific listings of operators, outfitters and facilities will be listed in the Sports & Recreation section of each destination chapter.

BICYCLING

Bicycling in Utah is limited only by your own level of ability and the weather. During the winter months most bicycling needs to be confined almost entirely to the warmer southwestern corner of the state. During the rest of the year there is opportunity for bicycling at all levels of difficulty. Bike routes and trails in park facilities or just along the roads in less developed areas can be appropriate even for novice bikers while some trails are a challenge for the heartiest and most experienced rider.

Bicycle Utah, *Tel. 435/649-5806,* is an organization of businesses and others who have banded together to promote bicycling throughout the state. There are more than a hundred member organizations. The association itself can provide more detailed answers to questions concerning riding in various parts of Utah. They also publish an annual biker's vacation guide.

Places to rent bicycles are common in Utah. If you are flying into the state and bringing a bike with you be sure that you comply with airline regulations for the transportation of bicycles.

BOATING

Besides the **Great Salt Lake** it isn't common to think of Utah as a watery place and even the Great Salt Lake probably doesn't evoke images of sailing to a lot of boating enthusiasts. But it is a popular venue for all kinds of water sports and it isn't the only place in Utah by any means to set sail or to launch a power boat.

Utah Lake near Provo, **Bear Lake** in the extreme northeast corner of the state, the **Flaming Gorge National Recreation Area**, and **Lake Powell** in the Glen Canyon National Recreation Area all have extensive facilities for boating. Many of Utah's rivers involve stretches of rapids so that boating on them is limited more to rafting, canoeing and kayaking than to sailing or motor boats.

FISHING

There are in excess of a thousand lakes and streams where fishing is allowed in Utah. Most of the boating venues indicated above are excellent places to fish as are the many streams that are noted for fly-fishing. The majority of the latter are located in mountain streams along the Wasatch Front or in the Uinta Mountains of the northeast. Fishing is allowed all year long in Utah.

Among the types of fish that can be caught are trout (rainbow, cutthroat, brown and mackinaw varieties), bluegill, striped bass, walleye and whitefish. Regulations can vary from one area to another but are always posted. For general information on fishing regulations it is best to inquire of the **Division of Wildlife Resources**, *1596 West North Temple, Salt Lake City UT 84116, Tel. 801/538-4700.*

GOLF

There are over 80 golf courses in Utah that are open to the visiting public. Courses are most numerous in the Salt Lake City-Ogden-Provo corridor, but many can also be found in the southwestern portion of the state. Golf can be played year-round in the latter region. Course layouts cover all levels of competency and many are situated in brilliant natural settings that enhance the enjoyment of playing a round. Numerous resorts offer golf vacation packages. A good source of further information is **Utah Golf**, *Tel. 801/538-1030.*

HIKING & BACKPACKING

The range of terrains for hiking in Utah is just about as huge as you can get. Whether it's in a national park (see later in this chapter) or a back country area, you'll find easy trails that any person can negotiate to some of the most difficult and challenging rocks in the world. Always be sure you have the proper gear and clothing when hiking and climbing. There are dozens of guide services and hiking vacation services in Utah and you'll find many of them in the chapters that follow.

HORSEBACK RIDING

Access into Utah's back country by horse is becoming a popular way to see some of the most remote areas. Stables and outfitters are located throughout the state. You should be aware that because a lot of the terrain throughout Utah can be of a difficult nature, the inexperienced rider will not find this state to be the best place to ride. However, see the sidebar below on guest ranches. Listings of stables and horseback riding outfitters can be found in the destination chapters.

BE A COWBOY OR COWGIRL...UTAH STYLE

While Utah is not typically western in the same way as Colorado or Wyoming, guest ranches have nonetheless become extremely popular and are now flourishing throughout the state. A lot of that popularity is due to the great scenery that can be explored on horseback, and many of the ranches are located in proximity to some of Utah's most beautiful natural wonders. If you're interested in this type of unique and enjoyable family vacation opportunity, see the listing of guest ranches in Chapter 15.

HOT AIR BALLOONING

This colorful and, for some, relaxing way to take in the scenery is available in many locations throughout the state but mostly in the mountain communities to the east and north of Salt Lake City. While many operate year round, they can be subject to frequent cancellations due to inclement weather–especially during winter.

HUNTING

Hunting in Utah is generally allowed by season in most public areas. However, there is no hunting in all national and state parks and monuments. Big-game hunting permits are issued through a drawing that is held in January but applications must be submitted from mid-October to mid-November. Non-resident licenses for small game are available from any office of the **Division of Wildlife Resources**, *Tel. 801/538-4700,* as well as from almost all sporting goods stores within Utah.

Among the species that can be hunted in Utah are antelope, deer, duck, elk, turkey, pheasant, dove, and several types of grouse and rabbits. Big game includes bears, bobcats and mountain lions. Professional hunting guide services and guest ranches specializing in hunting trips are popular with many sportsmen and women. It is best to contact the Division of Wildlife Resources if you intend to hunt while in Utah and aren't going to be on private hunting lands. Also be aware that airlines have strict regulations relating to the transporting of firearms.

NATIONAL & STATE PARKS, & PUBLIC LANDS

There are more than a hundred different natural and historic areas in Utah administered either by the federal or state government. These include both well known and off-the-beaten-track localities. Almost all of the best natural scenery, of which Utah has an abundance, is encompassed in these areas, which are listed under various designations, such as park, monument, recreation area or historic site. All are self explanatory except for monuments, which can be scenic, historic or otherwise.

Virtually all of the areas shown below are described in greater detail in the appropriate regional destination chapter. However, this section can serve as a checklist of places you want to see or as a means of categorizing what you want to do.

National Park Service (NPS) Facilities

• **Arches National Park**: Southeast region. Scenic (unusual geologic formations resulting from erosion).
• **Bryce Canyon National Park**: Southwest region. Scenic (vividly colored and unusual geologic formations resulting from erosion).
• **Canyonlands National Park**: Southeast region. Scenic (deep river gorges and colorful rock strata).
• **Capitol Reef National Park**: Southeast region (borders on southwest). Scenic (colorful rock formations and effects of erosion).
• **Cedar Breaks National Monument**: Southwest region. Scenic (unusual geologic formations resulting from erosion and vivid color rocks).
• **Dinosaur National Monument**: Northeast region. Natural history and scenic (remains of dinosaurs, river gorges and mountains). Partially in Colorado.
• **Flaming Gorge National Recreation Area**: Northeast region. Recreational and scenic (boating and water sports; lake in colorful canyon). Partially in Wyoming.
• **Glen Canyon National Recreation Area**: Southwest and southeast regions. Recreational and scenic (large man-made lake in colorful canyons). Partially in Arizona.
• **Golden Spike National Historic Site**: Northwest region. Historic (point where the two transcontinental railroads were linked up in the 19th century).

- **Grand Staircase-Escalante National Monument**: Southwest region with extension into southeast. Scenic (unusual and colorful rock formations). Mainly primitive; BLM administered.
- **Hovenweep National Monument**: Southeast region. Historic (remains of ancient Indian civilization). Consists of several scattered units, one in Utah but mainly in Colorado.
- **Natural Bridges National Monument**: Southeast region. Scenic (series of naturally formed rock bridges).
- **Rainbow Bridge National Monument**: Southwest region. Scenic (single large natural bridge) within the Glen Canyon National Recreation Area.
- **Timpanogos Cave National Monument**: Northwest region. Scenic (natural cavern high on mountainside).

National Forests (Department of Agriculture)
- **Ashley National Forest**: Northeast region.
- **Dixie National Forest**: Southwest region.
- **Fishlake National Forest**: Southwest and northwest regions.
- **Manti-La Sal National Forest**: Mostly the southeast region, some extension into northeast.
- **Sawtooth National Forest**: Mostly in Idaho. Small isolated section in northwest region.
- **Uinta National Forest**: Northeast region.
- **Wasatch National Forest**: Northwest region.

State Parks & Monuments
The state of Utah administers a total of 45 parks and other areas. Many are recreation oriented and are primarily "day use" facilities for residents. The locations below are of particular interest to visitors:
- **Anasazi State Park**: Southeast. Historic (ancient Indian civilization remains).
- **Antelope Island State Park**: Northwest. Scenic and recreational (large island in the Great Salt Lake).
- **Coral Pink Sand Dunes State Park**: Southwest. Scenic (large sand dunes with unusual color).
- **Dead Horse Point State Park**: Southeast. Scenic (adjacent and similar to Canyonlands National Park).
- **Edge of the Cedars State Park**: Southeast. Historic (ancient Indian civilization remains and museum).
- **Escalante State Park**: Southwest. Scenic (colorful rock formations).
- **Fremont Indian State Park**: Southwest. Historic (rock art archaeological site).

- **Goblin Valley State Reserve**: Southeast. Scenic (unusual geologic formations).
- **Goosenecks State Park**: Southeast. Scenic (series of "s"-bends in deep river gorge).
- **Great Salt Lake State Park**: Northwest. Recreational (on south shore of Great Salt Lake).
- **Iron Mission State Park**: Southwest. Historic (foundry built by early Mormon settlers).
- **Kodachrome Basin State Reserve**: Southwest. Scenic (unusually colored rock formations).
- **Rockport State Park**: Northwest. Recreational, scenic (mountain rimmed lake).
- **Snow Canyon State Park**: Southwest. Scenic (colorful rock formations).
- **Territorial State House State Park**: Southwest. Historic (first territorial capital)
- **This is the Place State Park**: Northwest. Historic (spot where Mormons first saw the Salt Lake Valley).
- **Utah Fieldhouse of Natural History**: Northeast. Natural history (museum).
- **Utah Lake State Park**: Northwest. Recreational (second largest lake in the state).
- **Wasatch Mountain State Park**: Northwest. Scenic and recreational (mountain scenery, golf, horseback riding, etc.).

Bureau of Land Management

The **Bureau of Land Management**, or BLM as it is more commonly known in the west, has jurisdiction over great tracts of land in Utah. Many but not all are of a wild nature and are hard to reach. They are generally far less developed than National Park Service facilities or state parks. Among the BLM areas in Utah are the Bonneville Speedway, Book Cliff Mountains, Calf Creek Recreation Area, Cleveland-Lloyd Dinosaur Quarry, Cottonwood Canyon, Devil's Rock Garden, Escalante Canyons, Fisher Towers, Grosvenor Arch, Needles Overlook, Price Canyon Recreation Area, the Red Cliffs, and the San Rafael Swell. BLM areas are usually free of charge.

Fees

Most National Park Service and state areas have a per vehicle admission charge. The prices shown in this book for the individual parks were accurate as of press time but have been increasing frequently during the past few years. Regardless of the cost, however, every one represents a bargain considering the wonders that are contained within their borders. And the price increases are based on new regulations that ensure that the fees will be used for maintenance and improvements in the park at which they are collected. That, at least, is a worthwhile cause.

If you are only going to be visiting a few NPS facilities you can simply pay the entrance fee at each one. On the other hand, if your itinerary includes several, then one of the three available "passports" is your best bet. The **Golden Age Passport** is available to any United States citizen aged 62 or over for a one-time fee of $10. **Golden Access Passports** are issued free of charge to any blind or disabled American.

For the general public there is the **Golden Eagle Passport**. This passport costs $50 and is good for one year. All three passports admit the bearer of the card and anyone traveling with him or her in a private passenger vehicle. They cover only park admission fees. Additional charges for tours or services within the parks operated by private concessionaires are not covered although discounts are frequently offered to passport holders. You can get the passports at any National Park Service regional office or at any NPS administered fee area.

Utah state parks are fee areas as well. Annual permits and family permits allow free day-use. For information on permits contact the **Utah Division of Parks & Recreation**, *1636 W. North Temple, Salt Lake City, UT 84116, Tel. 800/322-3770.*

ANOTHER TYPE OF PARK PASSPORT

Visitors who plan on seeing lots of park service areas in Utah as well as other states may wish to "collect" **passport stamps** *as proof of their visit. Each National Park Service facility (at the Visitor Center) provides a place where you can stamp your passport upon entry in a manner similar to going into a foreign country. The stamp contains the name of the facility as well as the date of your visit. You can collect the stamp on any paper or book of your choosing, but most people like to use the official park service passport booklet that is sold for this purpose. It looks almost like a real passport and makes a good record of your travels as well as an interesting conversation piece.*

OFF-ROAD, ATVS & FOUR WHEEL DRIVE VEHICLES

This category represents one of the most popular means of really getting into Utah's incomparable backcountry. Appropriate terrain exists in all portions of Utah and few states have more areas where off-roading is allowed and encouraged. Again, the terrain ranges from relatively simple to the most difficult. Off-roading in Forest Service and Bureau of Land Management administered areas is only allowed where designated.

Many Utah state parks also have designated off-road areas. Outside of these public lands, Utah allows all terrain vehicles and other off-highway vehicles in all places so long as individual land owners don't prohibit it. Be sure to always comply with restrictions on off-roading because you risk being saddled with a heavy fine. In addition, many restricted areas are there to protect fragile environments from the damage that can be done by these types of vehicles.

If you are hesitant about venturing out on your own in an ATV or off-road vehicle, then you should consider a guided tour with one of the many off-road operators that exist in all parts of the state. Rental vehicles are readily available.

RAFTING

Some of the nation's best white water rafting is available on several of Utah's wild rivers. Rafting takes place in the southeast region of the state on the Colorado, Dolores and San Juan Rivers as well as parts of the Green River, which extends into the northeast region. Whitewater is officially designated by "class," or the degree of whitewater. Class I is the most gentle, with successive classes becoming increasingly wilder through Class V. The **San Juan River** rafting experience is Class II while the **Green River** is Class III. Both the **Colorado** and **Dolores** vary depending upon the stretch of the river you're in. The range is from relatively mild Class II all the way up to Class V. If you've never rafted before it is probably best to start with a lower class. Mild float trips are also available on some of these rivers. These usually don't involve many rapids and when they do, they're only Class I.

Utah has almost 20 river outfitters that are associated through **Raft Utah,** *Tel. 801/566-2662.* Trips range from a half day through multi-day. All of these operators (listed in the appropriate destination chapter) have met the requirements and safety protocols established by government agencies. They all have excellent safety records and rafting is considered to be safe when in the hands of experienced and capable guides.

It is standard operating procedure in this industry for the price to include all protective gear and transportation to and from either their office or local hotels to the raft launch site. When planning your rafting adventure don't be afraid to ask the operator beforehand as many questions as you need to determine if it's the right trip for you.

SKIING

"The greatest snow on earth." That's an official state slogan. It even appears on Utah's license plates. So I guess they feel pretty strongly about it. I'm sure there are others, especially in Colorado or Switzerland, that would be glad to debate the matter but there is no denying that Utah is one of the outstanding places to ski in the entire world. The number of facilities may be less than in Colorado but the quality is definitely there.

Downhill skiing is especially popular in Utah, but there's also cross-country and other snow-related activities such as snowmobiling, bobsled, luge and ski-jumping. Helicopter skiing is for those who really want to get to some isolated places to experience the snow.

Utah's ski resort areas are located at altitudes that range from a low of about 7,100 feet above sea level to more than 10,000 feet. The ski season usually extends from November through April. During the months when the greatest amount of snow falls, accumulations can be as high as 100 inches per month. On an annual basis Utah's ski resorts receive an average of between 300 and 500 inches of the white stuff. Information on snow conditions can be obtained by calling *Tel. 801/521-8102*. General information is available from **Ski Utah**, *250 West 500 South, Salt Lake City UT 84101, Tel. 800-SKI-UTAH or 801/534-1779.*

TAKE ME TO THE GREATEST SNOW ON EARTH!

Just where you can find it? There are almost 20 major ski areas in Utah. The majority are located in the Wasatch Mountains in a north-to-south line that parallels the area from Ogden to Provo. Park City is probably the most famous of Utah's ski areas. A few others are located in the southwest. Complete listings of ski facilities by resort will be found in the regional destination chapters. A quick rundown on Utah's ski areas follows. The number in brackets for some listings indicates the distance in miles from Salt Lake City. Although Utah's ski resorts may not be quite as high priced as many in Colorado, they can still be very expensive. Since many are so close to Salt Lake City you can save some money by staying there or in other lower priced communities that are an easy commute to the slopes.

Northwest Region (Chapter 11): Alta [26], Beaver Mountain, Brighton [30], The Canyons [28], Deer Valley [34], Nordic Valley [49], Park City Mountain Resort [32], Powder Mountain [54], Snowbasin [52], Snowbird [24] and Solitude [28].

Southwest Region (Chapter 12): Brian Head and Elk Meadows.

In addition, cross-country skiing only is available at the northwest's Homestead [48], Sherwood Hills [66] and White Pine [32] as well as at Ruby's Inn in the southwest.

Excellent public transportation is available from Salt Lake City to almost all of the major Wasatch Range ski resorts for those who don't wish to drive through the mountains during the winter.

SPECTATOR SPORTS

Aside from a few minor college sports programs scattered about the state, spectator sports are limited to Salt Lake City region including Provo and Logan. Therefore, see Chapter 11 for details.

SWIMMING

All of the lakes that were mentioned in the boating section also are appropriate for swimming during the warmer months. In addition, there's hardly a hotel or large motel in the state that doesn't have at least a small swimming pool. If, by some chance, you happen to be in one that doesn't there's likely to be a municipal swimming pool located nearby.

TENNIS

Tennis courts are usually standard in the major resort properties and at many larger hotels. Non-guests are sometimes allowed to play for an additional fee. However, if you want to get in a game at more reasonable rates, then try one of the many public courts located in major communities and even some smaller ones. A sampling of them will be listed in the regional destination chapters but a good place to find additional courts is to peruse the local yellow pages.

9. MAJOR EVENTS

The calendar is filled with a variety of events big and small from one end of Utah to another. Some don't gain much notoriety outside of their local area while others are world famous. Try a sampling of both kinds for a real Utah experience. Because there are so many events in hundreds of communities, space limitations prevent listing all but some here. So I'll concentrate on those that have the broadest appeal. Many of these are important enough that travelers often time their visits to coincide with the event. Whatever locality you're in, however, it's always a good idea to check with the local chamber of commerce or visitors bureau as well as perusing magazines and newspapers to find out what's going on when you're in town. The chances are good that you may find something that tickles your fancy.

All of the events in this chapter take place each year but the exact dates will often vary from one year to the next. Again, the local chamber of commerce can provide you with more precise information.

JANUARY

Park City's **Sundance Film Festival** gets the year off to a fast start. The Sundance Resort is the spectacular setting for this festival.

Sports are a popular part of Utah's January special events as the **Utah Winter Games** take place at various venues throughout the state. These are an annual tradition in Utah and have nothing to do with the upcoming Winter Olympics.

The **Ogden-Hof Winter Carnival** features food, music, parades and a generally good time. Its name reflects Ogden's "sister" city in Germany.

FEBRUARY

A **Winter Festival** in Bryce takes place in the tiny community outside of the national park. Sports and entertainment play major roles in the goings on.

Park City returns to the calendar with its annual **Snow Sculpture Winterfest.** "Artists" create fantastic shapes and forms with snow and ice, some of which are really elaborate. A ski jumping contest is also part of the event.

The Brian Head ski resort hosts a number of events throughout the winter season. One of the last and best is on President's Day when they hold the **Fireworks & Torchlight Parade.** The pyrotechnics and lights, set against a beautiful mountain backdrop, are simply beautiful.

MARCH

The end of winter brings new reasons to celebrate at Brian Head as they get into the spirit of the warming trend with a popular **Spring Carnival** that features music and entertainment, plenty of food, and sporting events.

The **Easter Jeep Safari** (sometimes held in April depending upon when the holiday falls) is a Moab tradition. Everyone gets decked out in their finest spring regalia, decorates their jeep and heads out into the fantastic countryside. It's a sight.

The **US Mail Trail Ride** in Green River commemorates the old pony express days in a sort of way but it actually consists of many different equestrian events.

A **ski jumping championship** tournament is held in Park City as a way of closing out the ski season.

APRIL

Celebrations to the heritage of the pioneer spirit, specifically that of mountain men, is a popular theme in many parts of Utah. Among the biggest of this genre of events is the **Mountain Man Rendezvous** in Ogden.

A **Jeep Jamboree** in Blanding is on the same idea as the Moab Safari mentioned earlier but this one places more emphasis on jeep driving skills. It's a colorful event because of the nature of the people who take part. Classic car lovers and others who like to see cars on display more than spinning around will enjoy the **Rod Benders Car Show** in Moab.

MAY

The Great Salt Lake is the scene of the annual **Sailing Festival & Race Week.** Hundreds of colorful craft take part in the regatta and races. It's one of the largest inland sailing events in the nation.

Iron Country Cowboy Days in Parowan celebrates the early settlers of the Cedar City area and the importance of iron mining in the development of the region. Plenty of food and entertainment, including a rodeo, will keep visitors busy.

A reenactment of the link-up of the two transcontinental railroads that helped to usher in the growth of the west takes place each year along with steam train rides and demonstrations in the **Golden Spike National Historic Site Reenactment**.

JUNE

The world famous **Utah Shakespearean Festival** opens this month and continues through September in Cedar City. Formal plays, green shows and other events highlight this outstanding tradition.

The small town of Manti plays host to the annual **Mormon Miracle Pageant**. This is a history of the Mormon migration and settlement in Utah and involves a cast of about a thousand people.

Moab hosts the **Butch Cassidy Days**, an old west celebration loosely tied around the fact that the famous outlaw hid out in the rugged surrounding country. Other celebrations of a similar nature are scattered throughout the state. Another good one is in Vernal.

One day in June each year the state of Utah gives a gift to people by offering free admission to all State Parks.

JULY

Utah Pioneer Day Celebrations are held throughout the state all month long but especially around Pioneer Day (July 28th) in a tribute to those hardy souls who withstood travail and misfortune in settling the state. Historic reenactments, rodeos and general partying are a feature of most celebrations.

Logan hosts two important events during July. The first is the respected **Utah Festival Opera** and the other is the **Festival of the American West**. The latter runs into the second week of August and is one of the biggest exhibitions of western folk life. Native Americans, mountain men and cowboys all take part. Cook-offs and quilt making demonstrations are just two of the dozens of activities to be found.

The annual **Dinosaur Roundup Rodeo** is held in Vernal. Unfortunately, you'll have to settle for the usual rodeo bronco-busting and other type events since there aren't any live dinosaurs roaming around to be rounded up. This is, however, one of the biggest of the sanctioned professional rodeo events and has been a tradition for about fifty years.

Shakespeare isn't the only culture on hand in Cedar City. The **American Folk Ballet Summer Festival** adds to the fun in this attractive college town.

AUGUST

Strange as it may seem, Salt Lake City is the host of the **Utah Belly Dance Festival!** I'm surprised that this one hasn't become world famous. Kidding aside, you'll see some expert demonstrations of this ancient art form.

An **Art Festival** is hosted in Park City. The mountain town is filled with artists of all kinds. Musical entertainment and food vendors add to the joyful atmosphere.

An annual **Square Dance Festival** is held near Moab in the beautiful and isolated reaches of Dead Horse Point State Park. Nature at its best, on one hand, and colorful dancers on the other makes for a most unusual sight.

The **Weber County Fair** in Ogden is one of the biggest of the fairs that are held in every Utah county. Exhibits, western crafts, food and entertainment are on the agenda.

SEPTEMBER

If you want to see an Indian fair while in Utah your best bet is to go to Bluff for the excellent **Navajo Fair & Rodeo**. There are large selections of native crafts and jewelry, food, and entertainment as well as traditional rodeo events.

Many racing events are held from time to time on the Bonneville Salt Flats. One of the best is the **World of Speed** where vehicles traveling at the speed of jet planes whiz by in an exciting blur amid the desolate landscape.

A **Mountain Bike Event** and **Oktoberfest** are held in Brian Head as a way of getting ready for the upcoming ski season.

Salt Lake City hosts Utah's **State Fair** and this event has all the things associated with such events–agricultural exhibitions, contests of skill, music and entertainment, plenty of food and more. The **Greek Festival** highlights the city's large community of Greek ancestry.

Utah's largest Indian gathering takes place in Tooele with the **Native American Pow-Wow**. Visitors are welcome to enjoy the dancing, crafts and food.

OCTOBER

Three events are on tap in St. George during the month. These are the **St. George Marathon Race**, the **Jazz & Art Festival** and the **Utah Folklife Festival**. The three provide excellent variety but lots of fun in each case.

Many communities throughout the state hold their own version of **Oktoberfest**. Music, dancing and eating are all big activities. There's even beer at most of them!

NOVEMBER

An unusual event is the **Annual Bison Roundup** that takes place on Antelope Island in the Great Salt Lake. The island is home not only to bison but many other types of wildlife. They're all a part of this educational and interesting event.

The Christmas season gets off to an early start in Salt Lake City and Ogden. The former gets things going with the **Temple Square Christmas Lights**. Thousands of lights make the already beautiful buildings of Temple Square simply dazzling to look at. Ogden holds an **Old Christmas Parade and Village** that will delight all ages with its many lights and animated figures.

DECEMBER

Railroad buffs will enjoy train films and steam train rides at the **Railroad Film Festival** in Promontory Point.

The entire Moab area celebrates the season with the **Canyonlands Christmas Festival**. The emphasis is on old-fashioned methods of celebrating and amid the natural splendor of the region, makes for a less commercialized way of doing things. **Pioneer Christmas Days** in Salt Lake City is another harkening back to simpler times.

UTAH STATE HOLIDAYS

In the regional destination chapters you'll frequently read that some attractions are closed on state holidays. Rather than keep repeating the list of holidays every time that's the case, I'll list them all here:

New Year's Day
Martin Luther King's Birthday *(second Monday of January)*
President's Day *(2nd Monday of February)*
Memorial Day *(last Monday in May)*
July 4th
Pioneer Day *(July 28th)*
Labor Day *(1st Monday of September)*
Columbus Day *(2nd Monday of October)*
Veterans Day *(November 11th)*
Thanksgiving
Christmas

10. UTAH'S BEST PLACES TO STAY

For the most part Utah doesn't bring to mind images of famous world class lodging establishments, especially when compared to some of the neighboring states such as Arizona. However, there are quite a few wonderful places to spend a night or a week and you can generally do so for a lot less money than in just about any other part of the country. There are even a few places that are on a par with the competition anyplace in the world. If picking out a special lodging establishment to stay in is a key component of your travel plans then carefully reading the reviews in this chapter is the best place to begin your search.

It should almost be obvious that the better places are usually in the highest price category, although I've tried to cut across as many price ranges as possible without sacrificing high standards. The same can be said about geographic diversity. The types of establishments in my list of the best places to stay run the gamut from small bed and breakfasts to big city hotels to resorts. In fact, the only category of accommodations I consider to be "ineligible" for the best designation is guest ranches. The only reason I don't consider them isn't because some aren't special or memorable but because they appeal to a specific and relatively small segment of the traveling public.

Some of the things I look for in making my selections for this list include luxury of accommodations, outstanding service and the level of facilities that are available. But just as important are some intangible considerations, like how a place "feels" to me. If there is something that makes it unique or if there's something especially "Utahan" about it, that will also help. Sometimes just the physical setting of the property can be an important factor. After all, Utah is a state of such great natural beauty that a hotel or inn that fits right in with those surroundings is something to be commended.

While I love to rank things, it's almost impossible to separate first from second and so on in the group that qualifies as a Best Place to Stay. Therefore, the listing that follows is simply in alphabetic order.

ANNIVERSARY INN AT THE OLD SALT CITY JAIL, *460 S. 1000 East, Salt Lake City. Tel. 801/533-8184; Fax 801/328-5599. Toll free reservations 800/324-4152. 32 Rooms. Rates: $129-249 including Continental breakfast. Rates about $20 higher on weekends. American Express, Discover, MasterCard and VISA accepted. Located just to the east of downtown via 400 South to 1000 East and then south a half block.*

Not a very romantic name, I admit, to begin a list like this but once you get beyond the awful title things get a whole lot better in a hurry at this wonderfully unique Bed & Breakfast. The two part name can be explained this way–the owners thought that their establishment was a great way to spend a special occasion, such as an anniversary. That's the first part. The bad part of the name comes from the fact that the property was once used as the Old Salt City Jail Building (Salt City was a separate town before it was merged into the larger Salt Lake City). It was constructed in the 1890's and is listed on the National Register of Historic Places.

All of the units are multi-roomed suites with a different theme. The variation is what makes the Anniversary Inn so special. You could stay here a dozen times and no two experiences would be alike. Space limitations won't allow for a complete listing of the possibilities but some of the more interesting themes include Cape Cod, Fisherman's Wharf, Jackson Hole, a lighthouse, Napoleon Suite, an Opera House, a palace, Romeo & Juliet, South Pacific, Swiss Family Robinson, Treasure Island, and Venice. It almost sounds like a roster of theme hotels on the Las Vegas Strip! However, glitz isn't the product–instead, you'll get authentic looking architecture and furnishings and even the aroma and sounds associated with the theme of your accommodations. Every suite features stereo with surround sound, laser-disk movies, large (up to 46") screen television, and your own Jacuzzi. The linens and other accessories are all first quality and every bed at the Anniversary Inn is made up with triple sheeting. A delicious Continental breakfast is brought to your suite every morning. Age restrictions may apply so make inquiry beforehand if traveling with small children.

The public areas at the Anniversary Inn are also quite lovely although not extensive. Colorful and pretty grounds with flowers and mature trees enhance the classic Victorian style architecture. Complimentary snacks are available at several times each day. Unusual for a B&B is the presence of a full service restaurant. The Old Salt City Jail Restaurant is described in the *Where to Eat* section of the Salt Lake City chapter. The Inn has three stories but no elevator so elderly or disabled guests might want to request a room on the lower floor. Tours of the inn are given free of charge every Tuesday and Thursday afternoon at 2:30pm.

The Heers Family, which operates the Anniversary Inn at the Old Salt City Jail, owns another property with a similar style nearby. So, if this one is booked you can inquire about the Anniversary Inn at Kahn Mansion, *700 East at South Temple*. This is a smaller property (13 units) with much of the same charm as its bigger sister. The Kahn Mansion also dates from late 1800's and was owned by a wealthy early Salt Lake City merchant, Emmanuel Kahn.

GREENE GATE VILLAGE HISTORIC BED & BREAKFAST, *76 W. Tabernacle Street, St. George. Tel. 435/628-6999; Fax 435/628-6989. Toll free reservations 800/350-6999. 18 Rooms. Rates: $65-125 including full breakfast; rates run about $10 higher on weekends. Most major credit cards accepted. Located about two miles west of I-15, Exit 8 via St. George Blvd., then left on Main and right on Tabernacle.*

In 1877 Brigham Young decided that the gates and fences surrounding the St. George Temple should be painted green. He offered the excess paint to Mormon property owners so long as they used it to paint their gates green too. The Greene Gate Village is the only property left in the area from that era with its original gate. And it's still green! This unique B&B is, as the name says, a village consisting of nine meticulously restored houses that bring back the feel of the pioneer era while offering guests a host of modern comforts and amenities. Some of the houses are listed on the National Register of Historic Places. One was actually moved here from another site. Also located within the pretty tree shaded confines of the village is the Thomas Judd Store. Upon check in guests are invited to receive a free soda at the Judd store.

Every guest will delight in the sumptuous hot breakfast, which is highlighted by delicious pecan waffles, wonderful homemade breads and muffins and much more. The Bentley House even has a dining room where you can have dinner (Thursday through Saturday only by reservation). The Greene Gate also features an inviting swimming pool that can come in handy after a day of touring in the warm summer sun of Utah's Dixie.

The Carriage House at Greene Gate Village is a banquet center that can accommodate up to 80 people for meetings and dinner. It's extremely popular for family reunions but, of course, Mormon families are often quite large!

Despite the surprising number of guest facilities for a Bed & Breakfast, the real attraction at the Greene Gate are the delightful accommodations. The Orson Pratt House has four guest rooms (each named for people who actually lived there). The Robyn & Natalie, Linsey and Shanna rooms each have a fireplace and either microwave or kitchenette. The Shanna has a whirlpool tub. A couple of them are two-bedroom affairs. The Lysann Room in the Bentley House has a separate sitting room and a private balcony. The Trolley House has two units, each with fireplace. You'll also enjoy the comforts of the Christmas Cottage, Judd House, Green Hedge house, Grainery and Morris. Like the preceding descriptions, the accommodations are quite varied with some units being multibedroom or suite with sitting area. Some have fireplaces and their own whirlpool.

Two of the houses of Greene Gate Village are not located within the village itself. These include the Miles End House, *212 South 200 East*, and the Greenhouse, *162 South 300 West*. The latter is a complete home that has room for as many as 22 people. There are five bedrooms and three baths. A fireplace, whirlpool tub, kitchen and balcony are included as are your own private swimming pool and tennis court. For large groups traveling together it makes a unique vacation opportunity. The rates start at $225 per night for up to six people and you have to add $25 for each additional adult or $10 for children. The breakfast is not included for Greenhouse guests, however.

HOMESTEAD RESORT, *700 N. Homestead Drive, Midway. Tel. 435/ 654-1102; Fax 435/654-5087. Toll free reservations 800/327-7220. 148 Rooms. Rates: $109-259. Major credit cards accepted. Located a mile off of UT 113 via 200 West and 200 North to Homestead Drive.*

A classic and timeless country style inn that could be as much at home in the mountains of New England as it is in the beautiful Wasatch Mountains. The Homestead may well be "the" year round resort in Utah. It consists of many different buildings interconnected by beautiful walkways. Some of the structures are more than a hundred years old. All of them sit amid gloriously landscaped gardens in an even more gorgeous setting–the verdant green meadow that is the broad Snake Creek Valley. The valley is surrounded by the towering peaks of the Wasatch Range. All of the buildings and public areas have the graceful charm of an era gone by but with the modern amenities you expect in a first-class resort. You won't find massive public spaces but rather a cozy and home-like ambiance that produces a welcome atmosphere that is surpassed only by the exceptional warmth of the caring staff.

Considering that there are fewer than 150 guest rooms the accommodations are extremely varied. They range from suites with separate sitting area, fireplace and whirlpool tub to the spacious standard room to antique-filled bed and breakfast style facilities to one to four bedroom private homes. Among the amenities in many rooms regardless of class are kitchens, microwave ovens, coffee makers and safes. The furnishings are all on a traditional style but range from characteristic New England to Southwestern. There's even Victorian style if you choose the B&B-like Virginia House. Linens and toiletries are all of the highest quality but it's the little extra touches that really make the Homestead special—their delicious home made fudge and the tiny stuffed bunny that is the resort's mascot. Almost all guest facilities have a private entrance and a veranda from which you can soak up the magnificent scenery.

Dining at the Homestead is a top-notch experience. Simon's (see the *Where to Eat* section of Chapter 11 for details) offers impeccable food and service while Fanny's Grill is a more casual place to take any meal. Both restaurants have separate cocktail lounges. There is also a snack bar for quick meals located by the golf course.

Despite the warm surroundings that will surely tempt you to remain inside, the recreational opportunities at the Homestead are unsurpassed. Many of the facilities are on an extra fee basis and are open to the general public; however, discounts are given to Homestead guests. They're also available at no extra charge in some cases if you select one of the resort's many package plans.

The nature of the recreation varies by season although much is available year-round. There is a sauna, whirlpool, indoor swimming pool, two lighted tennis courts, hiking and jogging trails, in-room massage service, nature program and a children's playground. In the summer you can fish, mount up on a horse at the Homestead's Hitching Post Stable for a trail ride or take a horse drawn buggy or hay ride. During the winter the buggy ride becomes a sleigh ride. As a prelude to a chateaubriand dinner for two at Simon's, it's an unforgettable evening. You can take a snowmobile ride or go cross-country skiing, all on the Homestead's huge property. Downhill skiing is available nearby.

An unexpected outdoor treat is the Homestead Crater. Dominated by a 55-foot high rock dome, this natural mineral rich water hole has a number of activities. You can take therapeutic mineral baths, swim or snorkel or even scuba dive. By the way, tours of the Crater are offered every day.

For wonderful natural surroundings, great service and countrified elegance there are few places that can match the Homestead. All of this is within a drive from Salt Lake City of just over an hour. It makes the perfect vacation getaway in and of itself or a great base to take in a big chunk of Utah.

THE INN AT TEMPLE SQUARE, *71 W. South Temple, Salt Lake City. Tel. 801/531-1000; Fax 801/536-7272. Toll free reservations 800/843-4668. 90 Rooms. Rates: $130-170 on weekdays and $89-99 on weekends, all including breakfast buffet. Two-bedroom suites are available at $270. Most major credit cards accepted. Located in the heart of downtown across the street from the south side of Temple Square at the Crossroads Plaza shopping center.*

Dating from 1930, the Inn at Temple Square is an excellent example of Edwardian architecture and is reminiscent in style of the small elegant hotels of Europe. It has been faithfully restored to its original appearance. Noted for its fine service, this charming little hotel fits in exceedingly well with the classic surroundings of Temple Square. From the moment you approach the main entrance with its cobblestone courtyard and neatly planted flowers, you'll know this is a special place. The highly trained and personable hotel staff will gladly see to your every need.

The warm and intimate lobby is similar in appearance and comforts to a European grand hotel. Plushly furnished and dimly lit, it is a quiet haven that is literally steps away from the center of the city. Guest rooms are tastefully appointed with many individual differences. However, the elegance of 18th century Edwardian England is the overall theme. Some rooms have four poster beds. All feature a host of modern amenities.

For your dining pleasure the Carriage Court Restaurant features luxurious and private surroundings with excellent food and service to match. Both Continental and American cuisine are featured. A traditional style dinner is served every Sunday evening. See the *Where to Eat* section of Chapter 11 for more details. There aren't any recreational facilities in the hotel but this isn't meant to be a full service resort. For the business or vacation traveler who is seeking a refined, quiet atmosphere with excellent accommodations and outstanding service, the Inn at Temple Square has everything you could possibly need.

LITTLE AMERICA HOTEL & TOWERS, *500 South Main Street, Salt Lake City. Tel. 801/363-6781; Fax 801/596-5910. Toll free reservations 800/ 453-9450. 850 Rooms. Rates: $89-134. Major credit cards accepted. Located 5 blocks south of Temple Square at the corner of Main Street.*

One of America's premier city hotels, the Little America doesn't quite appear the part when you first see it. The 17-story high tower looks much like a modern high-rise luxury apartment building with its dark brown brick construction. But that appearance quickly changes when you step into the luxuriously appointed interior. The outstanding service for which the Little America is so famous begins with a warm welcome at the registration desk and will continue until the moment you check out. The Salt Lake City Little America is the flagship property in a small chain of the same name. They have three other Little Americas (two in Wyoming and one in Flagstaff, Arizona) as well as hotels going by other names in San Diego and Sun Valley, Idaho.

The lobby and other public areas feature some of the same exterior brick construction but are enlivened considerably by generous use of plants and flowers as well as beautifully domed stained glass ceiling areas. These feature western themes and are among the most brilliant I have seen anywhere. Much of the public spaces are taken up by meeting facilities as the Little America is also Salt Lake's most prestigious business address.

The wonderfully appointed guest rooms vary in style greatly so you could return time and again and experience a new feeling each time that you visit. But high quality furnishings and tasteful decor are evident in every room. There are three main classes of accommodations. The largest number of rooms are those in the tower but the lowest priced rooms are situated in two-story lodge style accommodations adjacent to the main building. The executive suites are larger and more luxurious facilities that occupy the top two floors of the tower. These feature Italian marble baths. Regardless of which level of accommodations you choose you can count on a great room at an affordable price with such nice touches as thick plush towels (robes in the Executive Tower), turndown service and immaculate housekeeping. Coffee makers, microwave ovens and in-room safes are some of the commonly found amenities.

The exquisite Little America Dining Room (see the *Where to Eat* section of Chapter 11) is an excellent choice for fine dining while the hotel's coffee shop offers much better than the usual fare found at these kinds of eateries. Live entertainment is featured at the Westgate Lounge. For recreation the Little America has both indoor and outdoor swimming pools (the outside version is large and is surrounded by many trees in a park-like setting), wading pool, health club and a spa with whirlpool and sauna. Off of the main lobby is a small shopping mall with several nice shops where you can purchase gifts for the friends back home. Upscale clothing shops are also featured.

There is plenty of on-site parking although a fee is charged. The location is excellent for touring downtown Salt Lake City (it's walking distance from Temple Square) and it's even close enough to the mountain resort areas that many skiers choose to stay here rather than in the usually more expensive ski resorts. Even with the extra transportation costs it will probably save you a considerable sum. All things considered, for the luxury you get the Little America almost has to be considered a real bargain.

THE LODGE AT BRIAN HEAD, *314 Hunter Ridge Road, Brian Head. Tel. 435/677-3222; Fax 435/677-3202. Toll free reservations 800/386-5634. 40 Rooms. Rates: High season (winter): $89-159 with higher end of scale on weekends; Low season (summer): $49-69, all rates including Continental breakfast. Many package plans with additional services are available. American Express, Discover, MasterCard and VISA accepted. Located just off Utah 143 about two miles north of the Cedar Breaks National Monument.*

I must first emphasize that the Lodge at Brian Head isn't on the same luxury level as some of the other places in this chapter. But it does have beautiful accommodations and a great location–all at what are bargain rates for a ski resort. It certainly is a best buy and worthy of inclusion among the best places to stay on that score alone.

The three-story white stone structure with blue trim sits attractively near the base of some of Brian Head's chair lifts. During the winter it blends in beautifully with the snow covered terrain. You can choose from the hotel rooms with queen beds or studio suites that have either king or queen beds. All rooms are attractively decorated, well maintained and comfortable. On premise facilities include a restaurant, heated indoor swimming pool, three Jacuzzi's, arcade room and a private club called the Club Royale Lounge. One of Brian Head's better night spots, temporary memberships are available to guests.

The Lodge is part of the larger community of Brian Head with several other lodging facilities, quaint shopping and almost unlimited recreational pursuits regardless of the time of the year. Guests at the Lodge can take advantage of all this via Brian Head's shuttle service. The staff will gladly arrange for your activities in the surrounding area.

NOVEL HOUSE INN, *73 Paradise Road, Springdale. Tel. 435/772-3650; Fax 435/772-3651. Toll free reservations 800/711-8400. 10 Rooms. Rates: $85-105 including full breakfast. Major credit cards accepted. Located off of Utah Highway 9 about one mile from the south entrance to Zion National Park.*

The name of this distinctive little place is based on the fact that all of the guest units are named for famous authors. These are Walt Whitman, Mark Twain, Louis L'Amour, Leo Tolstoy, Robert Louis Stevenson, C.S. Lewis, Rudyard Kipling, Charlotte Bronte, Jane Austin and Charles Dickins. Hmmm–my name seems to have been omitted. Oh, well, I won't take it personally. The decor in each room is reflective of the period and style associated with each of these great novelists. For instance, in the Kipling Room the four-poster bed has mosquito netting while the Tolstoy Room has an Anna Karenina armoire and czarist style bench. Every comfortable unit has, in addition to beautiful furnishings, a luxurious full bath and other modern amenities.

The exterior of Novel House doesn't prepare you for the interesting nature of the accommodations. The large modern two-story building is attractive but doesn't have the typical B&B appearance. It has been designed so that almost all of the rooms have an excellent view of the surrounding natural masterpiece–Zion National Park. You can watch the sun come up over Temple Mountain from your room or take in sunset over Watchman Mountain from the lovely covered porch.

Each day starts out with a delicious breakfast of muffins, sausage, quiche and much more accompanied by music that ranges from modern ballads to the classics. Winter menus aren't as extensive as during the summer months but are still more than adequate. In addition to breakfast Novel House offers a daily tea service along with cheese and other snacks. During the hotter months you can also sip on some refreshing homemade lemonade or punch. There's also a library, which you would expect in a place that is devoted to the great names of literature. Several board games can also be borrowed from the library to spend a few hours in the calm, quiet evenings of Springdale.

STEIN ERIKSEN LODGE, *7700 Stein Way, Park City. Tel. 435/649-3700; Fax 435/649-5825. Toll free reservations 800/453-1302. 131 Rooms. Rates: High season (early December through mid-April): $450-675 for rooms and $950-1,450 for suites, including a breakfast buffet; Low season (mid-April through early December): $175-200 for rooms and $250-300 for suites. Major credit cards accepted. Located via Deer Valley Drive to Royal street near the south side of town and following signs.*

This is one of Utah's highest priced (if not the most costly) ski resort lodge. So it had better offer something to justify those sky high rates. For the discerning traveler who demands the best, it certainly does. Built in the style of a Norwegian skiing lodge, the Stein Eriksen sits at the base of an aspen and pine covered mountain slope. The rarified air at this 8,200 foot elevation is as invigorating as the view. The luxury accommodations and outstanding service are on the same level. It's located in the heart of the Deer Valley Resort and has ski-in and ski-out facilities. It offers seclusion yet is in close proximity to all of the activities of Park City.

The recipient of many awards, the lodge is a member of the prestigious Small Luxury Hotels of the World. Beauty is everywhere, beginning with the impressive lobby. Highlighted by Scandinavian decor and color schemes, there's a warm fireplace and over the mantle a huge elk head against a stone chimney wall. The large dark wooden beams contrast nicely with the lighter colored sloped wooden ceiling. Plush furnishings add a warm home-style touch to the surroundings.

First class dining is available at the Glitretind Restaurant (described in the *Where to Eat* section of Chapter 11) and in the Troll Hallen Lounge.

The menu varies by season and features the freshest cuisine, magnificently presented and served on a table with freshly cut flowers. There is a heated outdoor swimming pool with a superb mountain view. It is glass enclosed so as to protect bathers from the sometimes strong mountain winds. Also on the premises are a whirlpool, sauna, and complete fitness center with massage facilities. Many more recreational services are available in the surrounding area and can be arranged for you by Stein Eriksen's attentive and knowledgeable concierge staff.

Guest accommodations consist of standard rooms, suites and grand suites. All are luxurious and spacious. All feature oversized bathrooms, coffee makers, in-room safe and plush furnishings. Suites have designer furnishings, European kitchens, fireplace, separate living area, two bathrooms (one with jetted tub), his and her dressing areas and wrap-around balconies. The Lodge's great service extends to the rooms where you'll be pampered with twice daily maid service.

Topping things off are a small shopping area with exclusive clothing and gift items, as well as a full service ski shop. Stein Eriksen Lodge offers many package plans according to season which may include meal and recreation options.

SUNDANCE, *State Highway 92, Sundance. Tel. 801/225-4107; Fax 801/226-1937. Toll free reservations 800/892-1600. 113 Rooms. Rates: High season (mid-December through March): $195-425; Low season (April through mid-December): $150-275. All rates including full breakfast. Most major credit cards accepted. Located northeast of Provo via US 189 and then left on Utah 92.*

Sundance will immediately appeal to many women when they hear that it is the "baby" of actor Robert Redford, who first conceived the idea in 1969 for a resort that would be in harmony with the beautiful natural surroundings. This village style resort is located in Sundance Canyon on the east facing slope of 12,000-foot Mount Timpanogos, the highest peak in the Wasatch Range. The property covers an impressive 6,000 acres and is a completely self-contained full service resort. But it's more than that. A community devoted to the performing arts, the culture of Native Americans and a place to protect and preserve the environment while still being enjoyed are all parts of the Sundance experience. It is a place where your physical being and spirit can be at one with nature. The canyon contains much wildlife and they can frequently be seen by Sundance guests.

The architecture is generally rustic western. Most of the buildings are hand hewn native woods with often massive beams and stone. Native American baskets, pottery, weavings and rugs highlight the decor in public areas.

Whether or not you're a guest at Sundance, one of its most important aspects is the now world-renowned Sundance Institute, which was added in 1981. Professional theater is offered during the summer in an outdoor amphitheater under the star-filled night sky of this beautiful mountain setting. There's daytime theater for children. The Sundance Film Festival has also become a respected event in the industry.

The basic accommodation is referred to as a "guest cottage," while for the upper end of the price scale you can treat yourself to the luxury of a multi-room mountain home. All are located either in the woods or streamside. They provide complete privacy in which to enjoy nature as well as the many modern amenities that Sundance offers. There are also some nice lodge units. Most units either have a kitchen or efficiency should you desire to eat in. Mountain homes generally have fireplaces and/or wood-burning stoves, whirlpool or steambath. In room coffee and tea, VCR and plush terry robes are just a few of the amenities. Interior styles range from the rustic to modern western. But always featured are large windows to let in the great outdoors and the varied earth-tone colors that are found throughout the southwest. Fabulous at any time of the year, perhaps nothing can be so special as a winter visit to Sundance when you return to your snow-covered cabin in a bright white meadow. At night the lights shine through the windows and create a uniquely beautiful picture.

Dining choices at Sundance are quite varied. The award-winning Tree Room Restaurant is described separately in the *Where to Eat* section of Chapter 11. The Foundry Grill offers excellent selections in a less formal atmosphere and the Sundance Deli is available for light meals or quick snacks. Regardless of where you dine the ambiance and food are wonderful. They claim that the great dining is due to the fresh ingredients and organic produce that are all grown on their very own Sundance Farms. Could well be but I think the fine western surroundings and outstanding service also have something to do with it. Sundance has a private club called the Owl Bar, which is delightful. Temporary memberships are available at a nominal cost. All of the dining is located in Sundance's own Village. Also within the Village is a most interesting shop called the General Store. High quality western and Native American goods are on sale. In fact, the General Store was such a success that the resort now offers much of the merchandise there to the general public through the Sundance Catalog.

With its unbeatable physical setting you would expect Sundance to have outstanding recreational facilities—and it does. It begins with a complete fitness center and ends with a full service massage facility. Fishing, hiking and horseback riding are popular during the warmer months while mountain biking is a year-round pursuit. Sundance also has one of Utah's finest skiing facilities and offers both downhill and cross-country varieties. Children certainly aren't ignored at Sundance as their Kid's Camp provides a whole day of fun-filled supervised activities.

With all of this to offer I would still, if asked what is the best thing about Sundance, answer by saying that you can explore the beauty of nature minutes from the privacy of your own room. The lush natural green carpet of the deep valley, rushing streams and brilliant gold colored peaks (except when they're entirely snow covered) make Sundance extra-special.

SUNFLOWER HILL BED & BREAKFAST INN, *185 N. 300 East, Moab. Tel. 435/259-2974. Toll free reservations 800/662-2786. 11 Rooms. Rates: High season (March through October): $115-155; Low season (November through February): $85-135, all rates including full breakfast. Discover, MasterCard and VISA accepted. Located about a quarter mile northeast of US Highway 191 via 100 North to 300 East.*

A classic and delightful bed and breakfast inn, the Sunflower Hill is located on a quiet residential street not far from the center of town. While the fantastic formations of the nearby national parks are not visible from the property, it does have its own kind of beauty. The many gables of the large red house sit attractively on nicely landscaped grounds amid mature shade trees. The covered front porch or chairs out on the lawn make a great place to relax after a day of activity in the nearby natural playgrounds. In addition, the warm and personal attention of your hosts will enhance your stay even further.

The eleven rooms range from standard to suite and on to deluxe and luxury. There isn't all that much difference in price so going for the top is a good idea but they're lovely whatever category you select. All feature beautiful antique beds while the deluxe rooms have their own whirlpool tubs and private balcony or patio. Light colored natural woods and bright and cheerful bedcovers and accessories make these units a joy.

The breakfast is huge and includes fresh fruit and homemade breads and pastries. Refreshments are served each evening and there is also an outdoor barbecue facility. An outdoor hot tub can be found on the grounds along with wooded pathways for just wandering around. But the best of the public areas may well be the large western styled lounging area with its massive fireplace and simple but comfortable furnishings. It's a great place for guests to gather during the evening and discuss their adventure-filled days in the surrounding country.

11. SALT LAKE CITY & THE NORTHWEST

With nearly eight out of every ten Utah residents residing in the Northwest region, it is no surprise that the urban-oriented traveler will find the largest and most interesting of Utah's cities right here. But you are never far from nature anywhere in Utah, and even the populated corridor that fronts the Wasatch Mountains is within minutes of dozens of interesting scenic attractions. While other regions of Utah may have the best and most unusual scenery, the northwest has a greater variety than any other part of the state. It has the largest lakes, desert and mountains, to name just a few.

Salt Lake City is the state's capital and largest community. It was founded on July 24, 1847 by a group of less than 150 people (only five of who weren't adult men) led by Brigham Young. They began the process of settlement the same day of their arrival. The center of the new town was to be the location of a temple and it remains so to this day...the famous square block known as **Temple Square**. Many more Mormon settlers soon followed the first party and they set about diligently building an agriculturally based community. The rest of the city's history parallels the remainder of Utah quite closely, but nowhere is the growth of the state as much in evidence as in this modern and bustling metropolis.

The city's setting is spectacular. The towering peaks of the **Wasatch Mountains** lie immediately to the east. Besides being a visually stunning backdrop for an emerging skyline of high-rise office towers, the mountains provide a year-round playground for both residents and visitors alike. The **Great Salt Lake** is to the northwest and the open expanse of the desert sits on the western edges of the metropolitan area. Several things are quickly in evidence to the visitor. The first, of course, is the aforementioned mountains. The second is the broad avenues that cover the city in a neat grid pattern. This was due to the foresight of Brigham Young, who decreed that the streets would have to be "wide enough for a team of four oxen and a covered wagon to turn around." Salt Lake City also possesses a clean and almost intangible orderly appearance. The city is also the cultural center of Utah as it is home to many venues for the performing arts as well as several outstanding museums. Sports and recreation, too, are an important part of the daily scene.

Getting back to the natural setting for a moment, one of the more interesting aspects of the city's location is the large number of canyons that lie immediately to the east of the city. They offer a different perspective than the "macro" city picture seen from the mountains or the mountains as seen from the city. Some lie partially within the city itself while others are in neighboring towns. All told, there are more than a dozen canyons. Among the more significant ones, listed from north to south, are **City Creek, Red Butte, Emigration, Parley's, Millcreek, Tolcats, Ferguson, Little Willow, Big Cottonwood, Little Cottonwood** and **Bells Canyons**. Many of these have attractions that are described in the *Seeing the Sights* section below. But all of them can be explored, some by car and others by foot, to get a full appreciation of the Salt Lake City area landscape.

Other interesting communities within the northwest are Ogden to the north and Provo to the south. The latter is the home of Brigham Young University and sits in close proximity to a scenic loop road. The ski resorts of Utah are concentrated in the mountains that parallel the three cities with the greatest number being located in and around Park City. The Great Salt Lake and the desert, as well as many other interesting natural and man-made attractions are ideally seen in short excursions from Salt Lake City.

ARRIVALS & DEPARTURES
By Air

The modern **Salt Lake City International Airport** is conveniently located less than five miles from the center of the city. Eleven different airlines serve about 21 million passengers each year on almost 400 daily flights. All major car rental companies have airport offices. If you are driving into town from the airport, pick up I-80 east bound immediately south of the airport exit.

There are several public transportation options from the airport. In addition to taxis or city bus you can use **Airport Limousine SLC, Inc.,** *Tel. 800/546-6871*; **Big City Transportation,** *Tel. 888/400-9592*; or the **Salt Lake Shuttle,** *Tel. 800/818-8944*. The latter also provides transportation to all ski resorts and other cities and towns along the Wasatch Front.

By Bus

   Greyhound, *Tel. 800/231-2222*, provides intercity service to Salt Lake City. Their terminal is located at *160 West South Temple* in the heart of downtown. Greyhound also serves Brigham City, Logan, Ogden, Orem, Provo and Wendover.

By Car

   Almost every person who is traveling to Salt Lake City by car will be coming in via means of one of two major Interstate highways. Those coming from either north or south will be on **I-15** while travelers from the east and west will be on **I-80**. The two converge for a three mile section that more or less parallels downtown. Exit 310 provides the best access into the center of the city. That exit leads directly into 600 South, which is about six blocks from the city center. The easiest method back to the freeway from downtown is via 500 South.

   I-15 also provides access to most of the rest of the region that lies in the Salt Lake City-Ogden-Provo corridor. US 89 closely parallels the Interstate and goes through many communities that lie along the highway. I-80 traverses the east-west axis of the northwest.

By Train

   The **Amtrak** station in Salt Lake City is located in **the Denver & Rio Grande Depot**, *Broadway and Rio Grande Street (two blocks west of 300 West)*. Service is once daily in each direction (east and west-bound). Amtrak also provides connecting bus service from the station to Ogden. There is direct train service to Provo. Contact Amtrak, *Tel. 800/USA-RAIL,* for schedules.

ORIENTATION

   Salt Lake City lies within a relatively narrow area that extends from the foothills of the Wasatch Mountains on the east to the Great Salt Lake Desert on the west. Areas to the north or south have the same geographic restrictions but part of the western edge to the north of the city is the Great Salt Lake itself. Various suburbs of Salt Lake City extend in both directions until they blend in with either Ogden in the north or Provo in the south. It is this corridor that constitutes home for the overwhelming majority of Utahans. By turning and facing the mountains, that is, standing towards the east, you should usually always be able to get your bearings.

   As was mentioned in the arriving by car section, Interstates 15 and 80 are the two main highways and they meet in Salt Lake City. I-215 is a soup-ladle shaped highway that starts in North Salt Lake at I-15 and runs parallel to I-15 before turning east and crossing it in the southern suburb of Midvale. It then turns north at the foothills of the Wasatch and ends at I-80 at the southeastern city limits. The only other controlled access highway is a small stretch of UT 201 on the southwest edge of the city that connects I-215 with I-15/80.

Just about all of Salt Lake City itself is a neat grid pattern that dates from the city's founding. This makes figuring out where you are and where you are going a snap with only a little bit of practice. Temple Square is the center of the city and all street numbering begins from that point. Most major streets are numbered such as 100, 200, 300 etc. (Sometimes there are streets like 320. This would usually be an unimportant street between the 300 and 400 blocks.) So, for example, "200 West 400 South" is located two blocks west of the temple and 4 blocks south. It can be a little confusing at first but is actually quite simple when you think about it for a while. Some residents tend to drop the last two digits so if you're told that something is on 8 North, it means 800 North.

Some important named streets are North Temple and South Temple (both running east to west and forming the northern and southern edges of Temple Square), West Temple and Main Street (running north to south and forming the west and east edges of Temple Square), and State Street which runs north to south a block east of Main Street. Some of the named streets have numeric equivalents as follows:
• State Street = 100 East
• West Temple = 100 West
• North Temple = 100 North

There are relatively few named streets, other than the above, which are of great significance. A number of these streets lie to the east or west of the capitol. The only other layout pattern that you need to be familiar with is an area to the immediate northeast of downtown that is known as the Avenue District. This is also a grid pattern but the grid is smaller than in the rest of the city. Within this district, which contains many historic houses, numbered avenues (1st, 2nd, etc.) run from east to west while lettered streets (A, B, etc.) run from north to south.

The majority of other communities and attractions in the northwest lie along a straight line extending in all four directions from Salt Lake City. Ogden and Provo are the two largest cities after Salt Lake City. Both also have orderly grid patterns for the most part. Provo uses a numbered quadrant system similar to Salt Lake while Ogden has numbered streets running east to west and named avenues (mostly of presidents) or boulevards running north to south.

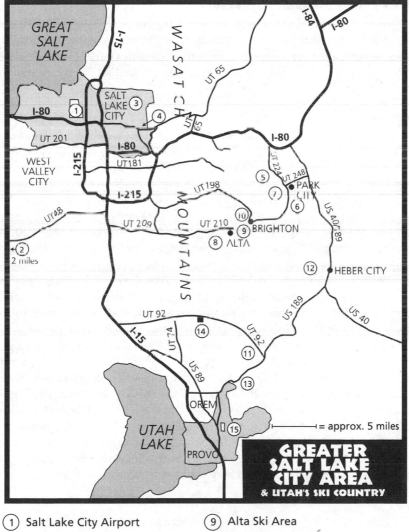

1. Salt Lake City Airport
2. Bingham Canyon Open Pit Copper Mine
3. University of Utah
4. This Is The Place State Park
5. Canyons Ski Area
6. Deer Valley Ski Area
7. Park City Mtn. Resort
8. Snowbird Ski Resort
9. Alta Ski Area
10. Brighton Ski Area
11. Sundance Resort
12. Wasatch Mtn. State Park
13. Bridal Veil Falls
14. Timpanogos Cave National Monument
15. Brigham Young University

GETTING AROUND TOWN

When you get into the sightseeing section of this chapter I'll give you specific instructions on how to reach all of the important attractions by foot (where appropriate), car and public transportation. But for now, here's some general information on getting around Salt Lake City and the northwest.

By Bus

The **Utah Transit Authority (UTA)** provides service within Salt Lake City and the entire Utah Valley, as well as in several neighboring counties on about a hundred different routes. There are four routes with service to Ogden and four to Provo. Most routes are wheelchair lift equipped and also have bicycle racks. Bus stops are marked by blue signs that list which route or routes stop there. Exact fare, bus tokens or a monthly pass is required when boarding. Many routes within the city operate until around midnight. Transfers from one route to another are issued upon request after paying the initial route fare. They are good for two hours.

The basic one-way fare within Salt Lake City is $1. Frequency of service depends upon the route but most lines serving the downtown area run every 20 to 30 minutes during the week with some even more frequently. Lines serving many of the outlying areas only have hourly runs or even less frequent service so they aren't always the ideal way to get around if you're on a tight schedule. Call *Tel. 801/287-4636* for route and schedule information. The UTA also maintains a **Transportation Information Center** in downtown Salt Lake City, *167 South Main Street*. There is a free ride zone within the downtown area. See the sidebar later in the chapter. Construction is now proceeding on a light rail system for downtown in the vicinity of Main Street. This might cause temporary detours on buses serving the area as well as traffic congestion. Ogden and Provo also have their own municipal bus systems.

By Car

Salt Lake City may be the biggest city by far in Utah but it isn't so heavily populated as to have massive traffic problems, at least compared with most major American cities. Of course, you won't hear that from the locals who often bemoan the urban growth and the accompanying traffic problems with heartfelt conviction that is hard for, say an easterner, to understand. Traffic congestion is mitigated to some extent by the fact that the metropolitan area is quite spread out considering the amount of people. Of course, you're going to encounter at least some delays going into or out of the downtown section during the rush hours. Not everyone is on vacation like you are and they have to get to work. Poor souls! The

Utah Department of Transportation is in the midst of a major four-year expansion and renovation of I-15 that will not be complete until sometime around 2001. Therefore, you can expect some delays or detours at times while negotiating I-15 through the Salt Lake metropolitan area.

On-street parking is controlled by meter in most sections of the city and generally has a two hour time limit. This is enforced rather strictly so don't be surprised to see a parking ticket if you run over. Meters stay in effect from about 8:00am to 6:00pm. The downtown area has many garages, including those at the Crossroads and ZCMI shopping centers adjacent to Temple Square. Garage parking in downtown usually runs about $1 an hour up to a daily maximum of $6 or less. Once you get out of the downtown area most attractions will have sufficient free parking.

By Taxi

As in most cities, traveling by taxi in Salt Lake City isn't the cheapest way of getting around. Fares begin with an initial flag drop of $1.25 and increase at $1.50 for each additional mile. Consult the Practical Information section at the end of this chapter for a complete listing of taxi cab companies operating in the Salt Lake City area.

WHERE TO STAY

Salt Lake City accommodations will be divided into two zones. The first covers downtown and the immediate adjacent areas. The second covers the rest of the city as well as several nearby suburban communities. After that there's an alphabetical listing of other localities throughout the northwest region.

SALT LAKE CITY–DOWNTOWN

Expensive

DOUBLETREE HOTEL SALT LAKE CITY, *255 S. West Temple. Tel. 801/328-2000; Fax 801/532-1953. Toll free reservations 800/222-TREE. 495 Rooms. Rates: $125-169. Major credit cards accepted. Located three blocks south of the west side of Temple Square and a block south of the Salt Lake Visitor Information Center.*

Ideally situated in the heart of downtown and close to everything, the Doubletree is one of the city's biggest and most luxurious hotels. Although I'm not frequently overly impressed by the all-too-often sameness of modern hotel high rises (this one is 18 stories), the Doubletree breaks the mold in several positive ways. The exterior is shining white and has its upper three floors jutting out over the rest of the structure; it is a handsome edifice to say the least.

The rooms are modern, spacious and quite attractive. If you're in the top half of the building you're likely to have good mountain or city views.

Executive level rooms are more plush. While mainly attuned to the needs of the business traveler the Doubletree does provide a number of facilities that the vacation traveler will also appreciate. These include two restaurants, cocktail, lounge, an indoor swimming pool and a complete fitness center with Jacuzzi and saunas. I always have to recommend at least one Doubletree Hotel to promote their fabulous fresh-baked chocolate chip cookies! But I wouldn't find fault with this property even if there weren't any cookies (perish the thought!). The level of service here is higher and more personable than at many so-called upscale chains, another strong point to its credit.

THE INN AT TEMPLE SQUARE, *71 W. South Temple. Tel. 801/531-1000; Fax 801/536-7272. Toll free reservations 800/843-4668. 90 Rooms. Rates: $130-170 on weekdays and $89-99 on weekends, all including continental breakfast buffet. Two bedroom suites are available at $270. Most major credit cards accepted. Located in the heart of downtown across the street from the south side of Temple Square at the Crossroads Plaza shopping center.*

A small luxury hotel in the grand European style, this Edwardian style structure dates from 1930 and has been beautifully restored. It's not a place with a lot of recreational facilities but, rather, a service oriented city center hotel with outstanding accommodations that are dignified and tastefully appointed. The location is within walking distance of most of Salt Lake City's most important sights as well as major shopping and entertainment venues. There's a good restaurant on the premises.

Selected as one of my Best Places to Stay (see Chapter 10 for more details).

THE MARRIOTT HOTEL, *75 S. West Temple. Tel. 801/531-0800; Fax 801/532-4127. Toll free reservations 800/345-4754. 515 Rooms. Rates: $99-189 with the higher range generally during the ski season. Major credit cards accepted. Located a block south of Temple Square near the Crossroads Plaza and across the street from the Salt Lake Visitor Center.*

Like all of the properties in the Marriott chain, this is a first class operation housed in a modern but otherwise rather dull looking 16-story high tower. It is connected to the Crossroads Plaza Shopping Mall so once you're settled in for the night you can quickly go buy something if the urge strikes. On a more practical level the Marriott features decent family dining at Allie's and more upscale fare at the popular JW's Steakhouse & Seafood Restaurant. There are also several fast food places on the premises including a Pizza Hut. Pitcher's Private Club offers temporary memberships to guests.

On the recreational side the Marriott boasts an indoor/outdoor swimming pool with hydrotherapy facilities and an excellent fitness center with saunas. Complimentary transportation to the airport is provided. First rate concierge service is a Salt Lake City Marriott hallmark. The hotel also offers a number of ski packages.

SALT LAKE HILTON, *150 W. 500 South. Tel. 801/532-3344; Fax 801/531-0705. Toll free reservations 800/421-7602. 366 Rooms. Rates: $155-179. Major credit cards accepted. Located five blocks south of Temple Square between 200 West and W. Temple.*

A nice first class hotel that's typical city-center Hilton. All of the rooms have been renovated within the past several years and they're quite nice. Those in the upper price range are unusually spacious. There are two restaurants (one of which provides a good view of the mountains), sauna, hot tub, swimming pool and fitness center. Like the Marriott, this hotel may be in the city but it offers plenty of plans for skiers. It also has facilities for skiers including rental and wax room on the premises. Room At the Top is an outstanding restaurant that is listed in the *Where to Eat* section that follows.

WOLFE CREST BED & BREAKFAST INN, *273 N.E. Capitol Blvd. Tel. 801/521-8710; Fax 801/596-1316. Toll free reservations 800/669-4525. 14 Rooms. Rates: $130 for one bedroom units, including full breakfast. Most major credit cards accepted. Located immediately to the southeast of the State Capitol. Take State Street north from downtown.*

Located in the historic Capitol Hill area just a few minutes walk from the state capitol and Temple Square, the Wolfe Crest is a large and luxurious turn-of-the-century mansion that has all the graciousness of that era in architectural style as well as service. Combine that with many modern hotel style amenities that aren't always found in a B&B and the Wolfe Crest becomes well suited to the tastes of the traveler looking for more than just a place to stay. The attractively decorated rooms vary in size quite a bit. The largest are definitely oversized but even the smallest are quite adequate. The Wolfe Crest also has some two-bedroom units that go for up to $400 per night. Located on the premises is a full service restaurant called The Porch. Breakfast is a delicious affair of fresh home-made goodies served in an attractive dining room.

WYNDHAM HOTEL, *215 W. South Temple. Tel. 801/531-7500; Fax 801/531-9282. Toll free reservations 800/WYNDHAM. 381 Rooms. Rates: $154; weekend rates from $79. Major credit cards accepted. Located at the Salt Palace Convention Center, two blocks west of Temple Square.*

Another modern high-rise, the Wyndham is an attractive hotel with first class facilities and accommodations at a good price. The rooms are spacious and attractively furnished in a modern style. All have coffee makers. Some have refrigerators and a few even have whirlpool baths. A complimentary newspaper is provided each morning. On the recreational side there's an indoor swimming pool, whirlpool and a small fitness center. Dining on the premises is available at the casual and pretty

City Creek Grill. The adjacent Creek Cigar & Martini Bar is a friendly little place to have a drink and socialize.

Moderate

ALPINE COTTAGES/SALTAIR BED & BREAKFAST, *164 S. 900 East. Tel. 801/533-8184; Fax 801/595-0332/. Toll free reservations 800/733-8184. 14 Rooms. Rates: $65-129; larger cottage units from $119-179. Rates include full breakfast in B&B units and Continental breakfast in cottages. Major credit cards accepted. Located nine blocks east of Temple Square via South Temple Street and then south two blocks.*

An interesting variety of accommodations can be found here in several adjacent Victorian style homes and cottages that have been nicely renovated. The B&B facilities are in a home dating from 1903. Cottage units are attractively furnished and have individual fireplaces and hot tubs. They also have full kitchen facilities. There are also a number of "executive suites" that are condominium style apartments with full kitchens accommodating up to four people. The Alpine is located on a quiet street away from the hustle of downtown but close enough to most of the major attractions that you could leave your car and walk or take a city bus. Hosts Nancy Saxton and Jan Bartlett are gracious folks who'll cook up some outstanding breakfast items if you're staying in the bed and breakfast units. There is one major shortcoming, however, in some of those B&B units–not all of them have private bath.

BEST WESTERN OLYMPUS HOTEL, *161 W. 600 South. Tel. 801/521-7373; Fax 801/524-0354. Toll free reservations 800/426-0722 or 800/528-1234. 393 Rooms. Rates: $109-149. Major credit cards accepted. Located four blocks south of the Salt Palace Convention Center complex between 200 West and West Temple Street.*

This modern 13-story high hotel is an imposing structure that's well situated for seeing downtown's major sights. The public areas aren't particularly elaborate but they're attractive and comfortable. The same can be said for the generally first-class rooms, which are quite spacious. Those on the upper floors have excellent city and/or mountain views. Some units have coffee makers and refrigerators. A few units at the top rate have whirlpools. Guests receive a morning newspaper each day. Recreational facilities include a swimming pool, Jacuzzi and a small fitness center. For dining and entertainment you can choose from Mulboon's, a good restaurant located on the Olympus' roof and providing outstanding vistas; or a more casual restaurant. Mulboon's also has a popular cocktail lounge. The Olympus provides courtesy airport transportation and offers a number of package plans during the skiing season.

THE CARLTON HOTEL, *140 E. South Temple. Tel. 801/355-3418; Fax 801/355-3428. Toll free reservations 800/633-3500. 45 Rooms. Rates: $74-99 including full breakfast. Most major credit cards accepted. Located one block east of Temple Square across the street from the ZCMI shopping center.*

Built in 1935, this small centrally located hotel is like staying at a European hotel with 19th century atmosphere. It has a charm and character that is in stark contrast to the many contemporary hotels of downtown Salt Lake City. While the accommodations and facilities are a couple of notches beneath the premier inns of the city, it is pleasant and comfortable. And at the prices charged it represents an excellent value considering that it's located so close to Temple Square. Most rooms have refrigerators. Facilities include a fitness spa with exercise room and sauna. There isn't any restaurant but plenty are located within a short walk. If you're planning a quiet evening in your room then you can choose a video from their library of more than 600 titles at no additional charge. The Carlton provides free airport transportation and also has several ski package plans.

LITTLE AMERICA HOTEL, *500 S. Main. Tel. 801/363-6781; Fax 801/596-5911. Toll free reservations 800/453-9450. 850 Rooms. Rates: $89-134. Major credit cards accepted. Located five blocks south of Temple Square at the corner of Main Street.*

The premier lodging address in Salt Lake City for quite a few years, the prestigious Little America Hotel combines modern facilities with old time service. Public areas and guest rooms are elegant in an understated and refined sort of way. Spacious rooms are located either in the 17-story high main tower or in lodge style accommodations around the perimeter. One of the city's better dining spots is the Little America Dining Room (see the *Where to Eat* section) and for entertainment there's the attractive Westgate Lounge.

Selected as one of my Best Places to Stay (see Chapter 10 for more details).

PEERY HOTEL, *110 W. 300 South. Tel. 801/521-4300; Fax 801/575-5014. Toll free reservations 800/331-0073. 77 Rooms. Rates: $99-149, including Continental breakfast. Most major credit cards accepted. Located two blocks south of the Salt Palace Convention Center complex between 200 West and West Temple Street.*

Another of Salt Lake City's older historic properties, the Peery is a registered landmark. The rooms aren't anything special but they're clean and comfortable. A couple of units have whirlpool tubs. An attractive pub style bistro is on the premises as is a fitness center with whirlpool. Parking is on a fee basis in an adjacent outdoor lot. If you're looking for a small quiet place to stay that has a good location and won't totally bust your budget, then the Peery is a good candidate.

Inexpensive
   ROYAL EXECUTIVE INN, *121 N. 300 West. Tel. 801/521-3450; Fax 801/521-3452. Toll free reservations 800/541-7639. 96 Rooms. Rates: $50-70 including Continental breakfast. Most major credit cards accepted. Located two blocks west of the northwest corner of Temple Square at the intersection of North Temple Street.*

   Providing basic accommodations at a most affordable price, the Royal Executive Inn is a better choice for the budget traveler than the lowest price chain motels. You'll get a good location and clean and comfortable rooms (some with microwave ovens and refrigerators) and a more than adequate Continental breakfast. This motor inn style facility also has a swimming pool and hot tub. Free airport shuttle service.

AROUND THE CITY
(Including Holladay, Midvale, Murray, Sandy, South & West Jordan and West Valley City)
Very Expensive
   ANNIVERSARY INN AT THE OLD SALT CITY JAIL, *460 South 1000 East. Tel. 801/363-4900; Fax 801/328-9955. Toll free reservations 800/324-4152. 32 Rooms. Rates: $129-249 including Continental breakfast. Rates about $20 higher on weekends. American Express, Discover, MasterCard and VISA accepted. Located just to the east of downtown via 400 south to 1000 East and then south one-half block.*

   A terrible name for a place to stay but everything else about it is superior. Unusually large for a B&B-style facility, the inn features a variety of themed suites ranging from literary topics to the most exotic destinations in the world. All of the creature comforts are in abundance–extra special things like surround stereo, gigantic screen television and more. In addition the more than adequate Continental breakfast, guests are treated to delicious snacks throughout the day. A smaller Anniversary Inn is located closer to downtown, *700 East at South Temple.* While not quite at the same level it will do nicely if the "Jail" location is booked.

   Selected as one of my Best Places to Stay (see Chapter 10 for more details).

Expensive
   BRIGHAM STREET INN, *1135 E. South Temple. Tel. 801/364-4461; Fax 801/521-3201. Toll free reservations 800/417-4461. 9 Rooms. Rates: $125-185 including Continental breakfast. American Express, MasterCard and VISA accepted. Located near downtown. Go east on South Temple from Temple Square for 11 blocks.*

   Well situated between downtown and the University of Utah campus, the Brigham Street Inn occupies a large Victorian mansion that is listed on the National Register of Historic Places. It is now more than a century old but it has been carefully restored and is an excellent example of turn-of-the century elegance. All of the units are attractively furnished in period decor. They aren't overly big but, on the other hand, they aren't cramped either. The largest unit (top end of rate scale) is a spacious suite complete with jetted tub. Many restaurants are located within a short distance.

LA EUROPA ROYALE INN, *1135 E. Vine Street. Tel. 801/263-7999; Fax 801/263-8090. Toll free reservations 800/523-8767. 9 Rooms. Rates: $155-225 including full breakfast. Major credit cards accepted. Located southeast of the city center. Take I-215 to Exit 8 and go north on 900 East to Vine Street and then turn right.*

A fabulous little hotel in the best tradition of the small European-style luxury inn, the La Europa Royale just barely missed making the Best Places to Stay list. It has some of the elements of a bed and breakfast and some of a hotel. The service is excellent and the rooms are first rate. Each features a working fireplace, a Jacuzzi that seats two people and a two-person shower. It's perfect for a romantic getaway (or perhaps just for those people who like to save water by showering with a friend). While all of the units are excellent the newly added luxury suites are even more special.

La Europa has one of the most beautiful breakfast rooms I've ever seen. The large and airy two-story high room has a white tiled floor and a semi-circular shaped bay that contains almost two dozen windows overlooking a pretty patio area. A warm fireplace on one side adds to the unique charm. For dinner, a number of restaurants are located within close proximity to the inn. A large video library is available.

PINECREST BED & BREAKFAST INN, *6211 Emigration Canyon Road. Tel. 801/583-6663. Toll free reservations 800/359-6663. 7 Rooms. Rates: $165-195 including full breakfast. American Express, Discover, MasterCard and VISA accepted. Located a few miles east of downtown. Take 900 South to 1300 East and then north to Sunnyside. Follow Emigration Canyon Road to the inn.*

Like the preceding facility, the Pinecrest could almost be another candidate for the best list. The setting is spectacular especially when taking into consideration that you're only 20 minutes from the city center. Pretty Emigration Canyon is filled with beautiful pine trees and the inn sits astride a picturesque stream. The historic house was once part of a huge estate and although that is no longer the case, the six acre Pinecrest continues to provide a high degree of privacy within the metropolitan area.

All of the units are spacious and nicely decorated. Three rooms either have private Jacuzzi or sauna. Two others are cottages with fireplace and full kitchen. Cooking breakfast in is always an attractive money-saving option but at the Pinecrest it's a tough choice for those staying in rooms with a kitchen–because then you miss out on the fabulous breakfast that's served overlooking the stream and a pretty pond. Getting to restaurants requires a short drive. Pinecrest is well situated for visitors who plan to spend a lot of time in Park City and the surrounding mountain resorts as well as in Salt Lake City.

Moderate

ALPINE ACCOMMODATIONS/CHALET OF SWITZERLAND, *4235 S. Lynn Lane, Holladay. Tel. 801/277-9300; Fax 801/278-6100. 4 Rooms. Rates: $60-140 including full breakfast. American Express, Discover, MasterCard and VISA accepted. Located southeast of downtown via I-80 to Exit 126 and then south via 300 East and Highland Drive to 4500 South. Then go east to Lynn Lane. Alternatively, take I-215 to Exit 5 and then go west on 4500 South to Lynn Lane.*

An authentic looking and attractive little Swiss chalet (your hosts even speak Swiss dialect German), Alpine Accommodations offers B&B style facilities as well as one large Alpine cottage unit that can sleep up to five people. The furnishings in each of the spacious units are attractive and comfortable. Jacuzzis and hot tubs are standard. Conveniently located to city sights and the ski areas.

CANDLEWOOD HOTEL, *2170 W. North Temple. Tel. 801/359-7500; Fax 801/359-7575. Toll free reservations 800/946-6200. 122 Rooms. Rates: $109. Major credit cards accepted. Located between downtown and the airport. Take North Temple west from downtown for about three miles.*

One of Salt Lake City's newest lodging facilities, the Candlewood offers a choice of studio and one bedroom suites, all with full kitchen. A CD player and VCR are standard. A nice feature is a comfortable recliner, something not often seen in hotels. Given the style of the accommodations the Candlewood is especially well suited to those planning to base their Utah visit in Salt Lake City. However, at this price and with the excellent rooms, it's a good choice no matter how long you plan to stay in the area. There isn't any restaurant but several are located within a short distance. Another possible drawback for some people is the lack of recreational facilities.

CASTLE CREEK INN, *7391 S. Creek Road, Sandy. Tel. 801/567-9437; Fax 801/567-9437. Toll free reservations 800/571-2669. 10 Rooms. Rates: $100-155 including Continental breakfast. Most major credit cards accepted. Located to the southeast of Salt Lake City. Take I-215 to Exit 8 and then proceed to 1300 East. Turn left (south) to intersection of S. Creek Road.*

A pretty little inn built in the style of a Scottish Castle, you could almost think that you're in Scotland given Castle Creek's appearance and its setting amidst a plethora of oak trees. Each unit is a luxuriously furnished suite with its own whirlpool tub and fireplace. Complimentary videos are provided to all guests. The authentic looking castle dining hall is the place where you'll be served breakfast - not quite as large as in a B&B, but generous enough to belie the "Continental" label.

MOUNTAIN HOLLOW BED & BREAKFAST, *10209 S. Dimple Dell Road, Sandy. Tel. 801/942-3428; Fax 801/943-7229. Toll free reservations 800/757-3428. 11 Rooms. Rates: $75-150 including full breakfast. American Express, Discover, MasterCard and VISA accepted. Located south of Salt Lake City via I-15 to Exit 297 and then east on 10600 South to S. Dimple Dell Drive.*

Nestled at the entrance to beautiful Little Cottonwood Canyon, making it convenient to Salt Lake City as well as the Alta and Snowbird ski areas, Mountain Hollow is a pretty old world style residence on a two acre estate. All of the units are spacious and wonderfully decorated in a traditional style. Floral pattern wallpaper, rich wood furniture and luxurious hand made quilts are just a few of the distinctive items to be found. The higher price range is for either mini-suite or luxury suite. Facilities at Mountain Hollow include a video library, game room and outdoor spa. Breakfast consists of a sumptuous buffet served in a pretty dining room. A charming place in a secluded location, the Mountain Hollow is a great place to use as a touring base or for a romantic get-away.

PARKWAY SUITES, *3850 W. Parkway Blvd., West Valley City. Tel. 801/977-0800; Fax 801/977-9298. Toll free reservations 800/251-0063. 31 Rooms. Rates: $89 (weekly rates available) including Continental breakfast. Most major credit cards accepted. Located southwest of downtown via I-215 to Exit 20 and then 2100 South east to 3800 and then south to Parkway Blvd.*

A good value for those seeking comfortable and spacious accommodations. Each of the units is a one bedroom suite of about 800 square feet situated around a nicely landscaped courtyard. The modern furnishings are both tasteful and attractive. All of the suites feature king size beds and full kitchens complete with microwave and dishwasher. The Continental breakfast may not be enough to satisfy those who like a big morning meal. Restaurants are located within a short drive.

UNIVERSITY PARK HOTEL & SUITES, *480 Wakara Way. Tel. 801/581-1000; Fax 801/584-3321. 220 Rooms. Rates: $129. Major credit cards accepted. Located to the east of the University of Utah. Take 500 South Street from downtown to Wakara Way and turn left.*

This is a typical modern motor hotel (seven stories) with large comfortable rooms that are a bit on the sterile looking side but more than adequate as a place to get some sleep. Recreational facilities include a swimming pool, whirlpool and fitness center. The on-premise restaurant serves nice breakfasts. It's alright for dinner too if you're looking not to have to travel after a busy day. I could be more enthusiastic about the

University Park if the prices were a little lower–given what's available elsewhere they're about $30 too high.

Inexpensive

DISCOVERY INN, *380 W. 7200 South, Midvale. Tel. 801/561-2256; Fax 801/561-4243. Toll free reservations 800/380-1415. 89 Rooms. Rates: $69-89. Major credit cards accepted. Located adjacent to Exit 301 of I-15, approximately ten miles south of downtown.*

Although most hotels in the Salt Lake City area aren't particularly high priced compared to many other American urban areas, decent inexpensive accommodations are still kind of difficult to find. The Discovery Inn, however, offers nicely decorated large rooms that are extremely well maintained at a most affordable rate. Some rooms have microwave ovens and/or refrigerators. A swimming pool, spa and sauna will be of interest to those looking for some end of day recreation in addition to a place to bed down for the night. There are quite a few restaurants located within a few miles of the inn.

SCENIC MOTEL, *1345 South Foothill Drive. Tel. 801/582-1527; Fax 801/582-1527. 23 Rooms. Rates: $44. American Express, Discover, MasterCard and VISA accepted. Located southeast of the University of Utah. From downtown take 500 South east to Foothill Drive.*

The accommodations are quite basic and there aren't any recreational facilities but if you're looking for a clean and comfortable budget priced facility then this will do nicely. Several restaurants are located within a short distance. The Scenic Motel has a good location that is convenient for getting into downtown as well as to the nearby mountains.

ALTA

Very Expensive

ALTA'S RUSTLER LODGE, *Little Cottonwood Canyon. Tel. 801/532-2020; Fax 801/742-3832. Toll free reservations 888/532-ALTA. 57 Rooms. Rates: High season (winter): $220-275; Low season (spring and fall): $195-245. All rates include breakfast and dinner [MAP]. Closed during the summer. Most major credit cards accepted. Located at the Alta ski area via I-215 to Exit 6 and then UT 210.*

A modern five story motor inn located at the base of the Alta ski area and providing ski-in/ski-out facilities, Alta's Rustler Lodge is the nicest of the ten or so lodging establishments located in Alta. A casual atmosphere prevails in the attractive public areas. The accommodations are generally spacious and nicely decorated. In addition to standard rooms the lodge features superior corner rooms, deluxe units and some suites. Some have balconies and the views are mostly quite good.

Dinner is included at the lodge's decent restaurant. In the evening there's friendly conversation and drinks at the Eagle's Nest Lounge. Recreational facilities include a complete fitness center with Jacuzzi and steam room and an outdoor heated swimming pool. Some children's programs are offered during holiday periods. A full service ski shop is located on the premises.

(Note: The Rustler Lodge has some budget units and six-bed dormitory style units with shared bath. I do not recommend these accommodations and the preceding description does not apply to them. However, if you're interested, the high season rates for these facilities range from $100 to $145 and from $90-115 during the low season).

BRIGHAM CITY

Inexpensive

CRYSTAL INN, *480 Westland Drive. Tel. 435/723-0440; Fax 435/723-0440. Toll free reservations 800/408-0440. 52 Rooms. Rates: $65 including Continental breakfast. Most major credit cards accepted. Located a mile east of I-15, Exit 364.*

One of Crystal's five properties in northwest Utah, the Brigham City inn offers (as do all the others) a number of nice amenities, including a microwave and refrigerator in every room along with a VCR (movie rentals cost extra but it's nice to be able to watch your day's camcorder results). There's also an indoor swimming pool, hot tub and small exercise room on the premises. They call the breakfast a "buffet" but it's more of an oversized Continental affair. Guest rooms are nicely decorated and have ample space. A number of larger suites are also available. Crystal is a notch above most standard chain accommodations and is a good value for the price. Restaurants are located within a short distance.

BRIGHTON

Expensive

THE INN AT SOLITUDE, *12000 Big Cottonwood Canyon. Tel. 801/536-5700; Fax 801/535-4135. Toll free reservations 800/748-4754. 46 Rooms. Rates: High season (late November through March 31st): $126-160 including Continental breakfast; Low season (April 1st through late November): $99. Higher rates for suites and during winter holiday periods. Major credit cards accepted. Located at the Brighton ski area. Take I-215 to Exit 6 and then take UT 210 to the junction of UT 190 and follow that through Big Cottonwood Canyon.*

For a major ski area there isn't much of a choice for lodging (perhaps because of its proximity to Salt Lake City). Most of it is overpriced considering the quality. The Inn at Solitude, although fairly high priced, is the exception. The newest and best property in Brighton, the Inn combines traditional European ski chalet styling with all of the modern conveniences. Guests can choose from either rooms or suites but all feature lovely decor along with refrigerator, VCR and such little extra touches as plush terry cloth robes. Recreational facilities include a full service health and fitness center with spa, heated swimming pool and Jacuzzi and, of course, easy access to the adjacent slopes.

The lobby lounge is an attractive place where people unwind after a busy day. You can do likewise in the library or in the private club (temporary membership required). The restaurant called The Round-house is an excellent place to eat and is described further in the *Where to Eat* section. The surroundings are luxurious.

Adjacent to the Inn at Solitude (and under the same management) is the Creekside Condominiums. Together with the Inn, the complex forms the Village at Solitude. Condo units range from one through three bedrooms and the prices are from $170 to $565 per night during the high season. The 18 unit building features home style alpine atmosphere with full kitchens, separate living areas, wet bar and private deck's plus their own hot tub. The facilities of the Inn are available to condominium guests.

HEBER CITY

Inexpensive

DANISH VIKING INN, *989 South Main. Tel. 435/654-2202; Fax 435/654-2770. Toll free reservations 800/544-4066. 34 Rooms. Rates: $55 during the summer and winter seasons; $45 during the spring and fall. American Express, Discover, MasterCard and VISA accepted. Located along the main road (UT 40) on the south side of town.*

This is a very attractive little motel, delightfully nestled in the pretty mountain community of Heber City and close to all of the Wasatch attractions and recreational activities. Not far from Salt Lake City either, the low rates (common to most Heber City properties) make it an excellent value and an ideal place to base yourself in if you want to save some money. The exterior architecture has some elements of rustic Scandinavian style but the rooms are of a more modern style. The furnishings are attractive and comfortable and there's plenty of space. Some units have full kitchen facilities while many others have a refrigerator. Among the amenities at the Danish Viking are an outdoor swimming pool, Jacuzzi and sauna. There are several decent eating places located within a short distance from the motel.

HYLANDER MOTEL, *425 S. Main. Tel. 435/654-2150; Fax 435/654-2109. Toll free reservations 800/932-0355. 22 Rooms. Rates: $49-59 including Continental breakfast. Major credit cards accepted. Located on US 40 in town.*

Considering the proximity of Heber City to the major mountain resorts, it's surprising to find so many bargains and the Hylander is another one. The rooms aren't great but they have enough space and are quite comfortable. The housekeeping, though, is immaculate. All rooms feature microwave ovens and refrigerators. Some have coffee makers. There aren't any recreational facilities so this is the place for those just looking for a clean and quiet place to spend a night or two. Restaurants are located nearby.

SWISS ALPS INN, *167 S. Main. Tel. 435/654-0722. 14 Rooms. Rates: $58-72. Major credit cards accepted. Located on US 40 in the center of town.*

You could pick either the Swiss Alps Inn or the two preceding entries blindfolded and you wouldn't go wrong in any case. The rooms are typical roadside motel fare, but then what else could you ask for at this price? It seems that motel builders in mountain towns often like to take European themes and that goes here as well. In this case the building features an authentic looking Swiss Alpine village style and is quaint and picturesque. Especially attractive features are the "clock tower" with its figures out on the balcony, the window shutters and flower garden. Facilities at the inn include a nice heated outdoor swimming pool and indoor Jacuzzi. Restaurants are within a short distance.

LOGAN
Moderate

CRYSTAL INN, *853 S. Main Street. Tel. 435/752-0707; Fax 435/787-2207. Toll free reservations 800/280-0707. 86 Rooms. Rates: High season (June 1st through August 31st): $79; Low season (all other times): $49. All rates include Continental breakfast. Major credit cards accepted. Located at the southern edge of town on the main highway.*

Everything that was said about the Crystal Inn in Brigham City also applies to this one so we won't bother repeating all of the features except to say that it's another good value. The location is within close proximity to a number of restaurants.

PROVIDENCE INN, *10 S. Main Street. Tel. 435/752-3432; Fax 435/752-3482. Toll free reservations 800/480-4943. 14 Rooms. Rates: $59-149 including full breakfast. Major credit cards accepted. Located in Providence, just south of Logan via UT 165 and then east on Providence Lane.*

A large B&B, the Providence Inn offers comfortable traditional accommodations. The large price range reflects the variety of rooms that range from small to large, from single room to suite. In addition to the delicious breakfast that's included with your stay, the Providence Inn features a very good moderately priced restaurant that is open for dinner.

MIDWAY

Very Expensive

HOMESTEAD RESORT, *700 N. Homestead Drive. Tel. 435/654-1102; Fax 435/654-5087. Toll free reservations 800/327-7220. 148 Rooms. Rates: $109-259. Major credit cards accepted. Located a mile off of UT 113 via 200 West and 200 North to Homestead Drive.*

A unique atmosphere, quality varied accommodations and lots of recreational facilities highlight this timeless country style inn that is tucked away in a beautiful mountain setting. Consisting of many different buildings connected by tranquil walkways and surrounded by the green carpeted Snake Creek Valley, the Homestead's gracious staff provides home-like ambiance to make your stay a memorable one. The pleasant decor ranges from New England to Southwestern to Victorian–no two rooms are alike but all have kitchens and safes. Many are multi-room units with fireplace or whirlpool tub.

For dining you can select from the first class Simon's (see *Where to Eat* section) or Fanny's Grill. Recreation is available year round and the nature of it does depend to a large extent on the season of your visit. An unexpected year-round sight is the natural mineral water hole called the Homestead Crater.

Selected as one of my Best Places to Stay (see Chapter 10 for more details).

HUCKLEBERRY COUNTRY INN, *1235 Warm Springs Road. Tel. 435/654-1400; Fax 435/654-6149. Toll free reservations 888/650-1400. 14 Rooms. Rates: $150-295 including full breakfast. American Express, MasterCard and VISA accepted. Located just out of town opposite the visitor center for Wasatch State Park.*

This B&B is situated high atop a grassy knoll with a fabulous view of the surrounding mountains. The big rambling house looks every bit like an elegant mansion from an era gone by and you'll feel that way from the moment you enter and see the winding staircase with its rich wood balustrade and the graceful balconies that overlook the downstairs public areas. It is located within minutes of just about any type of outdoor recreation you could want, regardless of the season.

Guest rooms are large and comfortable but are furnished on the simple side considering the richness of the house itself. Many, however, do have fireplaces and jetted tubs. A number of suites are also available. Breakfast is served in a large kitchen/dining room that is reminiscent of the 19th century. There's a pretty lounge with fireplace for relaxing during the evening. Huckleberry also serves dinner (by reservation) Thursday through Saturday evenings only. It's excellent.

KASTLE INN BED & BREAKFAST, *1220 Interlaken Lane. Tel. 435/654-2689; Fax 435/654-2689. Toll free reservations 800/561-2291. 5 Rooms. Rates: $100-155 including Continental breakfast. Most major credit cards accepted. Located in town.*

Midway, unlike nearby Heber City, is definitely not budget country. But if you want a nice little B&B that won't cost a fortune, then the Kastle Inn will do well. It's not the Homestead, of course, or even the Huckleberry for that matter, but the rooms are nicely decorated, large and comfortable. The two-turreted building gives the inn its name and we especially like the round Turret Room with its Jacuzzi and great views. The other rooms (Keepsake, Avonlee, Sweetbrier, and Lucerne) also have excellent vistas. Warm and friendly hospitality abounds. The breakfast is sufficient although not as complete as in most B&B's.

OGDEN

Expensive

HISTORIC RADISSON SUITE HOTEL, *2510 Washington Blvd. Tel. 801/627-1900; Fax 801/394-5342. Toll free reservations 800/333-3333. 144 Rooms. Rates: $124-149 including full breakfast. Major credit cards accepted. Located east of I-15, Exit 344 via 30th Street to Washington Avenue and then left.*

One of the first high-rise hotels in Utah, the Historic Radisson provides a pleasant combination of traditional atmosphere and modern amenities. The all-suite facility provides plenty of space and units on the upper floors have an excellent view of the Wasatch Mountains. The comfortably furnished accommodations include many units with coffee maker, refrigerator and microwave ovens. On the premises are a restaurant and coffee shop. Recreational facilities are limited to the swimming pool. Ski packages are offered.

Moderate

THE ALASKAN INN, *435 Ogden Canyon Road. Tel. 801/621-8600; Fax 801/394-4054. 12 Rooms. Rates: $85-165 including full breakfast. American Express, Discover, MasterCard and VISA accepted. Located in Ogden Canyon. Use Exit 347 of I-15 and travel east via 12th Street and Canyon Road.*

Situated in a pretty canyon that's within 15 minutes of the ski slopes, the Alaskan Inn is a nice place to stay regardless of the season or the reason for your visit to Ogden. Each room is decorated in an Alaskan or northern theme and boasts such features as Jacuzzi tubs, stereo and VCR. There's also a public hot tub. Breakfast can be served in the privacy of your own room.

BEST WESTERN OGDEN PARK HOTEL, *247 24th Street. Tel. 801/ 627-1190; Fax 801/394-6312. Toll free reservations 800/528-1234. 288 Rooms. Rates: $89-109 including full breakfast. Most major credit cards accepted. Located downtown. Use 24th Street exit of I-15 (#345) and drive east 1-1/2 miles to hotel.*

This Best Western is also Ogden's largest full-service hotel and it represents a good value for the money. All of the rooms are large and nicely decorated in a modern style. Those on the top floors facing the mountains have good views. In room amenities may include coffee makers or microwave ovens. A complimentary newspaper is provided each morning. The hotel has a good restaurant on the premises as well as a cocktail lounge. Recreational facilities consist of a heated indoor swimming pool, exercise facility and hot tub. Massage services are available at additional charge. The Ogden Park offers a number of ski season package plans.

PARK CITY
Very Expensive

THE LODGE AT MOUNTAIN VILLAGE (Resort Center), *1415 Lowell Avenue. Tel. 435/649-0800; Fax 435/649-1464. Toll free reservations 800/824-5331. 140 Rooms. Rates: High season (mid-December to March 31st): $250-650 with highest rates during holiday periods; Low season (April 1st to mid-December): $175-195. Most major credit cards accepted. Located at the base of the Park City ski area, four blocks off of UT 224.*

Prepare yourself for the highest priced hotels in Utah–Park City, unfortunately, has rates that are almost as high as many of the famous ski resorts in Colorado, although some relative bargains can be found here. So let's get started with the Lodge at Mountain Village.

This hotel is part of a village of lodging establishments collectively going by the name of David Holland's Resort Lodging. However, this description only applies to the main lodge. The Lodge features ski-in/ski-out access in the form of hotel rooms all the way to four bedroom condominium style units. Conveniently located at the base of the ski slopes, all of the accommodations boast attractive furnishings and decor. About two-thirds of the units have kitchen facilities. Some have fireplaces. The recreational facilities are extensive and include swimming pool, hot tub, fitness center and sauna. The on-premises restaurant is average or a little better but is casual and appropriate for family dining. It has a great view of the slopes. Within the village (all walking distance from the Lodge) is an almost uncountable number of additional eating places as well as excellent shopping.

THE OLD MINER'S LODGE, *615 Woodside Ave. Tel. 435/645-8068; Fax 435/645-7420. Toll free reservations 800/648-8068. 12 Rooms. Rates: High season (mid-November to mid-April): $200-250; Low season (mid-April to mid-November): $100-120. All rates include full breakfast. Most major credit cards accepted. Located two blocks west of Main Street via 4th Street.*

The best of Park City's half-dozen or so B&B's, the Old Miner's Lodge is a large old boarding house dating from 1889. It has been meticulously restored and is charmingly filled with all sorts of antiques and country style furnishings. Accommodations vary from bedrooms to two-room suites but all are spacious and exceedingly comfortable. The Lodge has a public hot tub. In addition to the bountiful breakfast, refreshments are served in the evening. Located close to the old time Main Street, you'll find plenty of restaurants and other diversions within walking distance. Minimum stay restrictions of up to four nights may apply during peak periods and small children aren't allowed.

RADISSON INN PARK CITY, *2121 Park Avenue. Tel. 435/649-5000; Fax 435/649-2122. Toll free reservations 800/333-3333. 131 Rooms. Rates: High season (mid-December to mid-March): $189 including full breakfast; Low season (mid-March to mid-December): $119. Major credit cards accepted. Located at the north end of Park City just off UT 224.*

This three-story lodge style facility is just far enough away from the heart of town to provide outstanding mountain views. Yet it's close enough to be within walking distance of many activities. The spacious guest rooms are among the best in Park City as long as you don't mind the relative drabness of modern styling. For dining, Radigan's (see the *Where to Eat* section) is excellent and pleasant evenings can be spent in Cooter's, one of the town's most popular lounges. Both have excellent mountain views. A beautiful indoor/outdoor swimming pool, sauna and several hot tubs provide plenty of recreational activity for guests.

SILVER KING HOTEL, *1485 Empire Avenue. Tel. 435/649-5500; Fax 435/649-6647. Toll free reservations 800/331-8652. 65 Rooms. Rates: High season (mid-November through March): $280-520 with higher rates at holiday periods; Low season (April through mid-November): $175. American Express, Discover, MasterCard and VISA accepted. Located off of UT 224 via Deer Valley Drive to Empire Avenue.*

Consisting of both hotel units and the Silver Cliff Village condo-minium style accommodations, Silver King is a beautiful property with striking views. Located adjacent to the Park City Mountain Resort ski area, all of the units have kitchen facilities. Besides hotel rooms there are one to three-bedroom suites. Some have their own spa but all have at least a jetted tub. Wood burning fireplaces are also standard. The spacious units feature pleasant light-colored woods and comfortable furnishings. The Silver King has a heated indoor/outdoor swimming pool, sauna and whirlpool facility. Massage service is available at an additional charge. There is no restaurant on the premises but plenty of good eating places are located within walking distance. Minimum stay restrictions apply at all times but they vary (generally three to five days) depending upon the time of year.

STEIN ERIKSEN LODGE, *7700 Stein Way. Tel. 435/649-3700; Fax 435/649-5825. Toll free reservations 800/453-1302. 131 Rooms. Rates: High season (early December to mid-April): $450-675 for rooms and $950-1,450 for suites, including full breakfast; Low season (mid-April to early December): $175-225 for rooms and $250-300 for suites. Major credit cards accepted. Located via Deer Valley Drive to Royal Street near the south side of town and follow signs.*

Utah ski country's highest priced establishment is also one of the state's best. A touch of Norway in the Wasatch Mountains, the lodge style facility features Scandinavian decor and color. There are a couple of excellent restaurants and lots of recreational facilities. During the warmer season the outdoor pool is beautifully framed by the magnificent mountains. All of the recreational opportunities of the Park City area are within minutes and you can make arrangements with the exceptional hotel staff. The accommodations are spacious and luxurious with many amenities. Suites are even more upscale with their multiple bathrooms, his and her dressing areas and wrap-around balconies. Although it's definitely not for the budget vacationer, the Stein Eriksen Lodge provides the facilities and atmosphere that the upscale sophisticated traveler is looking for.

Selected as one of my Best Places to Stay (see Chapter 10 for more details).

THE YARROW HOTEL, *1800 Park Avenue. Tel. 435/649-7000; Fax 435/6495-7007. Toll free reservations 800/927-7694. 181 Rooms. Rates: High season (mid-December through March): $240-269; Low season (April through mid-December): $108-120. Major credit cards accepted. Located on the main thoroughfare at the junction of UT 224 and 248.*

One of many attractive chalet style lodges in Park City, the Yarrow offers large and attractive rooms in addition to studio units and one-bedroom suites. There are many in-room amenities including refrigerators, coffee makers and fireplaces. A number of kitchenettes are also available. For dining and cocktails you can select from the Corner Cafe or Charlie's Place. Both have a pleasant atmosphere and the cafe's food is quite tasty. Recreational facilities at the Yarrow are a fully equipped exercise room and a heated outdoor swimming pool with hot tub. The hotel is located close to all of the dining and shopping options of Park City. Minimum stay requirements are imposed during the high season.

Expensive

EDELWEISS HAUS HOTEL, *1482 Empire Avenue. Tel. 435/649-9342; Fax 435/649-4049. Toll free reservations 800/438-3855. 45 Rooms. Rates: High season (mid-December to mid-April): $125-350; Low season (mid-April to mid-December): $69-129. American Express, Discover, MasterCard and VISA accepted. Located off of UT 224 via Deer Valley Drive to Empire Avenue.*

The Edelweiss is an attractive little facility that doesn't provide the full services available at many Park City lodging establishments, but it is more reasonably priced. There are only a few hotel style units; most are one or two bedroom condominium units (daily linen exchange at the front desk but maid service during your stay isn't provided in the condo units unless you pay an extra charge). All of the condominium units have full kitchens and working gas log fireplaces along with a balcony or terrace. The hotel units are also pretty and spacious and have microwave oven, coffee maker and a small refrigerator. The decor is attractive and the comfort level is high.

There's a large heated outdoor swimming pool and a Jacuzzi that accommodates up to 25 people along with a sauna. Garage parking. There isn't any restaurant on the premises but plenty of choices are available within a short distance as is shopping. The hotel is only a short walk from the Park City Mountain Resort lifts. Minimum stay restrictions imposed during the high season.

THE INN AT PROSPECTOR SQUARE, *2200 Sidewinder Drive. Tel. 435/649-7100; Fax 435/649-8377. Toll free reservations 888/870-4386. 200 Rooms. Rates: High season (late December to mid-April): $139 including Continental breakfast; Low season (mid-April to late December): $69. Major credit cards accepted. Located a half mile off of UT 248 via Sidewinder Drive.*

Another condominium style resort, the Inn at Prospector Square is close enough to town to offer all the conveniences and services of Park City but just far enough away from the center to provide a beautiful mountain setting. A collection of low-rise buildings, the Inn offers a diverse selection of accommodations including studios with kitchenettes, larger studio with open loft bedroom and kitchenette, and studio suites also with open loft. Two and three bedroom condominium units are also available. All have microwave, refrigerator, coffee maker and balcony. The condo units have fireplaces. Recreational facilities include a heated swimming pool, hot tub, sauna and complete fitness center. The on-premise Grub Steak Restaurant is adequate if you don't feel like walking or riding into the main part of town.

Moderate

CHATEAU APRES LODGE, *Lowell Avenue (Resort Center). Tel. 435/649-9372; Fax 435/649-5963. Toll free reservations 800/357-3556. 32 Rooms.*

Rates: $79-99 including Continental breakfast. Most major credit cards accepted. Located about a block from the base of the Park City ski area off of UT 224.

While I don't highly recommend this basic little place there is a strong need for some affordable accommodations in Park City for winter visitors and it does fit that bill, especially considering that it is walking distance from the ski slopes. The rooms are clean and comfortable and well maintained. The small informal lobby has a nice warm fireplace. In addition to the facilities described, the Chateau Apres has a number of dorm style units, which I wouldn't suggest despite their $25 price tag!

PROVO
Very Expensive
SUNDANCE, *State Highway 92, Sundance. Tel. 801/225-4167; Fax 801/226-1937. Toll free reservations 800/892-1600. 113 Rooms. Rates: High season (mid-December to mid-March): $195-425; Low season (mid-March to mid-December): $150-275. All rates include full breakfast. Most major credit cards accepted. Located northeast of Provo via US 189 and then left on UT 92.*

Established by actor Robert Redford, Sundance is one of the most beautiful and unique hotel properties to be found anywhere in America. Designed to blend in with and even complement the magnificent natural surroundings of Mount Timpanogos, Sundance is a community that is devoted to the performing arts, Native American culture and the environment. Rustic western architecture prevails while the decor is heavily southwestern and Native American. Luxurious accommodations range from the standard "guest cottage" to multi-room mountain homes. All have a feeling of seclusion and privacy. They also feature many amenities. There are several dining options ranging from a deli for quick snacks all the way up to the award winning Tree Room Restaurant (see the *Where to Eat* section). Several shops and an outstanding recreational program complete the picture.

Selected as one of my Best Places to Stay (see Chapter 10 for more details).

Moderate
PROVO PARK HOTEL & UTAH VALLEY CONFERENCE CENTER, *101 W. 100 North. Tel. 801/377-4700; Fax 801/377-4708. Toll free reservations 800/777-7144. 333 Rooms. Rates: $109-145. Most major credit cards accepted. Located east of I-15, Exit 268.*

The largest and nicest full-service hotel within Provo, this attractive nine-story facility offers absolutely outstanding views of either the mountains or valley from the upper floors. All of the rooms are attractively decorated in a modern style and offer plenty of space and a host of amenities including honor bar and coffee makers. Some units have microwave oven and refrigerator. Upscale suites are also available.

For your dining pleasure you can choose from the excellent Oak Grill (see the *Where to Eat* section) or a more casual eatery. There is also a private club for afternoon and evening socializing and cocktails. Temporary memberships are sold at a modest fee. The recreational facilities include a large fitness center, indoor and outdoor swimming pools, and a beautiful spa facility with sauna.

SNOWBIRD

Very Expensive

THE CLIFF LODGE & SPA, *Snowbird Village. Tel. 801/521-6040; Fax 801/742-3300. Toll free reservations 800/385-2002. 534 Rooms. Rates: High season (mid-December to early April): $209-419 Low season (mid November to mid-December and early to late April): $125-265 with higher rates for suites and condominium multi-bedroom units in both seasons. Closed at other times. Most major credit cards accepted. Located in Little Cottonwood Canyon via UT 210 from Exit 6 of I-215.*

Set against the base of the mountain, the Cliff Lodge provides a dramatic setting for Snowbird's premier lodging establishment. Soaring nine stories high, the hotel is divided into two wings. The east wing has canyon view and mountain view bedroom units, deluxe rooms (some with their own spa) and one and two bedroom suites. The west wing is known as the Cliff Club and has some bedroom and efficiency units in addition to one and two bedroom condominium units. All units, be it simple hotel room or large condo apartment, are spacious and attractively furnished.

The facilities and services of the Cliff Lodge are extensive. There are three different restaurants to choose from (including The Aerie and Steak Pit, which are described in the *Where to Eat* section). In addition, Rendezvous is a low-priced cafeteria style establishment with decent food for those on a budget or in a hurry. Extensive child care facilities and programs are available at the "Camp Snowbird"; there's also a large swimming pool and hot tub complex amid beautiful pine trees and great views (there is also a poolside cafe) and a game room. The Cliff Spa is a big rooftop facility that offers a separate pool, whirlpool, complete fitness center, massage and facial treatments as well as styling salons for men and women.

Some dormitory style units are available at much lower prices but are not recommended.

WENDOVER
Inexpensive
STATE LINE INN, *295 E. Wendover Blvd. Tel. 435/665-2226; Fax 435/ 531-4080. Toll free reservations 800/848-7300. 101 Rooms. Rates: $63-84 on weekends and $39-63 on weekdays. Most major credit cards accepted. Located just off of I-80, Exit 2.*

A simple two-story roadside motel with clean and comfortable rooms that will nicely fit the bill for those who don't wish to make the trip to and from Salt Lake City in a single day. No recreational facilities or restaurants on the premises but eating places are located within a short distance.

CAMPING & RV SITES
National Forests: There are almost 100 campgrounds in the national forests within a short drive from Salt Lake City in all directions except to the west. For information and central reservations, call *Tel. 800/280-2267.*

State Parks: Most state park campgrounds lie in the Wasatch Mountains to the east of Salt Lake but there are some in close proximity to the I-15 corridor as well, including locations in Provo (Utah Lake State Park) and Ogden (Fort Buenaventura State Park). A popular camping location is on Antelope Island State Park in the Great Salt Lake. State Park central camping reservations information number is *Tel. 800/322-3770.*

For **commercial sites**, try one of the following:
• **Camp VIP**, *1400 W. North Temple, Salt Lake City. Tel. 801/328-0224*
• **Century RV Park**, *1399 W. 2100 South, Ogden. Tel. 801/731-3800*
• **Heber Valley RV Park**, *UT 32, two miles north of US 40. Tel. 435/654-0721*
• **Hidden Haven Campground**, *2200 Rasmussen Road, Park City. Tel. 435/ 649-8935*
• **Lagoon's Pioneer Village Campground**, *135 N. Lagoon Drive, Farmington. Tel. 801/451–8100*
• **Lakeside Campground**, *4000 W. Center, Provo. Tel. 801/373-5267*
• **Mountain Shadows RV Park**, *13275 S. Minute Man Drive, Draper. Tel. 801/571-4024*
• **Mountain Spa**, *800 N. 200 East, Midway. Tel. 435/654-0721*

WHERE TO EAT
SALT LAKE CITY–DOWNTOWN
(Including Trolley Square)
Expensive
ABSOLUTE!, *52 West 200 South. Tel. 801/359-0899. Most major credit cards accepted. Lunch and dinner served nightly except Sunday.*

A European styled brasserie, Absolute! is a cozy and attractive restaurant with a cafe-like atmosphere. The varied menu includes fish and seafood, steaks and pasta dishes. All are nicely prepared and feature fresh vegetables and fruits. The desserts are excellent. The service is friendly but highly professional. Cocktail service. Validated parking available at the Bank of Utah building.

DIAMOND LIL'S RESTAURANT, *1528 W. North Temple. Tel. 801/ 533-0547. Most major credit cards accepted. Lunch and dinner served daily except Sunday.*

One of the better known and most popular of Salt Lake's restaurants, Diamond Lil's boasts an old west atmosphere and some of the best prime rib, steaks and ribs you can find. The homemade bread is great and so are their famous fresh baked pies for dessert. An efficient wait staff dressed appropriately to the restaurant's theme makes your evening even more pleasant. Full cocktail service is available.

THE GARDEN RESTAURANT, *15 E. South Temple (10th Floor of the Joseph Smith Memorial Building). Tel. 801/539-1911. American Express, MasterCard and VISA accepted. Lunch and dinner served nightly except Sunday. Reservations are suggested.*

The Joseph Smith Building was once the elegant Hotel Utah. I was sad to see it converted to an office building some years ago but at least they kept and even improved upon two of the hotel's restaurants (see also The Roof below). Located on the tenth floor and providing a fantastic view of Temple Square, the city and mountains, the Garden Restaurant features a beautifully decorated dining room with red tiled floor, white pillars and lots of greenery. During the warmer months the retractable glass roof is opened up and you dine under the skies amid the beautiful surroundings and feeling of outdoors without the noise of traffic and other annoyances often associated with outdoor street level dining. Despite all of the elegance the atmosphere and service is casual. The dinner fare consists mainly of American style favorites and is nicely prepared.

LITTLE AMERICA DINING ROOM, *501 S. Main Street, in the Little America Hotel. Tel. 801/596-5704. Major credit cards accepted. Breakfast, lunch and dinner served Monday through Saturday; brunch and dinner only on Sunday.*

Enjoy excellent Continental cuisine in an atmosphere of casual elegance. Extremely large selection of main courses, all deliciously prepared and served in adequate portions. Lunch is in the form of a buffet. Their fabulous Sunday brunch is popular with visitors and locals alike. Occasional entertainment is offered during dinner. Tableside cocktail service and separate lounge.

MARKET STREET GRILL, *48 Market Street. Tel. 801/322-4668. Most major credit cards accepted. Breakfast and dinner served daily. Sunday brunch.*

A local favorite, the Market Street Grill is Salt Lake City's best seafood restaurant. It's located in a restored building that's on the National

Register of Historic Places. Fresh fish from around the world is served daily. If you don't like fish or seafood that doesn't mean you shouldn't eat here–the Grill also has an excellent selection of nicely prepared prime rib, steaks and chicken. Children's menu available. If you get there early for dinner many of the specials are in the moderate price category. Cocktail service available.

NEW YORKER, *60 Market Street. Tel. 801/363-0166. Most major credit cards accepted. Dinner is served daily except on Sunday while lunch is available Monday through Friday only. Reservations are suggested. Private club (temporary memberships available for visitors).*

The New Yorker is one of the most elegant and sophisticated dining rooms in the city. Superb but rather stuffy service and rich tableware settings are in prominence. The cuisine is varied but concentrates on prime rib and other beef dishes along with one or two fish or seafood items each day. More on the casual style is the adjacent Cafe, which features pizza, pasta and salads along with several seafood dishes. (Hours for the Cafe vary so call ahead to confirm.) Complete cocktail service and bar.

THE ROOF RESTAURANT, *15 E. South Temple (10th Floor of the Joseph Smith Memorial Building). Tel. 801/539-1911. Most major credit cards accepted. Dinner served nightly except Sunday.*

The view is as spectacular as was described for the Garden Restaurant but this one doesn't have the retractable roof or quite the elegance of decor. But it is beautiful and serves the most elaborate buffet dinner in Utah, or maybe just about anywhere else for that matter. The selection is huge and there's sure to be something to please every taste. The quality of the food is equal to the best restaurants, something that can't be said all that often about buffets. The dessert selections are fantastic–especially noteworthy are the freshly baked pastries.

ROOM AT THE TOP, *150 W. 500 South (in the Salt Lake Hilton). Tel. 801/532-3344. Major credit cards accepted. Lunch and dinner served Monday through Friday; dinner only on Saturday; brunch and dinner on Sunday.*

On the top floor of the Hilton Hotel, Room At the Top offers excellent views of the city and mountains. Good selection of American dishes (beef and fish) nicely prepared and served by an efficient and thoughtful staff. The atmosphere is upscale casual. Cocktail service and entertainment in the piano bar.

Moderate

CAFE BACCHUS, *358 S. West Temple. Tel. 801/532-1055. Most major credit cards accepted. Lunch and dinner served nightly.*

Two separate dining rooms (the cafe and restaurant) but each is attractive and casual. Popular with "nouveau" cuisine lovers among the lunchtime office worker crowd, the Cafe Bacchus is a good choice for both lunch and dinner. Mediterranean style food creatively prepared and pleasing to the eye as well as the palate is the main fare. They also have several excellent coffee blends and delicious pastries. Cocktail service is available.

CARRIAGE COURT RESTAURANT, *71 W. South Temple (in the Inn at Temple Square). Tel. 801/536-7200. Most major credit cards accepted. Breakfast, lunch and dinner served daily (except no lunch service on Sunday). Reservations are accepted.*

A beautiful dining room with many chandelier fixtures and plush booth seating, the Carriage Court offers excellently prepared meals that are as traditional as the decor. The quiet surroundings and professional service will please those who appreciate dining in dignified but not overbearing surroundings. Health conscious selections highlight the menu but you'll also do well by selecting the chef's daily special.

CEDARS OF LEBANON, *152 E. 200 South. Tel. 801/364-4096. American Express, Diner's Club, MasterCard and VISA accepted. Dinner served nightly. Reservations are suggested.*

A delightful Mediterranean experience with delicious food that's actually good for you–the menu has been accepted by the American Heart Association. Vegetarian dishes from Lebanon, North Africa and the entire Mediterranean region are as beautiful to look at as they are good to eat. The service is excellent and the wait staff will be glad to explain what each dish consists of and how it's prepared. Besides the vegetarian fare there is a good selection of chicken and lamb dishes, mainly shishkabob style. For a really authentic experience you can opt to dine in the Moroccan Room where patrons take their meal while sitting on the floor! Cocktails are served.

DEE'S FAMILY RESTAURANT, *143 W. North Temple. Tel. 801/359-4414. MasterCard and VISA accepted. Breakfast, lunch and dinner served daily (open 24 hours on Friday and Saturday).*

Sure, great restaurants and unusual cuisine is a big part of a vacation. But sometimes you just want plain and simple food, warmly served and in ample portions to satisfy a huge appetite. When that's the desire in Salt Lake City, then Dee's is the answer.

DELLA FONTANA, *336 S. 400 East. Tel. 801/328-4243. Major credit cards accepted. Lunch and dinner served daily except Sunday.*

The city's most elaborate Italian restaurant, Della Fontana is housed in a former church building. The beautiful stained glass windows remain and there's even a waterfall flowing from the restaurant's ceiling! But the surroundings aren't the only thing that makes a visit to Della Fontana worthwhile. The food is among the best Italian to be found in Salt Lake City and the menu contains a sufficient selection of American cuisine to satisfy any non-Italian food lovers (is there such a person?) in your group. The service is efficient and professional. Cocktails are served.

DESERT EDGE BREWERY AT THE PUB, *273 Trolley Square. Tel. 801/521-8917. American Express, Discover, MasterCard and VISA accepted. Lunch and dinner served nightly.*

The microbrewery and pub craze has even hit conservative Salt Lake City with a big impact. Although the numbers of these institutions are relatively small by large city standards, there's still a good selection of them and Desert Edge is the best of the lot. Their brews have won several awards and the nouveau American cuisine is freshly prepared to order. The Trolley Square location adds to the ambiance. In addition to several different beers, the Desert Edge Brewery has full cocktail service.

LAKOTA RESTAURANT & BAR, *380 West 200 South. Tel. 801/519-8300 or 801/519-8400. American Express, MasterCard and VISA accepted. Lunch and dinner served nightly. Reservations are suggested. Private club (temporary memberships available for visitors).*

I haven't recommended a lot of places in the "private club" category because I don't think you should have to pay extra for the privilege of being able to order a drink at any time of the day. On the other hand some of the clubs are excellent restaurants that can't be ignored and Lakota is definitely in that class. The attractive dining room is modern and colorful–a bit on the eclectic side. The menu features American cuisine with an emphasis on southwestern fare. It's all beautifully prepared and wonderfully seasoned. The service by the highly professional but friendly staff is warm and gracious. In addition to tableside cocktail service Lakota has a "premium" bar that is popular among members. There's a branch of Lakota in Park City that's also very good but something about the Salt Lake City version strikes me as being a lot nicer.

LAMB'S RESTAURANT, *169 S. Main Street. Tel. 801/364-7166. Major credit cards accepted. Breakfast, lunch and dinner served daily except Sunday.*

Lamb's first opened in 1919 and claims to be the oldest existing restaurant in all of Utah. The decor, however, reflects the period of the 1930's and there's an excellent collection of photographs by Utahans from that era. American cuisine is featured and although it's quite good Lamb's long-standing reputation might be a little better than the actual dining experience. The service is friendly and efficient, the atmosphere casual. Cocktail service.

LA SALSA FRESH MEXICAN GRILL, *50 S. Main Street (in the Crossroads Plaza). Tel. 801/521-3300; or 532 East 400 South. Tel. 801/521-8200. Discover, MasterCard and VISA accepted. Lunch and dinner served daily.*

Either branch of this popular Mexican eatery is a colorful and delightfully tasty experience that is probably the best south-of-the-border cuisine in the city. The decor is that of an authentic Mexican "taqueria" and the cuisine is freshly prepared. Charbroiled chicken and steak are the top items in the hearty food category but La Salsa offers a wide variety of excellently prepared vegetarian dishes. There are always five different salsas offered each day ranging from mild to wild but all delicious. A good family dining spot with a friendly atmosphere.

MIKADO JAPANESE RESTAURANT & SUSHI BAR, *67 W 100 South. Tel. 801/328-0929. Major credit cards accepted. Lunch and dinner served daily.*

An excellent choice for authentic Japanese cuisine and sushi, Mikado also offers a number of dishes from around the Pacific Rim. They've been in business for about 40 years so they must be doing something right especially in view of the fact that until recently Japanese food wasn't something particularly in demand in Salt Lake City. You can dine at regular tables but for the true Japanese experience why not opt for the separate Japanese styled room. Full cocktail service is available.

PIÑA RESTAURANT, *327 W. 200 South. Tel. 801/355-7462. American Express, Diner's Club, MasterCard and VISA accepted. Lunch and dinner served Monday through Friday; dinner only on Saturday.*

Despite the name, Pina is not a Mexican or southwestern restaurant. The menu is extremely varied covering the gamut from American to Continental and even throwing in a few entrees that are appropriate to the name. Everything is freshly prepared and served by a gracious and friendly staff in a unique and lovely atmosphere that they refer to as "island colonial." They don't take themselves too seriously, though, as can be seen from the menu headings–things like "appeteasers, joy of grilling," and "sweet fantasies" for desserts. Cocktail service and bar.

XAO LI RESTAURANT, *307 W. 200 South. Tel. 801/328-8688. American Express, Discover, MasterCard and VISA accepted. Lunch and dinner served weekdays; dinner nightly.*

Salt Lake City's most elegant Chinese restaurant, Xao Li features beautiful surroundings and excellent service. Szechuan dishes are the house specialty but many less spicy Mandarin-style entrees are also on the menu. Succulent large shrimp mixed with Chinese vegetables and surrounded by a ring of sliced lemons is both beautiful to look at and delicious to eat. Cocktail service.

Inexpensive
CUTLER'S COOKIES & SANDWICHES, *20 West 200 South. Tel. 801/596-8851. Most major credit cards accepted. Breakfast, lunch and dinner served daily.*

While this may not be the best place for a gourmet at dinner time (or someone who's just plum hungry), the menu of soups and sandwiches makes it a great place for lunch. The large variety of sandwiches are all nicely stuffed and the soups are always hot and fresh. And those cookies–they're simply great!

FRONTIER PIES RESTAURANT & BAKERY, *735 W. North Temple. Tel. 801/521-4700. American Express, Discover, MasterCard and VISA accepted. Breakfast, lunch and dinner served daily.*

The whole family will enjoy dining in this family style eatery that's decorated in pioneer theme. Traditional American favorites are the main menu items but Frontier is best known locally for their fresh homemade soups and pies–so you better leave some room for dessert.

THE OLD SPAGHETTI FACTORY, *189 Trolley Square. Tel. 801/ 521-0424. Discover, Diner's Club, MasterCard and VISA accepted. Lunch and dinner served nightly except dinner only on Sunday.*

Part of a national chain with locations in major cities, the Old Spaghetti Factory, for those of you unfamiliar with it, is always housed in historic refurbished locations. In this case, it sits in the middle of Trolley Square. Indeed, part of the restaurant is an old trolley car. The place is filled with unusual antiques and bric-a-brac and is quite a sight. Spaghetti and other pasta dishes with a variety of sauces is the feature, which makes it a good place to take children. Very casual and lots of fun. The food is good, served in generous portions, and the price is almost ridiculously low. Wine is served.

AROUND THE CITY
Very Expensive
LA CAILLE RESTAURANT, *9565 Wasatch Boulevard. Tel. 801/942-1751. Most major credit cards accepted. Dinner served nightly; Sunday brunch. Reservations are suggested.*

This may well be the city's premier gourmet dining experience–it's certainly among the priciest. However, for those who appreciate great food and service in beautiful surroundings then it's worth the price. Set amid expansive and gorgeously landscaped grounds, La Caille reflects the style and atmosphere of a well-to-do 18th century country French manor house. The cuisine features provincial French entrees along with a varied selection of other Continental dishes. The service is impeccable and tends toward the formal but the overall atmosphere is one of casual elegance. The elaborate Sunday brunch is something special. Cocktail service. La Caille is superb but definitely not the best choice for young children.

Expensive
LOG HAVEN, *6451 E. Millcreek Canyon. Tel. 801/272-8255. Most major credit cards accepted. Dinner served Monday through Saturday; Sunday brunch.*

For less money than La Caille will set you back, Log Haven offers an exceptional dining experience. I'm not the only one to rank this place as the best dining spot in Salt Lake City. It has been recognized as one of the state's premier dining establishments by a number of sources, including the respected Zagat survey. Secluded on a 40-acre site in picturesque Millcreek Canyon only four miles from downtown, Log Haven is an authentic log-style mansion that was built way back in 1920. It was completely renovated in the mid-90's and sits majestically among towering pine trees, beautiful wildflower meadows and several waterfalls. While the interior is nothing short of magnificent a special treat comes during summer when you're able to dine outside on the pretty patio surrounded by the wonderful setting that I've just described.

The cuisine is Continental with a hint of nouveau American flare that makes the beef, fish or whatever you're having taste out of the ordinary. Delicate seasonings are a hallmark of Log Haven's skilled chefs. All of the vegetables are freshly cooked. The service is as excellent as the food and surroundings. Cocktail service and children's menu available.

MILLCREEK INN, *in Millcreek Canyon off of 3800 South. Tel. 801/278-7927. Major credit cards accepted. Dinner served Tuesday through Sunday.*

There are a lot of similarities between Log Haven and Millcreek Inn—the rustic atmosphere in a "wilderness" setting close to the city center as well as the fine food and service. Millcreek is, however, a notch below the former in just about every category. This doesn't mean that it isn't an excellent choice. It most definitely is. The prices are also a tad below Log Haven so on a value basis it is just about equal. The menu at Millcreek consists of both American and Continental entrees. When it comes to atmosphere you'll have to choose between the pretty outdoor patio (at least during the summer months) or the cozy and relaxed indoor dining rooms with their warm fireplaces. Full cocktail service.

POMODORO, *2440 E. Fort Union Boulevard. Tel. 801/944-1895. Most major credit cards accepted. Dinner served nightly except Monday. Reservations are suggested.*

This is Salt Lake's most upscale Italian restaurant and the food is delicious. There are all of the traditional favorites along with some novel twists courtesy of California influenced chefs. The dining room is attractive and the service first-rate. Pomodoro has one of the most extensive wine lists of any restaurant in the city along with full cocktail service.

Moderate

ARCHIBALD'S RESTAURANT, *1100 West 7800 South, West Jordan. Tel. 801/566-6940. Most major credit cards accepted. Lunch and dinner served daily but closes at 5:00pm on Sundays.*

Archibald's is located in a registered historic landmark dating from way back in 1877. The former mill is part of Gardner Village, a collection of interesting and attractive shops that provides a most pleasant atmosphere. An attentive and friendly staff serves excellent American cuisine. The menu includes a number of health conscious entrees. Full cocktail service is available. Children's menu.

MICHAELANGELO RISTORANTE, *2156 South Highland Drive. Tel. 801/466-0961. American Express, Discover, MasterCard and VISA accepted. Lunch and dinner served nightly.*

While Pomodoro may be more of an "in" place with the chic crowd, Michaelangelo is high on my list if you're looking for authentic Italian cuisine. Tuscan regional and northern Italian specialties highlight the extensive menu in this attractive and friendly place. Cocktail service is available.

OLD SALT CITY JAIL, *460 S. 1000 East (in the Anniversary Inn). Tel. 801/355-2422. Major credit cards accepted. Dinner served nightly. Reservations are suggested.*

As delightful a place as the Inn in which it's located, the Old Salt City Jail allows diners to take their grub in an authentic former prison. Your host is the "sheriff" and he'll even sing a song or two for you as you dine on well prepared and delicious steak, prime rib or varied seafood selections. A bountiful salad bar is part of every meal at this jail. Cocktail service.

SANTA FE RESTAURANT, *2100 Emigration Canyon. Tel. 801/582-5888. MasterCard and VISA accepted. Lunch and dinner served Monday through Friday; dinner only on Saturday; Sunday brunch.*

One of my favorites in Salt Lake City, Santa Fe is another of several great eateries near town but situated in an almost idyllic natural setting. This one is two miles up the canyon and is inside a pretty southwestern-style lodge. It offers excellent views of the mountains and canyon either from the indoor dining room or the outdoor decks. Massive fireplaces and original southwestern works of art highlight the interior decor of this showplace restaurant. The cuisine is traditional southwestern although a number of American entrees are also available. All are a feast for the eyes as well as the palate. Cocktail service is available tableside or you can socialize in the adjacent private club (temporary membership is required for the latter).

WAGONMASTER STEAK COMPANY, *5485 South Vine, Murray. Tel. 801/269-1100. Most major credit cards accepted. Dinner served nightly except Sunday.*

Considering that Salt Lake City is the west it isn't that well represented by the usual number of great western steakhouses that are so commonly found in other mountain states. Well, the Wagonmaster will more than make up for the more limited numbers of this genre. Thick juicy steaks and prime rib prepared exactly to your specifications are what draw locals and visitors alike to this casual and fun restaurant. The decor features Dodge City covered wagons and the staff of cowboys and Indians makes it a great place for children as well as grown-ups hunting for that perfect piece of beef. Cocktail service is available.

ALTA
Moderate

ALTA LODGE RESTAURANT, *Alta Ski Area. Tel. 800/707-2582. Discover, MasterCard and VISA accepted during the summer only. Breakfast, lunch and dinner served daily during the winter; Dinner and Sunday brunch only during the summer. Reservations are suggested.*

A lot of Salt Lake City residents make the ride from the city to Alta to take in the spectacular setting of the Alta Lodge Restaurant. The food and service also have to be extra special to make the ride and you'll find both at this fine restaurant, which features imaginative preparation of a wide variety of American and regional cuisine using the freshest ingredients. The service is highly personalized and efficient. The popular Sunday brunch is outstanding. Cocktail service.

BRIGHAM CITY
Moderate

MADDOX RANCH HOUSE, *2 miles east of I-15, Exit 364 (Perry). Tel. 435/723-8545. American Express, Discover, MasterCard and VISA accepted. Lunch and dinner served Tuesday through Saturday.*

This authentic former ranch house contains several different dining rooms so that you eat in a casual but very private atmosphere highlighted by excellent service. The food, while not outstanding, is well prepared traditional American favorites like beef and chicken (the fried chicken, however, is great). This is a nice place for family dining.

Inexpensive

IDLE ISLE CAFE, *24 S. Main Street. Tel. 435/734-2468. Discover, MasterCard and VISA accepted. Lunch and dinner served daily except Sunday.*

More than a restaurant, the Idle Isle is also a candy factory that has been around since the 1920's. You can purchase candy on your way out, something that children will no doubt appreciate. The old time atmosphere of the restaurant is delightful, especially the old time soda fountain. Entrees consist primarily of traditional American dishes that are served in substantial portions especially when considering the modest price. The service is efficient but friendly.

BRIGHTON/SOLITUDE
Very Expensive
THE ROUNDHOUSE AT SOLITUDE, *12000 Big Cottonwood Canyon, Solitude. Tel. 801/536-5709. Most major credit cards accepted. Dinner served nightly. Reservations are required.*

An extra special dinner experience for those willing to pay the price. The Roundhouse is a casual but elegant facility located 12 miles into Big Cottonwood Canyon and then atop a mountain peak. The name comes from the circular construction. Seating is around the outside edge so that no matter what table you're at you have a simply wonderful view of the Wasatch Mountains. Getting there is half the fun–you're escorted by a host in a modern version of the open sleigh–a snow cat! Once at the Roundhouse you'll experience fine service and gourmet preparation of regional American and Continental cuisine. Full cocktail service is available. While the cuisine and style of the restaurant isn't ideally suited to families with small children, the trip there is definitely fun for all ages.

HEBER CITY
Moderate
HUB CAFE, *1165 S. Main Street. Tel. 435/654-5463. Most major credit cards accepted. Breakfast, lunch and dinner served daily.*

A typical small town family style restaurant that's unpretentious and affordable. They have a nice selection of American cuisine for dinner and boast an impressive selection of sizable sandwiches for lunch. In fact, the Hub is a good place for tasty food, quick service and comfortable surroundings no matter what meal you're ready for.

Inexpensive
DON PEDRO'S FAMILY MEXICAN RESTAURANT, *42 W. Main Street. Tel. 435/654-0805. Discover, MasterCard and VISA accepted. Lunch and dinner served daily.*

Don Pedro offers authentic and well prepared Mexican food that's not too spicy. There's plenty to eat and the prices are a bargain. The service is friendly and efficient and the atmosphere is attractive. Children's menu.

LOGAN
Moderate

THE COPPER MILL RESTAURANT, *55 N. Main Street (third floor). Tel. 435/752-0647. Most major credit cards accepted. Lunch and dinner served daily except Sunday.*

A nice casual atmosphere highlights this downtown eatery that features such popular American staples as prime rib and chicken as well as a decent selection of seafood. Some menu items edge into the expensive category. They have a large salad bar and good desserts. Wine is served but no liquor. Children's menu.

ZANAVOO, *4880 East Highway 89. Tel. 435/752-0085. American Express, Discover, MasterCard and VISA accepted. Dinner served nightly except Sunday.*

Considering the reasonable prices at Zanavoo, this is a highly rewarding dining experience. The chef prepares excellent American cuisine and it's served by a professional staff in a rustic atmosphere that is most attractive.

MIDWAY
Very Expensive

SIMON'S, *700 N. Homestead Drive, Midway, in the Homestead Resort. Tel. 435/654-1102. Major credit cards accepted. Dinner served nightly; Sunday brunch. Reservations are suggested.*

The premier restaurant in the top rated Homestead Resort, Simon's is a wonderful dining experience. Simon's captures the atmosphere of a rich country home. Fireplaces, fine linen and cutlery, fresh flowers and candlelight provide a warm and intimate feeling. The view out the windows is one of tranquility. The cuisine is American but with a flair reminiscent of the great restaurants of Europe. Some Continental dishes are also featured, including Simon's specialty of the house–chateaubriand. There is much table-side preparation. A formal but friendly and most gracious wait staff will tend to your needs and help ensure a most enjoyable dinner. Complete cocktail service. Simon's also has a children's menu and although sophisticated dining of this nature is usually considered adult territory, the staff will go out of their way to make children feel comfortable.

During the winter months Simon's is noted for something that even tops dining there at other times of the year. Dinner can be preceded by a sleigh ride through the Homestead's extensive grounds on groomed trails. The chateaubriand is part of this special. Another Simon's tradition, regardless of the time of the year, is their bountiful Sunday brunch. It's a colorful feast for the eyes and an impossible task to sample all of the imaginatively presented food.

OGDEN
Moderate

BAVARIAN CHALET, *4387 Harrison Blvd. Tel. 801/479-7561. American Express, Discover, MasterCard and VISA accepted. Dinner served Tuesday through Saturday. Reservations are suggested.*

The best German food in Utah is served at the pleasant and attractive looking Bavarian Chalet. Although the German specialties of the house are the featured attractions on the extensive menu you can also select from a number of nicely prepared American entrees including steak and fish. A number of pasta and vegetarian dishes are available as well. Portions are more than ample. The service is quite good. Cocktail service. Children's menu.

CAJUN SKILLET, *2550 Washington Blvd. Tel. 801/393-7702. American Express, MasterCard and VISA accepted. Lunch and dinner served daily except Sunday.*

Good cajun style cooking isn't found all that often in Utah, but the Cajun Skillet will do nicely if that's what you're in the mood for. Fish and seafood dishes are the main feature of the menu. For the more adventurous diner I suggest trying the delicious alligator dinner. Trust me, it's a lot better than it sounds. The surroundings are attractive and the service more than adequate. Cocktail service.

PAVILION RESTAURANT, *247 24th Street. Tel. 801/627-1190. Major credit cards accepted. Lunch and dinner served daily except Sunday.*

A large selection of entrees is the strong point of this modern downtown restaurant that features good food and service at affordable prices. The veal cutlet a la parmesan is excellent. Cocktail service.

PARK CITY
Very Expensive

GLITRETIND, *7700 Stein Way, in the Stein Eriksen Lodge. Tel. 435/ 649-3700. Major credit cards accepted. Dinner served nightly; Sunday brunch. Reservations are suggested.*

In a resort known for upscale dining, Glitretind is the leader of the fine dining category. An atmosphere of understated elegance prevails in this immaculate dining room that overlooks an exquisitely beautiful alpine mountain vista. The table is set with the finest china and cutlery and enhanced by freshly cut flowers. Your waiter is a professional who has a complete understanding of the complex menu and will serve you in a gracious manner. Continental cuisine is featured and the chef changes the menu with the passing of each season.

Regardless of what's on the menu, though, it will be beautifully prepared and delicately seasoned. The only negative for me, besides the price, is that bigger appetites may not be satisfied. I know that's supposed to be the way it's done in finer restaurants but would a little more food hurt? Oh, well, hungry folk will just have to spend a little more and sample one of the delicious and sinfully rich desserts. Full cocktail service. Children's menu available.

Expensive

GOLDENER HIRSCH, *7570 Royal Street East. Tel. 435/649-7770. American Express, MasterCard and VISA accepted. Winter: Breakfast, lunch and dinner served daily; Summer: lunch on Friday and Saturday only, dinner Thursday through Sunday (with some exceptions); Sunday brunch. Reservations are suggested during the winter but call in summer to confirm hours.*

A fine restaurant with a casual atmosphere, the Goldener Hirsch features a mainly Continental menu with a good selection of lighter health conscious entrees. If the name sounds vaguely familiar that's because it's taken from a famous restaurant in Salzburg, Austria. The decor has been copied to a large degree and makes for a delightful setting. The food is excellent and so is the service but the latter definitely isn't stuffy or overbearing. There is tableside cocktail service as well as a separate lounge. Children's menu is available.

THE MARIPOSA, *Silver Lake Village off of Royal Street. Tel. 435/645-6715. Most major credit cards accepted. Dinner served nightly except Monday during the winter season. Call at other times to confirm hours. Reservations are suggested.*

It's too bad that the Mariposa has somewhat erratic operating hours during the summer months because this is a good restaurant that isn't quite as highly priced as many of the best dining spots in Park City. The varied menu selection features cuisine that ranges from classic European to nouveau American, all deliciously prepared and attentively served by a knowledgeable staff. The Mariposa is especially known for its excellent appetizers. Cocktail service.

Moderate

CISERO'S, *306 Main Street. Tel. 435/649-5044. Most major credit cards accepted. Lunch and dinner served nightly.*

Cisero's is one of Park City's most popular establishments and it earns that distinction. They have great Italian fare that's highlighted by fresh seafood. "Cioppino" is Cisero's own home-made fresh pasta dish and it is excellent. The atmosphere is equally inviting as the food. It occupies an historic building that dates from 1906 and it has been extensively remodeled. The main dining room is on the street level and features the full menu along with cocktail service and a children's menu. On the lower level is a lively club (temporary membership required). In addition to drinking and socializing, the club offers a limited menu of lighter fare. Cisero's is an excellent choice not only because of the good food and service but due to the fact that it is one of the more affordable full service restaurants in Park City.

THE PANTRY, *1895 Sidewinder Drive, in the Olympia Park Hotel & Convention Center. Tel. 435/649-2900. Most major credit cards accepted. Breakfast and dinner served nightly. Reservations are suggested.*

Like Cisero's, the Pantry provides good food at reasonable prices, something that's not always that easy to find in this town despite the presence of almost a hundred restaurants. Many are very high priced while the cheaper ones are the fast food variety–and that certainly rules out the possibility of "good" food! The Pantry offers nicely prepared American fare in adequate portions that's served by a friendly and efficient staff. Outdoor dining available in season. Cocktail service tableside or in the separate lounge called The Pub. Children's menu. One of the better family dining spots around.

RADIGAN'S, *2121 Park Avenue, in the Radisson Park City. Tel. 435/ 649-5000. Major credit cards accepted. Breakfast, lunch and dinner served daily.*

While some of the entrees edge into the expensive category, Radigan's is a decent family restaurant (they have one of the better children's menus in Park City) that serves an excellent variety of American cuisine. The desserts are outstanding and may well be the best feature of Radigan's for those who like the big finish for their meal. The restaurant is also quite attractive and during the warmer months you can dine outside on the patio. Cocktail service.

TEXAS RED'S PIT BARBECUE, *440 Main Street. Tel. 435/649-7337. Discover, MasterCard and VISA accepted. Lunch and dinner served daily.*

This may be the only full service restaurant in town that has at least several entrees that fall into the inexpensive category although, on the whole, it has to be included in the moderate priced group. Just about everything at Texas Red's is pit cooked, as the name implies, and with their savory sauce it makes for a delicious meal whether you get the ribs, pork, chicken or whatever. The brisket of beef is especially good. Also outstanding is their home-made chili–it's on the hot side but if that's you're liking, then go for it. A sizzling tongue for the next few hours will be a constant reminder of a good meal!

Texas Red's is also a good place for lunch as they have an excellent selection of sandwiches, salads and soups. Cocktail service. Children's menu. A fun atmosphere that's good for the whole family.

PROVO

Expensive

THE TREE ROOM, *State Highway 92 in the Sundance resort. Tel. 801/ 225-4107. Most major credit cards accepted. Dinner served nightly. Reservations are suggested.*

This is one of the most beautiful dining rooms you'll encounter no matter where you travel even though it isn't in the elegant class. What it does offer is a thoroughly rustic atmosphere with wood paneled walls and beamed ceilings. Native American art work and western memorabilia (some of the latter from Robert Redford's own personal collection) adorn walls, shelves and fireplace mantles. It's almost like a western museum. Amid all of this are tables surrounded by high-backed chairs, elegant linens and tableware that somehow fit in nicely with the otherwise casual surroundings.

The food doesn't take a back seat to the setting at the Tree Room. Exquisitely prepared southwestern fare dominates the menu along with fresh seafood and wild game dishes. Savory sauces add a special flavor to whatever you order as do the fresh vegetables and herbs that are organically grown locally, sometimes on the grounds of the Sundance resort. The service is outstanding. Full cocktail service. Children's menu. Perhaps the most surprising thing about the Tree Room is that it isn't even more expensive.

Moderate

MAGLEBY'S, *1675 N. 200 West. Tel. 801/374-6249. Major credit cards accepted. Lunch and dinner served nightly except Sunday.*

A most attractive if not somewhat eclectic decor, Magleby's features everything from old time lamp posts to big windows with colorful flower boxes. The well prepared food runs the gamut from steaks and seafood to pasta. They have an excellent salad bar and the locals also come to Magleby's for the delicious desserts. Cocktail service.

OAK GRILL, *101 W. 100 North, in the Provo Park Hotel & Utah Valley Conference Center. Tel. 801/370-3547. Major credit cards accepted. Dinner served nightly; Sunday brunch.*

An attractive dining room with a casual feel, the Oak Grill is a popular restaurant for couples and families that serves a good variety of American cuisine. Their extensive Sunday brunch is excellent. Service is first rate but in a relaxed and friendly manner. Sometimes the Oak Grill has a live piano player tapping out soft melodies while you dine. Cocktail service and children's menu available.

SNOWBIRD

Expensive

THE AERIE RESTAURANT, *Snowbird Ski Area, in the Cliff Lodge. Tel. 801/521-6040. Most major credit cards accepted. Breakfast and dinner daily; Sunday brunch during the summer. Reservations are suggested.*

Snowbird's Cliff Lodge and the surrounding village have about a half dozen restaurants in all price ranges and all of them are good. But, so you won't think I have a financial tie-in with them, I'll only give special praise to two of them. Aerie's is the most attractive of the lot and also presents diners with fabulous views. Continental cuisine is featured; the most popular dishes are fresh seafood and lamb. There's a casual atmosphere and good service. Cocktail service tableside and in the separate lounge. Temporary membership is required only if you are going to consume alcoholic beverages.

THE STEAK PIT, *Snowbird Ski Area, in the Cliff Lodge. Tel. 801/521-6040. Most major credit cards accepted. Dinner served nightly.*

This is one of the better steak houses in Utah and many Salt Lake City residents make the drive to Snowbird to eat here. Thick, juicy and tender prime rib is the star attraction although the seafood and fish are also quite good. The decor is rustic and the atmosphere relaxing and casual. The service is efficient and unhurried. Cocktails are served.

WENDOVER

No doubt if you stay overnight in Wendover you'll want to eat something. There isn't any place in town that I can recommend, especially for dinner. Your best bet is to go a few blocks over the state line into Nevada and eat at one of the casino restaurants.

SEEING THE SIGHTS

You will probably be surprised at the large number of interesting attractions to be found within Salt Lake City as well as the surrounding areas. Unless you are going to be spending at least a few days in the area you won't be able to do them all. To make things easier for you I've divided seeing the sights of the Northwest into two major sections. The first is Salt Lake City itself. That has been further divided into a downtown tour and one that takes in the remainder of the city. All of the other sights of the northwest are seen via daily excursions from Salt Lake City although you could easily stay overnight in one or more other communities if you're making a loop or simply don't want to drive back and forth every day.

The first Salt Lake City tour is best done on foot because it covers a relatively small area in the middle of the city. Although the second tour is more easily done by car it is possible to reach just about every point of interest by the city's extensive network of buses. However, that is a lot more time consuming. Likewise, many of the attractions in the excursion section are accessible by bus but, again, a car is much more convenient. If you are using the UTA buses to get to places on Tour 2 the appropriate line will be indicated after each attraction.

SALT LAKE CITY

Tour 1: Downtown Salt Lake City

Approximate duration (by foot including sightseeing time) is a full day. Begin at the Salt Lake City Visitor Information Center, 90 S. West Temple Street (corner of 100 South) in the Salt Palace.

The **Visitor Information Center** is always a good place to begin a walking tour because you can get brochures and ask any questions you might have of the helpful staff. The Center is located in the huge complex known as the **Salt Palace Convention Center**. It's beginning to show its age a bit but it remains one of the premier facilities of its kind in the United States. Then walk north one block to South Temple and you will be facing the beautiful **Temple Square**. This is literally and figuratively the heart of Salt Lake City.

The most sacred place on earth to the Mormon faithful, Temple Square is also one of the most fascinating places to visit regardless of your religious affiliation or convictions. You should be aware that at all LDS (Latter Day Saints) facilities you're likely to encounter some attempts, subtle or otherwise, to interest you in converting to Mormonism. If you find this annoying or worse, simply excuse yourself in a polite way and move on. In many ways, Temple Square is reminiscent of a grand European city center with a magnificent cathedral dominating the surroundings. Within the ten acres of Temple Square are the Mormon Temple, Tabernacle, Assembly Hall and Visitors Center. The splendid park-like grounds of Temple Square contain the Sea Gull Monument as well as numerous other statues and monuments.

A good place to start is at the **LDS Visitor Center** on the northwest corner of the square. The center has beautiful murals depicting scenes from both the Old and New Testaments and the stunning Christus statue. Another visitor center at the southwest corner features film presentations on various aspects of the Mormon faith. Presentations last about 30 to 45 minutes and are only recommended if you are especially interested in theology. The **Tabernacle**, constructed entirely of wood, is one of the largest self-supporting domed facilities in the world and, considering that it was built in the 19th century, is an engineering marvel. The acoustics are absolutely remarkable. During tours you will witness a demonstration of the proverbial pin being dropped. If you have really good hearing you may be able to detect it. Regardless, the acoustic qualities are something special and so is the magnificent pipe organ. The famous building is, of course, the home base for the equally well known **Mormon Tabernacle Choir**.

The **Mormon Temple** is the focal point of the square and is one of the finest religious structures in the world. Construction began in 1853 and took forty years to complete. Six soaring towers that slowly narrow to a graceful point highlight the striking gray colored edifice. The east tower is the biggest and soars to a height of 210 feet. On top of the tower is a brilliant gold-leaf covered statue of the Angel Moroni, of special significance to the Mormon faith. The interior of the temple is closed to the general public. It contains all that is sacred to the Mormons and is used for important ceremonies including marriages. The temple is architecturally splendid during the day but it takes on a special appearance during the evening when it is illuminated. In fact, the entire square is gorgeous at night. The **Assembly Hall** is frequently the venue for free concerts, generally on the weekends.

Temple Square and the Visitor Centers are open daily from 8:00am through 10:00pm, Memorial Day through Labor Day and from 9:00am to 9:00pm the remainder of the year. There is no admission charge. Free guided tours of the square are offered at about ten minute intervals (depending upon traffic). They depart from the flagpole and last approximately 45 minutes. For information call Tel. 801/240-2534. Recitals at the Tabernacle are open to the public, also free of charge. Inquire as to schedule. Mormon Tabernacle Choir rehearsals are held on Thursday evenings at 8:00pm and the public is invited. The Sunday morning Choir broadcast takes place from here as well. Visitors must be inside by 9:15am. For inquiries relating to the Choir, call Tel. 801/240-8096. The LDS church also provides a general information number for all church related attractions. The number is Tel. 800/537-9703.

Several other facilities related to the LDS church are in the vicinity of Temple Square. The **Family History Library**, *35 N. West Temple*, is across the street from the southwest corner of the square and contains one of the largest collections of genealogical information in the world. It is mainly of interest to those who wish to do research on their family lineage. If that appeals to you then consult the sidebar. Next door to the library is a facility of more general interest. This is the **Museum of Church History And Art**, *45 N. West Temple*. The museum traces the history of the Mormon faith from its earliest days through the present time. It does so though many exhibits and displays as well as through sculpture and paintings depicting Mormon history and theological themes. You can see the exhibits on your own or via a guided tour. *Tel. 801/240-3310. The museum is open weekdays from 9:00am until 9:00pm and on weekends and holidays from 10:00am to 7:00pm. There is no admission charge; tours are also free.*

DOWNTOWN SALT LAKE CITY

⊢———⊣ = Approx. 1/4 mile

① Beehive House
② Brigham Young Monument
③ Cathedral of the Madelene
④ Council Hall
⑤ Crossroads Plaza
⑥ Delta Center
⑦ Eagle Gate
⑧ Family History Library

⑨ Hansen Planetarium
⑩ LDS Church Office Bldg.
⑪ Lion House
⑫ Museum of Church History and Art
⑬ Pioneer Memorial Museum
⑭ Pioneer Park
⑮ Promised Valley Playhouse
⑯ Salt Palace Convention Center/Visitors Info

⑰ Rio Grande Depot (Amtrak)
⑱ State Capitol
⑲ Temple Square
⑳ Triad Center
㉑ Tracy Aviary
㉒ Trolley Square
㉓ Union Pacific Depot
㉔ ZCMI Center

MORMON GENEALOGY & YOU

Tracing one's ancestors is an interesting hobby for many people. For the Mormons it is almost a sacred duty. Mormons believe that they must be "sealed" with their ancestors. So, being able to determine exactly who your ancestors were becomes of great importance. Whether you're Mormon and need to find out about your ancestors or you're not a Mormon and simply would like to know about your heritage, the facilities of the Family History Library are open to one and all. Records include microfilm, computers, books and family registries. The major part of the genealogical collection focuses on the United States, Great Britain and Mexico, although information on other parts of the world is being added at a furious pace. The records begin in 1550 and go through 1910. The library staff will assist you in conducting your search.

Call them at Tel. 801/240-3702. There is no charge for using the facilities. Inquire as to research hours.

Now work your way around to the east side of Temple Square. On Main Street between North and South Temple Streets is the **Brigham Young Monument**. The monument also pays homage to the Ute Indians native to the area as well as the fur trappers who explored the region prior to the arrival of the Mormons. At the corner of South Temple and Main Street is the **Joseph Smith Memorial Building**. The building, which is listed on the National Register of Historic Places, used to be the Hotel Utah. It was a grand old place much in the tradition of Denver's Brown Palace and some of the finer hotels in Europe. The main legacy of the hotel that still remains are two excellent restaurants on the roof which provide outstanding views of Temple Square. Within the building are more genealogical research facilities and a theater showing a 50-minute long film about the pioneers. It is entitled *Legacy.* Tours of the building are also offered. *Tel. 801/539-1911. Call for tour information. Film times and ticket information can be obtained by calling Tel. 801/240-4383.*

Just east of the Joseph Smith Building at *63 E. South Temple* is the **Lion House**. The house was built in 1855 and was the residence of Brigham Young. The building is not open to the public except for a restaurant on the lower level. The **Beehive House**, next door at *67 E. South Temple,* was also a home for Mr. Young. I guess he didn't like to move too far. This building served as the official residence of the Utah Territorial Governor, a post first held by Brigham Young. The house is a registered national landmark and has been carefully restored and furnished in period. *Tel. 801/240-2671. Free guided tours lasting about 30 minutes are offered. The house*

ABOUT THOSE SEA GULLS

A lot of people wonder about that Sea Gull monument in Temple Square (not to mention the already forgotten fact that the sea gull is the Utah state bird). After all, Salt Lake City is pretty far from the sea. Maybe so, but they do like to frequent the nearby Great Salt Lake. Okay, that's reasonable, but a monument to some birds? Well, it seems that the early settlers had a few problems during their second year in the Salt Valley, such as frost and drought. But no problem was worse than the plague of grasshoppers that nearly destroyed the entire harvest and could have led to the disbanding of the young settlement. But the sea gulls came to the rescue. They came in from the lake and munched on those little buggers so that enough of the crop was saved to get the pioneers through the winter. So, in gratitude for a job well done we have the sea gull as the state bird and the nice monument in Temple Square.

is open weekdays from 9:30am to 6:30pm, Saturdays from 9:30am to 4:30pm and on Sunday from 10:00am until 1:00pm June through August. The remainder of the years it is open daily from 9:30am to 4:30pm except on Sunday when it is open from 10:00am to 1:00pm. Closed New Year's, Thanksgiving, and Christmas.

As you leave the Beehive House along South Temple and approach the corner of State Street you can't help but notice the impressive **Eagle Gate** spanning the street. The gate was originally built to denote the entrance to Brigham Young's personal property. Although several gates have been built on the site the current one measures 76 feet across and is topped by an eagle whose wings spread 20 feet. The eagle alone weighs about two tons. Now turn north (left) on State and proceed to North Temple. Walk to the left once again until you reach the entrance of the **LDS Church Office Building**, *50 E. North Temple*. The sleek and beautiful building is the administrative headquarters of the world-wide Mormon church and is also the tallest building in Salt Lake City. The main lobby contains a huge mural of Christ and the Apostles. There is an observation deck on the 26th floor that offers panoramic views of the city and nearby mountains. Lovely gardens are located on the building's plaza level. *Tel. 801/240-2452. The building is open to the public weekdays from 9:00am until 4:00pm. Closed holidays. There is no admission charge. Guided tours that include an explanation of the mural are also offered.*

Now it's time to get away from Mormon Church history and attractions for a while. Continue west on North Temple to the corner of Main Street and turn right. Proceed four blocks up to Capitol Hill. But before you get to the capitol stop at the **Pioneer Memorial Museum**, *300 North Main*. The building is designed in the style of an old theater that no longer exists. It contains almost 40 different rooms that depict all aspects of life in 19th and early 20th century Utah. A separate building houses a collection of old vehicles. *Tel. 801/538-1050. The museum is open daily from 9:00am until 5:00pm except for Sunday when it opens at 1:00pm. It is closed Sunday except during the period from June through August. There is no set admission charge but donations are requested.*

After leaving the museum cross the street into the park which houses the **State Capitol**. The 1915 capitol building cost $2.75 million, a staggering sum of money at the time. Constructed mainly of Utah granite and Georgia marble for decoration, the Renaissance Revival structure also has traces of the ornate Corinthian style of architecture. The huge dome is covered with copper. From the hilltop entrance there is an excellent view of the city. The grounds surrounding the capitol are lovely and include hedges in the shape of Utah. On the inside visitors will see the impressive main hall and rotunda. Many murals adorn the walls and ceilings. There are also exhibits about each of Utah's counties and the state reception area is open for public viewing when not in use. The legislative chambers can only be seen by 30-minute guided tour. *Tel. 801/538-3000. Tours are offered every half hour weekdays from 9:00am through 4:00pm, Memorial Day to the Friday before Labor Day. At other times of the year the hours vary and it is best to call in advance for information. Admission is free.*

If you have children you might want to make a detour to the **Children's Museum of Utah**, *840 North 300 West*. Walk west from the Capitol to 300 and then turn right for five blocks. The "hands on" museum emphasizes exhibits in science and is geared toward children under 12. *Tel. 801/328-3383. Museum hours are daily except Sunday from 9:30am to 5:30pm. It is open on Friday evenings until 8:00pm. Admission is $4 for adults and $3.75 for children ages 2 through 13.*

Now reverse your route to the state capitol. From that point, whether or not you visited the children's museum, go just south on the east side of State Street to **Council Hall**, *300 North State*. The handsome structure dates from the late 19th century and once served as the city hall as well as a territorial headquarters. Many furnishings from the 1860s are on display. The Utah Travel Council is now housed here and you can get information on all parts of the state from the helpful staff. *Tel. 801/583-1030. Council Hall is open weekdays from 8:00am until 6:00pm and from 10:00am to 5:00pm on weekends and holidays. There is no admission charge.*

The area behind Council Hall is **Memory Grove Park** and **City Creek Canyon**, a lovely long and narrow park that extends to the mountains. You can relax for a while or walk the many trails. For visitors, though, several memorials to Utah veterans and a Liberty Bell replica are of interest. Leave the park via the east side and you will be on Avenue A.

Walk south (to the right) to 1st Avenue and turn right once again until you reach the **Mormon Pioneer Memorial Monument**, *110 E. 1st Avenue*. The small monument site also contains the grave of Brigham Young and some of his family members as well as a pioneer poetess named Eliza Snow. Then walk back to Avenue A, turn right and go one block to South Temple and turn left. Between B & C Streets at *331 E. South Temple* is the **Cathedral of the Madeleine** which was built in 1900. The large cathedral features two 220-foot high towers. The ornate interior has beautiful stained glass, Venetian mosaics, extensive use of marble, and many statues carved from oak. A recent restoration program has returned the cathedral to tip-top condition and its original splendor. *Tel. 801/328-8941. The cathedral is open Monday to Friday from 8:00am until 5:30pm and there is no admission charge.*

A smaller cathedral dating from 1870 is located nearby at *231 E. 100 South*. Take 300 East one block south to 100 South and turn right. The Episcopal **Cathedral Church of St. Mark** is the oldest non-Mormon church in Utah. The Scottish pipe organ dates from the late 1850s. *Tel. 801/322-3400. Open weekdays from 9:00am to 4:00pm. Donations are appreciated.*

Now walk west on 100 South back to State Street and turn right, proceeding to about mid-way down the block to the **Hansen Planetarium**, *15 S. State Street*. The complex houses a museum with exhibits on the earth and space. The planetarium features a trip to the planets of our solar system in the Star Chamber. It's mildly interesting but not much different than dozens of other planetariums throughout the country. However, science lovers will like it and if you have children it is definitely educational. The laser shows are the best feature. *Tel. 801/538-2104. Open Monday through Saturday from 9:30am to 9:30pm (till midnight on Friday evening) and on Sunday from 12:30pm to 6:00pm. Call for schedule of star and laser shows. The planetarium and museum are free of charge but the Star Shows cost $4.50 for adults and $3.50 for seniors and children ages 4 to 12. Laser shows are $6-7.50 for adults and $5 for seniors and children.*

Four blocks south on State Street between 400 and 500 South is Washington Square and the location of the **City & County Building**. The huge granite structure served as the state capitol from 1896 to 1915. Today it is just an office building but the exterior architecture as well as the pretty square with its fountains and ponds is worth a brief look. Now it's on to the last stop of our downtown tour. Walk west on 400 South until you reach 400 West. That's correct...remember the grid! Turn right and go one block to 300 South and then left to the **Rio Grande Depot**. The Depot, among other things, houses the **Utah State Historical Society Museum**. In a setting of a restored train station, the museum has various exhibits about Utah covering the different groups who have settled in the state. *Tel. 801/533-3501. Museum hours are Monday through Friday from 8:00am until 5:00pm and on Saturday from 10:00am to 3:00pm. There is no admission charge.*

To make your way back to the origination point of this tour return east on 300 South for four blocks to West Temple. Turn left and in two blocks you'll be back at the Visitor Center and Salt Palace. It's been quite a day!

DARTING AROUND DOWNTOWN

The Utah Transit Authority offers a "Free Ride Zone" in downtown Salt Lake City. Although most of the attractions are close together, this service can come in handy for some of the longer walks or if you're feet are just getting a bit too tired. The zone encompasses all bus routes in an area bordered by N. Temple, 200 East, 400 South and W. Temple. It isn't a huge area but does contain a large majority of the attractions on the downtown tour.

Tour 2: Around the City
Approximate duration (by car including sightseeing) is a full day. Begin at Liberty Park, located at the intersection of 500 East and 900 South. Take any major north-south street from the downtown area to 900 South and then head east to 500 East. Major attractions that can be reached by Utah Transit Authority bus from downtown will be indicated by the route numbers.

Liberty Park is a large and attractive municipal park with recreational facilities and the pretty *Seven Canyon Fountain* as well as another historic home of Brigham Young. The main point of interest, however, is the **Tracy Aviary** located about four blocks south of 900 Street on 500 East. The aviary was built in 1938 and is one of the oldest facilities of its kind in the world. The bird collection numbers more than 800 and features exotic as well as endangered species from every corner of the globe. *Birds of a Feather* is an interesting show that is presented several times a day. *Tel. 801/596-0900. The aviary is open daily from 9:00am until 6:00pm except from November to March when it closes at 4:30pm. It is closed only on Christmas. Admission is $3 for adults and $1.50 for seniors and children ages 4 through 12. Bus #10.*

Head south one block to 1000 South and take that west to 900 West and the **International Peace Gardens**. The gardens, which are part of Jordan Park, are divided into 14 sections with each one representing the culture of a different nation. The pathways through this colorful and imaginative floral display make for a tranquil walk. *Generally open from May through October although the exact dates vary from year to year. There is no admission charge. Bus #17 or 81.*

One of the longer rides of the day will lead to the next area of multiple attractions. Head back toward the east on 900 South for about 2-1/2 miles to 1300 East. Turn left (north) and travel for a half mile to 400 South. A final right will bring you to University Street and the campus of the **University of Utah**. The state's largest public institution of higher education occupies an attractive 1,200 acre campus at the foothills that begin to rise over Salt Lake City.

Two buildings that should be visited here are the **University Museum of Natural History** and the **Utah Museum of Fine Arts**. The natural history facility is one of the finest of its type and takes visitors through about the last 200 million years of Utah's history through large dioramas and interactive exhibits. Children are likely to be most impressed with the excellent dinosaur exhibit but the Native American section is also of special interest. *Tel. 801/581-4303. Museum hours are Monday through Saturday from 9:30am until 5:30pm and on Sundays and holidays from noon to 5:00pm. The admission is $3 for adults and $1.50 for seniors and children under age 13.* The Fine Arts museum is best known for its collection of Renaissance paintings, tapestries and furniture although there is also much work from Asia, Africa and the Americas. *Tel. 801/581-7332. Museum hours are weekdays from 10:00am to 5:00pm and weekends from noon until 5:00pm. It is closed on state holidays. Admission is free. All university points of interest by Bus #'s 1 through 5 as well as 7, 8 and 11.*

Also on the campus is the **Red Butte Garden & Arboretum**. This extensive portion of the college's land contains over 300 different types of trees. You can pick up a brochure at the visitor center that describes many of them as well as getting a map that will take you through the 25 acres of gardens and along some of the more than four miles of nature trails. Concerts are sometimes held on the grounds. *Tel. 801/581-5322. The gardens are open daily from 9:00am until dusk from April through October and there is no admission fee.* Other sights on the campus that may be of interest to some are the university stadium and special events center.

The southern boundary of the university is 500 South. Make your way to that street and turn east. Where the street turns and changes names to Foothill Drive make a left onto Wasatch Drive, which separates the university campus from the **Fort Douglas** military reservation. Many of the buildings on the base date from the 19th century and represent a large variety of architectural styles. However, the only facility open to the public is the **Fort Douglas Military Museum**. The collection covers a wide spectrum of United States military history although much emphasis is placed on Utah. An especially popular exhibit is the display of uniforms that begins in the pre-Civil War era and comes right up to the present time. A number of armored vehicles and artillery weapons are also on display. *Tel. 801/588-5188. The museum is open Tuesday through Saturday from 10:00am until 4:00pm (closes for lunch between noon and 1:00pm) except on Federal holidays. There is no admission charge. Bus #'s 1 through 3.*

Make your way back to Foothills and continue south on that street for a short time until you reach Sunnyside Avenue. Turn left and follow Sunnyside until you get to the **This is the Place State Park**, *2601 E. Sunnyside*. Located at the entrance to scenic **Emigration Canyon**, the park commemorates the arrival of Mormon pioneers in 1847. This is where Brigham Young is said to have uttered the famous words by which the park is known and the Mormons began to set up shop in their new home. It ended a 1,300 mile journey from the persecution found in the Midwest. Some historians say it's 2,000 miles, since the Mormon Church was actually founded in New York. Either way it is a beautiful and interesting place to visit.

The centerpiece is the large and inspiring "This is the Place" Monument, built in 1947 to commemorate the 100th anniversary of Brigham Young's arrival. The many figures on and around the monument's white marble base represent more than just the Mormon pioneers. Spanish explorers, fur trappers, Native Americans and others who have been important influences on Utah history are also given their due. Also in the park is **Old Deseret**, a recreation of a pioneer community that is typical of many in Utah during the period from 1847 through 1870. It contains several adobe structures, commercial buildings and some actual homes that have been relocated here from towns throughout the state. One of them is Brigham Young's first farmhouse and it is furnished in period. The park also has a visitor center with exhibits. *Tel. 801/584-8391 or 801/584-8392 for Old Deseret. The park is open daily from 10:00am until 6:00pm but the visitor center closes an hour earlier. Old Deseret is open Tuesday through Saturday from 11:00am until 5:00pm (until 8:00pm on Thursday) from early April to early October. The admission is $5 for adults and $2 for seniors and children ages 3 through 11. Admission to the park itself is free. Bus #3 and 4.*

Across the street from the park on the south side of Sunnyside is the **Hogle Zoological Gardens**, *2600 E. Sunnyside Avenue*. A first-rate zoo, Hogle features hundreds of animals from all over the world in natural settings. The collection of reptiles is unusual. Butterfly World is an enclosed area where you get close up to many colorful species. A children's zoo is especially good for young ones although the entire facility is a great place to take the kids. *Tel. 801/582-1631. Zoo hours are daily from 9:00am through 6:00pm June through August. Closing time is at 4:30 or 5:00pm at other times. It is closed only on New Year's Day and Christmas. The* *adult admission price is $5 but seniors and children ages 4 through 14 pay only $3. Bus #3 and 4.*

Work your way back to Foothills Drive and turn south into the beginning of I-215. Take the highway to Exit 9 and proceed north via Union Park Avenue to 6400 South and then to 900 East and the **Wheeler Historic Farm**, *6351 South 900 East.* This dairy farm will give you an excellent understanding of late 19th and early 20th century farming activities. Located on the farm are animals that are used exactly as they would have been over a hundred years ago. The "farmers" who work today at Wheeler do so in a style of dress and with implements that also would have been in use in times past. During the summer months farming demonstrations are given. A special treat for children but maybe for grown-ups as well is the gathering of eggs, milking the cows and feeding of animals that takes place each day at 5:00pm. There is also a guided tour of a 1898 farmhouse. Wagon rides (sleigh rides during the winter) are offered as are dances and special events in connection with seasonal holidays. In addition to the farm and its buildings, the 75-acre tract also has a nature preserve. *Tel. 801/264-2241. The farm is open Monday through Saturday from 9:30am until 8:00pm between Memorial Day and Labor Day and until 5:30pm from April 1 to Memorial Day and the day after Labor Day through the end of October. At other times it is open from 1:00pm to 5:30pm. The adult admission fee is $3 while seniors and children ages 3 through 11 pay $2. Bus #11 and 44.*

After leaving the farm go north on 900 East for about 1-1/2 miles where it runs into Van Winkle Expressway. That, in turn, becomes 700 East. Stay on the latter for about 3-1/2 miles to the intersection of 600 South and the final stop on this tour, **Trolley Square** *(Bus #'s 21, 44 and 89).* This is a shopping center and will be discussed as such in the appropriate section, but it is also much more than that. It was built in 1908 to house Salt Lake City's municipal trolley vehicles. The style, considering it was an industrial building, is quite elaborate and the plant equipment, trolley cars, antique lighting and generous use of beautiful stained-glass have all been meticulously restored. It's also a good place to have dinner to end off a long day of touring. You can return to the downtown area or get to the freeway system via 500 South Street westbound.

THE NORTHWEST:
EXCURSIONS FROM SALT LAKE CITY

There are four suggested excursions from the capital that will lead you to the many sights of the northwest. Some can be done either as a day trip or overnighters while others are best done in two to three days. They can also be easily combined with or without overnight stays in Salt Lake

City. The eastern and southern excursions are especially simple to link together.

North: Ogden & Golden Spike Country

Our first excursion covers about 255 miles not counting some suggested side trips and extensions. Because of the distance and the number of attractions it isn't possible to do this one in a single day unless you leave some things out. We begin by traveling north on I-15. If you are traveling with children you might want to stop at the **Lagoon Amusement Park** adjacent to Exit 326 in Farmington (see the Sports & Recreation section for details). On North Main in Farmington is the **Utah State University Botanical Gardens** whose colorful rose, annual, perennial and vegetable gardens are a pleasant sight. They're open all year during daylight hours. Then it's back north on I-15 for another short ride.

At Exit 335 you'll travel east to **Antelope Island State Park** via UT 108 and 127. The largest island in the **Great Salt Lake**, it is separated from the mainland by a causeway that is over seven miles long. The park occupies the entire island and on its 28,000 acres are a visitor center, bathing beaches, camping facilities and over 20 miles of hiking trails. But the best part is that Antelope Island is home to many species of animals, birds and waterfowl. Among them is a herd of more than 600 bison. A yearly roundup of the bison takes place each November and attracts a horde of visitors. Expected to reopen sometime in 1999 is the **Fielding Garr Ranch**, a sheep ranch that dates from 1848. The park attracts many visitors who come to see the brilliant sunsets. *Tel. 801/773-2941. Daily vehicle use charge of $3.* Several private concessionaires conduct tours for visitors. These include wagon rides and dinner cruises on the *Island Serenade*. You can get information on these and other activities at the visitor center.

A JOURNEY ON SKYLINE DRIVE

*Those of you looking to see some nice scenery and combine it with a ride that is sure to give you a thrill or two can detour from the main route beginning in Bountiful at Exit 320 and then via Ward Canyon Road to the loop known as **Skyline Drive**. It ends in Farmington. Covering about 24 miles, the unpaved road offers excellent views of alpine terrain and the Great Salt Lake, including Antelope Island. The road isn't always in the best of condition and should be avoided during or after rainy weather. Four-wheel drive is absolutely necessary as the road has steep grades. Drive extra slow due to rough gravel.*

1. Dinosaur Park
2. Fort Buenaventura
3. Hill Aerospace Museum
4. Ogden Nature Center
5. Union Station

Upon completion of your visit to Antelope Island, return to I-15 north for the final six miles into Ogden. Your first stop is immediately off of Exit 341. The **Hill Aerospace Museum** is located adjacent to the entrance of the sprawling Hill Air Force Base. The huge museum houses more than a hundred different aircraft in both indoor and outdoor facilities as well as many weapons and military hardware. Some of the most popular aircraft on display are the sleek SR-71 Blackbird, a B-17 Flying Fortress, the famous P-51D Mustang fighter and a B-52 bomber. Young boys are especially thrilled with the exhibits but only a little bit more than their fathers are. A short film depicting the history of Hill Air Force Base is shown continuously. *Tel. 801/777-6818. The museum is open daily from 9:30am to 4:30pm (and till 5:30 on weekends) except for New Year's Day, Thanksgiving and Christmas. There is no admission charge.*

Return to I-15 and go north for three exits (#345) and follow 24th Street east to **Fort Buenaventura State Park**, *2450 A Avenue*. The park contains a replica of a frontier stockade built around 1840. The original fort, which burned to the ground in 1852, was the first permanent settlement in the Great Basin. *Tel. 801/621-4808. Open daily from 8:00am until 8:00pm April through September and until 5:00pm in March and October through November. There is a $3 vehicle charge.*

Now it's time to head into the heart of Ogden. Continue east on 24th Street until Wall Avenue and make a right turn. Go south one block to **Union Station**, the city's premier cultural venue and which is listed on the National Register of Historic Places. In addition to theaters, restaurants and excellent gift shops, the ornate Mediterranean style building has a number of interesting museums. These are the **Browning Firearms Museum** (the largest collection of Browning Company firearms in the world); the **Browning-Kimball Car Collection** (classic vehicles from the early 1900's); the **Natural History Museum** (concentrating on local geology); and two railroad museums.

The first is the **Eccles Railroad Center** with a large display of working-order rolling stock while the second, the **Wattis-Dumke Model Railroad Museum**, contains eight model train layouts that trace the transcontinental railroad's route. *Tel. 801/629-8535. All museums are open Monday through Saturday from 10:00am until 5:00pm and Sunday from 11:00am to 3:00pm year round except that it is closed on Sunday from after Labor Day to the Sunday before Memorial Day. Also closed on New Year's Day, Thanksgiving and Christmas. The combined admission is $3 for adults, $2 for seniors and $1 for children ages 1 through 11.*

You can walk or ride to the next attraction via 25th Street east for five blocks to Jefferson and then right one block to the **Eccles Community Art Center**, *2580 Jefferson Avenue*. The art exhibit features works by Utah artists but the building itself, an elaborate Victorian mansion, is also of interest. *Tel. 801/392-6935. Open weekdays from 9:00am until 5:00pm and on Saturday from 10:00am until 4:00pm. Admission is free.* Next proceed north on Jefferson to 22nd Street and back west to Grant Avenue and the **Daughters of Utah Pioneer Museum,** *2148 Grant Avenue.* The museum is dedicated to the pioneering spirit of Miles Goodyear who settled in the area in 1836. The cabin dates from 1845 and is reputedly the oldest existing homestead in the state. Photographs and exhibits trace the life and times of the noted fur trapper. *Tel. 801/393-4460. The museum is open daily except Sunday from 9:00am until 5:00pm from the middle of May through the end of September. There is no admission charge.*

Now drive east on any numbered street to Harrison Boulevard and turn left. Stay on Harrison until Ogden River Parkway and turn right. Your next stop is **Eccles Dinosaur Park,** *1544 East Park Boulevard,* picturesquely situated alongside the river in full view of the mountains. You'll go back millions of years in time as you stroll the grounds that are filled with more than a hundred life size and authentic looking dinosaurs. In fact, they're so real looking that small children could be a little frightened at first. The creatures are all shapes and sizes and span the Cretaceous, Jurassic and Triassic geologic eras. I'm sure your kids will want one of the many dinosaur items available for purchase at the large gift shop. *Tel. 801/393-DINO. Park hours are Monday through Saturday from 10:00am to 8:00pm and Sunday from noon to 6:00pm, Memorial Day through Labor Day and 10:00am to 6:00pm (from noon on Sunday) in the spring and fall. Closed from November through February. The admission is $3.50 for adults, $2.50 for seniors and $1.50 for children ages 3 through 17.* If you want to take in a bit of scenery you can proceed further east on the Ogden River Parkway until reaching Ogden Canyon Road. The latter goes to the Pineview Reservoir and the Ogden Valley ski areas. The views are lovely at any time of the year.

The last stop in Ogden is reached by taking Canyon Road (which becomes 12th Street) west to the **Ogden Nature Center** located at *966 W. 12th Street.* The facility has several pretty nature trails and is a wildlife sanctuary. Special programs and tours are usually offered. *Tel. 801/621-7595. The center is open daily except Sunday from 10:00am until 4:00pm and a small donation is requested.*

Continuing west on 12th Street, you'll soon return to I-15. Not that you should need a break from travel because the ride is short, but you might want to briefly stop in Brigham City (off of Exit 364) to take a quick look at the **Brigham City Tabernacle.** Otherwise, take US 91 north from Brigham City through the forested mountains on the way to Logan. But before you reach Logan, you should definitely consider an interesting little detour via UT 101 east for 15 miles through scenic **Blacksmith Fork**

Canyon to the unique **Hardware Ranch**. This is an elk feeding station and you can observe the animals in their natural habitat via sleigh rides during the fall and winter. During the summer months, unfortunately, not as much is going on at the Ranch although it still makes an interesting visit. Return through the canyon to the junction of US 89/91 and go north for the final ten miles into Logan.

The town has another Daughters of Utah Pioneer Museum and an Eccles Art Gallery, but of most interest is the **Ronald B. Jensen Living Historical Farm**, on US 89/91 south of town. Covering a picturesque 126 acres, this living history museum is a recreation of a 1917 Mormon farm. The more than dozen buildings are authentic, having been moved to this location from surrounding areas. There are guides in period costumes and graduate students from Logan's Utah State University give frequent demonstrations of farming. *Tel. 435/245-4064. The farm is open Tuesday through Saturday from 10:00am until 4:00pm and on Saturday until 5:00pm, June through August. The admission is $5 for adults, $4 for seniors and students with identification and $3 for children ages 2 through 12. There is also a $15 family rate.*

Not included in the mileage for this excursion is an 80-mile round-trip from Logan through the northern reaches of the Wasatch-Cache National Forest to Garden City and beautiful **Bear Lake**. Along the route you'll pass towering cliffs and thick forests all the while traveling alongside the rushing Logan River. The route (part of US 89) has been designated as the **Logan Canyon Scenic Byway** and passes 9,029-foot high Temple Peak. The lake itself extends into neighboring Idaho and is one of the largest in the state and has all sorts of water sports and recreational facilities which are available in a number of state parks that surround the lake. The most significant of these is **Bear Lake State Park**, located two miles north of Garden City. The park has wonderful lake views and is popular with scuba divers who like to explore the exquisite turquoise waters around Cisco Beach.

From Logan travel west on UT 30 to I-15 and go south to Trementon. From there take UT 102 for eight miles to UT 83 and then north five miles to the signed cutoff for **Golden Spike National Historic Site**. Situated on Promontory Summit overlooking the Great Salt Lake, the site commemorates the historic events of May 10, 1869 when the Central Pacific and Union Pacific Railways were linked together to form the nation's first transcontinental railroad. A golden spike was driven to mark the link-up point. A reenactment of that event is held each year on the anniversary date. Various railroad festivals are held at different times throughout the summer. Working replicas of the two locomotives that took part in the original event can be visited from May to October. From spring through early fall visitors can drive their cars over the original railroad grades. (The railroad is no longer in this spot because it was relocated further south to avoid some difficult mountain climbs.) There is also a visitor center that documents the meeting of the railways and its effect on Utah and the nation. *Tel. 435/471-2209. The site is open daily from 8:00am to 6:00pm, Memorial Day through Labor Day and until 4:30pm the remainder of the year. Admission is $7 per vehicle (summer) or $4 per vehicle (other times) to those not holding a valid park service passport.*

About two miles from the historic site is the plant of the Thiokol Corporation, a major manufacturer of rocket engines. The **Thiokol Rocket Display** is outside the entrance. You can inquire as to if there are going to be any rocket tests in the area. If so, they are visible from the highway.

Make your way back to I-15 and head south for the return to Salt Lake City. A final stop that may interest you is the so-called **Fruitway** on US 89 between Brigham City and Willard. The 18-mile stretch that closely parallels the Interstate is the heart of a major fruit growing area. You can purchase orchard fresh fruits from dozens of roadside stands that set up shop right along the road from July through September. The area is especially well known for its delicious peaches but apricots, cherries and many other fruits are also available.

THE EAST: THE WASATCH & UTAH SKI COUNTRY

Covering about 150 miles through the magnificent Wasatch Mountains that form Salt Lake City's background, this trip is ideally suited to be done in a single day. We leave the city by taking I-15 south to I-215 (Exit 302) and then driving south on the latter for about four miles to Exit 6. You'll already be on the edge of the mountainous **Wasatch-Cache National Forest** but before we get into the main part of the excursion we'll follow UT 210 east into **Little Cottonwood Canyon**. The 15-mile dead-end road leads to the ski resorts of **Snowbird** and **Alta**. Alta had its origins in 1865 as a silver mining town but the boom only lasted until 1873. During that time there were more than 100 murders and the community ranked as one of the west's wildest, something out of character for most of Utah's pioneer communities. It became a virtual ghost town in a few years until the opening of the first ski resort in 1940.

Today the town has about 600 residents and in the summer months it is a popular area for outdoor recreation. After your visit retrace the route on UT 210 to the intersection of UT 190. Head to the east once again, this time into **Cottonwood Canyon** via a road that goes by the same name before reaching **Brighton**, another small town, ski area and year-round playground. At an altitude of 8,700 feet, Brighton affords great views of the mountains and valley. The **Mount Millicent Chairlift** provides summer sightseers with the best opportunity to take in the panorama. The summer operating season depends upon how early and late the snowfall occurs but you can always count on May through October. *Call the Brighton ski area, call Tel. 801/532-4731 for information on hours and fares.*

Both Little and Big Cottonwood Canyons, like all the canyons leading eastward into the Wasatch from the Salt Lake City area have lovely scenery including rushing creeks alongside the canyon roads. From Brighton the road climbs further and twists through the mountains to Park City. About five miles of the road through Guardsman Pass (closed during the winter) is unpaved but doesn't require any special vehicle or driving skills to negotiate, at least if the weather has been good. For those who don't want to get to Park City via that kind of road then it may be best to see the aforementioned canyons either on a separate short excursion from Salt Lake City or as part of the southern excursion that follows. If you skip this portion then go to Park City via I-80 and UT 224.

Park City also had its beginnings in the silver mining days but snow has been a more enduring draw in the long run. It is probably Utah's most famous winter resort area but there's plenty to see and do during any month of the year. In addition to exploring some of the beautiful resorts that surround the town (**Park City Mountain Resort**, **Deer Valley** and **The Canyons**, all described in the *Where to Stay* section), Park City itself is a quaint and attractive community in a beautiful mountain setting. It has become something of an art town as well. The latter aspect is in evidence at the **Kimball Art Center**, *638 Park Avenue (UT 224)*, which features two galleries that display the works of the many artists who now reside in Park City. The *Nightlife & Entertainment* section below outlines some of the many goings on in Park City which range from popular to classical.

For those whose interests lie more in history then the **Park City Museum & Territorial Jail**, *528 Main Street*, is the place to see. The museum chronicles the development of the area from the silver mining era through the growth of skiing by means of exhibits and artifacts. The jail, more appropriately called a dungeon, has been preserved to appear just as it did when it housed some of Utah's more notorious residents. It was also used to detain labor leaders during the late 19th and early 20th centuries. *Tel. 435/649-6104. Museum hours are Monday through Saturday from 10:00am until 7:00pm and on Sunday from noon to 6:00pm year round except for May and October when its open daily from noon to 5:00pm. There is no admission charge.*

Just outside town on UT 224 is the interesting **Park City Silver Mine Adventure**. After donning protective helmets and clothing, visitors descend 1,500 feet inside the mountain and travel by mine train for more than a half mile. It's the real thing and one of the better mine tours to be found anywhere. It's also "spooky" enough for kids to have a real good time. Surface exhibits, including interactive computers, tell the story. An 1880s homesite is also on the grounds as are a pretty cafe for lunch and an excellent gift shop. *Tel. 800/467-3828. Open daily from noon through 6:00pm. Some extension of hours during holiday periods. Admission is $14 for adults and $11 for seniors and children ages 4 through 12 (children under 4 are not allowed in the mine). A ticket allowing access only to surface exhibits costs $8 for adults and $6.50 for seniors and children. Credit cards.*

At the north end of Park City take UT 248 east for a few miles to the junction of US 40. From there it's 15 miles south (although the route will be marked east) to **Heber City**. Here you can board the **Heber Valley Railroad** for a journey back in time, especially if your train is pulled by the 1907 Baldwin Locomotive #618. The line also operates three diesel-electric locomotives. The Heber Valley Railroad operates all year long but schedules and destinations vary. Trips last from one to four hours depending upon routing. The longer trip goes as far as Provo Canyon. The train travels through excellent mountain and canyon scenery. *Tel. 435/654-5601. Call for exact schedules since, although it operates daily, some days may be pre-booked for groups. Reservations are strongly suggested. Adult fares range from $9 to $17 depending upon trip length. Senior fares are $8-15 and children pay $5-10. Credit cards.*

A few miles east of Heber City via UT 113 is beautiful **Wasatch Mountain State Park**. The largest facility in the Utah State Park system at 22,000 acres, Wasatch Mountain covers an area of heavily forested mountain slopes. There are all sorts of recreational pursuits year-round, including a golf course. The vistas from the many trails and roads are excellent. The most heavily visited site in the state park system, Wasatch is especially known by the locals for the breathtaking display of color in the fall. *Tel. 435/654-5400. $4 per vehicle daily use fee.*

Return to Heber City and then follow US 40 west to I-80. The Interstate traverses scenic **Parley's Canyon**. At the end of the canyon Salt Lake City will suddenly appear before your eyes, an impressive sight.

If you want to make a more extended trip that covers the first two excursions the best place to link them up is by taking I-80 east from the junction of US 40 instead of west back towards Salt Lake City. At Exit 120 take I-84 east. This road leads to Ogden where you can pick up the first excursion. Along the way at the town of Devil's Slide (Exit 111 of I-84) you should take a short detour to see **Weber Canyon** and the 40-foot high rock walled gorge known as the **Devil's Slide**. The chute-like chasm is several hundred feet long.

THE SOUTH: BINGHAM CANYON & PROVO

This 155-mile excursion can be done in a single day if you wish but making it an overnight trip will allow you to explore more in depth and at a leisurely pace. If you decide to include the two Cottonwood Canyons on this excursion instead of the previous one to avoid the rough road or other reasons, then an overnight trip is definitely a better idea.

Leave Salt Lake City by traveling south on I-15. Get off at Exit 301 and follow UT 48 (Bingham Highway) west for 14 miles to the **Kennecott Copper's Bingham Canyon Mine**. Almost an eighth of America's copper needs are met at this one facility which helps you clearly understand that it is one of the largest open pit mines in the entire world. Covering almost 2,000 acres, the multi-level terraces that have been carved out stretch for approximately 2-1/2 miles across and measure a half-mile deep. Your stay here begins with the visitor center where exhibits tell the story of copper mining, production and use. But the highlight is certainly the observation area from which you can see the entire huge excavation. Mammoth dump trucks look smaller than little toys as they drive along the terraces that provide access to the bottom of the pit. While you might think that an open pit mine would be ugly, quite the contrary is true: the colorful layers of rock have a sort of beauty to them. While you may not want a big hole like this in your neighborhood, Kennecott has by most accounts, been a good community neighbor to Bingham Canyon. *Tel. 801/252-3000. The visitor center and observation area are open daily from 8:00am until 8:00pm, April through October. The charge for admission is $3 per vehicle.*

Return the opposite way to I-15 and proceed south once again for about 15 miles to Exit 287. Follow UT 92, which is known as the **Alpine Scenic Loop**, one of Utah's many scenic byways. The road is closed during the winter. About seven miles after beginning this route the road enters the green clad mountain slopes of the **Uinta National Forest**. Following the American Fork Creek for another two miles you arrive at the **Timpanogos Cave National Monument**. The cave is located inside of 11,750-foot high Mt. Timpanogos. Before you get all excited about visiting the cave, be aware that the cave entrance is reached only by a fairly difficult 1-1/2 mile foot trail. Although it is paved, no strollers or wheelchairs are allowed. It is steep in some places. The walk to the cave, the tour of the cave, and the return trip requires about three hours. A visitor center at the base has presentations on the cave and tickets for tours are sold here.

The cave is 1,800 feet long and has a temperature of 45 degrees. It's kind of a sticky feeling though, as the humidity is always a muggy 100 percent! In fact, so much dripping is taking place that beautiful dripstone formations are still growing, but not exactly right before your eyes. There are three separate caves that have been connected by man-made tunnels. Beautiful crystals and helicites are seen in abundance as well as the more usual cavern stalactites and stalagmites. *Tel. 801/756-5238. Open daily 7:00am to 5:30pm from mid-May through mid-October. Cave tours are $6 for adults and $5 for children ages 6 through 15. Discounts are given for Golden Age Passport holders. Cave tours, which leave frequently, are limited to 20 people and tend to fill up quickly. In order to avoid long lines, especially on weekends, you can purchase tickets up to 30 days in advance.*

Continue with UT 92 after your Timpanogos visit. The next ten miles steadily twist and climb before an almost continuous drop through one of the highest regions of the almost million acre Uinta National Forest. It makes for a splendidly scenic ride and one that shouldn't present any great difficulty for most drivers. On the eastern slope of Mt. Timpanogos in Sundance Canyon is the famous **Sundance** resort. Founded by actor Robert Redford in 1969, the resort is more than a year-round playground as it promotes the performing arts and the environment. In the rustic western architecture are venues for film, theater, art and children's programs. Details on the resort can be found in the *Where to Stay* section above but it's worth exploring even if you don't intend to stay there or patronize one of the fine restaurants. Shortly after Sundance UT 92 ends at US 189. Turn to the right and follow that road south for the few miles to Provo. This short stretch traverses pretty **Provo Canyon** along the **Provo Canyon Scenic Byway**. Within the canyon just a few miles north of Provo is lovely **Bridal Veil Falls** that cascades more than 600 feet down a rocky mountainside in a double cataract. As you enter Provo from the northeast you'll see the **Mormon Temple** which commands an excellent view of the city.

The major point of interest in Provo is **Brigham Young University**, the largest institution of higher education in the state and one of the biggest church-sponsored universities in the world. The campus sits near the base of the Wasatch Mountains and covers well over 600 acres. Points of interest (besides the several fine museums that we'll get to in a moment) are the 60,000-seat football stadium (always filled for Cougar home games) and the huge whitewashed "Y" on the mountainside which is painted annually by the poor freshmen, and the 112-foot high **Centennial Carillon Tower**. The Tower contains more than 50 bells and ring periodically throughout the day. Campus tours are available at the Hosting Center but are primarily of interest to prospective students. It's a good idea to get a campus map in order to find your way easily to the four major museums that are of more general interest.

The **Monte Bean Life Sciences Museum** is a natural history museum without the rocks–it focuses solely on birds, animals, insects and so forth through mounted specimens and interesting exhibits. Children will most likely be especially pleased by the live reptile shows that are offered weeknights at 6:30 and 7:30pm or on Saturday at 1:30pm. *Tel. 801/378-5051. Museum open weekdays from 10:00am until 9:00pm and on Saturdays from 10:00am to 5:00pm. There is no admission charge.* The **Earth Science Museum** provides the other half of the natural history picture. It is noted for the excellent collection of dinosaur fossils that date from the Jurassic period. *Tel. 801/378-3680. Museum hours are weekdays from 9:00am to 5:00pm and Saturdays from noon to 4:00pm. Admission is free.* The **Museum of Art** has a varied and extensive collection of European and American paintings, pottery, sculpture and musical instruments. Some of the works on display were done by university faculty or students. *Tel. 801/378-2787. Museum hours are weekdays from 10:00am until 6:00pm (until 9:00pm on Monday and Thursday evenings) and on Saturdays during the fall and winter from noon until 5:00pm. There is no admission charge.*

The fourth museum (and probably the best of the group) is located slightly off-campus. The **Museum of Peoples and Cultures**, *700 N. 100 East Street*, has items from many ancient civilizations throughout the world but emphasizes both ancient and more modern Native American groups. The Mayan collection is one of the best in the nation. Among the North American peoples represented are the Basketmakers, Anasazi, Pueblo, Shoshone and Utes. The displays are excellent and this is a wonderfully educational experience for school age children. *Tel. 801/378-6112. The museum is open weekdays from 9:00am until 5:00pm. Closed on state holidays and the last half of December. Like all the BYU museums, admission is free.*

Of brief interest in the center of downtown is the **Utah County Courthouse**, *Center Street and University Avenue*, about a mile south of the BYU campus. The ornate building was constructed of local limestone during the 1920's and the rotunda has several huge paintings. The **McCurdy Historical Doll Museum**, *246 N. 100 East* (one block east of University Avenue) will be appreciated by children of all ages, even those in their 70's! The dolls are arranged according to themes, some of which are First Ladies, Native American dolls and, since this is Utah, biblical women. One of the best is the huge collection representing folk dresses from all over the world. All in all the museum has more than 3,000 dolls. *Tel. 801/378-6112. The museum is open Tuesday through Saturday from 1:00pm until 5:00pm. The adult admission price is $2 and children ages 3 through 11 are charged $1.*

At the west end of Center Street, four miles from the heart of downtown, is **Utah Lake State Park**. The park offers many types of recreation, both land and water based. It also offers excellent vistas of Utah Lake, the largest fresh-water lake in the state and the second biggest overall at almost a hundred thousand acres. The point where the Provo River enters the lake is a popular spot with bird watching enthusiasts. Many varieties of shorebirds as well as raptors can usually be seen in the area.

If you want to take a scenic drive that adds about 90 miles to the previously mentioned length of this trip, then go for the **Mount Nebo Scenic Byway**. Proceed south on I-15 from Prove to Payson and then follow the 38-mile long byway to Nephi. From there you return to Provo via the Interstate northbound. The paved byway (closed in winter due to snow) offers fabulous views of the Wasatch Mountains and the vast Utah Valley including Utah Lake. At its maximum elevation the road reaches an altitude of more than 9,000 feet.

The east and south excursions come within 15 miles of one another so they make the most logical ones to combine into a single longer trip if you are so inclined. That short stretch between them is traversed by US 189 between Heber City on the east journey and the junction of UT 92 near Provo on the south trip. If you're returning to Salt Lake City from Provo it's less than an hour ride along I-15.

THE WEST: THE LAKE'S SOUTH SHORE & THE SALT FLATS

Our final excursion is the longest at approximately 265 miles. It has the fewest number of attractions so that it can be done in one long day. But, again, making it overnight would be a better way to do it. Take I-80 in a westerly direction. Our first stop will be to visit the south shore of the **Great Salt Lake**. The best place to see the lake is from the **Great Salt Lake State Park** also known as **Saltair**. Use Exit 104 for access, which is located about 17 miles west of Salt Lake City. There is a beach where you can go swimming or floating (see the sidebar). The area also has an amusement park and various musical and other events are frequently held.

Now head west once again on I-80 for another short distance to Exit 99. About three miles further along UT 138 near Stansbury Park is the **Historic Benson Grist Mill**. The site contains the 1854 mill that was built by LDS church apostle Exra Benson to meet the needs of the early Mormon settlements in this area. Several log cabins and a blacksmith shop are also open for inspection. The museum depicts area history and has a gift shop. *Tel. 435/882-7678. Open Tuesday through Saturday from 10:00am until 4:00pm, May through October. Admission is free.* A few miles further south in the many-voweled town of Toole is a small local pioneer museum and the **Tooele County Railroad & Mining Museum**, *Vine Street and Broadway, center of town.* Located in a former railroad depot dating from 1909, the museum has a fairly good collection of railroad cars and engines

A LITTLE MORE SALT, PLEASE...

*The **Great Salt Lake** is, with the exception of the Dead Sea, the saltiest body of water on earth. It occupies about ten percent of an area that was once a fresh water inland sea known as Lake Bonneville. That lake reached depths of about a thousand feet but the Salt Lake is less than 30 feet at its deepest points. In most places it is around ten feet deep. It does make up for lack of depth by the rest of its dimensions. The lake measures more than 70 miles long and nearly 30 wide, making it the largest natural lake west of the Mississippi River.*

So just how salty is it? Depending upon the depth and other environmental factors it can range between 15 and 25 percent salt. That is more than five times as salty as the ocean and if you've ever tasted that, well.... In fact, the Great Salt Lake is so salty that the only thing that can live in it is a type of algae and brine shrimp. The salt content is so high because the lake has no natural outlet and is fed by mineral rich streams. People like to go swimming in the lake because of the water's buoyancy. Even the inexperienced usually have no problem floating in the water by the beaches of Antelope Island and the south shore.

as well as a simulated mine. *Tel. 435/882-2836. Museum open during the summer season; call for exact dates which vary from year to year. Donations.*

Return towards I-80. On the way back is a little side trip for the more adventurous traveler. The contrast of desert and surrounding mountains can be seen no better than from atop **Deseret Peak**, an 11,000-foot high summit amid the Wasatch-Cache National Forest. It's a three-hour climb to the top but those who make the trek will be rewarded with a magnificent view of the Skull Valley salt flats, the southern edge of the Great Salt Lake and the snow white desert. The trailhead can be reached by following the paved road leading off of UT 138 at the town of Grantsville. That community is about 11 miles from Tooele.

Back on the Interstate now, the highway will skirt the south shore of the Great Salt Lake for about 20 miles before crossing Skull Valley and the Cedar Mountains and finally entering the barren **Great Salt Lake Desert**. It is about 75 miles from the end of the lake to the town of Wendover on the Nevada border. Although Wendover doesn't have much to see or do, it's a welcome sight to some travelers after the virtually service-absent stretch of highway. You can eat, fill up the car or stay overnight if this isn't a day trip. On the Nevada side of the border another town of the same name has gambling in a few small casinos that aren't anything like Las

Vegas. As for the desert itself, the lack of civilization is one of the attractions. There's a solitude about it that you don't often see (as long as you ignore the sounds of the Interstate highway). The scenery isn't gorgeous but is attractive in a unique sort of way.

The big attraction out here not counting the solitude that some people do come to see is the **Bonneville Speedway** and **Salt Flats** that are located off of Exit 4, just a five minute ride east of Wendover. The area's topography shows it to be part of the remains of ancient Lake Bonneville with the addition of silt from millions of years. The surface is extremely hard and mainly flat which make it ideal for racing. Most of the land speed records have been set here in "cars" that are more like jet aircraft or rockets. Races and other events are held here at various times throughout the year (see the Major Events chapter for a sampling). At other times you can drive your own car on the Salt Flats and make believe you're a famous racer. But do be careful because you aren't really that racer, now are you?

Return to Salt Lake City via I-80 eastbound.

NIGHTLIFE & ENTERTAINMENT
SALT LAKE CITY

There is a common impression, although a wrong one, that Salt Lake City is devoid of after hours activities and culture. It's not New York or Los Angeles but the sidewalks are not brought in at sundown and there's plenty of ways to enjoy yourself out on the town. And the cultural life is rich and rewarding. Much of that is due to the Mormon tradition of placing great importance on the arts.

This section will be divided into two categories. The first is the performing arts and the second, "Out on the Town," will list some of the more popular nightspots. For both categories it is a good idea to check on current schedules at the Visitor Information Center or in newspapers or magazines.

Performing Arts

Ballet West, *50 West 200 South, in the Capitol Theater. Tel. 801/355-ARTS.* One of the premier ballet companies in America, Ballet West offers performances of the classics as well as original works developed specifically for this company.

Hale Center Theater, *2801 South Main. Tel. 801/484-9257.* A variety of offerings including drama, musicals and comedies. Some Saturday matinee performances are also given.

Promised Valley Playhouse, *132 S. State Street. Tel. 801/240-5696.* A beautifully restored theater from the early 1900's, the Playhouse presents a variety of theater events suitable for the entire family. That would be expected since the Mormon Church directs the theater company.

Utah Opera Company, *50 West 200 South, in the Capitol Theater. Tel. 801/355-ARTS.* Each annual season offers four opera classics with internationally recognized stars.

Utah Symphony, *123 W. South Temple, in Maurice Abravanel Concert Hall. Tel. 801/533-5626.* An excellent orchestra performs in what is considered to be one of the finest venues from an acoustic standpoint in the entire world.

In addition to the above you might be interested in performances of the **Repertory Dance Theater**, *Tel. 801/534-1000* or the Broadway theater productions frequently offered at the **Salt Lake Community College Grand Theater**, *Tel. 801/957-3322.*

Out on the Town

Keep in mind that popular tastes can change frequently and without apparent explanation. Therefore, while all of the establishments listed here can be considered as "in spots" at press time, one never quite knows when a nightclub can lose favor with the public. All of the places in this section that serve alcoholic beverages (other than beer) are private clubs, which mean that you have to pay the temporary membership fee of five bucks.

Cheers to You, *110 West 600 South. Tel. 801/575-6400.* Classic oldtime bar where you can even buy beer "by the yard." Wine coolers. No hard alcohol but lot's of fun nonetheless.

Dead Goat Saloon, *165 S. West Temple. Tel. 801/328-GOAT.* Live nightly music, satellite TV and pool tables. Again, beer but no other alcoholic beverages. This place has been around since the mid-'60s so they must be doing something right.

Port O'Call Social Club, *78 West 400 South. Tel. 801/521-0589. [Private Club.]* This large and popular club features live music, game room, pool tables and more than 25 television screens. They also have decent food for a place of this type. Stays open every day of the year until 2:00 in the morning.

The Zephyr Club, *301 S. West Temple. Tel. 801/353-5646. [Private Club.]* The Zephyr is one of the top entertainment spots in Salt Lake. The main attraction is the name bands that are brought in from all over the country. The surroundings are beautiful and the ambiance is casual.

One place that's almost a cross between the performing arts and going out on the town is the **Off Broadway Theater**, *272 South Main Street, Tel. 801/355-4628.* The fare ranges from full length Broadway style comedies to improvisation. Combine this with a drink at one of the above and you're in for a nice night.

ELSEWHERE IN THE NORTHWEST

The mountains in and around Park City offer a great deal more entertainment possibilities then you might expect. Besides the lounges in the ski resorts (especially during the winter months), Park City, like the ski centers of Colorado, has become a performing arts center as well. The two most important events take place during the summertime. These are the **Music in the Mountains Festival** and the **Institute at Deer Valley Dance Company Residencies**. Music in the Mountains includes concerts performed on a mountain slope at the beautiful Deer Valley Resort's amphitheater, at the City Park bandstand and other venues, *Tel. 435/649-6100*. The Dance Company program is held from June through August. Live theater productions are also offered through **Park City Performances**, *Tel. 435/649-9371*. Weekly information on the performing arts in Park City can be obtained by calling the Park City Arts Council, *Tel. 435/645-0110*.

Theater, music and dance are a part of the college scene in Provo's **Brigham Young University** and Ogden's **Weber State University**. Ogden also has a **Symphony & Ballet Association**, which sponsors a number of events, *Tel. 801/399-9214*; and the **Terrace Plaza Playhouse**, *99 W. 4700 South, Tel. 801/393-0070*.

Ogden's (and maybe Utah's) most beautiful indoor venue for entertainment is the 1924 Art Deco **Peery's Egyptian Theater**. Call the Weber State University Project Office for performance information, *Tel. 801/626-6895*.

SPORTS & RECREATION

Amusement Parks

Lagoon Amusement Park, *Lagoon Drive, Farmington. Tel. 801/451-8000*. One of the largest amusement parks in the nation. Water park and land based rides and attractions. Recreated pioneer village.

Laser Quest Salt Lake City, *7202 South 900 East, Midvale. Tel. 801/567-1540*. High-tech interactive laser tag.

Raging Waters, *1200 West 1700 South. Tel. 801/972-3300*. Water theme park. Over 30 different slides and attractions.

Seven Peaks Water Park, *1330 East 300 North, Provo. Tel. 801/373-8777*. More than 40 attractions.

Bicycling

Salt Lake City and the northwest are ideally suited to bicycle touring and its popularity will be in evidence by all the riders you'll see throughout the area. Opportunities begin in the city itself. The broad, straight streets make it easy for bikers to get around and to use it as a means of transportation from one attraction to another. Nice rides within the city limits can be taken in **City Creek Canyon**. Other favorite venues for bicyclists are the three-mile long **Ogden River Parkway** in Ogden and **Big** and **Little Cottonwood Canyons** to the southeast of Salt Lake City.

Longer routes are the 34-mile **Great Salt Lake Bicycle Route** and the hundred miles of bike trails on the **Utah Lake Loop** near Provo. Also in the Provo area are **Mount Nebo** and **Provo Canyon, Wasatch Mountain State Park** and roads in the Park City/Deer Valley area. Because of the mountainous terrain on some of the latter routes and the high altitude, these are for the more experienced rider. An easier route and one of the most popular is to ride on the trails of **Antelope Island State Park** including along the seven mile causeway that connects it to the mainland.

Bike rentals in Salt Lake City and the surrounding area are available at:
• **Canyon Bicycles**, *3969 S. Wasatch Boulevard, Tel. 801/278-1500; and 1122 E. Draper Parkway, Draper, Tel. 801/676-8844*
• **Cole Sport**, *1615 Park Avenue, Park City, Tel. 435/649-4806*
• **Guthrie Bikes & Boards**, *156 E. 200 South, Tel. 801/363-3727; and near the University of Utah at 1330 E. 200 South, Tel. 801/581-9977*
• **Jan Mountain Outfitters**, *1600 Park Avenue, Park City, Tel. 435/649-4949.*
• **Wild Rose Sports**, *702 3rd Avenue, Tel. 800/750-7377*

For guided bike touring (and rentals) you can contact **Sport Touring Ventures**, *4719 Silver Meadows, Park City. Tel. 435/649-1551.*

Boating

Boat tours on the Great Salt Lake as well as dinner cruises are offered from Antelope Island State Park by **Salt Island Adventures**, *Tel. 888/SALT ISLE.*

Lakes with marinas and boat ramps can be found at the following:
• **Bear Lake: Bear Lake State Park**, *Garden City. Tel. 435/946-3343.*
• **Great Salt Lake: Antelope Island State Park**, *Syracuse. Tel. 801/773-2941*; **Willard Bay State Park**, *Brigham City. Tel. 435/734-9494.*
• **Utah Lake: Utah Lake State Park**, *Provo. Tel. 435/375-0731*

Additional boating facilities can be found in some of the mountain lakes to the east of Salt Lake City. One of the most popular is **Strawberry Reservoir,** located about 25 miles east of Heber City via US 40.

Fishing

There isn't any fishing in the Great Salt Lake, of course, but the lakes and streams in the mountains in and around Park City and other resorts offer plenty of great fun for anglers. In addition to the boating sites above (except for the Salt Lake), fishing is available in all mountain state parks (especially **Rockport** and **Jordanelle**), throughout Bear Lake, Utah Lake, Strawberry Reservoir, and the Provo and Weber Rivers.

Golf

- **Bonneville Golf Course**, *954 Connor Road, Salt Lake City. Tel. 801/583-9513*. 18 holes.
- **Brigham Willows Golf Course**, *900 N. Main, Brigham City. Tel. 800/418-5301*. 9 holes.
- **Eagle Mountain Golf Course**, *960 E. 700 South, Brigham City. Tel. 800/269-3212*. 18 holes.
- **Eaglewood**, *1110 East Eaglewood Drive, North Salt Lake City. Tel. 801/299-0088*. 18 holes.
- **East Bay Golf Course**, *1860 S. East Bay Blvd., Provo. Tel. 801/373-6262*. 18 holes.
- **Glenmoor**, *9800 S. 4800 West, South Jordan. Tel. 801/280-1742*. 18 holes.
- **Mount Ogden Golf Course**, *3000 Taylor Avenue, Ogden. Tel. 801/629-8700*. 18 holes.
- **Nibley Park Golf Course**, *2780 S. 700 East, Salt Lake City. Tel. 801/483-5418*. 18 holes.
- **Ogden Golf & Country Club**, *4197 Washington Blvd., Ogden. Tel. 801/621-2060*. 18 holes.
- **Park City Municipal Golf Course**, *1451 Thaynes Canyon Drive, Park City. Tel. 435/649-8701*. 18 holes.
- **Park Meadows Country Club**, *2000 Meadows Drive, Park City. Tel. 435/649-2460*. 18 holes.
- **Rose Park Golf Course**, *1386 N. Redwood Road, Salt Lake City. Tel. 801/596-5030*. 18 holes.
- **Seven Peaks Resort**, *1455 E. 300 North, Provo. Tel. 801/375-5155*. 18 holes.
- **Valley View Golf Course**, *2501 East Gentile, Layton. Tel. 801/546-1630*. 18 holes.
- **University Golf Course**, *100 S. 1900 East, Salt Lake City. Tel. 801/581-6511*. 18 holes.
- **Wasatch Mountain State Park**, *Highway 113, Midway. Tel. 435/654-0532*. 27 holes.

Hiking & Backpacking

Many of the locales that were suitable for bike riding are also excellent for hiking. The best places for hiking in the northwest are in the state parks and national forests along the Wasatch Range extending from the Idaho state line all the way to the southern edge of this region below

Provo. During the warmer months when there isn't any skiing, the many ski resort areas in and around Park City are popular places for hiking. **Big Cottonwood Canyon** and **Little Cottonwood Canyon** near Salt Lake City and **Provo Canyon** are excellent places to begin hikes. Many trails leading off of these will present a challenge to even the most experienced back-country hiker.

Horseback Riding
• **Homestead Stables**, *700 N. Homestead Drive, Midway. Tel. 435/654-1102*
• **Red Pine Adventures**, *Park City. Tel. 800/417-7669*
• **Rocky Mountain Recreation of Utah**, *Park City. 435/645-7256*

Hot Air Ballooning
• **ABC Ballooning**, *Park City. Tel. 800/820-2223*
• **The Great Balloon Escape**, *Park City. Tel. 435/645-9400*
• **Howling Dog Balloon Adventure**, *Park City* and *Ogden. Tel. 800/745-4426*
• **Park City Balloon Adventures**, *Park City. Tel. 800/396-8787*

Skiing
The mountains to the east of Salt Lake City are one of the world's premier winter ski centers. All of the ski facilities listed below have equipment rentals and sales on site or nearby. The types of skiing available are shown by the following abbreviations:

DH–Downhill
SB–Snowboarding
XC–Cross-country

The numbers under "terrain" indicate the approximate percentage of runs for each level of experience; that is, Beginner (B), Intermediate (I) and Advanced (A).

ALTA SKI AREA, *Alta. Located in Little Cottonwood Canyon east of Salt Lake City via I-215 and UT 210. Main Tel. 801/742-3333; Snow Report Tel. 801/572-3939.*

Base elevation, 8,530 feet; top elevation, 10,550 feet. Full day adult lift ticket price is $28. [DH.] 40 runs. Terrain: B=25, I=40, A=35. 6 double, 2 triple and 5 surface tow lifts. Usual season is mid-November through mid-April. Ski school and full children's program.

BEAVER MOUNTAIN, *Logan. Located 27 miles east of Logan via US 89. Main Tel. 435/753-0921; Snow Report Tel. 435/753-4822.*

Base elevation, 7,200 feet; top elevation, 8,800 feet. Full day adult lift ticket price is $22. [DH, SB.] 22 runs. Terrain: B=35, I=40, A=25. 3 double chair lifts. Limited night skiing. Usual season is early December through March except for Christmas Day. Ski school. Some children's programs.

BRIGHTON SKI RESORT, *Brighton. Located in Big Cottonwood Canyon east of Salt Lake City via I-215 and UT 190. Main Tel. 800/873-5512; Snow Report Tel. 801/532-4731.*

Base elevation, 8,755 feet; top elevation 10,500 feet. Full day adult lift ticket price is $32. [DH, SB, XC.] 64 runs. Terrain: B=21, I=40, A=39. 2 high speed, two triple and 3 double lifts. Night skiing. Usual season is early November through late April. Extensive ski school program. Limited children's programs but all children under ten ski for free.

THE CANYONS, *Park City. Located just north of Park City off of UT 224. Use Exit 145 on I-80 if coming from Salt Lake City. Main Tel 800/754-1636; Snow Report Tel. 435/649-5400.*

Base elevation, 6,800 feet; top elevation, 9,380 feet. Full day adult lift ticket price is $52. [DH, SB, XC.] 74 runs. Terrain: B=16, I=38, A=46. 1 gondola, 6 quads and 2 double lifts. Limited night skiing. Usual season is mid-December through mid-April. Ski school and extensive children's programs.

WINTER ADVENTURES

For the thrill seeker who finds that "normal" skiing isn't quite enough adventure, Utah's ski country offers several options on the wilder side. The first is helicopter skiing. Fly into the back country and ski some of the most challenging of slopes in rarified air and gorgeous, uncrowded surroundings. This service can be arranged through **Diamond Peaks Heli-Ski Adventures***, Tel. 888/740-4631,* **Timberline Helicopter Skiing***, Tel. 801/658-0125 and* **Wasatch Powderbird Guides***, Tel. 801/742-2800. A little more on the mild side is snow cat skiing. The idea is basically the same– use a means of transportation that can bring you outside of the normal ski area boundaries for a truly unique skiing experience. The Deer Valley, Powder Mountain and Snowbird ski areas offer this service (as does Brian Head in the southwest region).*

Snowmobiling tours can be arranged in Park City through **Snowest Snowmobile Tours***, Tel. 800/499-7660. Guided tours of one, two or three hours are available and no previous experience is required. Finally, have you ever thought about learning how to ski jump? Not me, but I'm sure plenty of you would like to do it. Then visit the* **Utah Winter Sports Park***, Tel. 801/658-4200. Lessons are available.*

DEER VALLEY RESORT, *Park City. Located on UT 224 in Park City. Main Tel. 800/424-DEER; Snow Report Tel. 435/649-2000.*
Base elevation, 7,200 feet; top elevation, 9,400 feet. Full day adult lift ticket price is $54. [DH, XC.] 67 runs. Terrain: B=15, I=50, A=35. 2 double, 9 triple and 3 quad lifts. Usual season is early December through mid-April. Extensive school and children's programs.

PARK CITY MOUNTAIN RESORT, *Park City. Located on UT 224 in Park City. Main Tel. 800/222-PARK; Snow Report Tel. 435/647-5449.*
Base elevation, 6,900 feet; top elevation, 10,000 feet. Full day adult lift ticket price is $52. [DH, SB.] 93 runs. Terrain: B=16, I=45, A=39. 3 high speed, 2 quad, 5 triple and 4 double lifts. Night skiing. Usual season is mid-November through mid-April. Ski school. Some children's programs.

POWDER MOUNTAIN, *Eden (Ogden Canyon). Located east of Ogden via 12th Street and then following signs through Ogden Canyon. Main Tel. 801/745-3772; Snow Report Tel. 801/745-3771.*
Base elevation, 7,600 feet; top elevation, 8,900 feet. Full day adult lift ticket price is $29. [DH, SB, XC.] 72 runs. Terrain: B=10, I=60, A=30. One triple, 2 double, 2 surface and 1 platter lift. Night skiing. Usual season is mid-November through April. Extensive ski school and children's programs.

SNOWBASIN RESORT, *Huntsville. Located 17 miles east of Ogden via Ogden Canyon and UT 226. Main Tel. 435/399-1135; Snow Report Tel. 435/399-0198.*
Base elevation, 6,400 feet; top elevation, 8,800 feet. Full day adult lift ticket price is $30. [DH, SB.] 39 runs. Terrain: B=20, I=50, A=30. 4 triple and 1 double lift. Usual season is late November through April. Ski school. Some children's programs.

SNOWBIRD SKI & SUMMER RESORT, *Snowbird. Located in Little Cottonwood Canyon east of Salt Lake City via I-215 and UT 210. Main Tel. 800/385-2002; Snow Report Tel. 801/742-2222, Ext. 4285.*
Base elevation, 7,760 feet; top elevation, 11,000 feet. Full day adult lift ticket price is $39 to $47. [DH, SB.] 66 runs. Terrain: B=25, I=30, A=45. High speed tram, one quad and 7 double lifts. Night skiing. Usual season is mid-November through April. Extensive ski school and children's programs.

SOLITUDE SKI RESORT, *Solitude. Located in Big Cottonwood Canyon east of Salt Lake City via I-215 and UT 190. Main Tel. 800/748-4SKI; Snow Report Tel. 801/536-5777.*
Base elevation, 7,988 feet; top elevation, 10,035 feet. Full day adult lift ticket price is $36. [DH, SB.] 63 runs. Terrain: B=20, I=50, A=30. One high speed quad, 2 triple and 4 double lifts. Usual season is early November through late April. Ski school. Limited children's programs.

SUNDANCE RESORT, *Sundance (near Provo). From Salt Lake City take I-15 south to Exit 287 and follow UT 92. From Provo, use US 89 through Provo Canyon and then UT 92. Main Tel. 800/892-1600; Snow Report Tel. 801/225-4100.*

Base elevation, 6,100 feet; top elevation, 8,250 feet. Full day adult lift ticket price is $35. [DH.] 41 runs. Terrain: B=20, I=40, A=40. 2 double and 2 triple lifts. Night skiing only at separate Nordic facility. Usual season is mid-December through April. Ski school and children's programs.

In addition to the above areas that have Nordic style cross-country skiing, Nordic only ski facilities are available at the following locations: **Homestead Cross-Country Ski Center**, *Midway, Tel. 800/327-7220*; and **Sherwood Hills**, *Wellsville, Tel. 800/532-5066*. The Solitude and Sundance resorts both have cross-country facilities that are near but separate from the main ski resort. Many of Utah's ski resorts have major expansions planned. Most will coincide with the increase in traffic that is expected in conjunction with the 2002 Winter Olympic Games but at least some additional facilities will be on line before that time.

The **Utah Winter Sports Park**, 30 miles east of Salt Lake City via I-80 and UT 224, will be the host of several events during the 2002 Winter Olympics. The Park is already open and the winter facilities that are

GETTING TO THE SLOPES

If the purpose of your Utah visit is to ski then you don't even have to rent a car to get to all of the ski areas described above. There's an extensive network of public transportation from Salt Lake City and within the ski area itself. The Utah Transit Authority (UTA) has frequent service (up to every half-hour at peak times) to all of the resorts in Big and Little Cottonwood Canyons for under $10. That covers Alta, Brighton, Snowbird and Solitude. Call Tel. 801/BUS-INFO for information and schedules.

*Private bus, van and limo service is also available. Among the options are **All Resort Express**, Tel. 800/457-9457 ($20 to all Park City resorts); **Canyon Transportation**, Tel. 800/255-1841 (all locations, prices vary); **Five Star Transportation**, Tel. 888/965-1155 (all locations, prices vary); **Lewis Brothers Stages**, Tel. 800/826-5844 (all locations from $10-20 one way) and **Park City Transportation Services**, Tel. 800/637-3803 (all locations, prices vary).*

Within the Park City area there is free courtesy transportation from the slopes into town and back. Similar services are provided in other areas where there are multiple resorts such as in Big and Little Cottonwood Canyons and in Ogden Canyon. Inquire at your hotel.

available include Nordic jumping hills, bobsled and luge. It is currently open to the public five days a week but the schedule will vary as the Olympics get closer. Tours of the facility are also given if you're interested; *Tel. 435/649-5447*.

Spectator Sports

Professional Sports: On the "major league" level the only team in town is the beloved **Utah Jazz** of the National Basketball Association, who play in downtown Salt Lake City's **Delta Center** from November through April plus the playoffs. The team has been one of the best throughout the 1990s but a championship has eluded them. The "Jazz" name is as inappropriate as you can get but is a remnant of the team's origins in New Orleans. At least they have a stylized mountain on their uniforms. For ticket and schedule information, call *Tel. 801/355-DUNK*.

Minor league baseball is provided by the **Salt Lake Buzz**, the Triple-A farm club of the Minnesota Twins. Their season at **Franklin Quest Field**, *77 West 1300 South* runs from April through August. *Tel. 801/485-3800*. Minor league ice hockey can be seen from October through March in suburban West Valley City via the International Hockey League's **Utah Grizzlies**, *Tel. 801/988-8000*.

College Sports: The **University of Utah** has a full program of men's and women's intercollegiate athletics. Men's football and basketball are the most popular. The basketball program has met with great success in recent years as the team has consistently reached later rounds of the NCAA championship tournament. However, like their professional brethren, the Jazz, they have yet to win the big one. Contact the university's athletic department for schedules and ticket information for all **Utes** home games, *Tel. 801/581-3542*. All events are held on campus. Provo's **Brigham Young University** has an equally large intercollegiate program. In fact, the **Cougars** of BYU are the archrivals of the University of Utah. The football team has a proud tradition of winning teams that include many bowl game appearances, high national rankings and even a national championship. The football team has sent many players to the National Football League. Steve Young is probably the most famous sports alumnus. Alas, the last few years haven't been particularly successful. The popularity of BYU sports in Provo is exemplified by this city of less than 100,000 people having a football stadium that seats 66,000 and a basketball arena that holds 23,000 (making it one of the largest basketball courts in the nation). *Tel. 801/378-3384*. Utah State University in Logan is the other school with a major sports program. Call *Tel. 801/750-1657* for information.

Other Spectator Sports: The **Suntana Raceway** in Springville (just south of Provo) has NASCAR Winston Cup racing, the only such venue in Utah. Races are usually held on Saturday evenings. *Tel. 801/298-2980.*

Swimming

See the *Boating* section above. All of those areas are great for swimming. In addition, the **Great Salt Lake** is a unique place to swim because of the natural buoyancy of the lake. The touring section had additional information on the swimming areas on the lake's south shore nearest to Salt Lake City.

Tennis

Numerous privately operated tennis clubs that allow visitors can be found in the Yellow Pages. However, a cheaper alternative is to make use of the courts that can be found in many city parks. The nearest to downtown and one of the best facilities is located in **Liberty Park**.

THE 2002 SALT LAKE CITY WINTER OLYMPIC GAMES

*Perhaps the ultimate spectator sporting event is coming to Salt Lake City: the **2002 Winter Olympic Games**. It's not too early to start thinking about the Games if you plan on attending, although ticket information for the various events will not be available until the beginning of 2000.*

Most of the venues for the games are already in existence, although a lot of construction is also taking place in and near Salt Lake City. In all there will be five indoor venues located within the city and five outdoor venues in the mountains. The Olympic Village will be adjacent to the main stadium on the University of Utah campus.

The events will include figure skating, ice hockey, speed skating, curling, biathlon, cross-country and Nordic combined events, bobsled, luge, ski jumping, slalom giant slalom, freestyle skiing, downhill skiing and even snowboarding.

For information on the games you can write to: Salt Lake Organizing Committee, Public Information Department, 257 E. 200 South, Suite 600, Salt Lake City, UT 84111. Tel. 801/322-2002. Their web site is www.slc2002.org.olympics.

SHOPPING

SALT LAKE CITY & SUBURBS

While Salt Lake City isn't a shopping mecca by any means (especially for those who are used to the southwestern and Native American items so commonly found in Arizona and New Mexico), it is large enough to have a fairly diverse selection of stores and goods. There are some good places to purchase craft items, jewelry and fine arts. Mormon handicrafts are prized among some people for their high quality. I'll suggest here a few of the better places to find unusual items.

If you're looking for craft items, try the **Quilted Bear Antique & Craft Mall**, *145 West 7200 South, Midvale*, a collection of small shops featuring just about anything you could possibly be looking for. **Mormon Handicraft**, *36 S. State Street* and **Q Street Fine Crafts**, *88 Q Street* (in the Avenue section east of downtown) are both good choices as well. High quality Native American goods can be found in abundance either at the **Nizhoni Trading Company**, *Cottonwood Mall* or in downtown's **TP Gallery**, *252 South Main*. Nizhoni is Salt Lake's largest Indian goods dealer while the TP Gallery concentrates on Zuni, Navajo and Hopi items. They have an excellent selection of *kachina* dolls. Southwestern items are in abundance at the **Southwest Shop**, *914 East 900 South*, while those interested in spiffy western apparel, boots and equestrian supplies should check out **A.A. Canister**, *3615 S. Redwood Road*. **Honest Jan's Hills House Antiques**, *126 South 200 West*, has a great selection of antique American furniture and will ship anywhere.

If you're hunting for the right Utah souvenir I suggest that you go to **Salt Lake To Go**, in the visitor information center at *90 S. West Temple*. Items range from the usual tee shirts and junk to some really nice stuff. Also in that category is the **Souvenir Shop at Temple Square**, in the ZCMI Center Mall. Perhaps the most unusual Utah gifts can be found at **Wild Earth Images**, *606 Trolley Square*. They feature nature photography with Utah and other western scenery that is about as good as you can get without seeing the real thing.

Salt Lake City doesn't have a fine arts district but there are a number of excellent art galleries for those who seek that special painting for their home. Try **Thomas Chanced** (Trolley Square), **Aperture Gallery**, *307 W. 200 South* and the **Phillips Gallery**, *444 East 200 South*. Utah artists' works are featured at **Dolores Chase Fine Art**, *260 South 200 West*. Finally, the **Simantov Oriental Rug Gallery**, *341 S. Main Street*, also has Navajo rugs in addition to Oriental rugs.

A place that has to be included in the unusual category even though it's a mall is **Trolley Square**, *600 South at 700 East*. I've already mentioned it in the sightseeing section because it is something worth seeing even if you don't come here to shop. About 80 specialty shops are housed in three interconnected historic trolley barns. There are many restaurants and entertainment programs are often featured. Finally, **Gardner Village**, *1100 W. 7800 South, West Jordan,* is a quaint village of shops that surround a large former mill dating from 1853. It is listed on the National Register of Historic Places. The pioneer architecture is authentic and most of the shops in the attractively landscaped setting feature quality gifts and home furnishings. There's also a museum and restaurant.

For the more mundane shopping experience (that is, compulsive shoppers who just can't stay away from the big regional malls) here's a quick rundown on some of the major shopping areas.

Crossroads Plaza, *50 South Main.* About 145 stores in the heart of downtown anchored by upscale *Nordstrom.* There are many restaurants to choose from that are well suited for lunch.

ZCMI Center Mall, *South Temple & Main.* Across the street from Crossroads Plaza, this 80-store mall is located in an historic building that has been thoroughly modernized. Nice food court. ZCMI is the name of one of the department stores and stands for Zion's Cooperative Mercantile Institution. It has the distinction of being the first department store in the United States, having been established by the Mormon Church way back in 1868. ZCMI also has branch locations in almost all of the area's major shopping malls.

South Towne Center, *10600 South & State Street.* The largest shopping center in Utah with over 150 stores, including four department stores, more than 20 restaurants and 10-screen motion picture theater. It's only about 15 minutes south of downtown.

Other suburban malls are the **Cottonwood Mall**, *4835 S. Highland Drive*; **Fashion Place** (in Murray); the **Valley Fair Mall** (West Valley City) and the **Factory Stores of America** outlet shops in Draper.

ELSEWHERE IN THE NORTHWEST

The most unique shopping in the area around Salt Lake City is in Park City. Many interesting shops are located along historic Main Street. Fine quality boutiques and gift shops are easy to find. You might also want to check out the 50 outlet stores at the **Factory Stores at Park City**, *6699 N. Landmark Drive.*

The city of Ogden also has an historic shopping district, which you'll find along 25th Street. There are several antique shops. The heart of the district is between Wall and Grant Avenues, just east of the Union Station museum complex. Ogden also has two malls. These are the **Ogden City Mall**, *24th & Washington*; and the **Newgate Mall**, *36th & Wall.*

PRACTICAL INFORMATION

Airport, *Salt Lake City International,* Tel. *801/575-2408*

Airport Transportation
Airport Limousine SLC, Inc., *Tel. 800/546-6871*
Big City Transportation, *Tel. 888/400-9592*
Park City Transportation Services, *Tel. 800/321-5554*
Salt Lake Shuttle, *Tel. 800/818-8944*

Bus Depot
Brigham City, *888 S. Main,* Tel. *435/734-9497*
Logan, *18 E. Center,* Tel. *435/752-8568*
Ogden, *2501 Grant Avenue,* Tel. *801/393-6868*
Orem, *721 N. State St.,* Tel. *801/225-2150*
Provo, *124 N. 300 West,* Tel. *801/373-4211*
Salt Lake City, *160 W. South Temple,* Tel. *801/355-4684*
Wendover, *Tel. 435/665-2322*

Hospital
Ogden: *Ogden Regional Medical Center, 24th Street and Washington Boulevard,* Tel. *801/627-2800*
Provo: *Utah Valley Medical Center, 1034 N. 500 West. Tel. 801/373-7850*
Salt Lake City: *LDS Hospital, 8th Avenue & C Street,* Tel. *801/321-1100; University of Utah Hospital, 50 N. Medical Drive (1800 East),* Tel. *801/581-2121*

Hotel Hot Line
Park City Mountain Reservations, *Tel. 800/453-5789*
Utah Hotel & Lodging Association, *Tel. 801/359-0104*

Municipal Transit Information, *Utah Transit Authority,* Tel. *801/262-5626*

Police (non-emergency)
Brigham City: *Tel. 435/723-3421*
Ogden: *Tel. 801/629-8221*
Park City: *Tel. 435/645-5050*
Provo: *Tel. 801/379-6210*
Salt Lake City: *Tel. 801/799-3000*

Taxi
Ogden: *Yellow Cab,* Tel. *801/394-9411*
Provo: *Yellow Cab,* Tel. *801/377-7070*

Salt Lake City: *City Cab Company, Tel. 801/363-8400; Ute Cab Company, Tel. 801/359-7788; Yellow Cab, Tel. 801/521-2100*

Tourist Office/Visitors Bureau
Brigham City: *6 N. Main Street, Tel. 435/723-3931 or 888/503-0351*
Logan: *160 N. Main Street, Tel. 435/752-2161 or 800/882-4433*
Ogden: *2501 Wall Avenue, Tel. 801/627-8288 or 800/ALL-UTAH*
Park City: *1910 Prospector Avenue, Tel. 435/649-6100 or 800/453-1360*
Provo: *2545 N. Canyon Road, Tel. 801/377-2262*
Salt Lake City: *90 S. West Temple, Tel. 801/521-2822*

Train Station
Provo, *600 South 300 West*
Salt Lake City, *90 S. West Temple Street, Tel. 801/521-2868*

12. SOUTHWEST UTAH: COLOR COUNTRY

I can't take any credit for the "**Color Country**" name that is applied to this region of Utah. It's been an official promotional title for a long time. And why not? The nation's, if not the world's, most spectacular array of colors are abundant in the rocks and mountains of southwestern Utah. So are fantastic shapes and forms that simply defy description. In fact, with only a few communities of any significant size, the southwestern part of Utah, Color Country, is synonymous with outstanding scenery. Whether the formations themselves or their colors are more spectacular is a subject that can be debated without end. Perhaps there is no answer. One thing is certain–the combination of form and color is without parallel anywhere else on earth and it makes Color Country a unique and unforgettable adventure.

These wonderful sights are concentrated on lands specifically set aside for our enjoyment of them. **Bryce Canyon** and **Zion National** parks, **Cedar Breaks** and the new **Grand Staircase-Escalante** national monuments, **Kodachrome Basin**, and **Coral Pink Sand Dunes** state parks as well as many others await your inspection. But you don't even have to enter these natural reserves to see nature's handiwork. Just about any road in the southwest will place you in a position to view great scenery at every turn. Some of the best routes have been designated as scenic byways while scenic backways clamor for the attention of the more adventurous motorist.

The scenery dominates but it isn't without some competition. Small cities such as **St. George** and **Cedar City** have a wealth of attractions, too. The latter, for instance, is host to a summer-long Shakespeare Festival that is among the best of its type in the world. They and many small towns trace their origins to Mormon pioneers in the second half of the 19th century. The communities of the southwest as well as the natural preserves provide an abundance of all kinds of recreational activities throughout the year.

① Anasazi Indian Village
State Park

② Brian Head Resort

③ Bryce Canyon
National Park

④ Capitol Reef
National Park
(See Southeast Chapter)

⑤ Cedar Breaks
National Monument

⑥ Coral Pink Sand Dunes
State Park

⑦ Escalante Petrified
Forest State Park

⑧ Kodachrome Basin
State Park

⑨ Kolob Canyons
Section of Zion Natl. Pk

⑩ Rainbow Bridge
National Monument.

⑪ Snow Canyon
State Park

⑫ Zion National Park

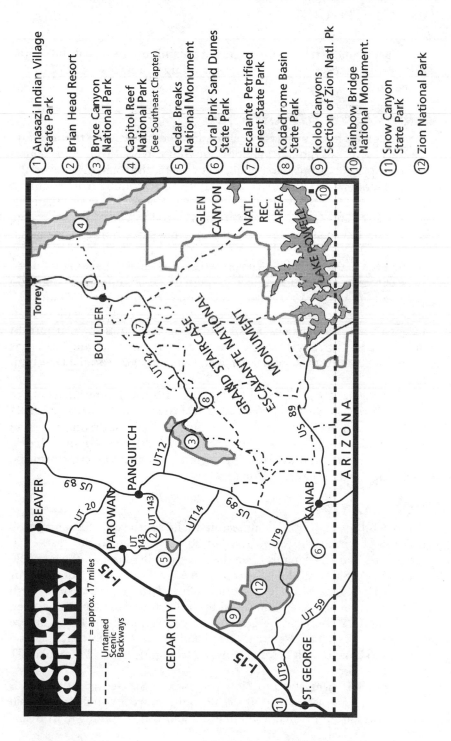

While accommodations in this region are mainly on the casual and simple side, there are several major resorts, including **Brian Head**, one of Utah's best skiing venues.

ARRIVALS & DEPARTURES

I'm going to be using **St. George**, located in Utah's extreme southwestern corner, as the starting point for your travels through this region for a couple of reasons. First of all, it is on I-15, the main highway in the state. It's where you will arrive in Utah if you're coming from southern California. St. George is much nearer to Las Vegas (125 miles) than it is to Salt Lake City (310 miles), so you can fly into Las Vegas and avoid a big drive. This especially makes sense if your Utah trip is going to be limited to the southwest and southeast regions where the majority of the great scenery is. On the other hand, if you do originate in Salt Lake City you can still easily access the southwestern loop. In that case you will join the loop at Cove Fort along I-15 about 25 miles south of the town of Fillmore.

St. George does have some scheduled air service. SkyWest flies to Salt Lake City and Los Angeles out of the St. George Municipal Airport. In nearby Cedar City, SkyWest offers service to Salt Lake City and Las Vegas from the Cedar City Regional Airport. Car rentals are available at both locations.

For those of you who will be coming into the southwest from the southeast region, the two virtually touch at the town of Torrey on UT 24 just west of Capitol Reef National Park. Finally, for those driving into Utah from Arizona (and points east of Arizona via I-40), you can immediately begin seeing the southwest touring region as soon as you cross over the Utah line north of Page, Arizona.

ORIENTATION

I-15 is the major north-south route in the southwest, although US 89 pretty well parallels most of it about 30 or so miles to the east. Utah highways 12 and 24 roughly form the eastern side of the southwest while UT 9 and US 89 travel along the southern edge. Your Color Country tour route is a loop that, with a few detours, follows I-15 from St. George north to the junction of I-70 and then east for a short time to near Salina, then UT 24 and 12 through the Grand Staircase region and Bryce before reaching US 89 near Panguitch. Then head south on US 89 to Kanab and beyond to Lake Powell before returning to slightly beyond Kanab to UT 9.

This route brings you to Zion and back to St. George. If it sounds confusing just look at a map. It's really quite simple. You'll also see that where you start or finish doesn't matter. So if you're coming in from any other Utah region or places I haven't even mentioned, the southwest loop is still the way to go.

GETTING AROUND

The southwest's biggest city (St. George) has less than 40,000 people; the second place community is home to less than half that amount. So, you won't find much in the way of public transportation. As indicated earlier, St. George and Cedar City are the only places you can expect to fly into via scheduled service. There is no train service and although Greyhound does stop in many towns in the southwest, the attractions are mostly out of town–mainly way out of town, so you still need wheels to get around.

The only alternative to your own or a rental vehicle as a means to see most of the southwest's natural attractions is an escorted tour. Three good choices are **Bryce Canyon Scenic Tours**, *Tel. 800/432-5383*; **Color Land Tours**, *Tel. 800/900-TOUR*; and **R & R Tours**, *Tel. 800/765-7710*. All do require that you make your way by public transportation to the St. George area (to Bryce for the first). They emphasize the southwest's national parks.

WHERE TO STAY
BEAVER
Inexpensive

BEST WESTERN PARADISE INN, *1451 N. 300 West. Tel. 435/438-2455; Fax 435/438-2455. Toll free reservations 800/528-1234. 53 Rooms. Rates: $50-68. Major credit cards accepted. Located just east of I-15, Exit 112.*

Beaver is a good place to stay if you're looking for inexpensive accommodations while on a ski trip to southern Utah or as a gateway to the national parks of the southwest part of the state. The Paradise Inn's location right off of the Interstate makes it even better in that regard. The motel itself is a fairly typical two-story roadside affair with clean and comfortable rooms that are a little bit bigger and better than average. The Paradise has an on-premise restaurant and a heated indoor swimming pool with spa.

BICKNELL/LOA/TORREY
Moderate

ROAD CREEK INN, *90 S. Main, Loa. Tel. 435/836-2485; Fax 435/836-2490. Toll free reservations 800/388-7688. 15 Rooms. Rates: $69-79. American Express, Discover, MasterCard and VISA accepted. Located in the center of town on UT 24.*

This quiet little place offers decent accommodations at a reasonable price. There aren't any recreational facilities so this is the type of motel that's strictly for the traveler making his or her way through the scenic wonders of Utah and looking for a clean and comfortable place to spend the night. There is, however, a restaurant that is open for breakfast and dinner which comes in handy before or after a long travel day and you're not looking for some fancy dining.

SKY RIDGE BED & BREAKFAST, *950 E. Highway 24, Torrey. Tel. 435/425-3222; Fax 435/425-3222. 5 Rooms. Rates: $82-120 including full breakfast. MasterCard and VISA accepted. Located in town on the main highway about three miles west of Capitol Reef National Park.*

A small but delightful B&B that is a surprising find out here in the relative middle of nowhere. All of the rooms are spacious and attractively decorated. Only a few of them have air conditioning but that shouldn't be too much of a problem since the evenings in Torrey generally aren't that hot. Perhaps the greatest pleasure of staying at Sky Ridge is to wake up to the fabulous breakfast that your hostess, Sally, has become locally famous for. There's everything from fresh fruit to quiche and homemade granola to made to order omelets.

Inexpensive

AQUARIUS MOTEL, *240 W. Main Street, Bicknell. Tel. 435/425-3835; Fax 435/425-3486. Toll free reservations 800/833-5379. 26 Rooms. Rates: $ 37-48. Major credit cards accepted. Located in the center of town on UT 24.*

Considering the bargain price the Aquarius is one of the best lodging establishments in the vicinity of Capitol Reef and the northeast corner of this touring region. All of the rooms are over-sized and nicely furnished. There's an indoor heated swimming pool as well as a children's wading pool and a spa. Some units have kitchen facilities. The on-premise restaurant is an attractive facility with good food and reasonable prices.

AUSTIN'S CHUCKWAGON LODGE, *12 W. Main, Torrey. Tel. 435/ 425-3335; Fax 435/425-3434. 21 Rooms. Rates: High season (April through October): $58; Low season (November through March): $45. American Express, MasterCard and VISA accepted. Located in town about a mile west of the junction of UT 12.*

It seems that the way to characterize all of the motels in this area is by saying they're small, clean and comfortable. That applies to Austin's, too, a thoroughly modern facility with nice furnishings. There isn't any restaurant but they do have a grocery store which sells, among other things, excellent baked goods. You could easily make yourself a nice in-room breakfast with that.

WONDERLAND INN, *Junction of UT 12 and 24, Torrey. Tel. 435/425-3775; Fax 435/425-3212. Toll free reservations 800/458-0216. 50 Rooms. Rates: High season (mid-March through October): $58-70; Low season (Novem-*

ber through mid-March): $40-48. Major credit cards accepted. Located about three miles west of Capitol Reef National Park.

Just when I got finished saying that everything in the area is small, along comes Wonderland Inn. Not that it's big, but 50 rooms for these parts is almost like a mega-resort. Conveniently located at the junction of the two main roads, the inn sits pleasantly atop a small knoll and offers an excellent view of the surrounding area. The grounds are attractively landscaped. Guest rooms are large and quite a bit more attractive than the typical small motel. There are some multi-room units and a few upgraded rooms with Jacuzzi. Many rooms either have a balcony or patio. Among the amenities are an indoor swimming pool with spa and sauna and a nice restaurant offering tasty food at an excellent price.

BRIAN HEAD

Very Expensive

CEDAR BREAKS LODGE, *223 Hunter Ridge Road. Tel. 435/677-3000; Fax 435/677-2211. Toll free reservations 888/AT CEDAR. 178 Rooms. Rates: High season (early November through mid-April): $150-450; Low season (mid-April to early November): $99-200. American Express, MasterCard and VISA accepted. Located just off of UT 143 about two miles north of the Cedar Breaks National Monument.*

This is an older property that has recently completed a major renovation and the results are pleasing, to say the least. It offers, among other things, ski-in/ski-out facilities but it's a good choice year round because of its proximity to so many natural wonders. The guest accommodations are all suites that are spacious and beautifully decorated. All of the shopping, restaurants and other services of the Brian Head village are within walking distance (or via the free shuttle bus during ski season). There are two restaurants on the premises, one of which is listed in the *Where to Eat* section; however, both of them are quite good. The Pinnacle Breaks Private Club, where temporary memberships are available to guests, rounds out the dining and entertainment scene. For recreation guests can opt for the new Day Spa or the heated indoor swimming pool.

Expensive

THE LODGE AT BRIAN HEAD, *314 Hunter Ridge Road. Tel. 435/677-3222; Fax 435/677-3202. Toll free reservations 800/386-5634. 40 Rooms. Rates: High season (winter): $89-159 with higher end of scale on weekends; Low season (summer): $49-69. Many package plans with additional services available. Most major credit cards accepted. Located just off of UT 143 about two miles north of the Cedar Breaks National Monument.*

What is most remarkable about the Lodge at Brian Head is that you get first-class accommodations at a price, considering the location, which is almost too low to believe. This attractive lodge is located near the Brian Head resort chair lifts and features hotel rooms or suites, all attractively furnished. There's a good restaurant and quite a few recreational amenities. The Lodge is part of the larger Brian Head Village, which has interesting shopping opportunities.

Selected as one of my Best Places to Stay (see Chapter 10 for details).

BRYCE (RUBY'S INN) & BRYCE CANYON NATIONAL PARK

Moderate

BEST WESTERN RUBY'S INN, *State Highway 63, Ruby's Inn (Bryce). Tel. 435/834-5341; Fax 435/834-5265. Toll free reservations 800/528-1234. 369 Rooms. Rates: High season (May 1st to October 15th): $70-125; Low season (October 16th to April 30th): $44-100. Major credit cards accepted. Located about a mile north of the entrance to Bryce Canyon National Park on UT 63, just south of the junction of UT 12.*

This is the largest lodging establishment in the vicinity of Bryce Canyon and one of the best so long as the modern style is okay–some people staying by national parks prefer to have a more rustic experience. If so, then consider the Bryce Canyon Lodge below. Ruby's Inn, however, has a long history. The family that operates it has been associated with tourism at Bryce since 1916 when they built a ranch and became frequent hosts for visitors to the marvels of nature that surrounded them. Their first motel was built three years later on land that would soon be taken over by the national park service so they moved the "tourist rest" to it's present site. Since then it has been rebuilt several times, growing larger each time.

The stone and wooden main building that fronts the highway contains most of the guest services, including the restaurant (see the *Where to Eat* section) and Ruby's General Store. This large emporium carries everything from film (and has a one-hour film developing service on the premises) to tacky souvenirs to the finest Native American arts and crafts and high quality western wear and jewelry. You'll be amazed at the selection. Just browsing around is a worthwhile way to spend a half-hour or more during the evening. The general store also carries a good selection of groceries if you like to snack or dine in your room. The inn's spacious and attractive main lobby is typically western with its wooden furniture, lots of exposed beams and a massive stone fireplace. Across the street is a western style shopping town. A beauty salon and liquor store is also on the premises. Activities that can be arranged at the Inn include helicopter rides, mountain biking, rodeo, horseback riding and snowmobiling during the winter. Chuckwagon dinners are also an option.

The rooms are located in six different lodge buildings spread out over a big area plus a few units in the main lodge. They're all quite spacious and nicely decorated. Some two-bedroom suites are available and many rooms have their own spa. A public hot tub is also available in addition to separate indoor and outdoor heated swimming pools. While Ruby's Inn isn't a luxury level establishment and doesn't quite make the "best" category, it is most certainly far more than just a motel. It's really almost a full service resort facility.

BRYCE CANYON LODGE, *Bryce Canyon National Park. Tel. 435/834-5361; Fax 435/834-5464. Reservations, Tel. 303/297-2757. 114 Rooms. Rates: $78-88. American Express, Discover, MasterCard and VISA accepted. Closed from November through March. Located inside of Bryce Canyon National Park just off of the main road.*

This is the only lodging establishment within the confines of the park and it is, appropriately, a large but thoroughly rustic looking two-story structure that is surrounded by towering trees at one of the more heavily forested areas of the plateau. Originally constructed in the 1930's, it has been restored to the elegance of that area. Even the same manufacturer that decorated the lodge with hickory furniture was used to refurnish it. Despite the natural surroundings the entire place has an atmosphere of luxury and time-softened livability. The architect, Gilbert Stanley Underwood, designed several national park lodges in the southwest and is recognized for his brilliant way of blending in man-made structures with beautiful surroundings. The building is a National Historic Landmark.

The accommodations are varied. More than half of the units are motel style rooms in the main lodge. The Lodge also has several deluxe suites and studio units. Especially nice, though, are the forty cabin units, which offer even more atmosphere that will enhance your stay in the marvelous company of nature. Regardless of the type of unit you choose you'll find rich looking furniture and comfortable surroundings. In fact, this place barely missed being included on my Best Places to Stay list but I wouldn't be surprised if you put it on yours. The Bryce Canyon Lodge Dining Room is an excellent restaurant that is described in the *Where to Eat* section. The Lodge also has an interesting gift shop with Native American items featured. Trail rides within the national park can be arranged at the activities desk in the Lodge's attractive main lobby.

Inexpensive

BRYCE CANYON PINES, *State Highway 12. Tel. 435/834-5441; Fax 435/834-5330. Toll free reservations 800/892-7923. 50 Rooms. Rates: High season (April through mid-November): $65-75; Low season (mid-November through March): $35. Most major credit cards accepted. Located on UT 12 about six miles west of Bryce Canyon National Park.*

Only a few minutes from the national park entrance, Bryce Canyon Pines is one of several inexpensive lodging options in the area but the only one with standards high enough to make it fit for a listing in this book. The guest rooms are fairly spacious and nicely decorated. There are a couple of kitchen units that have fireplaces ($95 in the high season). The on-premise restaurant is adequate but is closed during the winter season. The motel features an indoor heated swimming pool. Trail rides can be arranged by the motel staff.

CEDAR CITY
Moderate
ABBEY INN, *940 W. 200 North. Tel. 435/586-9966; Fax 435/586-6522. Toll free reservations 800/325-5411. 81 Rooms. Rates: High season (April through mid-September): $59-81; Low season (mid-September through March): $ 59-69. All rates including Continental breakfast. Major credit cards accepted. Located immediately to the east of I-15, Exit 59.*

A convenient right-off-the-highway location and nicely decorated rooms with either king or queen size beds make this a good choice in Cedar City. Every room features a microwave oven and refrigerator. A few units have individual spa facilities at a higher rate. In addition to the Continental breakfast, a full service restaurant is located within walking distance. The Abbey Inn also has a heated indoor swimming pool and whirlpool.

BEST WESTERN EL REY INN, *80 S. Main Street. Tel. 435/586-6518; Fax 435/586-7257. Toll free reservations 800/528-1234. 73 Rooms. Rates: High season (mid-May through September): $74-99; Low season (October through mid-May): $56-88. All rates including Continental breakfast. Major credit cards accepted. Located in the center of town (use Exit 57 of I-15 if coming from the south and Exit 59 from the north) via Business I-15.*

Everything here is quite similar to the preceding entry and it's almost a toss-up as to which one is better. Microwave and refrigerator equipped rooms are standard and a small number of whirlpool units are also available. The main difference here is that a few of the rooms are on the small size while some are oversized. All are nicely furnished, clean and comfortable. For recreation there's an outdoor swimming pool during the summer, game room and a small exercise facility. Several restaurants are located within a short distance. A complimentary morning newspaper is furnished to each guest.

ESCALANTE

Inexpensive

PROSPECTOR INN, *380 W. Main. Tel. 435/826-4653; Fax 435/826-4285. 51 Rooms. Rates. $50. American Express, Discover and VISA accepted. Located at the west end of town along the main highway.*

There are relatively few lodging establishments along most of scenic Highway 12 that are worthy of mention. Escalante has about a half-dozen undistinguished places. Not that there's anything special about the Prospector, but it's definitely the best of the lot. All of the rooms have been recently refurbished and they're clean and comfortable as well as mildly attractive. A small restaurant and gift shop are on the premises.

KANAB

Moderate

BEST WESTERN RED HILLS, *125 W. Center Street. Tel. 435/644-2675; Fax 435/644-5919. Toll free reservations 800/830-2675 (direct to hotel) or 800/528-1234 (Best Western central reservations). 75 Rooms. Rates: High season (June through October): $82-92; Low season (November through April): $47-57, with slightly higher rates during the second half of April. All rates include Continental breakfast. Major credit cards accepted. Located in the center of downtown via US 89.*

For the best rooms in town the Red Hills is clearly the leader. All of the units are large and attractively decorated in a modern style with some southwestern influence. A number of rooms have a microwave oven and refrigerator. The cleanliness and housekeeping are excellent. There's a pretty outdoor swimming pool and hot tub in the courtyard. Several restaurants are located within a short distance.

SHILO INN, *296 West 100 North. Tel. 435/644-2562; Fax 435/644-5333. Toll free reservations 800/222-2244. 119 Rooms. Rates: High season (May through October): $70-94; Low season (November through April): $45-75. All rates including Continental breakfast. Major credit cards accepted. Located on US Highway 89.*

Shilo is a small western chain that offers decent accommodations at an affordable rate. This modern three-story motor inn is typical of the entire chain and is one of the nicer looking places to stay while in Kanab. The rooms are large and comfortably furnished but like many of the inexpensive cookie-cutter chain properties can be rather sterile looking. A few rooms have kitchen facilities. There isn't any restaurant on the premises but several are located within a short ride.

Inexpensive

PARRY LODGE, *89 E. Center Street. Tel. 435/644-2601; Fax 435/644-2605. Toll free reservations 800/8748-4104. 89 Rooms. Rates: High season*

(May through October): $57-65; Low season (November through April): $46. American Express, Discover, MasterCard and VISA accepted. Located in the center of town on US 89.

Not that the rates for any motel in Kanab are high but at these prices I couldn't ignore the Parry Lodge because the quality level is darn close to the preceding listings. There aren't any recreational facilities or other amenities but if you're looking for a clean and comfortable place to stay at a budget price then there's absolutely nothing wrong with the Parry Lodge. The on-premise restaurant is good and also very affordable. If you stay at the Red Hills or the Shilo you might well wind up here for dinner.

MARYSVALE
Moderate
BIG ROCK CANDY MOUNTAIN RESORT, *Sevier Canyon. Tel. 435/ 326-2000; Fax 435/326-4378. Toll free reservations 888/560-ROCK. 16 Rooms. Rates: $59-89. MasterCard and VISA accepted. Located on US 89 about six miles north of the town of Marysvale.*

Located in the shadow of the mountain of the same name, this resort consists of about an equal number of motel style units or private riverfront cabins with full kitchen facilities. The accommodations are pleasant but nothing to write home about. However, the setting is lovely and there are lots of activities at Big Rock Candy Mountain that are conducive to a fun-filled family vacation. Among the activities are hiking, horseback riding, river rafting, fly fishing and ATV trails. There's also a nice "swimmin' hole" that kids will especially enjoy. The resort also features a decent restaurant (which is a good thing because it's the only one in town) with patio dining during the summer and a small general store.

PANGUITCH
Inexpensive
ADOBE SANDS MOTEL, *390 N. Main. Tel. 435/676-8874; Fax 435/ 676-8874. Toll free reservations 800/497-9261. 33 Rooms. Rates: $42-59 with the upper range during the summer months. Discover, MasterCard and VISA accepted. Located on US 89 on the north side of town; about 20 miles from Bryce Canyon National Park.*

You won't find anything fancy in Panguitch but decent low-cost lodging is easy to come by. The Adobe Sands is a typical family style one-story roadside motel that's well kept and comfortable. There are a couple of larger family units and about a dozen "economy" units that are on the small side. The rest are standard motel fare. There's a small heated swimming pool and a barbecue area. Restaurants are located within a short distance.

PANGUITCH INN, *50 N. Main Street. Tel. 435/676-8871; Fax 435/676-8340. Toll free reservations 800/331-7407. 24 Rooms. Rates: High season (July through mid-October): $45-59; Low season (mid-October through June): $35-49. Major credit cards accepted. Located on US Highway 89 in the center of town about 19 miles from Bryce Canyon National Park.*

The Panguitch Inn is a restored commercial building dating from the 1920's. It features nicely decorated rooms, all with coffee maker. Several large family units are available. All have queen or king beds. The Panguitch Inn has indoor parking. Restaurants are located within walking distance.

RICHFIELD/SALINA
Inexpensive
IMA HENRY'S HIDEWAY, *60 N. State Street, Salina. Tel. 435/529-7467; Fax 435/529-3671. Toll free reservations 800/341-8000. 32 Rooms. Rates: $38-46 with the higher rates during the summer. American Express, Discover, MasterCard and VISA accepted. Located in the center of town on US 89 about three miles north of I-70, Exit 54.*

No, Ima isn't Mr. or Mrs. Henry's first name. It's actually an abbreviation–IMA Lodging owns about a half dozen small properties in Colorado and Utah. They say that it stands for "inviting, memorable and affordable." The last is definitely true while the other two are more a matter of opinion although the Hideway is an attractive and pleasant facility. The rooms are cozy and comfortable. Some have microwave oven and refrigerator but all have a coffee maker. There's a swimming pool and hot tub on the premises as well as a reasonably priced restaurant featuring family dining.

ROMANICO INN, *1170 S. Main Street, Richfield. Tel. 435/896-8471. Toll free reservations 800/948-0001. 29 Rooms. Rates: $36-46 with the higher rates during summer. Most major credit cards accepted. Located in the center of town just off of I-70, Exit 37.*

A nice little motel with a good location that's close to restaurants and shopping as well as convenient to the highway. The Spanish style exterior is pretty. A few rooms have a microwave and refrigerator. The units are all attractive and well kept but some are on the cramped side. Try to get one of the bigger ones. There isn't any swimming pool but a hot tub is available.

ST. GEORGE
Moderate
GREENE GATE VILLAGE HISTORIC BED & BREAKFAST INN, *76 W. Tabernacle Street. Tel. 435/628-6999; Fax 435/628-6989. Toll free reservations 800/350-6999. 19 Rooms. Rates: $65-125 including full breakfast.*

Most major credit cards accepted. Located about two miles west of I-15, Exit 8 via St. George Blvd., then left on Main and right on Tabernacle.

An historic property that dates from the late 1870s, the Greene Gate comprises nine meticulously restored houses and is on the National Register of Historic Places. There are an unusual number of amenities and public facilities for a B&B such as a swimming pool and a general store but the best part of the Greene Gate is its delightful accommodations. Many rooms have working fireplaces and some are multi-room suites or private cottages.

Selected as one of my Best Places to Stay (see Chapter 10 for details).

HILTON INN, *1450 S. Hilton Drive. Tel. 435/628-0463; Fax 435/628-1501. Toll free reservations 800/662-2525. 100 Rooms. Rates: $70-100. Major credit cards accepted. Located immediately west of Bluff Street via Exit 6 of I-15.*

Not the familiar high-rise big city style Hilton, but rather a two-story motor inn facility, the Hilton Inn of St. George is an attractive place that is surprisingly affordable for this chain. Set around a tropical courtyard that's pretty and relaxing, your best bet is to get a room that faces in rather than towards the street. All of the accommodations are spacious and nicely decorated with furnishings that are beyond the quality usually found in motor inns. Recreational facilities include lighted tennis courts, a spa and sauna. A complete health club is located near the inn and is available to Hilton guests. The on-premise Tony Roma's Restaurant is a plus for those who like ribs or steak. Some other menu choices are also available. The Hilton offers various golf package plans at an adjacent course.

Inexpensive

BEST WESTERN CORAL HILLS, *125 E. St. George Boulevard. Tel. 435/673-4844; Fax 435/673-5352. Toll free reservations 800/542-7733 (direct to hotel) or 800/528-1234 (Best Western central reservations). 98 Rooms. Rates: $54-75 including Continental breakfast. Major credit cards accepted. Located about two miles west of I-15, Exit 8.*

There are no fewer than three Best Western motels in St. George but the Coral Hills is definitely the best of the group. The rooms are surprisingly good as they are quite large, attractive and meticulously well maintained. All rooms have refrigerators. Even the Continental breakfast is better than the usual that can be expected in that genre. The Coral Hills features both indoor and outdoor swimming pools (plus a wading pool for small children), a spa and small exercise room. There are several family suites available that have an in-room spa. There is no restaurant on the premises but several decent eating places are located within a short distance.

RANCH INN, *1040 S. Main Street. Tel. 435/628-8000; Fax 435/656-3983. Toll free reservations 800/341-8000. 52 Rooms. Rates: $44-64 including Continental breakfast. Most major credit cards accepted. Located west of I-15, Exit 6, via Bluff Street to Main.*

While there isn't anything exceptional about the Ranch Inn you shouldn't have any complaints about it–especially at the budget rate they offer. The rooms are clean and comfortable and all have queen beds and a coffee maker. More than half of the units have a kitchenette so you can save even more money if you decide to cook in. A small heated swimming pool is available as is a Jacuzzi and sauna. Restaurants are in close proximity.

SEVEN WIVES INN, *217 N. 100 West. Tel. 435/628-3737; Fax 435/673-0165. Toll free reservations 800/600-3737. 13 Rooms. Rates: $65-75 including full breakfast. Major credit cards accepted. Located about two miles west of I-15, Exit 8 via St. George Blvd. and then right on 100 West.*

This is an attractive and small B&B that will appeal to those with a sense of history. Located in a pioneer era three story structure (no elevator), it was the first B&B in the southern part of the state. The rooms are comfortable and are furnished with antiques that, although aren't original, do date from the era in which the inn was constructed. The breakfast is large and delicious. For other meals there are many restaurants located within a short distance.

SINGLETREE INN, *260 E. St. George Boulevard. Tel. 435/673-6161; Fax 435/674-2406. Toll free reservations 800/528-8890. 48 Rooms. Rates: $48-58 including Continental breakfast. Most major credit cards accepted. Located about 1-1/2 miles west of I-15, Exit 8.*

A nice friendly place at an extremely attractive price. Guest rooms are basic to a little better. The higher priced rooms may have a microwave oven or refrigerator as well as a comfortable recliner. That's something you don't see often in lodging establishments but should. The Singletree has a small swimming pool as well as a Jacuzzi. The attractive grounds feature comfortable seating in a pretty shaded area. Plenty of restaurants are nearby.

SPRINGDALE
Moderate

CLIFFROSE LODGE, *281 Zion Park Boulevard. Tel. 435/772-3234; Fax 435/772-3900. Toll free reservations 800/243-8824. 36 Rooms. Rates: High season (April through October): $68-145; Low season (November through March): $45-75. American Express, Discover, MasterCard and VISA accepted. Located about a quarter mile south of Zion National Park's south entrance gate.*

The Cliffrose is one of the most attractive little motel properties you'll find and it couldn't be better located for Zion National Park visitors.

You'll have great canyon views from almost anywhere on the five acre property that sits astride the Virgin River. The beautiful lawns and grounds are generously planted with trees and colorful flower gardens. Although the rooms don't quite live up to the standards set by the landscaped grounds and setting, they are rather nice and are well maintained. The Lodge features a large swimming pool and a children's play area. There are quite a few restaurants along the main highway through Springdale.

HARVEST HOUSE BED & BREAKFAST, *29 Canyon View Drive. Tel. 435/772-3880; Fax 435/772-3327. 4 Rooms. Rates: $95-100 including full breakfast. Discover, MasterCard and VISA accepted. Located on UT Highway 9 about a half mile from the entrance to Zion National Park.*

An enticing B&B for the traveler who wants to be alone. With only four guest rooms you can be assured of privacy and personalized service when you want it. Each bedroom is attractively decorated and features a queen sized bed. In addition to the excellent breakfast that is served in the home style dining room, guests may choose from a variety of hot and cold beverages at any time of the day from the well stocked wet bar. Children under six years of age are not allowed at the Harvest House. Restaurants are located within a short drive.

NOVEL HOUSE INN, *73 Paradise Road. Tel. 435/772-3650; Fax 435/ 772-3651. Toll free reservations 800/711-8400. 10 Rooms. Rates: $85-105 including full breakfast. Major credit cards accepted. Located off of Utah Highway 9 about one mile from the south entrance to Zion National Park.*

The unusual name of this large B&B is based on the fact that each of the rooms is named for a famous author. And the decor in the room is themed to the writings or times of its namesake, which makes the accommodations at Novel House diverse and unique. The exterior design is modern and attractive considering the more traditional interior. Most units have a great view of the surrounding area, including portions of Zion National Park. Great breakfasts and refreshments throughout the day are part of the Novel House experience. For quiet moments you can catch up on some reading at the inn's extensive library.

Selected as one of my Best Places to Stay (see Chapter 10 for more details).

ZION PARK INN RESORT, *1215 Zion Park Boulevard. Tel. 435/772-3200; Fax 435/772-2449. Toll free reservations 800/934-7275. 120 Rooms. Rates: High season (April through mid-October): $89-94; Low season (mid-October through March): $68-77. Most major credit cards accepted. Located in town about two miles from the south entrance to Zion National Park.*

Springdale's largest lodging establishment and one of the nicest, the Zion Park Inn is a modern facility with a rustic look that fits in quite well with the spectacular Zion countryside that's behind the inn (the front, unfortunately, faces the main street which is kind of commercialized). All of the rooms are quite spacious and nicely decorated. A few units have efficiency kitchens. On the premises are the excellent Switchback Grille (see the *Where to Eat* section for further details), an outdoor swimming pool and hot tub as well as a large gift shop. The package store sells just about anything you might need including groceries for in-room cooking or making a box lunch to take into the park.

Inexpensive

CANYON RANCH MOTEL, *668 Zion Park Boulevard. Tel. 435/772-3357; Fax 435/772-3057. 22 Rooms. Rates: $44-68 with higher end of scale during the summer season. American Express, Discover, MasterCard and VISA accepted. Located on Utah Highway 9 about one-quarter mile from the south gate to Zion National Park.*

Definitely not in the luxury category but a real good value and convenient for national park visitors. The small establishment consists of cabins arranged around a pretty lawn that has excellent views of Zion. Some of the cabins are new while others have been recently remodeled. Either way they're all clean and comfortable. There's an outdoor swimming pool and Jacuzzi. Restaurants are located within a short distance.

TERRACE BROOK LODGE, *990 Zion Park Boulevard. Tel. 435/772-3932; Fax 435/772-3596. Toll free reservations 800/342-6779. 26 Rooms. Rates: High season (April through October): $68; Low season (November through March): $57. American Express, Discover, MasterCard and VISA accepted. Located on UT Highway 9 about a mile south of Zion National Park entrance.*

The Terrace Brook is an attractive facility with a wide variety of accommodations. These include nice sized single rooms as well as some two and three bedroom units (priced up to $94 for a maximum of six people) and a few with kitchen facilities. The lodge is spread out over a fairly large area considering it only has 26 units. Some rooms are equipped with coffee maker and microwave oven. A number of rooms are on top of a hillside with great mountain views. If possible you should try and get one of them. Terrace Brook has a barbecue area and an outdoor swimming pool that's solar heated. The pool is open from April through October. There isn't any restaurant at the lodge but several are located within a short drive.

ZION NATIONAL PARK

(*See also Springdale*)
Moderate

ZION LODGE, *Zion National Park. Tel. 435/772-3213; Fax 435/772-2001. 121 Rooms. Rates: High season (March through November): $75-110; Low season (December through February): $54-80. Most major credit cards* *accepted. Located in Zion National Park along Zion Canyon Road about four miles north of the south entrance gate.*

This is the only lodging within the borders of Zion National Park and while it doesn't save that much time over staying in Springdale, it is a delightful place that doesn't cost much more than an in-town location. The historic lodge is located in a relatively broad portion of usually narrow Zion Canyon and offers outstanding vistas in all directions. It was originally built in the 1920's and is another of the architectural masterpieces of Gilbert Stanley Underwood. A serious fire in 1966 shut it down but it was quickly rebuilt in order to have in-park accommodations. It was not until 1990, however, that it was finally restored to the original "classic rustic" appearance that Underwood had created.

Accommodations consist of 41 cabins and 80 newer motel style units. Both are nice but the cabins give you a more "natural" experience with their solid wood beams and casual western furnishings. Facilities at Zion Lodge include an excellent restaurant (see the *Where to Eat* section), snack bar, and a fine gift shop. The activities desk at Zion Lodge is a focal point for arranging in-park activities.

CAMPING & RV SITES

National Parks and other federal lands: Two campgrounds are available at Bryce Canyon National Park, three at Zion National Park and another at Cedar Breaks National Monument. For information and reservations contact the superintendent's office of each area. The Dixie National Forest has campgrounds in each of the four major sections that cover most of southwest Utah and more are in the Fishlake National Forest in the region's northern section. Information is available by calling *Tel. 800/280-2267.*

Other campgrounds are maintained by the Bureau of Land Management. Information can be obtained from the Cedar City District office, *Tel. 435/586-2401* and the Richfield District office, *Tel. 435/896-8221.* The Cedar City District covers all of Utah's "Dixie" region as well as large portions of the Grand Staircase-Escalante National Monument. The Richfield office handles the west-central portion of the state.

State Parks: Escalante State Park has camping as does Gunlock and Snow Canyon State Parks in the St. George area. The central reservations office can be reached at *Tel. 800/322-3770.*

For **commercial camping** and **RV sites**, try:

•**Beaver Canyon Campground**, *1419 E. Canyon Road, Beaver. Tel. 435/438-5654*

•**Broken Bow RV Camp**, *495 W. Main, Escalante. Tel. 435/826-4959*

•**Cedar City KOA**, *1121 N. Main, Cedar City. Tel. 435/586-9872*

•**Crazy Horse RV Campark**, *625 E. Highway 89, Kanab. Tel. 435/644-2782*
•**Panguitch Big Fish KOA**, *555 S. Main, Panguitch. Tel. 800/562-1625*
•**Redlands RV Park**, *650 W. Telegraph, St. George. Tel. 800/533-8269*
•**Ruby's Inn RV Park & Campground**, *Bryce. Tel. 135/834-5301*
•**Sand Creek RV Park & Campground**, *540 W. Highway 24, Torrey. Tel. 435/425-3577*
•**Zion Canyon Campground**, *479 Zion Park Blvd., Springdale. Tel. 435/772-3237*

WHERE TO EAT
BRIAN HEAD
Expensive
SUMMIT DINING ROOM, *223 W. Hunter Ridge Road, in the Cedar Breaks Lodge. Tel. 435/677-3222. American Express, MasterCard and VISA accepted. Dinner served nightly. Reservations are suggested during the winter season.*

An attractive setting for dinner with excellent views and friendly, efficient service. The food certainly isn't great but there's a good selection available. Perhaps the biggest problem is that the operators don't quite know if they want a simple family restaurant or a fine dining experience. They try to do both and only partially succeed. Cocktail service is available.

Moderate
MOUNTAIN VIEW CAFE, *508 North Highway 143. Tel. 435/677-2411. Most major credit cards accepted. Breakfast, lunch and dinner served daily.*

A better choice than the above especially when you take price into consideration. The Mountain View strives only for family style dining and you'll receive nice portions of well-prepared American favorites in a pretty cafe with some great views.

BRYCE (RUBY'S INN) & BRYCE CANYON NATIONAL PARK
Moderate
BRYCE CANYON LODGE DINING ROOM, *in the Bryce Canyon Lodge, Bryce Canyon National Park. Tel. 435/834-5361. American Express, Discover, MasterCard and VISA accepted. Breakfast, lunch and dinner served daily. Closed during winter. Reservations are required.*

This very attractive restaurant is one of the few original buildings remaining from the earliest days of the park lodge. The decor remains 1930's style and the service is also typical of fine dining in that era. Given all that you may be a little disappointed in the food, which is certainly good but nothing special. The cuisine is basically American with a few southwestern entrees usually available. Cocktail service. For those who plan to do some serious exploring in Bryce, the restaurant will prepare box lunches to go.

RUBY'S INN RESTAURANT AND STEAKHOUSE, *Junction of Highways 12 and 63 in the Best Western Ruby's Inn. Tel. 435/834-5341. Major credit cards accepted. Breakfast, lunch and dinner served daily.*

It's difficult to write about this restaurant because it seems to change so often...perhaps because the proprietors want to keep it fresh for return visitors to Bryce and Ruby's Inn. However, I feel comfortable recommending it because no matter what they do with it the atmosphere is attractive and the food and service is always good. Steaks and southwestern cuisine are featured attractions but the menu is quite diverse. During the summer season you have the option of ordering off of the menu or partaking of the buffet. While I'm an admitted buffet lover, I advise going with the menu because the value usually associated with buffets isn't there in this case. Also, the selection isn't that great on the buffet and the food seems to me to be a notch below what comes fresh out of the kitchen.

Inexpensive

HAROLD'S PLACE, *On Highway 12. Tel. 435/676-2350. MasterCard and VISA accepted. Breakfast, lunch and dinner served daily. Closed November through February.*

Surprisingly reasonable prices are the biggest plus for Harold's Place which offers a large selection of American dishes in an attractive dining room with rustic decor. This is a good place for family dining especially in view of the excellent children's menu. The homemade pies for dessert are delicious.

CEDAR CITY

Moderate

ADRIANA'S RESTAURANT, *164 S. 100 West. Tel. 435/865-1234. American Express, Discover, MasterCard and VISA accepted. Lunch and dinner served daily except Sunday. Reservations are suggested*

This is the most delightful dining spot in Cedar City. The traditional old world setting is in keeping with the Utah Shakespeare Festival but it makes an attractive motif year round. Even the waitresses are appropriately costumed in period garb. The service is excellent but quite casual. The menu selection is large and includes pasta, ribs and prime ribs in addition to several English and other old world items. Wine is served.

MILT'S STAGE STOP, *Utah Highway 14, approximately 5 miles east of town. Tel. 435/586-9344. Most major credit cards accepted. Dinner served nightly. Reservations are suggested.*

While Adriana's is my first choice for dining in Cedar City if you like thick and juicy steaks, first quality prime rib or fresh seafood, you certainly can't go wrong with this place either. In fact, the locals have consistently made Milt's their "best" choice. The attractive mountain setting and the bountiful salad bar can't help but add to the enjoyment, as does the efficient and friendly wait staff. Cocktail service.

SULLI'S STEAK HOUSE, *301 S. Main Street. Tel. 435/586-6761. American Express, Discover, MasterCard and VISA accepted. Dinner served nightly.*

Sulli's menu is quite similar to that at Milt's and you would be hard pressed to choose between them as to quality as well. Their salad bar is somewhat smaller and the downtown location doesn't quite have the great atmosphere but these are only minor complaints. Sulli's has a children's menu and full cocktail service. The adjacent **SULLIVAN'S CAFE** (inexpensive to moderate) serves a simpler more family oriented menu and also includes a salad bar. In addition, the cafe serves breakfast and lunch.

Inexpensive
JIMMY'S RESTAURANT, *453 S. Main Street. Tel. 435/865-6613. Discover, MasterCard and VISA accepted. Breakfast, lunch and dinner served daily.*

You would never know it from the name but Jimmy's is a Mexican restaurant. The decor is semi-southwestern and the menu includes all of the traditional Mexican favorites nicely prepared and served in generous portions.

ESCALANTE
Moderate
COWBOY BLUES DINER, *530 West Main. Tel. 435/826-4251. MasterCard and VISA accepted. Lunch and dinner served daily except Sunday.*

A super casual and friendly little place serving good southwestern specialties along with some American entrees in pleasant surroundings. Prices for some dinners are in the inexpensive category. Children's menu.

PONDEROSA RESTAURANT, *45 North 400 West. Tel. 435/826-4658. Most major credit cards accepted. Breakfast, lunch and dinner served daily.*

This is not part of the inferior steak chain that goes by the same first name. The Ponderosa has been established in Escalante for some time although the current owners have only been there a few years. They are

Imi and Suzane Kun who hail from Budapest, Hungary. Now, Escalante isn't where Hungarians usually wind up but their presence has certainly brightened the local dining scene as they feature both American and European cuisine. Go for the European, especially Hungarian, specialties–you won't be sorry. Cocktails are served.

KANAB
Moderate
HOUSTON'S TRAIL'S END RESTAURANT, *32 E. Center Street. Tel. 435/644-2488. American Express, Discover, MasterCard and VISA accepted. Breakfast, lunch and dinner served daily. Closed January and February.*

This downtown eatery has an attractive and casual western decor to go along with its menu of mainly steak and seafood. There is a smattering of Mexican and other southwestern dishes as well. All of the food is well prepared and efficiently served. There's a salad bar and a children's menu.

PANGUITCH
Moderate
COWBOY'S SMOKEHOUSE, *95 N. Main Street. Tel. 435/676-8030. Discover, MasterCard and VISA accepted. Dinner served nightly except Sunday. Closed November through January.*

For a great taste of the old west the Cowboy's Smokehouse is the place to go. The dining room looks like a hangout for cowboys with its authentic old west artifacts and numerous game trophies. The menu is exactly what you would expect given the surroundings–deliciously prepared mesquite barbecued dishes like pork ribs and smoked turkey as well as ribs. The brisket of beef is as good as it gets. There's a children's menu which comes in handy considering the oversized portions that are served. Beer is served but no other alcoholic beverages are available.

Inexpensive
GRANDMA TINA'S SPAGHETTI HOUSE, *523 N. Main Street. Tel. 435/676-2377. MasterCard and VISA accepted. Breakfast, lunch and dinner served daily. Closed November through March.*

All sorts of spaghetti and pasta dishes are the star attraction at Grandma Tina's where the atmosphere and service is as warm and friendly as the name implies. Their sauces are homemade from an old family recipe and are simply delicious. The pizza is also good. Children's menu.

RICHFIELD/SALINA

Expensive

TOPSFIELD STEAK HOUSE, *1200 S. Main Street, Richfield. Tel. 435/ 896-5437. Most major credit cards accepted. Dinner served nightly.*

Who said that excellent steak houses have to be confined to the big cities? Topsfield belies that with expertly prepared choice cuts of beef served thick and juicy to your specifications. They also have a decent selection of fresh seafood. Portions are generous. Complete cocktail service available.

Moderate

PEPPERBELLY'S MEXICAN RESTAURANT, *680 S. Main Street, Richfield. Tel. 435/896-6476. Major credit cards accepted. Lunch and dinner served nightly except Sunday.*

The atmosphere is unusual for a Mexican restaurant–it's decorated like a small town gasoline filling station from the 1950's and the result is a fun, casual atmosphere that's good for the whole family. The strictly Mexican cuisine is excellent and not too hot although they'll be glad to spice it up if that's what you want.

ST. GEORGE

Expensive

SULLIVAN'S ROCOCO STEAK HOUSE, *511 S. Airport Road. Tel. 435/673-3305. Most major credit cards accepted. Lunch and dinner served Monday through Friday; dinner only on Saturday and Sunday.*

Sitting atop a small hill at the west end of town, Sullivan's patrons are treated to an excellent view as well as fine food. The decor is attractive and even on the fancy side considering the otherwise casual atmosphere. Although it's primarily a steak place Sullivan's menu does offer a substantial number of other dishes including seafood and chicken. Children's menu. Cocktail service.

Moderate

ANDELIN'S GABLE HOUSE, *290 E. St. George Boulevard. Tel. 435/ 673-6796. American Express, Discover, MasterCard and VISA accepted. Lunch and dinner served daily except Sunday. Reservations are suggested.*

A charming family restaurant featuring old world decor and fine service, Andelin's is the top spot in St. George if you're looking for excellent seafood. The menu also includes many traditional American favorites. Children's menu is available.

DICK'S CAFE, *114 E. St. George Boulevard. Tel. 435/673-3841. Most major credit cards accepted. Breakfast, lunch and dinner served daily.*

This small cafe is a nice family restaurant featuring a good variety of steak, seafood and chicken dishes. The service and decor are both pleasant. Some entrees are in the inexpensive price category.

SCALDONI'S GOURMET GROCER & GRILL, *929 W. Sunset Boulevard. Tel. 435/674-1300. American Express, Discover, MasterCard and VISA accepted. Lunch and dinner served daily; dinner only on Sunday. Reservations are suggested and required on weekends.*

The "grocer" part of the name of this local award winning restaurant (and it's deserved) refers to the extensive take-out section that features some rather unusual gourmet items. The sit-down menu does, too, with an interesting assortment of entrees ranging from Italian to Californian. Many items are seasonal and are prepared with the freshest ingredients. The health conscious diner will find plenty to select from at Scaldoni's. The atmosphere is relaxed and pleasant and during the warmer months you can dine outside on the patio. A children's menu is available and cocktails are served. For lunch Scaldoni's is known for their great sandwiches.

SPRINGDALE
Moderate

MAJESTIC VIEW, *2400 Zion Park Boulevard. Tel. 435/772-3000. Most major credit cards accepted. Lunch and dinner served daily but closes at 7:00pm during the winter months.*

Formerly the Log House Restaurant, this attractive steak and seafood restaurant is a casual and friendly place that's good for family dining. Although the food and service are both good, one of the biggest draws is the excellent view of a portion of Zion National Park, especially from the pleasant outdoor dining patio that's open during the summer season. Part of the restaurant has an interesting wildlife exhibit.

SWITCHBACK GRILLE, *1149 Zion Park Boulevard, in the Zion Park Resort. Tel. 435/772-3777. Most major credit cards accepted. Breakfast, lunch and dinner served daily.*

One of the nicest dining rooms in Springdale, the Switchback Grille features a large menu of steak, seafood and Italian entrees as well as some lighter dishes. The service is good and the ambiance is warm. Cocktails are served.

Inexpensive

PIONEER FAMILY RESTAURANT, *828 Zion Park Boulevard. Tel. 435/772-3009. Most major credit cards accepted. Breakfast, lunch and dinner served daily except Sunday.*

Prices for dining in Springdale aren't that high considering the location right outside a major national park. Even so, for those on a tighter budget and looking for relative bargains, the Pioneer Family Restaurant provides good food (American favorites), selection and service in a comfortable dining room. Children's menu.

ZION NATIONAL PARK
Moderate

ZION LODGE RESTAURANT, *in the Zion Lodge inside Zion National Park. Tel. 435/772-3213. Most major credit cards accepted. Breakfast, lunch and dinner served daily.*

The only restaurant within the park, the Zion Lodge Restaurant is a traditional American restaurant serving mainly steak and seafood although the menu includes a number of lighter meals including salads. (For those who are looking for lunch on the run there's a sort of fast food section that's open during the afternoon). The rustic decor and fine service, along with the well prepared meals, make this a pleasant and satisfying dining experience. Cocktail service. Box lunches are available for those who'll be out exploring the park at lunch time.

SEEING THE SIGHTS

I suggest heading north on this route through the southwest only because that will leave the best attractions for the second half of the trip. Otherwise, it doesn't matter. You could easily start from the end and work your way back to my beginning.

ST. GEORGE & VICINITY

The area around St. George is often referred to as "Utah's Dixie." Part of the reason is the generally mild winters compared to the rest of the state. But there's also an historic aspect to the name. During the Civil War it was impossible to secure cotton so the Mormon settlers planted their own and even made a cotton mill until the war was over. The cotton industry, such as it was, doesn't exist any more but the Dixie name still holds sway. Now with about 45,000 residents, St. George is by far the largest city in the southern half of Utah and it is growing at a fairly brisk pace.

Downtown St. George is easy to get around. It uses the hundred number grid like the one in Salt Lake City. The main east to west thoroughfare is St. George Boulevard. 400 East Street is the most important north-south artery in the city center. I-15 has exits on the east side of St. George at the northern and southern ends of town.

We'll begin our tour downtown. Use the Bluff Street Exit off of I-15 and hang a right on Main Street. In a few blocks you'll reach the city center. The first stop will be to take a quick look at the **Mormon Temple**,

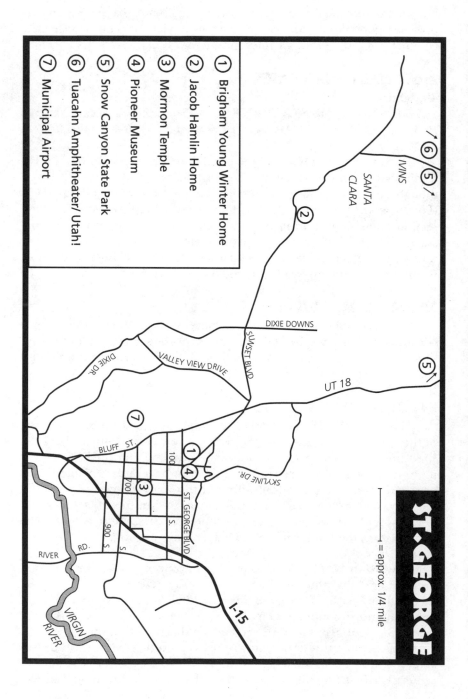

① Brigham Young Winter Home
② Jacob Hamlin Home
③ Mormon Temple
④ Pioneer Museum
⑤ Snow Canyon State Park
⑥ Tuacahn Amphitheater/ Utah!
⑦ Municipal Airport

ST·GEORGE

⊢ = approx. 1/4 mile

IVINS

SANTA CLARA

DIXIE DOWNS

SUNSET BLVD

DIXIE DR.

VALLEY VIEW DRIVE

UT 18

BLUFF ST.

100

700

900 S

S.

RIVER RD.

ST. GEORGE BLVD.

SKYLINE DR.

I-15

VIRGIN RIVER

300 East and 400 South. It's not nearly as large or ornate as other temples but the brilliant white structure has a simple elegance to it. It also has the distinction of being the first Mormon temple to be completed in Utah. It dates from the 1870's. Go back to Main Street, turn right and proceed four blocks to Tabernacle Street where you'll find the **LDS Tabernacle**. The handsome red brick building features large trusses, hand-carved spiral staircases and a clock made in England. Many of the buildings on the surrounding streets date from the same period. You can take a brief walk up Main to St. George Boulevard, then west one block to 100 West and north to 300 North. In this vicinity are more than a dozen homes and businesses of historic significance, some of which are not open to the public.

Two places that you should stop to visit are the **Brigham Young Winter Home**, *67 W. 200 North (corner of 100 West)* and the **Pioneer Museum**, *143 N. 100 East (just north of St. George Blvd.).* Young's home was completed in 1871 with an addition a couple of years later. This not only enabled him to escape the harsher winters up north but also allowed for his personal supervision of the construction of the St. George Temple. The house is furnished in period. *Tel. 435/673-2517. The house is open daily from 9:00am to 8:00pm during the period between Memorial Day and Labor Day and 9:00am to dusk the remainder of the year. Guided tours are given with the last tour beginning one hour prior to closing. Free admission.*

The museum was built in the 1930s but is more reminiscent of the 19th century style seen in much of St. George. That's appropriate because the collection is devoted to the early pioneer period from St. George's founding in 1847 until the construction of the temple. *Tel. 435/628-7274. Museum hours are daily except Sunday from 10:00am until 5:00pm. It is closed Thanksgiving and the last three weeks of December through New Year's Day. There is no set admission charge but donations are requested.* You should be able to complete the downtown St. George tour in a couple of hours, including seeing both of the above facilities.

After leaving the museum drive west on St. George Boulevard until it ends at Bluff Street. Turn right and proceed eight blocks to Sunset Boulevard. Turn left (westbound) and follow Sunset through the adjoining town of Santa Clara and the **Jacob Hamblin Home**. The restored home was constructed in 1862 and is one of the oldest pioneer structures in the vicinity. Hamblin was a church missionary and colonizer but is best known for his good relationship with the Native Americans of the region. He successfully negotiated several treaties and prevented hostilities on more than one occasion. Interesting 30-minute tours of the home, which is furnished as it would have been in the 1880s, are given. *Tel. 435/673-2161. Open daily from 9:00am until dusk and there is no admission charge.*

UTAH!...THE PLAY

*Off of UT 91 near Ivins about a half hour west of St. George in a beautiful canyon of red rocks is the site of an outdoor musical presentation called **Utah!** The elaborate show features a cast of more than 80 talented performers who tell the story of how the Mormon pioneers withstood one hardship after another to settle the state. (There is no effort to convert show viewers to Mormonism—just lively song and dance.) The cast shares the bill with numerous excellent special effects that include live galloping horses, the burning of a village and a flood that sweeps across the stage towards the audience. The amphitheater follows the natural slope of the canyon and the stage extends all the way to the canyon's red walls. In fact, some of the action takes place on the rocks. The theater complex goes by the name Tuacahn, meaning Canyon of the Gods.*

Get there well before the show so you can take some time to explore the surroundings. In fact, the grounds are open during the day so you might want to take a look even if you aren't going to the show. For information, call Tel. 800/SHOW-UTAH. Performances are held daily except Sunday at 8:30pm from mid-June through early September. There is pre-show entertainment from 6:30 to 7:30 and an optional dinner package is available. Reservations are suggested. Ticket prices vary from $15-25 for adults and $9-16 for children under 12 depending upon the seat location. Credit cards.

*Tuacahn's plans for 1999 and beyond calls for an extended season that will alternate three different shows. In addition to Utah!, two new shows will be added: **How the West Was Won** and **King of Kings**. Call the box office for further information on the two newest shows.*

A little bit further west on Sunset Boulevard will bring you to the junction of UT 18. Turn north and in a few miles you'll get your first true taste of Color Country when you enter **Snow Canyon State Park**. The beautiful park is known for its vivid and contrasting colors. There are both red and white sandstone rock formations as well as black lava beds, all of which explains the areas geological history. The road starts above the canyon and provides a splendid overall panorama before you descend into the canyon itself for a more close up look at the high rocky bluffs with their intricate shadings and vertical fault lines. There are several trails of varying length. Horseback riding in Snow Canyon is also popular. You can drive through the park and make some nice photo stops in less than an hour but much more time can be spent if you want to hike the canyon. *Tel. 435/628-2255. Open at all times. There is a $4 daily vehicle use charge.*

Reverse your route back into St. George. Take St. George Boulevard east until it ends at River Road and then turn left. The street will change names to Red Cliffs Drive as it parallels the highway. At the town of Washington, a few miles up the road, you can make a brief stop to see the **Washington Cotton Mill**. It's generally closed to the public but has been expertly restored and will give you an excellent idea of what it looked like during the 1860's. Then go back a block to the entrance of I-15. Go north on the highway for a few miles to Leeds (Exit 22). Two miles north is the ghost town of **Silver Reef**. It was another wild-west boomtown that produced millions of dollars in silver during the 1870's and 1880's. There isn't too much left (that's why it is called a ghost town, after all) but the Wells Fargo building has been restored to its original condition. It houses a small museum and art gallery.

Go back to the highway and take I-15 north again to Exit 40 and the **Kolob Canyons** section of Zion National Park. Most of Zion National Park is located east of St. George and will be seen as the last attraction on the southwest loop before returning to St. George. The major portion of the park and Kolob Canyons are not directly connected by road. The surprising thing about Kolob Canyons is how little known it is to people outside of Utah. While it isn't as spectacular as the more famous Zion Canyon it is, nonetheless, a beautiful sight and extremely convenient to visit. In fact, it begins the second you leave I-15. A small visitor center is located adjacent to the exit.

The five mile drive from the visitor center to the Kolob Canyons Viewpoint climbs through magnificent forests of juniper, pine and fir along steep red rock walls. From the several pull outs along the road are excellent views of the narrow "finger canyons" that have been carved over the ages by streams. The road has some steep grades and sharp turns but doesn't present any special problems. Allow about an hour to see the Kolob Canyons section. See Zion National Park later in this chapter for basic information on the park. Upon returning to the Interstate you'll go north 17 miles to Cedar City.

CEDAR CITY

The second largest city in southwest Utah, Cedar City began as an iron mining community but is now mainly a college town. **Southern Utah University** has their campus here and is a focal point for visitors as well as students and residents. More than 6,000 students are enrolled. It is best known as the home of the renowned Utah Shakespearean Festival, which will be detailed in a few moments. Of interest on the campus is the **Braithwaite Fine Arts Gallery**, *351 W. Center*, which has a permanent collection as well as exhibits by local and nationally recognized artists. *Tel. 435/586-5432. The gallery is open daily except Sunday from noon to 8:30pm* *during the summer and on weekdays from noon until 7:00pm the rest of the year. It is closed on state holidays. Admission is free.* While on campus you should also take a few moments to see the **Old Sorrel** statue, which represents the founding of the university. The life size sculpture shows a proud horse pulling a wagon and its riders from out of a tough spot.

The university and city are deservedly proud of the outstanding **Utah Shakespearean Festival** that is held each summer. It attracts more than 135,000 visitors from all over the world. Each year six different Shakespeare plays are selected and play in nightly rotation before starting over again the following week. A separate theater presents a number of non-Shakespearean works also on a rotating basis. But the plays aren't the only "thing," to paraphrase Bill S., that make the festival so special. Part of the fun is that you watch the show in an open-air theater that is almost exactly like the original Globe Theater. Even more fun is the free "greenshow" that is held each evening prior to the main performance. It is like a medieval English festival complete with jugglers, musicians and story tellers all appropriately dressed in period garb. Children may not be thrilled with an evening of Shakespeare but all ages can be delighted by the merry-making during the greenshow. Other aspects of the festival include back stage tours and Renaissance style meals. *Tel. 800/752-9849. The festival runs from late June through early September. Performances are held nightly except Sunday at 8:30. There is also a 2:00pm matinee performance. Children under five are not allowed to attend performances. Tickets cost between $10 and $40. Reservations are strongly advised.*

Located to the northwest of the town center via UT 91 is the **Iron Mission State Park**, *635 N. Main.* The earliest Mormon settlers in the area found extensive deposits of iron and Brigham Young decided that it would be a good idea to exploit the discovery. The foundry opened in 1851 and was the first one to be built west of the Mississippi River. Steel forging continued until 1858. The iron mission is gone although there is a large diorama of what it would have looked like. On the grounds today is a large collection of horse-drawn vehicles representative of the period from 1870 through about 1930. The stagecoaches are probably of most interest, especially one that is riddled by bullets possibly fired by Butch Cassidy or one of his group. Allow at least a half an hour to visit the park. *Tel. 435/586-9290. The park is open daily from 9:00am until 7:00pm June through August and until 5:00pm the remainder of the year. It is closed on New Year's Day, Thanksgiving and Christmas. There is a $3 daily vehicle use charge.*

Leave Cedar City to the east by way of UT 14. The road starts to climb sharply the minute you leave town. In 18 miles you'll reach the junction of UT 148. A left turn here will immediately bring you to the entrance of the next destination, Cedar Breaks. However, before we get to that I'll mention a little side trip that might interest you. If you continue on UT

14 past the UT 148 junction, the highway passes through a particularly pleasing area of the Dixie National Forest. Of most interest is the section between the village of **Duck Creek** and **Navajo Lake**. The latter is locked in by a natural lava dam. The entire area is of geologic interest because the last known eruptions took place less than 2,000 years ago, recent in geologic terms. There is relatively little vegetation although it is taking hold. This results in some picturesque rock outcroppings.

CEDAR BREAKS & BRIAN HEAD

Cedar Breaks National Monument is a well deserved member of Color Country and a sort of miniature Bryce. It is a natural amphitheater that is three miles wide and cut to a depth of more than 2,300 feet. The Native Americans of the area referred to it as a "circle of painted cliffs." The Anglo name comes from the juniper trees near the base of the cliffs. Early settlers thought they were cedars. The amphitheater's rim sits majestically in the rarified air of the 10,000-foot level. The shapes of the rocks are of great interest but the red, yellow and purple colors resulting from different minerals in the rock are Cedar Break's most impressive feature.

A short road leads to several viewpoints along the rim. The rim contains a variety of wildlife and lovely wildflower meadows during the summer months. There's a small visitor center that explains the geological history of Cedar Breaks. Allow about 45 minutes for your visit unless you plan to do a lot of walking within the Monument. *Tel. 435/586-9451. The visitor center is open daily from 8:00am until 6:00pm from Memorial Day through Labor Day and to 5:00pm through mid-October. It is closed the rest of the year. Road access to Cedar Breaks depends upon snow levels but it is usually open to traffic from late May through October. During the winter it can only be reached by snowmobile or by cross-country skiing. Admission is $4 per vehicle to those not holding a national park service passport.*

Exit from Cedar Breaks on the north side and pick up UT 143 which will soon bring you to **Brian Head**, one of Utah's great skiing resorts and a beautiful spot at any time of the year. At an altitude of about 9,600 feet, Brian Head offers mountain biking, hiking and fishing during the warmer months as well as great views. See the *Sports & Recreation* section for further information on these activities. Brian Head Peak reaches the lofty height of 11,300 feet.

About 15 miles north of Brian Head on UT 143 is Parowan. Another early Mormon settlement, Parowan today is a small community that has a great view of the mountains. The town square looks much as it did more than a hundred years ago. The **Old Rock Church** is of interest. You can also visit the **Parowan Heritage Park**, *west of town on UT 91*, near the now dry lake bed of what the first settlers named the "Little Salt Lake."

PAROWAN TO RICHFIELD

The northern end of Parowan sits at the junction of I-15 where you can start driving north. A relatively short scenic side trip can be made at Beaver (Exit 112). The downtown section of Beaver has more than 30 historic buildings that date from the pioneer era, many of which have unusually interesting architecture. UT 153 east heads into **Beaver Canyon** along the Beaver River. There are several picnic areas, trails and areas for off-roading in the pine and aspen forests. Wildlife is commonly seen in the canyon. The road ends after 17 miles at the **Elk Meadows Ski and Summer Resort** in the shadow of two 12,000-foot high mountains. Hikers enjoy the resort during the warmer months.

After returning to I-15 and continuing in a northerly direction for 23 miles to Exit 135, follow signs south for two miles to **Cove Fort Historic Site**. The fort was built in 1867 as a way station for travelers between Fillmore and Beaver. That 60-mile trip usually took about two days. A volcanic and limestone rock wall that was quarried at nearby sites surrounds the twelve room fort. The walls measured 18 feet in height. All of the rooms have been restored to the 1870's period with authentic furnishings. *Tel. 435/438-5547. The fort is open daily from 8:00am until an hour before sunset (except in bad weather) and there is no admission charge.*

Once you're finished with Cove Fort the tour route picks up I-70 a mile south of the fort. Go east through the picturesque high country of the Fishlake National Forest and its **Pahvant Range** and the **Clear Creek Canyon**. Use Exit 17 and follow signs for the short distance to the **Fremont Indian State Park**. Besides the visually splendid sights of Clear Creek Canyon, the canyon is a major archaeological site of ancient Native American culture with excellent examples of rock art. The so-called Fremont Indians drew their art on the canyon's walls. Pictographs are paintings while petroglyphs were chiseled into the rock. Both types are in evidence although archaeologists have yet to figure out their significance or meaning. The visitor center has a good museum. A dozen trails varying from wheelchair accessible to quite difficult stretch through the two miles of the canyon that the park occupies. Of most interest are **Spider Woman Rock** and **Cave of the Hundred Hands**. An especially scenic area of Clear Creek Canyon called **The Narrows** lies just west of the park along UT 4. Allow at least an hour for your visit to the state park and nearby canyons. *Tel. 435/538-7221. Park open daily during daylight hours; visitor center from 9:00am to 6:00pm during the summer with shorter hours at other times. Daily vehicle use charge of $5.*

Work your way back to I-70 and go east for one exit (#23) and the town of Sevier. Turn south on US 89 for a few miles to the unusual **Big Rock Candy Mountain**. The well-known rock formation is caramel candy

FILLMORE...& MORE

It's just not possible to include everything there is to see on a loop unless that loop is going to be a zillion miles long. So here's another side trip for those with some extra time. About 30 miles north of Cove Fort via I-15 is the town of Fillmore, once the Utah Territorial capital. The story of that era is told at the **Territorial Statehouse State Park**, *the oldest public building in Utah still standing. Various exhibits are contained within. Visitors will probably comment upon seeing the old statehouse that it's rather small and not at all stately looking for a capitol building. That's because it was never finished. Fillmore was selected to be the capital because of its central location. The building was to have consisted of four wings with a central area covered by a Moorish-style dome. Only one wing was completed when construction was halted in 1855. The territorial legislature only met there once before the capital was relocated back to Salt Lake City in 1858.*

Call 435/743-5316. Park open daily, Memorial Day to Labor Day, from 8:00am until 8:00pm except Sunday when the hours are from 9:00am to 6:00pm. At other times it is open daily except Sunday from 9:00am to 6:00pm. Admission is $2 per person or $5 vehicle use charge.

The area to the west of Fillmore contains a number of interesting volcanic formations. The closest and most easily reached is **Red Dome Volcano**, *a 4,000-year old eruption site. Take UT 100 five miles west from Fillmore then south about four miles, the last two of which are unpaved. There are eerie views into the crater but they do require some difficult walking. Sturdy shoes are a must.*

If you're coming to the southwest region from Salt Lake City this isn't a side trip at all. Your route will be on I-15 through Fillmore in order to reach the southwest loop.

colored and thus worth a brief stop to take a look at. The surrounding commercial development is of less interest but there is ample opportunity for river sports, biking and hiking. Just a little further south in Marysvale is **Bullion Canyon**, so called because there were many gold mines in the area at one time. Some of the mills and mines can be visited. If you're interested then inquire in town.

Return to Sevier and rejoin I-70 east for 14 miles to Richfield (Exit 37), Sevier county's seat and largest community, Richfield is a focal point for equipment rentals to go into the surrounding back country. A listing of some is in the *Sports & Recreation* section.

THE PAIUTE ATV TRAIL

*The rugged and isolated country of this portion of Utah makes it extremely popular for people who love to ride all terrain vehicles, or ATV's. Richfield is the biggest community along the **Paiute ATV Trail**, a 200-mile long loop that crosses three mountain ranges, several canyons and even a small desert. Most of it is within the boundaries of the Fishlake National Forest. There are also countless side routes that can be explored off of the main trail. In addition to Richfield, you can access the trail from Salina, Circleville, Marysvale and a number of other small communities. Elevations range from 5,100 feet to 12,000 feet. The Trail is host to the annual **Rocky Mountain ATV Jamboree** each September. Late spring, summer and fall are good times to go ATV-ing on the Paiute. The fall colors are gorgeous and make it one of the most popular times to take a ride. In addition to ATV rentals, you can find trail guide services if you're unsure of your navigating abilities.*

RICHFIELD TO TORREY

Take UT 119 west from Richfield for about seven miles until it ends at the junction of UT 24. Turn right and follow the latter route to **Torrey**, a distance of about 50 miles. This is one of the few stretches of road in the southwest that doesn't have too much to see on it, but it isn't all that long and the scenery isn't unpleasant (there are views of forested mountains). The town of Loa is named for Hawaii's Mauna Loa. A Mormon missionary was quite impressed with the big Hawaiian mountain and named the town after it. There's a fish hatchery in Loa that's open to the public that is mildly interesting if you've never been to one of these facilities.

About four miles east of Torrey via UT 24 is the entrance to the **Capitol Reef National Monument**. This spectacular natural area is part of the Southeast region and is described in the next chapter. I mention it now because if you don't intend to travel in the southeast it is worth going the few miles into that region to see it. However, for now let's continue on our southwest sojourn by taking UT 12 south from Torrey.

REMARKABLE UTAH 12

Also known as the **Panguitch-Escalante-Boulder Scenic Highway** and the **Utah 12 Scenic Byway**, this road is one of the most fabulous in the nation no matter what name it goes under. This entire section of the trip could also be called the **Grand Staircase-Escalante National Monument** but see the sidebar for more about that. UT 12 between Torrey and Bryce Canyon covers 108 miles of spectacular and often unbelievable scenery. (It continues past Bryce for another 14 miles but I'm getting a bit ahead of myself again.)

Along the route you'll encounter numerous sights to marvel at as you pass by and many more that require stopping. The Byway also has several places of historic interest on its course through canyons, forests, mountains and rock cliffs. All are splashed with an array of colors as you would expect from a road through Color Country. There are even a few small towns along the way. The road is not a difficult one to drive but does require a degree of caution because of frequent turns and some steep grades. It definitely doesn't call for four-wheel drive or high clearance vehicle although the former is always helpful.

THE GRAND STAIRCASE-ESCALANTE NATIONAL MONUMENT

America's newest national monument, **Grand Staircase-Escalante** *was established by presidential proclamation in 1996. There was a great deal of politics involved in its creation (and much opposition from within Utah) but I won't get into that. Covering a vast 1.7 million acres (larger than the state of Delaware), the monument stretches from the western edge of Capitol Reef National Park, all along the northern side of the Glen Canyon National Recreation Area and west to a line about level with Bryce Canyon National Park. The first part of the name comes from the series of terrace like rock formations that gradually rise along the Colorado Plateau. Most of this multi-colored and rugged landscape is comprised of the* **Kaiparowits Plateau.** *In its rocks and magnificent scenery are recorded 200 million years of earth's history. Not only is the land rugged but it is mostly remote and undeveloped. It was the last area of the continental United States to be mapped. Many areas of the Monument were previously Bureau of Land Management facilities and, in fact, Grand Staircase is the only National Park Service facility to be administered by the BLM.*

Future development of visitor facilities is uncertain. The only services available now are in the nearby communities of Boulder, Escalante, Cannonville and Tropic on UT 12 on the Monument's northern edge and in Kanab and Big Water on US 89 on the south side. The only roads that penetrate the interior are backways, several of which are briefly described in the next sidebar. If you plan to hike in Grand Staircase be sure to carry at least one gallon of water per person for each day and wear clothing that will protect you from the sun if you're exploring during the hotter months. Also be aware of abandoned mines which can be dangerous and the hazard of flash floods in narrow canyons. The latter can occur in a matter of minutes during or after a heavy thunderstorm, even a brief one.

A few miles south of Torrey is the first point of interest on UT 12. The road crosses 9,670-foot high **Boulder Mountain** on the **Aquarius Plateau**. Several roadside pullouts are located along this section. You can see a distance of more than a hundred miles to such sights as the Waterpocket Fold and Navajo Mountain. The next stop is just before the town of Boulder at the **Anasazi Indian Village State Park**. The site dates from around 1050 and is believed to have been the home of about 200 members of the Kayenta Anasazi. The partially excavated village includes the ruins of almost 90 different rooms. Many artifacts found at the site are in the adjacent museum and there is also a recreation of a full-size six-room dwelling. *Tel. 435/335-7308. The park is open daily from 8:00am to 6:00pm from the middle of May to mid-September and from 9:00am until 5:00pm the rest of the year. The admission is $2 per person plus a $5 vehicle use fee (for up to 9 people).*

South of Boulder the road swings around the **Calf Creek Recreation Area** on a section called the "Million Dollar Road to Boulder." It was built in the 1930s by the Civilian Conservation Corps, and replaced hazardous routes that were previously traveled only by riders on mules or pack horses. The spectacular scenery of **Escalante Canyon** is best seen from one of several pullouts. Within the recreation area are picnic tables, a great place for a break, and a six-mile trail through sandy terrain to 126-foot high **Lower Calf Creek Falls**. It's beautiful but if you want to do it then add at least 2-1/2 hours to the time frame for UT 12 mentioned at the end of this section.

Escalante is the largest town on Byway 12. It was settled in 1876 by Mormon farmers. Today, almost a hundred historic homes from the early days of Escalante remain. Most are located within a block or two of UT 12, which is Main Street. You can get a brochure outlining a walking tour at the information center on Main between Center and 100 East Streets.

Right after the town of Escalante is the **Escalante Petrified Forest State Park**. In addition to a reservoir for swimming, fishing or boating, the park has fine examples of 160 million year old petrified wood. These can be seen via a self-guiding nature trail. *Tel. 435/826-4466. Open all year during daylight hours. There is a $4 daily vehicle use charge.* The 30-mile stretch between the park and the town of Henrieville is still scenic but not quite as spectacular as the portion of the route we've been following up to now.

A few miles beyond Henrieville you'll reach the tiny town of Cannonville. Turn off here to the south via Cottonwood Wash Road and drive nine miles along a paved narrow road to fantastic **Kodachrome Basin State Park**. The name of this place should give you an idea of what to expect. Dozens of huge sandstone formations, mostly shaped like chimneys, dominate the scene and appear as shades of gray, white and red. The colors change with the movement of the sun throughout the day so it can look completely different from one visit to the next. No matter what time of day it is, though, the sight is both strange and beautiful. The park contains numerous tranquil coves. Picnicking is popular as is horseback riding. *Tel. 435/679-8562. Open at all times. There is a $4 daily vehicle use fee.*

Once you return to UT 12 from Kodachrome Basin it's only a 12 mile ride through the towns of Cannonville and Tropic before you reach the semi-town of Bryce (also known as Ruby's Inn) along UT 63. This short

BACKWAYS TO ADVENTURE ALONG UTAH 12

The wonderful sights along UT 12 are certainly enough to make for an eventful day. Some people, however, may want to see even more. Or maybe they're a little disappointed that UT 12 wasn't difficult enough. Okay, so you want something a bit more adventurous. Well, there's plenty of that, courtesy of many scenic backways that lead off of UT 12. The four that are mentioned here are among the most popular. All are unpaved and a couple are downright difficult, even for the most experienced driver. Do not attempt any of them without a four-wheel drive, high clearance vehicle. And don't try them during or right after a big rain.

*The **Burr Trail** is a 66-mile long route (one way) that passes striking scenery such as Capitol Reef's Waterpocket Fold and vast areas of wilderness before ending at Lake Powell's Bullfrog Marina.*

***Hell's Backbone** is considered by the experts to be one of the wildest roads in America. It travels along a narrow crest with precipitous drop-offs on both sides. The scenery along the way is breathtaking. You can return to UT 12 by reversing your route once you've reached the road's highlight—the **Hell's Backbone Bridge**, or you can continue to the **Posey Lake Road Scenic Backway** that will bring you to UT 12 at Escalante. If you do the latter, however, than you miss UT 12 between Boulder and Escalante which is one of the most beautiful stretches of the byway.*

*The 60-mile road to the **Hole-in-the-Rock** also encompasses some great scenery and ends at an historic Mormon settlement on what is now Lake Powell. If you don't want to go the entire distance you might try driving as far as the **Devil's Rock Garden**, an area of highly unusual rock formations that almost look as if they've been planted. It is only 18 miles from Escalante.*

*Finally, the road that leads to Kodachrome Basin State Park continues for ten miles further to **Grosvenor Arch**, a remarkably beautiful and large natural rock arch.*

side road off of UT 12 leads directly into your next adventure and one that is likely to be a highlight regardless of what else you see in Utah. You should allow at least a half a day to traverse UT 12 and the sights along the route but that doesn't include any time for one or more backways.

BRYCE CANYON NATIONAL PARK

Whatever I say about **Bryce Canyon National Park** can't possibly do it proper justice. Its endless sights are vivid in my memory from many trips there and I have pictures of it in front of me as I write. Yet, both leave me at a loss for words. How do you describe something that defies description, that must be seen to be believed? You can see the Grand Canyon, Yellowstone, Yosemite and a host of other magnificent places but most experienced travelers will happily tell you that Bryce cannot be beat. I concur. Exactly what is it that will leave you standing on the rim of Bryce, mesmerized so that you barely can pull yourself away from the breathtaking scene played out before you? It's enough to bring tears to the eyes of grown men....I know, because I'm one of its victims!

Bryce is the product of millions of years of erosion. Wind and rain have carved thousands upon thousands of rock spires known as **hoodoos**. The cliffs of Bryce are predominantly pink but there are varying shades of red, yellow, brown and lavender resulting from minerals in the rock. The colors are brilliant at all times but especially at sunrise and sunset. Bryce is named after an early Mormon farmer named Ebenezer Bryce. It's not apparent whether or not he fully appreciated the scenery but he is said to have commented that the area was "a hell of a place to lose a cow." No doubt! It was established as a national park in 1928 and attracts more than 1-1/2 million visitors each year. In a geological sense Bryce is not a canyon at all but rather several horseshoe shaped amphitheaters that have been carved out of the Paunsaugent Plateau by the action of the Paria River. The Native Americans of the area were more accurate in their name for Bryce–it translates something as "red rocks standing like men in a bowl shaped canyon." Unfortunately that name, although highly descriptive, is a little cumbersome. It would also be too long to get it onto a small map so we'll have to stick with Bryce Canyon.

The park is at an elevation of about 9,000 feet at the rim level but drops to as low as 6,600 feet at the bottom of the cliffs. The road rises about a thousand feet from the entrance to the highest point, which is located at the far end of the road. Seeing the park is extremely easy–you can do it with hardly any walking at all. On the other hand, for the nature enthusiast some of the trails are long and extremely challenging. While you will have a wonderful visit to Bryce just by driving the park's road and taking the short walks to the almost 20 overlooks, the Bryce experience

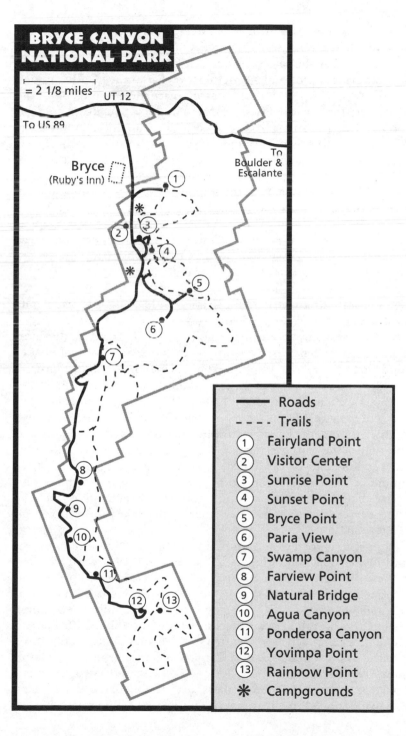

BRYCE CANYON NATIONAL PARK

= 2 1/8 miles

UT 12

To US 89

Bryce
(Ruby's Inn)

To Boulder & Escalante

—— Roads
- - - - Trails
1 Fairyland Point
2 Visitor Center
3 Sunrise Point
4 Sunset Point
5 Bryce Point
6 Paria View
7 Swamp Canyon
8 Farview Point
9 Natural Bridge
10 Agua Canyon
11 Ponderosa Canyon
12 Yovimpa Point
13 Rainbow Point
✳ Campgrounds

isn't complete without venturing down beneath the rim. We'll soon take a look at the road and the trails in succession. A visitor center is located about a mile south of the park's entrance. Services within the park include lodging, dining, camping and a general store. Park rangers offer guided hikes and talks during the summer season. A schedule is available at the visitor center. Horseback riding is also a popular activity. Wildlife is common. The largest animal you're likely to see is a mule deer but many small mammals will be seen scurrying about on the rim because they know that uneducated visitors will feed them. But don't. They are wild and can bite. Also, human food isn't good for them.

The dead-end road that runs through Bryce is 18 miles long. Including a few short spur roads you will only have to drive about 45 miles to cover the entire road system. The road does have some rises and drops as well as many turns but it is simple to negotiate. Exercise caution near overlooks as other visitors may be on or very near the road. Trailers are not allowed south of the Sunset Campground.

First, let's talk about the driving tour of Bryce. As soon as you pass through the entrance to the park there is a cutoff leading just over a mile to **Fairyland Point**. Because of its location many visitors miss it entirely, which would be a shame because Fairyland is just that. It is one of the finest views in the park. The vista encompasses the many unusual shapes contained in the Fairyland Amphitheater (such as the "Sinking Ship"). A little south of the Visitor Center there is a loop off the main road that takes you to **Sunrise Point** and to most of the park's services. Immediately to the south of Sunrise (but on the main road) is **Sunset Point**. These two points mark the ends of Bryce Amphitheater, the largest in the park and certainly one of the most spectacular. The view of multi-colored hoodoos is almost endless and you can also see the sharp drop off from the rim as the amphitheater curves away from you. Also take notice here, and elsewhere, of dark spots on the rocks. Upon closer examination you'll see that they are trees that somehow have managed to take root and grow on uneven terrain.

The final spur road comes up in a jiffy south of Sunset Point. This leads to **Inspiration Point** and via a T-shaped end to **Bryce Point** and **Paria View**. The former two look back into the Bryce Amphitheater and the perspective, especially at Bryce Point, is far different from those at Sunrise and Sunset. Paria View looks out on another spire filled amphitheater but has a beautiful backdrop consisting of the **Table Cliffs Plateau** and the **White Cliffs**. Once you return to the main road it's about three miles to the next overlook, **Swamp Canyon**. There are quite a few more overlooks between this point and the road's end but the best are **Farview Point** with its "big picture" view of areas surrounding Bryce, the so-called **Natural Bridge** that's actually an arch (you'll learn the difference when we explore the southeast) and **Ponderosa** and **Agua Canyons**. The latter two are extremely colorful both because of the rocks themselves and the heavy concentration of pine trees. The road ends at **Rainbow Point** where you can take in a view that covers (during clear weather) almost a hundred miles. Steep slopes and many more hoodoos are in evidence.

I know you'll be disappointed at the end of the road because your appetite for more will be unsatiable. So, stop at some of your favorite points on the way back. With the shifting sun they're likely to appear differently than at your first glance. That's one of the things that make a visit to Bryce so special.

Now for the trails. There are almost 50 miles of trails and they can be divided into two groups. The first are the easy trails that go along the rim. The second constitute the under the rim group and can be quite strenuous, especially on the way up. A couple of cautions: It is dangerous to throw anything into the amphitheaters while you're on the rim or on the upper portions of any below the rim trails. Hikers below can be injured. Secondly, the trails that descend beneath the rim often have steep drop-offs. Use caution and know your own limits. Again, because of the high altitude you'll tire easily unless you are in tip-top shape.

The **Rim Trail** extends for 11 miles along the plateau and affords wonderful views at virtually every step. It roughly parallels the road, and like the road, has a dead end rather than looping back a different way. So pick and choose your spots to walk the rim. The most popular area to do so is the approximately half-mile long section between Sunrise and Sunset Points. Not only is this one of the most beautiful areas of the Park, but the trail is reasonably level and paved. It is even well suited to physically impaired visitors. If you only have the time or inclination to walk a single trail in Bryce, do make it this one.

All of the trails that descend into the "canyon" are collective referred to as the **Under the Rim Trail**." However, although they're all interconnected you can do various sections of one or more depending upon how much time you have and your hiking capabilities. The easiest trail to go below the rim is the **Queen's Garden Trail** (begins at Sunrise Point). It's two miles long and drops 320 feet. Openings in the rocks allow you to get a wonderful view of some formations, including one of "Queen Victoria." The **Navajo Loop Trail** covers a distance of only 1-1/2 miles but it descends more than 500 feet. It leads to a section of the amphitheater known as Wall Street because of the high and almost perpendicular cliffs. It also goes to a formation called Thor's Hammer. Other trails vary in length from about a mile to eight miles. A couple of them descend as much as 900 feet. If that doesn't give you pause, just think about the fact that you have to come up the same 900 feet on the return trip. The rewards certainly justify the trek for those that can handle it. The scenery from under the rim is remarkable and completely different than from above. You'll often find yourself totally surrounded by the colorful and wildly shaped rocks. Some are relatively small and some are huge but each is beautiful in its own way.

You can make a quick jaunt through Bryce in under three hours if you are pressed for time. However, a full day is required to do a thorough exploration. If you are going to be trying some of the longer below the rim trails than more than a day should be allocated.

General Information: Tel. 435/834-5322. Write to the Superintendent, Bryce Canyon National Park, Bryce Canyon, UT 84717. Admission is by $10 pass good for 7 days or $20 annual permit for those not holding a valid park service passport. The visitor center is open daily from 8:30am to 4:30pm with extended afternoon hours in the peak travel season. It is closed only on New Year's Day, Thanksgiving and Christmas. The park is open all year but may be temporarily closed due to heavy snows. Regardless of the snow level, it remains open in the winter to cross country skiers, an unusual and exciting way to see the park. Horseback rides are offered by **Canyon Trail Rides***, Tel. 435/679-8665, from April through October.*

Upon leaving Bryce Canyon National Park return to UT 12 and turn left (west). You'll pass through a beautiful area known as **Red Canyon**. Located in the **Dixie National Forest** immediately to the west of Bryce, Red Canyon has magnificent vermilion colored rocks and tall ponderosa pines. There is a trail system and information kiosks along the road. The easiest walk is the **Bird's Eye Trail**. It's less than a mile and offers close up looks at the formations. The road itself offers excellent views and contains several tunnels that have been cut through the red rock.

BRYCE IS A WINTER WONDERLAND

The arrival of winter at Bryce Canyon brings with it a special magic. The clearest days, and therefore the best distant views, occur most often during the colder months. The lack of visitors creates a quiet solitude that brings the awe-inspiring surroundings up another notch. The snow atop the pinnacles has most often been described as icing on a cake. Touring the park on a pair of snowshoes or by cross-country skiing is a delight.

Many of the viewpoints near the road are kept open all year long although spur roads are usually closed. Because you can't reach all of the park's attractions during the winter I don't suggest a first time visit to Bryce during this period. If you do plan a winter trip always call in advance to check on conditions. There is a lot of snow during the winter and into early spring and it can sometimes close most of or even the entire park for days.

KANAB/LAKE POWELL & RAINBOW BRIDGE

UT 12 ends at US 89 where you should turn south. The 42-mile long stretch to Mt. Carmel Junction passes through several small towns. On your left will be nice views of the high plateau country on which Bryce lies. At Mt. Carmel Junction US 89 crosses UT 9. That road leads to Zion and on to St. George. However, unless you're cutting your southwest journey short, we'll ignore it for now and continue on US 89. About two miles past Mt. Carmel Junction is a paved cut-off road that leads several miles to the **Coral Pink Sand Dunes State Park**. Sand and high winds in this area between two mountains have caused the growth of dunes. The unusual color of the dunes is a result, once again, of minerals in the Navajo sandstone rock that has been pulverized over millions of years. A number of red rock formations serve as a lovely background to the unusually colored dunes. Boardwalks traverse several sections of the dunes. *Tel. 435/874-2408. The park is open at all times and there is a $4 daily vehicle use charge.*

You can return to US 89 the opposite way you came in or you can cut off a few miles by taking an unpaved road that ends up at US 89 at a point several miles south of where you left it. Either way your next stop is in Kanab, the only sizable community in this section of the southwest. But a little before you get into town (five miles north to be more exact) is **Moqui Cave**. The small cave contains a collection of Native American artifacts as well as colorful fluorescent minerals. It's only mildly interesting but children will probably like it. *Tel. 435/644-2987. Hours are daily except Sunday from 9:00am until 7:00pm during the period from Memorial Day through Labor Day and until 6:00pm during April to Memorial Day and after Labor Day to the end of October. Closed at other times. The adult admission charge is $3.50 while seniors pay $3 and children $1.50-2.50 depending upon age.*

In town are two attractions. The **Heritage House**, *100 S. Main Street*, was constructed in 1894 in Victorian style using materials available locally. The contents of the house include items from the original owners as well as from other old homes throughout Kanab. *Tel. 435/644-3506. House open Tuesday through Friday from 2:00pm to 6:00pm and on Saturday from 10:00am until 4:00pm. There is no admission charge.* The area around Kanab has beautiful scenery and has attracted motion picture makers for many years. This aspect of Kanab's economy is reflected at the **Frontier Movie Town**, *297 W. Center Street*. There's a museum as well as the original sets used in several motion pictures. During the evening a western style dinner show is presented (*Tel. 800/551-1714 for reservations. The cost is about $25. Credit cards*). *Tel. 435/644-5337. Movie Town is open daily from 8:00am until 11:00pm and there is no admission charge.*

From Kanab resume your journey on US 89. Along the way you'll travel through interesting and colorful scenery consisting mainly of the

Vermilion Cliffs. It's about 75 miles to just past the Arizona state line and the town of Page, base community for activities in the **Glen Canyon National Recreation Area** and **Lake Powell**. Although you generally will have to cross into Arizona in order to explore the region, almost all of Lake Powell and the surrounding recreation area lie within Utah. Nature, of course, recognizes no borders. (If you have your own boat to explore Lake Powell there are launching sites on the Utah side of the border.)

Within Page is the impressive **Glen Canyon Dam** that is situated in a deep red walled canyon. Self-guiding dam tours to the powerhouse are available. Several different boat rides on Lake Powell are offered. The options include a short one-hour trip that will acquaint you with the beautiful scenery from out on the water, a half-day trip or a full day. The latter are preferable because they visit the Rainbow Bridge National Monument. The longest trip obviously goes further but unless you have lots of time the half-day tour is the best choice for most visitors.

Lake Powell is 186 miles long and because of its many side canyons and coves has a coastline that measures a staggering 1,960 miles! Within the canyons are many Indian ruins. The deep blue waters of Lake Powell contrast with the dark red Navajo sandstone rock walls and, in the almost constant summer sunshine, is a gorgeous sight to behold. Unless you have your own boat you must travel on the lake via the National Park Service concessionaire, Lake Powell Resorts & Marinas, or Aramark. *Tel. 800/ 528-6154. Call for schedules and prices. Reservations are suggested. Departures are from the Wahweap Marina located between Page and the Utah line.* Another popular activity on Lake Powell is house boating. It's a pleasant and leisurely way to take in the terrific scenery. If you're interested in spending a few days out on the lake in this manner, Aramark is again the place to contact.

Rainbow Bridge National Monument is located in one of Lake Powell's twisting side canyons and is not visible until you are practically right on top of it. That makes the sight of this gigantic formation even all the more impressive. It is the largest natural bridge in the world, measuring 290 feet in height above the lake and 275 feet across. In addition to the sheer size Rainbow Bridge is special because of the near perfection of its form–the shape of the arch is almost exactly like that of a rainbow. Rainbow Bridge is sacred to many Native American tribes. For most visitors it is only accessible by boat on Lake Powell. (The land route through Arizona is by a rough 14-mile trail that must be done on foot or via horseback. Either way it is only for the most fit adventurers.) From the boat dock the trail to the bridge is short and easy. Be sure to walk directly beneath the bridge and look up.

Clearly visible from many parts of the lake but especially in the vicinity of Rainbow Bridge (out on the main lake, not in the side canyons) is the massive block of sandstone known as **Navajo Mountain**. This landmark sits just on the Utah side of the border. It can only be reached, however, by trail from Arizona–the same general land route to Rainbow Bridge mentioned in the preceding paragraph. The mountain is sacred to the Navajo and climbing on it is not allowed. Besides its historic, cultural and scenic interest, Navajo Mountain is actually massive enough to generate storms in the area. This probably helps to explain why the Native Americans were so in awe of it and have given it sacred status.

In addition to the boat tours from Wahweap, Lake Powell/Rainbow Bridge excursions also leave from Utah's Bullfrog Marina, further up the Colorado. See Chapter 13 if you want to make this excursion part of your southeast loop.

After completing your visit to the Lake Powell area make your way back on US 89 to Mount Carmel Junction. Then head west on UT 9. It's only about a dozen miles to the east entrance of Zion National Park. The road is known as the **Zion-Mount Carmel Highway** and is part of the larger **Zion Park Scenic Byway**. The Zion-Mount Carmel Highway, besides passing through some wonderful scenery (especially as it approaches Zion Canyon), is considered to be one of the great highway engineering works in the nation.

ZION NATIONAL PARK

Established in 1909, Zion is one of the nation's oldest national parks and one of America's greatest natural treasures. **Zion National Park** contains the most diverse landscape of Utah's many natural areas. Within its borders you'll encounter terrain that ranges from desert to lush vegetation, from barren rock to waterfalls cascading down rocky faces and vegetation clinging to the walls. There are colorful and unusual formations, many of which are especially noted for their mammoth size. Above all it is a landscape of cliffs and canyons that has been cut over eons via the action of the Virgin River, a process that continues to this day. At its mouth the Zion Canyon is about a half mile wide but by the time it reaches the end of the car accessible portion of the canyon it has narrowed down to only 300 feet. And it gets even narrower beyond that.

Part of the fun of seeing Zion, beyond the fantastic scenery, are the many fanciful names that have been given to the parks most notable formations. Some are perfectly descriptive but all are sure to inspire the imagination almost as much as the forms themselves. You'll meet all of them very soon.

Visitor services within Zion National Park are extensive but especially during the summer. Lodging, dining, camping and picnic grounds are available as is guided tram tour through Zion Canyon (extra fee charged) for those who don't want to make the canyon drive on their own or who arrive by other means than a private automobile. Park rangers conduct an extensive program of guided walks and talks that are both entertaining and highly informative. See the schedule posted at the Visitor Center at the southern entrance of Zion Canyon. Our tour will begin with the Zion-Mt. Carmel road section first and then go on into Zion Canyon. Should your tour be originating from the west side of the park (from the direction of St. George) you can do them in the reverse order.

As you enter Zion you will pass through the **White Cliffs** and soon reach the **Checkerboard Mesa**, an unusual gently sloping sandstone mountain with a pattern of cracks and grooves crossing it. It looks like an army of chiselers were kept busy for months but in reality it is all nature's own fabulous handiwork. The road will begin to twist in earnest after the Mesa and you'll drive through the first of two tunnels. This one is relatively short. Just before the second tunnel is a parking area for the **Canyon Overlook**. The mile-long round trip is relatively easy as it only ascends about 160 feet. At the end of the mostly fenced in trail, which has some steep drop-offs for the vertigo inclined, is a breathtaking view of portions of the Zion and Pine Creek Canyons.

Back on the road again you will soon enter the final tunnel called, appropriately, the Long Tunnel. As you drive through notice the areas of rock on the tunnel walls that have been cut out like windows. In the old days before there was much traffic you could stop your car in the tunnel and have a look. But that's dangerous and illegal now because Zion is heavily visited. The tunnel is only wide enough for two automobiles to pass in opposing directions. There are restrictions on vehicles wider than 7'10" or higher than 11'4". Vehicles exceeding those dimensions must be escorted through the tunnel for a fee. Inquire at the entrance station.

Emerging from the 5,600 foot Long Tunnel you'll enter one of the most exciting parts of a visit to Zion–the descent through the **Pine Creek Canyon** into Zion Canyon. You do so through a series of six switchbacks and average five percent grade. It's worthwhile to stop at one of the switchback pullouts for a longer look at the magnificent scene before you. High cliffs and colors of every sort surround you on all sides. After the final switchback it's about a half mile to the junction of the road into Zion Canyon. The canyon is to the right but you might want to make a short detour to the left first because that is where Zion's Visitor Center is located. If you are pulling a trailer or traveling in a camper that is longer than 21 feet you cannot travel into Zion Canyon. Use the shuttle service.

The six-mile long (each way) **Zion Canyon Scenic Drive** will bring you up close to many of Zion's most famous and beautiful formations. You have to get out frequently to see things as the narrow canyon walls that enclose you on both sides prevent getting a good view from inside of your

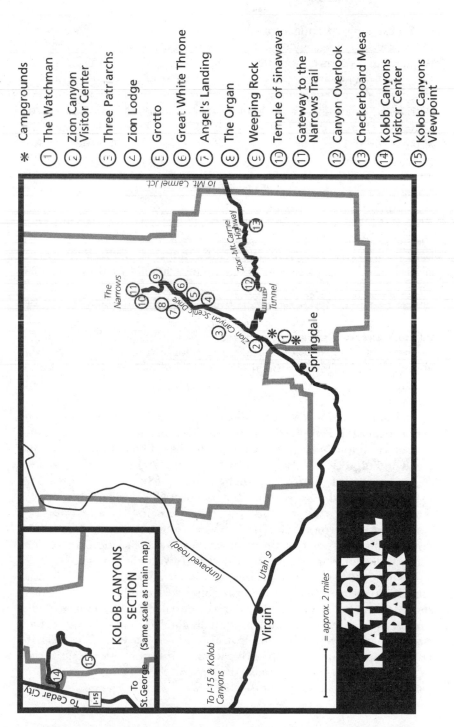

* Campgrounds
① The Watchman
② Zion Canyon Visitor Center
③ Three Patriarchs
④ Zion Lodge
⑤ Grotto
⑥ Great White Throne
⑦ Angel's Landing
⑧ The Organ
⑨ Weeping Rock
⑩ Temple of Sinawava
⑪ Gateway to the Narrows Trail
⑫ Canyon Overlook
⑬ Checkerboard Mesa
⑭ Kolob Canyons Visitor Center
⑮ Kolob Canyons Viewpoint

ZION NATIONAL PARK

KOLOB CANYONS SECTION
(Same scale as main map)

To Cedar City
I-15
To St. George

To I-15 & Kolob Canyons

Virgin

Utah 9

(unpaved road)

= approx. 2 miles

Springdale

Zion Canyon Scenic Drive

The Narrows

Tunnel

Zion-Mt. Carmel Highway

To Mt. Carmel Jct.

car unless you're driving a convertible with the top down. There are also many trails in the canyon that range from easy ten-minute walks to journeys that require more than a single day. The first pullout is at the **Court of the Patriarchs**. Cross the footbridge over the North Fork of the Virgin River for a closer look. Several tiers of mountains rise behind the Patriarchs. At another footbridge just to the south of Zion Lodge is the trail to the **Emerald Pools**. The trail is a little over a mile long and takes about an hour. It isn't overly difficult if you go only as far as the two lower pools and its pretty waterfall although there are some steep drop-offs. The larger upper pool requires a more difficult hike of another mile. The upper pool sits at the base of a huge cliff.

Soon after on the right side of the canyon drive is the **Great White Throne**, a 6,700-foot high monolithic rock that is almost pure white at the top but gradually changes to a shade of red as it works down toward the base. Then, as the road follows a bend in the river you'll be able to see several other famous monoliths including **Angel's Landing** and **The Organ**. By the way, most of the formations were named by a Methodist minister named Frederick Fisher, thus the heavy influence of religious themes. Immediately opposite The Organ is the parking area for the easy half-mile nature trail called **Weeping Rock**. It leads to rock that is always covered with the tears of a slowly dripping spring. This results in an abundance of vegetation on the rocks including colorful wildflowers during the spring and summer months. It makes for one of Zion's more unusual sights.

A little beyond the Weeping Rock area the Zion Canyon road will end at the beautiful **Temple of Sinawava**. This big natural amphitheater contains a couple of large stone pillars that have been dubbed **The Altar** and **The Pulpit**. What else? As beautiful as this sight is, it is not the end of your visit to Zion Canyon. From the Temple of Sinawava is the two-mile long **Gateway to the Narrows** trail. You'll probably think that the canyon is already kind of narrow at this point but it gets almost claustrophobic if you enter the Narrows itself. The Gateway is mostly paved and reasonably level and disabled persons can go on it if they have someone to assist them. You'll walk along the Virgin River past cliffs with hanging gardens.

Where the pavement ends the **Narrows** itself begins. This is a much longer and more difficult trail that requires rock climbing and wading in several feet of water. Proper clothing is essential. Be advised that thunderstorms can cause violent and potentially fatal flooding in the narrow canyon. This is especially true in the Narrows but can also affect the Gateway section as well. Do not attempt to enter either one in bad weather. You should also make inquiry at the Visitor Center about conditions before attempting the Narrows.

Now it's time to retrace your route on the Zion Canyon Scenic Drive. South of the visitor center on the way out of the park there is a good view of the **Watchman**, the sentinel mountain that stands guard over Zion Canyon. You should allow at least a half-day to see Zion. That will allow time for the drives and several of the shorter trails. Avid hikers will be able to spend several days considering the fact that Zion contains about 65 miles of trails.

Perhaps the only complaint you'll ever hear from visitors to Zion is that traffic along the Zion Canyon Scenic Drive was bumper to bumper. The Park Service has been aware of this problem for quite some time and beginning in May of 2000 is going to do something about it. From that time on visitors to the canyon will have to leave their cars at a new visitor and transportation center being built just outside the park in Springdale. Shuttles will carry you into the canyon and make frequent stops. This should actually enhance your visit to Zion as it will reduce congestion and allow you to spend more time seeing things rather than waiting for one of the increasingly scarce parking spots. Traffic on the Zion-Mount Carmel Highway will not be affected by this change. In addition, park visitors who are staying within the canyon at Zion Lodge will still be allowed to take their cars into the canyon.

General Information: Tel. 435/772-3256. For information write to Super-intendent, Zion National Park, Springdale UT 84767. The visitor center is open daily from 8:00am until 7:00pm from Memorial Day through Labor Day and from 9:00am to 5:00pm the remainder of the year. Zion can be visited at all times but there is snow during the winter months that may restrict activities. Admission is by seven-day permit costing $10 per private vehicle; $20 annual permit or a national park service passport. For horseback riding trips make inquiry at Zion Lodge.

After leaving Zion, travel 35 miles west on UT 9 back to I-15. From there it's only a five minute jaunt south into St. George and your starting point. Most of UT 9 has pleasant scenery consisting of distant mountains and red colored cliffs.

NIGHTLIFE & ENTERTAINMENT

You may have been surprised at the variety of entertainment options available in Salt Lake City. Well, the southwest (along with the remainder of the state) is definitely more in keeping with the "roll in the sidewalks" view of Utah after dark. Bars and lounges can sometimes be found in the larger hotels but don't expect to find nightclubs catering to out-of-town visitors. An exception is in the Brian Head ski resort near Cedar City. There are several clubs with live entertainment. The winter season is the most active. Nonetheless, despite the limitations, there are some things you can look forward to doing once the sun goes down.

CEDAR CITY

The previously described **Utah Shakespearean Festival** is an outstanding way to spend an evening or two.

ST. GEORGE

The outdoor musical *Utah!* that was described under seeing the sights is the premier theater event in town. Concerts and other events of general interest are sometimes held in St. George's **Dixie Center**, *700 East, Tel. 435/628-7003.*

SPRINGDALE

The nightlife in this small town on the edge of Zion National Park is mostly related to its location. The **Zion Canyon Cinemax** shows large screen 70-millimeter movies that chronicle the history of the region and the natural wonders of Zion. *Tel. 435/772-2400.* From May through September you can attend *The Grand Circle: A National Park Odyssey* at the **O.C. Tanner Amphitheater**. This impressive sound and light show begins at dusk and is projected on a 960 square foot screen with the towering rocks of Zion Canyon as a background. *Tel. 435/652-7994.*

SPORTS & RECREATION

Bicycling

Color Country possesses some of the most beautiful biking opportunities in America that range from easy to challenging. Because traffic is generally light in this region you could choose almost any road to lead you to scenic adventures. Among the most popular biking routes are along scenic byways such as Utah Highways 9 and 12 and in Bryce and Zion National Parks. Summer bikers might appreciate the cooler temperatures along trails in the Dixie National Forest. More difficult routes can be found along the route from Cedar City to Cedar Breaks or in the Brian Head area.

Bike rentals are available from the following locations:
- **Best Western Ruby's Inn**, *Bryce. Tel. 435/834-5341*
- **Bike Zion**, *1458 Zion Park Blvd., Springdale. Tel. 435/772-3929*
- **Brian Head Sports**, *Brian Head resort. Tel. 435/677-2014*
- **Cedar Cycles**, *38 E. 200 South, Cedar City. Tel. 435/586-5210*
- **Georg's Ski Shop & Bikes**, *Brian Head resort. Tel. 435/677-2013*
- **Moak's Bicycle Warehouse**, *1060 E. Tabernacle, St. George. Tel. 435/673-0878*
- **Mountain Bike Heaven**, *25 E. Center Highway 89, Panguitch. Tel. 435/676-2880*

Organized bike tours are available through the **Red Rock Bicycle Company**, *146 North 300 East, St. George, Tel. 435/674-3185* and the **Franklin Quest Institute of Fitness**, *202 North Snow Canyon Road, Ivins, Tel. 800/407-3002.*

Fishing
• **Big Rock Candy Mountain**, *Marysvale. Tel. 888/560-ROCK*
• **Boulder Mountain Flyfishing**, *Boulder. Tel. 435/335-7306*
• **Fremont Indian State Park**, *Sevier. Tel. 527-4631*

Golf
• **Canyon Breeze**, *Highway 153, Beaver. Tel. 435/438-9601.* 9 holes.
• **Cedar Ridge Golf Course**, *200 East 900 North, Cedar City. Tel. 435/586-2970.* 18 holes.
• **Coral Cliffs Golf Course**, *East Highway 89, Kanab. Tel. 135/644-5005.* 9 holes.
• **Entrada**, *2511 W. Entrada Trail, St. George. Tel. 435/674-7500.* 18 holes.
• **St. George Golf Club**, *2190 South 1400 East, St. George. Tel. 435/634-5851.* 18 holes.
• **Southgate Golf Club**, *1975 S. Tonaquint Drive, St. George. Tel. 435/628-0000.* 18 holes.
• **Sunbrook**, *2240 W. Sunbrook Drive, St. George. Tel. 435/634-5866.* 18 holes.

Hiking & Backpacking
During the narrative tour of the southwest you've already been introduced to the myriad hiking adventures that are available in this region. More experienced hikers will want to sample one or more of the following:
• **Kolob Canyons (Kolob Arch) Trail**, *Zion National Park.* 14 miles.
• **Narrows of the Virgin River Trail**, *Zion National Park.* 13 miles.
• **Under the Rim Trail**, *Bryce Canyon National Park.* 22 miles.

Other good hiking trails can be found in the Dixie National Forest (especially Red Canyon) and in the **Paria Canyon Wilderness** (38 miles east of Kanab off of US 89). Adventure hikes are the name of the game in many portions of the Grand Staircase-Escalante National Monument. Maps can be obtained from the BLM office in Escalante. Back country permits are required.

Horseback Riding
The Brian Head resort, Bryce and Zion national parks are the most popular venues for horseback riding in the southwest, but any part of the

region is well suited to this method of exploration. Try one of the following outfitters:
• **Bryce-Zion Grand Trail Rides**, *Tropic. Tel. 435/679-8665*
• **Escalante Scenic Trail Rides**, *Escalante. Tel. 435/826-4630*
• **Pack Saddle Trips**, *Hurricane. Tel. 435/635-4950*
• **Ruby's Outlaw Trail Rides**, *Bryce. Tel. 800/468-8660*
• **Scenic Safaris**, *Cannonville. Tel. 435/679-8787*

Hunting
The best hunting in the southwest is concentrated in the Fishlake National Forest. Hunting trips can be arranged through **Snow King Outfitters**, *Richfield, Tel. 435/896-8398.*

Off Road, ATV's & Four Wheel Drive Vehicles
Few places can compare with the **Paiute ATV Trail**, the 200-mile long route that was described in detail in a sidebar earlier in this chapter. Other good places to off-road in the southwest include the **Burr Trail** (leading south from Boulder); in the **Coral Pink Sand Dunes State Park**; and the road to **Hole-In-the-Rock** from Escalante. Guided tours and rental vehicles are available from the following:
• **Bushwackers ATV Rental**, *Marysvale. Tel. 435/326-4549*
• **Great Western ATV**, *Bryce. Tel. 800/432-5383*
• **Mount Holly Outfitters**, *Beaver. Tel. 435/438-2440*
• **Rainbow Country Tours**, *Escalante. Tel. 800/252-8824*

Skiing
All of the ski facilities listed below have equipment rentals and sales on site or nearby. The types of skiing available are shown by the following abbreviations:

DH–Downhill
SB–Snowboarding
XC–Cross-country

The numbers under "terrain" indicate the approximate percentage of runs for each level of experience; that is, Beginner (B), Intermediate (I) and Advanced (A).
BRIAN HEAD RESORT, *Brian Head. Located 12 miles from I-15, Exit 75 via UT 145. Main Tel. 800/272-7426; Snow Report Tel. 435/677-2055.*
Base elevation, 9,600 feet; top elevation, 10,920 feet. Full day adult lift ticket costs $35. [DH, SB, XC.] 53 runs; Terrain: B=30, I=40, A=30. 5 triple and one double lift. Night skiing available. Usual season is early November through late spring. School for skiing and snowboarding. Full children's ski program.

ELK MEADOWS, *Beaver. Located off of I-15, Exit 112 via UT 153. Main Tel. 888/881-SNOW; Snow Report Tel. 435/438-5433.*
Base elevation, 9,100 feet; top elevation, 10,400 feet. Full day adult lift ticket costs $30. [DH, SB.]35 runs; Terrain: B=14, I=62, A=24. 3 quad and 2 double lifts. Usual season is late November through mid-April. Lessons and children's program.

In addition to the above ski areas, the **Best Western Ruby's Inn** outside of Bryce Canyon National Park offers Nordic style cross-country skiing amid the spectacular terrain of Bryce. Call *Tel. 800/468-8660* for season and information.

SHOPPING

There isn't a whole lot of great shopping in the southwest. Most of what is available is concentrated in the St. George and Cedar City areas. St. George's two biggest retail establishments are the **Red Cliffs Mall** and the **Zion Factory Stores**. Both are located within a few hundred yards of one another on River Road/Red Cliffs Drive adjacent to I-15. Use the St. George Boulevard exit. The former is a fairly good-sized regional mall while Zion features 50 outlet stores with nationally known name brands. Downtown Cedar City has a number of interesting shops. Neither community has much Utah-related shopping but if you're looking for western wear then check out **Jolley's Ranchwear**, *52 North Main, Cedar City.*

You can sometimes find interesting gift shops in the small towns along UT 12. The best are in Escalante. Of special note are the Native American flutes at **Bear Flutes**, the **Crooked Thunder Trading Post** and **The Tribe**. There are also several art galleries featuring western paintings. Almost all of the shopping is along Main Street. The town of Springdale (just outside the main entrance to Zion National Park) and Ruby's Inn by Bryce Canyon National Park have plenty of souvenir shops that boast a variety of quality merchandise and cheap trinkets. The "general store" inside of the Best Western Ruby's Inn is huge and probably has the best selection.

PRACTICAL INFORMATION
Airport
    Cedar City, *2221 W. Kitty Hawk Drive, Tel. 435/586-3033*
    St. George, *Airport Drive, 435/634-3830*

Bus Depot
    Beaver, *935 N. Main, Tel. 435/438-2229*

Cedar City, *1355 S. Main, Tel. 435/586-9465*
Fillmore, *590 N, Main, Tel. 435/743-6876*
Parowan, *20 N. Main, Tel. 435/477-3421*
St. George, *1235 S. Bluff St., Tel. 435/673-2933*

Hospital
    Cedar City, *Valley View Medical Center, 595 S. 75 East, Tel. 435/586-6587*
        Kanab, *Kane County Hospital, 221 W. 300 North, Tel. 435/644-5811*
        St. George, *Dixie Regional Medical Center, 554 S. 400 East, Tel. 435/634-4000*

Hotel Hot Line, *Southern Utah Tourist Information & Services, Tel. 800/765-7710*

Police (non-emergency)
    Beaver, *Tel. 435/438-2358*
    Cedar City, *Tel. 435/596-2955*
    Kanab, *Tel. 435/644-5807*
    St. George, *Tel. 435/634-5001*

Taxi
    Cedar City, *Cedar City Cab, Tel. 435/559-8294*
    St. George, *Pete's Taxi, Tel. 435/673-5467*

Tourist Office/Visitors Bureau
    Cedar City, *585 N. Main Street, Tel. 435/586-4484*
    Escalante, *360 W. Main Street, Tel. 435/826-4810*
    Kanab, *78 S. 100 East, Tel. 435/644-5033 or 800/733-5263*
    Panguitch, *55 S. Main Street, Tel. 435/676-8826 or 800/444-6689*
    St. George, *97 E. St. George Boulevard, Tel. 435/628-1658*

13. SOUTHEAST UTAH: CANYON LANDS

While the southwest part of Utah has enough scenery to satisfy the toughest critic, the southeast doesn't have to play second fiddle to anyone. Some of the most awesome sights in nature can be found here. Colorful rock formations are to be found, certainly, but not in the same variety and quantity as in the neighboring region. What the southwest does have in abundance are magnificent canyons forged by the cutting action of several rivers, including the mighty Colorado. Canyons are such an integral feature of the southwest that I've decided to refer to the whole thing as **Canyon Lands**. (Canyonlands as a single word refers to a specific national park that is a highlight of the southwest. It is sometimes used in that form to reflect the dominant feature of the entire region. However, to avoid confusion I separate it when I'm not talking about the national park.)

Other impressive canyons can be seen in portions of the **Glen Canyon National Recreation Area**, along the **San Juan River** where they wind in sharp turns such as in the **Goosenecks State Park**, and in the incomparable **Dead Horse Point State Park** located next to **Canyonlands** itself. Unlike the Grand Canyon and many other canyons found elsewhere, the wonderful gorges of Utah's southeast aren't limited to the canyon itself. Because of the lay of the land you will often see spread before you a vast panorama of canyon in the foreground and rocky plateaus beyond with slight indentations that are actually other canyons. It is a scene like no other on earth.

The southeast also has a lot more than canyon after canyon amid plateau after plateau. Unusual geological formations are another important and widespread feature. Among the best known are **Arches National Park** and **Monument Valley** (the latter shared with Arizona), but there are many others. Just to whet your appetite with the names of a few, there are the **Fisher Towers**, **Goblin Valley**, **Mexican Hat** and the **Natural Bridges**

National Monument. The southeast is generally arid and harsh looking but it can be unexpectedly diverse, such as in the forested high country of the **Manti-La Sal National Forest**.

All of that scenery, of course, means great outdoor sporting adventures are available. The southeast has just about everything except skiing but whitewater rafting is probably the most popular. Those whose interests lie to man-made things will have much less to choose from. The entire region has less than 50,000 people and the largest community is home to only about 15,000 residents. The history of the area is closely tied to the Native Americans (a part of the Navajo Indian reservation extends into Utah's extreme southeast) and several ancient sites can be explored. Other towns have played roles in the exploration and settlement of the west.

ARRIVALS & DEPARTURES

It's likely that you'll be arriving in the southeast by car since common carrier transportation is limited, to say the least. But let's get them out of the way first. Air service via Alpine Air is available on a scheduled basis to Moab from Salt Lake City. Amtrak has one daily train to Green River and Greyhound serves Green River and a few other towns. However, they all leave you with the problem of getting around once you arrive.

The most direct route by car from Salt Lake City is I-15 to US 6 and then US 6/191 to I-70 near Green River. While Green River is the nearest point to Salt Lake City on the loop and can be your starting point for touring the southeast, I'm using Moab (54 miles southeast of Green River via I-70 and US 191) as the point of origination because it is the largest community in the heart of the canyon country. Moab is also convenient for travelers coming in from the east (from Colorado) via I-70 to Exit 212 and then UT 128 on into town.

Those coming in from Arizona will use US 163 and join the loop as soon as they cross into Utah at Monument Valley. Travelers from the west, including those who just explored southwest Utah will link up with the southeast loop via UT 24 at the town of Torrey near Capitol Reef National Park.

ORIENTATION

It's hard to get lost in the southwest because there are no large cities and not even that many important roads. Not counting a few relatively short rides that divert from the loop here and there, the southeast uses I-70 as its northern edge, US 191 as the long east side, US 193 and UT 261 for the small southern point and then UT 95 and UT 24 on the west edge of the loop.

The only towns of significance in the southeast are Green River in the north; and Moab, Monticello and Blanding on the east. The southern and western portions of the loop don't have any towns with so much as 2,500 people. For your information, however, some of the towns you'll pass through include Bluff, Mexican Hat, Gouldings and Hanksville.

GETTING AROUND

As just indicated, once having arrived in the southeast you absolutely need a car if you want to get around in an independent fashion. The only places you can count on to be able to rent a car in are Moab and Green River. While there are many operators offering day tours by any number of means of travel, there are few comprehensive regional tours. If that, however, is what you're seeking, then you might want to make inquiry with one of the following, all of which operate out of Moab:

• **Adrift Adventures**, *Tel. 800/874-4483*
• **Moki Treks**, *Tel. 435/259-4859*
• **Royal Coaches**, *Tel. 435/259-5353*

WHERE TO STAY
ARCHES/CANYONLANDS NATIONAL PARKS

There are no accommodations within either park. See Moab below.

BLANDING
Inexpensive

GRAYSON COUNTRY INN, *118 E. 300 South Street. Tel. 435/678-2388. Toll free reservations 800/365-0868. 10 Rooms. Rates: $49-59 including full breakfast. American Express, MasterCard and VISA accepted. Located immediately to the east of US Highway 191.*

An historic home from the area's pioneer days is now a pretty bed and breakfast inn that provides very comfortable accommodations at an extremely attractive rate. The rooms are spacious and furnished mostly in period. A couple of units have either efficiency or full kitchen facilities. The only drawback to the Grayson is that some rooms are not air conditioned. As this can be a problem during the hot southeastern Utah summers, you should be certain to book a room that does have air conditioning. The breakfast is a bountiful home-cooked affair. The restaurant selection in Blanding isn't extensive but several places are located within a short distance.

BLUFF
Inexpensive
RECAPTURE LODGE, *202 E. Main Street. Tel. 435/672-2281; Fax 435/672-2284. 28 Rooms. Rates: $42-48. American Express, Discover, MasterCard and VISA accepted. Located along US Highway 191 in town.*

Most of the accommodations in Bluff are of the small and quaint cottage variety or even more basic roadside motel units. Actually, the same can be said of most towns in the sparsely settled southeast so you had better get used to non-luxury living for a while. The Recapture Lodge is, believe it or not, Bluff's biggest lodging facility and the "fanciest." Your friendly hosts, Jim and Luanne Hook, will take a personal interest in your comfort and vacation activities by helping you to arrange area trips such as four wheel drive tours and even llama pack trips!

The lodge itself is a rustic style facility on nicely tree-shaded grounds. The rooms are clean and comfortable and perhaps a little bit above the "basic" level. There are some kitchen units as well as rooms with microwave and refrigerator. There isn't any air conditioning but you do have "swamp coolers." This air and water system is quite common in the older lodging establishments of southeastern Utah and while it doesn't provide the power of air conditioning it will generally do except during the hottest weather. A restaurant is located within walking distance of the lodge.

CAPITOL REEF NATIONAL PARK
There are no accommodations within the park. See Hanksville below or listing in the preceding chapter under Bicknell.

GREEN RIVER
Moderate
BEST WESTERN RIVER TERRACE, *880 E. Main. Tel. 435/564-3401; Fax 435/564-3403. Toll free reservations 800/528-1234. 51 Rooms. Rates: High season (April through mid-October): $79-120; Low season (mid-October through April): $59-89. Major credit cards accepted. Located in town along the I-70 business loop.*

The River Terrace is a slightly better than standard fare highway motel that offers nice sized comfortable rooms. The big swimming pool area (seasonal) is the inn's most attractive feature. Most rooms have hair dryers as well as an iron and ironing board. There are some third floor units but there isn't any elevator. Restaurants are located within a short distance.

HANKSVILLE

Inexpensive

FERN'S PLACE MOTEL, *99 E. 100 North. Tel. 435/542-3251 8 Rooms. Rates: $35-50. Located in town along the main highway.*

This isn't my idea of the ideal place to stay but for those traveling to or from Capitol Reef and needing accommodations on the west side of the park, there aren't any other nearby towns besides Hanksville and the choices here are severely limited. The rooms are clean and comfortable enough (some have kitchen facilities) for you to get a good night's rest. And that, after all, is all you're generally looking for in a town like Hanksville.

MOAB

Expensive

SUNFLOWER HILL BED & BREAKFAST INN, *185 N. 300 East. Tel. 435/259-2974; Fax 435/259-3065. 11 Rooms. Rates: High season (March through October): $155; Low season (November through February): $125. All rates include full breakfast. Discover, MasterCard and VISA accepted. Located about a quarter mile northeast of US Highway 191 via 100 North to 300 East.*

The greatest variety and highest levels of accommodations in the southeast can be found in Moab and the Sunflower Hill gets us off to a great start. This classic B&B facility features interesting architecture with many gables and is situated on attractively landscaped grounds. Bright and attractively decorated rooms with antique beds and colorful accessories will greet you upon the completion of a busy day in the nearby national parks. Besides the huge breakfast the Sunflower offers guests refreshments each evening. For relaxation try the outdoor hot tub or the tranquil wooded pathways. On cooler evenings you can warm yourself by the massive fireplace in the western style lounge.

Selected as one of my Best Places to Stay (see Chapter 10 for more details).

Moderate

AARCHWAY INN, *1551 N. Highway 191. Tel. 435/259-2599; Fax 435/259-2270. Toll free reservations 800/341-9359. 97 Rooms. Rates: High season (mid-March through October): $96; Low season (November through mid-March): $64. All rates include Continental breakfast. American Express, Discover, MasterCard and VISA accepted. Located on the main highway at the north end of town.*

What look's like a spelling error is more likely an attempt to ensure the first spot in any alphabetical listing of Moab accommodations. While it may not be Moab's best it is one of the nicest and newest places in town.

All of the units are extremely spacious and attractively decorated in a modern fashion. About a dozen rooms are upgraded "luxury" units with a private whirlpool at a slightly higher rate. Many units have a microwave oven and refrigerator. For recreation there's a heated swimming pool, Jacuzzi and a small exercise facility. The location at the northern end of town means that you'll have to make a short drive in order to obtain a choice of eating places.

CASTLE VALLEY INN, *424 Amber Lane. Tel. 435/259-6012; Fax 435/ 259-1501. 8 Rooms. Rates: $80-145 including full breakfast. Discover, MasterCard and VISA accepted. Located 15 miles north on US 191 and then east on UT 128 to the La Sal Mountain Loop Road. Take that road for just under two miles following signs.*

Not that Moab is such a big and busy place that you might want to avoid the heart of town, but the Castle Valley Inn has a secluded setting near the Colorado River that's definitely in touch with the natural surroundings. It certainly offsets the extra twenty minutes or so it will take to get to Arches and Canyonlands (as well as to restaurants). On the other hand, if you're exploring the La Sal Mountains area then the location is practically perfect.

This is a pretty little B&B with some units consisting of individual bungalows while others are in the main house. Three of the eight rooms have full kitchens. Try to get a room that has air conditioning since it can get real hot in this area and it takes quite a while for it to cool down in the evening. There is a two-day minimum stay on weekends and some restrictions on children so inquire before making your reservation.

LANDMARK MOTEL, *168 N. Main Street. Tel. 435/259-6147; Fax 435/259-5556. Toll free reservations 800/441-6147. 36 Rooms. Rates: High season (April through October): $86; Low season (November through March): $58. Most major credit cards accepted. Located in town on US Highway 191.*

One of the more attractive looking motels in Moab from the outside (the rooms aren't bad either), the Landmark is an "L"-shaped two story building with a semi-colonial look. Within the "L" is a large pool and recreation area that has a full size pool with water slide, child's wading pool and a hot tub. A few rooms have kitchen facilities. Restaurants are located within a short distance.

MOAB VALLEY INN, *711 S. Main Street. Tel. 435/259-4419; Fax 435/ 259-4332. Toll free reservations 800/831-6622. 127 Rooms. Rates: High season (March through mid-November): $85-125; Low season (mid-November through February): $67-80. All rates include Continental breakfast. Most major credit cards accepted. Located about a mile south of the town center on US Highway 191.*

There's nothing special about the Moab Valley Inn but it offers another reasonably priced choice and you may well need one in Moab because accommodations can fill up rather quickly with all of the great attractions at it's doorstep. The rooms are clean and well kept but a little on the small side. Some units have kitchen facilities. Restaurants are located within a short distance.

RAMADA INN MOAB, *182 S. Main Street. Tel. 435/259-7141; Fax 435/259-6299. Toll free reservations 800/228-2828. 84 Rooms. Rates: High season (mid-April through mid-November): $52-99; Low season (mid-November through mid-April): $35-89. Most major credit cards accepted. Located along the main highway in the center of town.*

While Ramada isn't an upscale chain, this is one of the most luxurious places to stay in Moab. The rooms are large and quite attractive. They feature modern furnishings and pictures of some of the famous nearby landmarks. Some rooms have balconies although the views aren't anything to speak of. For recreation you'll find a heated swimming pool and hot tub. Dining at the Ramada is one of the reasons to stay here. In addition to the informal and quick Pancake House, the Arches Dining Room is probably the best restaurant in town (see the *Where to Eat* section for details on the latter). The Ramada has three floors but no elevator, so if you have difficulty negotiating steps be sure to stay on one of the lower floors.

Inexpensive

RED STONE INN, *535 S. Main Street. Tel. 435/259-3500; Fax 435/ 259-2717. Toll free reservations 800/772-1972. 50 Rooms. Rates: High season (March through September): $60-65; Low season (October through February): $35-50. American Express, Discover, MasterCard and VISA accepted. Located along US Highway 191.*

The Red Stone is definitely the best buy in Moab. Not that the other lodging prices are high, especially for these days, but at the prices charged here you simply can't go wrong. It's one of the newer motels in town and the name aptly describes the attractive exterior appearance. Some rooms have kitchenette facilities. There's a nice looking barbecue and picnic patio area although there isn't any swimming pool or other recreational facilities. Restaurants and shopping are located close by, as the inn is only a few blocks from the center of town.

MONTICELLO

Moderate

GRIST MILL INN, *64 South 3rd East. Tel. 435/587-2597. Toll free reservations 800/645-3762. 9 Rooms. Rates: $66-86. Most major credit cards accepted. Located just to the east of US Highway 666.*

A delightful little B&B, the Grist Mill Inn was originally the Monticello Flour Mill when it was built in 1933. It served that function until as recently as the mid-1960's. Six of the guest rooms are in the old mill itself while an additional three are located in the adjacent granary. Every room is quite spacious and attractively decorated. The Grainery rooms all have kitchen facilities. The attractive public areas include a large sitting room with a fireplace, television room and a library. There's a hot tub on the premises and the screened porch area is a great place to relax after a busy day. A bountiful breakfast is served each morning in the dining room. Dinner is available by advance reservation or you can take advantage of some of the nearby restaurants in Monticello. Finally, a pretty gift shop on the premises offers authentic country crafts and other items of interest.

Inexpensive

BEST WESTERN WAYSIDE INN, *197 E. Central Street. Tel. 435/587-2261; Fax 435/587-2920. Toll free reservations 800/528-1234. 38 Rooms. Rates: High season (May through September): $69-74; Low season (October through April): $45-49. Major credit cards accepted. Located on US Highway 666 immediately east of the junction of US 191.*

This is an exceptionally well-kept little motel that although not particularly attractive, represents an outstanding value. The rooms, which are all recently remodeled, vary quite a bit in size and decor so you might want to take a look before checking in or just go for the higher rates–for a few extra dollars you'll be sure of getting a better room. All units have coffee makers and some have a microwave oven or refrigerator. A complimentary newspaper is given to all guests. There's a swimming pool and hot tub during the warmer months. Restaurants are available within a short drive.

TRIANGLE H MOTEL, *164 E. US 666. Tel. 435/587-2274; Fax 435/587-2175. Toll free reservations 800/657-6622. 26 Rooms. Rates: $24-59 with higher end of scale during the summer months. Major credit cards accepted. Located just to the east of the junction of US 191.*

While the Wayside is a little nicer you certainly can't go wrong for the rate charged at Triangle H. It's a small, friendly, family run motel that's clean and comfortable–nothing more and nothing less. No recreational facilities. Restaurants are nearby.

MONUMENT VALLEY/GOULDINGS
Moderate

GOULDING'S TRADING POST & LODGE, *1000 Main. Tel. 435/727-3231; Fax 435/727-3344. Toll free reservations 800/874-0902. 62 Rooms. Rates: High season (mid-April to mid-October): $108-128; Low season (mid-October to mid-April): $72-92. Major credit cards accepted. Located two miles west of US 163 opposite the entrance to the Monument Valley Navajo Tribal Park and just north of the Arizona state line.*

Perched on a low rock ledge within a stone's throw from Monument Valley, you couldn't ask for a much better setting for a place to stay than Goulding's. But it isn't only the location–this is a real nice lodge with a variety of services available. Originally started as a Navajo trading post, Goulding's has developed into a miniature town and the base for a lot of activities in the Monument Valley area. The front desk can arrange valley tours. An area museum is on the premises and a multimedia presentation entitled "Earth Spirit Show" is offered each evening.

Most of the rooms are in a modern and attractive two-story lodge featuring southwestern decor, but there are also a few separate cabins. All of the lodge units have excellent views. The **Stagecoach Dining Room** offers good meals in pleasant surroundings. It's the best place to eat in the area and that would probably be true even if it weren't the only place to eat. A quick cafe is also located in the trading post, which has an excellent selection of gifts, especially authentic Navajo arts and crafts.

CAMPING & RV SITES

National Parks and other federal lands: There are campgrounds in Arches, Canyonlands and Capitol Reef National Parks. Reservation information can be obtained through the park superintendent's office. In addition, the Bureau of Land Management operates many campgrounds throughout the southeast. Information is available from the Moab District office, *Tel. 435/259-6111.*

State Parks: Camping is available in Goblin Valley, Goosenecks and Dead Horse Point State Parks. The number for reservations is *Tel. 800/ 322-3770.*

For **commercial camping** and **RV sites**, try:
- **Goulding's Monument Valley**, *1000 Main, Monument Valley. Tel. 435/ 727-3235*
- **Kampark**, *861 S. Main, Blanding. Tel. 435/678-2770*
- **Jurassic RV Park**, *100 S. Center, Hanksville. Tel. 800/524-3433*
- **Mountain View RV Park**, *632 N. Main, Monticello. Tel. 435/587-2974*
- **Shady Acres RV Park**, *360 E. Main Street, Green River. Tel. 800/537-8674*
- **Turquoise RV Park**, *US 191 & 5th West, Bluff. Tel. 435/672-2219*
- **Valle's Trailer Park**, *US Highway 163, Mexican Hat. Tel. 435/683-2226*

WHERE TO EAT
BLANDING
Moderate

OLD TYMER RESTAURANT, *733 S. Main Street. Tel. 435/678-2122. American Express, Discover, MasterCard and VISA accepted. Breakfast, lunch and dinner served daily; closed Sunday during the winter months.*

A pleasant family style restaurant with comfortable surroundings that are a reflection of its name. The service is warm and friendly. Definitely the best place to eat in Blanding, the Old Tymer offers a surprisingly large menu that includes steak and prime rib, Mexican and chicken. There's a nice salad bar and a children's menu.

BLUFF
Moderate
COTTONWOOD STEAKHOUSE, *US Highway 191. Tel. 435/672-2282. MasterCard and VISA accepted. Dinner served nightly except Sunday.*

Standard fare steak and prime rib served in nice sized portions at a reasonable price in simple but attractive surroundings. The Cottonwood certainly isn't the best steakhouse in Utah but the choices in Bluff aren't very good when it comes to dinner time and this is the best of the lot.

GREEN RIVER
Moderate
TAMARACK RESTAURANT, *870 East Main. Tel. 435/564-8109. MasterCard and VISA accepted. Breakfast, lunch and dinner served daily.*

The nicest restaurant in town, this riverside eatery with a view serves well prepared American fare. Lunch buffet available. The service is friendly and efficient.

HANKSVILLE
Moderate
REDROCK RESTAURANT, *Center, on UT Highway 24. Most major credit cards accepted. Breakfast, lunch and dinner served daily. Closed in winter.*

The choices in Hanksville are exceedingly slim. This restaurant, adjacent to the campground of the same name offers decent American cuisine in reasonably attractive surroundings. When it's closed the only other choices are in the fast or semi-fast food category.

MOAB
Moderate
THE ARCHES DINING ROOM, *196 S. Main Street, in the Ramada Inn. Tel. 435/259-7141. Major credit cards accepted. Breakfast, lunch and dinner served daily.*

Long established as one of the more popular restaurants in Moab, the Arches serves typical American fare prepared in a simple style. The dining room is decorated with large pictures of some of the famous formations in Arches National Park. Children's menu. Beer and wine are served.

CENTER CAFE, *92 E. Center Street. Tel. 435/259-4295. Discover, MasterCard and VISA accepted. Dinner served nightly; closed in December. Reservations are suggested.*

Moab's finest dining spot, the Center Cafe is an extremely attractive restaurant with many colorful works of art and other interesting decor. The menu is the most eclectic in town and includes American cuisine along with some Continental dishes as well as a few entrees from just about all over the world. All are wonderfully prepared using the freshest quality ingredients that result in a plate that is delightful to look at and delicious to eat. The dishes vary from game dishes to seafood to gourmet pizza. The bread and pastries are all homemade and are a great part of the Center Cafe dining experience. Full cocktail service is available. Quite a few entrees do drift into the expensive category.

GRAND OLD RANCH HOUSE, *1266 Highway 191 North. Tel. 435/259-5753. Major credit cards accepted. Dinner served nightly. Reservations are suggested.*

Located in a former home that is now listed on the National Register of Historic Places, the Grand Old Ranch offers fine dining at a reasonable price. The fare is American and features prime rib, steak and seafood. It is well prepared and graciously served. A children's menu is available. Cocktail service.

SUNSET GRILL, *900 North Highway 191. Tel. 435/259-7146. Major credit cards accepted. Dinner served nightly.*

Located in an elaborate historic home that once belonged to a local uranium mining baron, the Sunset Grill is another excellent choice for dining in Moab. (At least there's one city in the region with an outstanding choice of restaurants!) An excellent panoramic view of the town can be had from the restaurant's hilltop location. Most of the menu is devoted to steak and seafood but there's also an excellent selection of pasta dishes. The food is delicious and the service is first-rate. Children's menu. Cocktail service.

MONTICELLO
Moderate

MD RANCH COOKHOUSE, *380 S. Main Street. Tel. 435/587-3299. MasterCard and VISA accepted. Breakfast, lunch and dinner served daily. Closed mid-November through February. Reservations are suggested.*

Here's an interesting place that can be enjoyed by grown-ups and children. The atmosphere recreates a western ranch. The emphasis is on casual fun. The cooking is a simple home style that is quite tasty and won't leave you wondering what was in it. Portions are quite generous. Many of the American menu items are western in nature including the trout.

Buffalo meat and burgers are served and you should try them–they're delicious. The desserts are excellent. Children's menu. Several entrees are available in the inexpensive price range.

Inexpensive
WAGON WHEEL PIZZA, *164 S. Main Street. Tel. 435/587-2766. No credit cards. Lunch and dinner served daily.*

As a former New Yorker I usually have trouble endorsing a lot of the so-called pizza that's found out west but this place does get it right. They also have a good selection of other pasta dishes and sandwiches. It's especially good for lunch although if you can make a dinner out of pizza then this is the place in southeast Utah to do so.

SEEING THE SIGHTS
MOAB & THE MANTI-LA SAL LOOP

Moab, population about 5,000 (second largest city in the southeast) has a wonderful setting, situated along the Colorado River at the base of rocky red cliffs for which the area is famous and also bordering on the high La Sal Mountains. It has seen a variety of eras in its history starting with outlaw days, movie making, and uranium mining. But tourism has been the longest lasting and the most important. It is the surrounding areas that have all the attractions, however. The town itself is a base for seeing some of the best things nature has to offer. In town is a small museum of local archeology and history. It is called the **Dan O'Laurie Memorial Museum**, *118 Center Street in the heart of town. Tel. 435/259-7985. Open daily except Sunday during the period April to October from 1:00pm to 8:00pm. Check for hours at other times. There is no set admission fee but donations are requested.*

An entertaining evening for adults and children can be had by attending the **Bar M Chuckwagon**, *just north of town on US 191.* A recreated western town is the scene of a nightly gunfight prior to dinner. That consists of a simple but hearty western meal served chuck-wagon style. It is followed by a cowboy stage show that's lots of fun. *Tel. 888/269-2697. Grounds open at 6:00pm and dinner begins at 7:30pm. Open daily except Sunday from June through September and on Friday and Saturday evenings only during April and May. The admission is $16 for adults and $8 for children ages 4 through 10. Credit cards.*

The two most important attractions in the Moab area are Arches and Canyonlands National Parks. However, before addressing them I'll take you on a less widely known but beautiful loop through the **Manti-La Sal National Forest** and another scenic byway. I should also mention at this point that Moab makes a great base for seeing a sizable portion of the

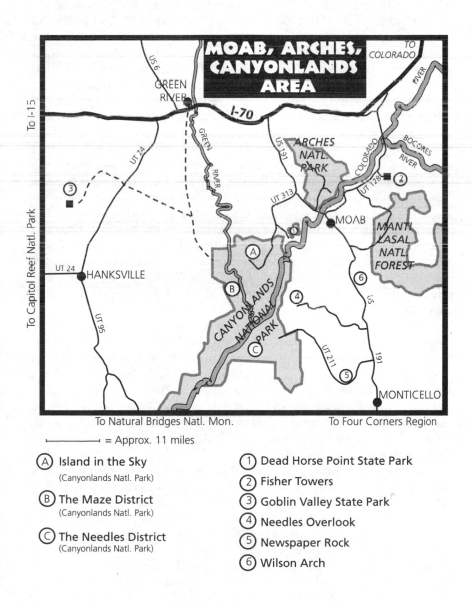

MOAB, ARCHES, CANYONLANDS AREA

To Natural Bridges Natl. Mon.   To Four Corners Region

⊢————⊣ = Approx. 11 miles

(A) **Island in the Sky**
(Canyonlands Natl. Park)

(B) **The Maze District**
(Canyonlands Natl. Park)

(C) **The Needles District**
(Canyonlands Natl. Park)

① Dead Horse Point State Park

② Fisher Towers

③ Goblin Valley State Park

④ Needles Overlook

⑤ Newspaper Rock

⑥ Wilson Arch

southeast. A full day can easily be spent at several places that are a drive of an hour or less from Moab.

Only three miles north of Moab, just before reaching the bridge over the Colorado River, is the junction with UT 128. Turn right and you're immediately on the **Colorado River Scenic Byway**. The road twists and turns along the winding course of the Colorado River not far above the water's level. The river isn't particularly wide at this point nor does it possess any special beauty. In fact, more often than not it will be kind of murky and muddy looking. Maybe not what you would expect from the mighty Colorado but the surrounding scenery more than makes up for it. Huge red sandstone walls tower above you on both sides and there are many side canyons that can be explored by trail.

About 18 miles up the byway you'll come upon the **Fisher Towers**, a cluster of red rock monoliths that soar almost 1,500 feet above the surrounding valley floor. Titan, the name given to one of the towers, is the highest in the group. The towers are clearly visible from the byway but you can get right up to them via a three mile graded dirt road. A two-mile long trail at the base of the towers allows for even more exploration. Then you can head back on UT 128. The **Castle Valley** will now be on your left. Many motion pictures have been made in this scenic valley which has several interesting rock formations including **Castle Rock**, the **Priest**, and **The Nuns**. All can be clearly seen from the **Manti-La Sal Loop Road** which branches off of UT 128.

The Loop road ascends the lower elevations of the La Sal Mountains, second highest range in Utah. In contrast with the arid terrain around most of Moab, this route will take you through thick forests, past cool looking lakes and streams and provide many excellent vistas of the canyon country. A small portion of the road is unpaved but it doesn't present any unusual difficulties. The Manti-La Sal road ends at US 191, which you can take back north to Moab. The entire loop covers a distance of approximately 60 miles. Along with the Colorado River Scenic Byway you can do it in a half-day jaunt from Moab.

But before returning to Moab there is one more attraction that's located on US 191 a little bit south of the junction with the loop road. The **Hole 'N The Rock** is a strange dwelling to say the least. Covering some 5,000 square feet, the "house" was carved out of a large sandstone rock formation over a period of some 20 years by a husband and wife team. Many of the furnishings, especially the paintings, were also done by the builder. They also carved the likeness of Franklin Roosevelt that appears on the face of the rock. It isn't a place of beauty but if you like to see something that's different then this fits the bill. *Tel. 435/686-2250. Tours of the house leave at frequent intervals daily from 9:00am until 6:00pm from Memorial Day through Labor Day and until 5:00pm the rest of the year. Closed*

New Year's Day, Thanksgiving and Christmas. Adult admission is $2.50 while children ages 6 through 12 pay $1.50.

ARCHES NATIONAL PARK

The entrance to **Arches National Park** sits at the base of a huge red rock plateau just five miles north of Moab via US 191. The park contains the greatest concentration of natural rock arches in the world. The exact number is subject to interpretation since various "experts" disagree as to how big a space has to be created to constitute an arch. The most conservative figure is about 1,500 but common practice claims more than 2,000 arches are present within the park's borders. Either way it's a lot, and you couldn't possibly see let alone count them all anyway. But Arches National Park is a whole lot more than arches. Within it you'll also find impressive and beautiful canyons of red rock and dozens of unusually shaped rock formations resulting from the various processes of erosion. There are also distant views of mountains and the ever present canyon lands.

ARCHES & BRIDGES...WHAT'S THE DIFFERENCE?

We've already encountered some natural bridges in our travels up to this point. Many people are under the impression that natural arches and natural bridges are the same thing and that the terms are interchangeable. While they may look alike a geologist would likely become violent at the thought of thinking they're the same. Lucky for you I'm not a geologist. The basic difference is in the process that forms the arch or bridge. Bridges are formed by the cutting action of water from a stream or river. The water literally cuts through the rock and only a section remains on top. While bridges are formed from the bottom up, arches are formed from the top down. Rain and wind are the two driving forces in the creation of an arch. The structure of the rock as well as other factors allows the top portion of the arch to remain intact while the area beneath it gets eroded away. The process is a slow but constant one. Many of the arches and natural bridges in existence today will eventually collapse. But others are being formed and will take their place.

Arches National Park is quite easy to see from your car and through a series of short walks. But there are also many miles of trails including some that are long and challenging. They range from a quarter of a mile to more than four miles long. The formations of Arches are a photographer's delight and while any time of the day is good the light in the morning or early evening is best if you want to capture the full flavor of the fiery red color of the rock. The road system within Arches covers about 45 miles of paved routes. In addition there are several primitive often sandy back roads that traverse even more remote sections of the park. Four-wheel drive is required on the latter. Arches is hot during the summer months and the sun is particularly relentless. Therefore, it is important to carry water if you're going to be doing any hiking. Visitor facilities in Arches are not that extensive. There is a walk-in campground on a first come-first served basis and a visitor center but no lodging or dining. Park rangers conduct various programs and guided walks. A schedule is posted at the Visitor Center.

As soon as you leave the Visitor Center the park road rises quickly and steeply to the top of the plateau. There's a good view of the US 191 corridor as you ascend. Upon reaching the top the remainder of the road is generally level although there are some dips and rises throughout as well as a few sharp turns but it is quite easy to drive. The first stop you reach will alone make a visit to Arches a worthwhile venture. This is the **Park Avenue Viewpoint and Trailhead**. The area is so named because of the large number of tall red sandstone formations that flank either side of a narrow valley. Indeed, they are reminiscent of the skyscrapers of Manhattan if you use a little imagination! The trail is a mile long and isn't difficult since it only involves a short drop to the canyon floor. However, it's two miles long if you return the same way. The far end of the trail comes out a little further up the road so if the driver is willing to forgo the trail, all the other passengers can walk it and meet up at the end. Or maybe one hearty soul can make the round trip by foot and get the car for everyone else.

The only point of interest on the road between the two ends of the trail is the **La Sal Mountain Viewpoint**, maybe the best spot in the park for taking in the distant panorama of mountains. At the north end of the Park Avenue trail are several interesting formations. These include **The Organ**, the **Courthouse Towers** and the **Three Gossips**. The shapes are almost self evident from the names but the last one is worthy of special mention. The cluster of three slender rock towers with head-like tops really does look a lot like three people (in the old days I would have said three women but I have to be fair, don't I?) standing around and discussing the doings or misdoings of the park's visitors.

Immediately beyond this area you'll pass a jumble of rocks known as the **Tower of Babble** before coming to the pretty **Petrified Dunes Viewpoint**. This is the most wide open space in Arches and the colorful terrain will make you think you're not even on earth! Up ahead on the road is the amazing **Balanced Rock**. How it doesn't tumble is beyond me. It's easily visible from the parking area or you can take the very short trail that surrounds it. Just past Balanced Rock is a split in the road. Go to the right on the 2-1/2 mile spur that leads to the **Windows Section** of Arches, certainly one of the more amazing sights anywhere in the park. Along the road are several more unusual formations including **Ham Rock**, the **Garden of Eden**, and **Parade of Elephants**. At the end of the road is a parking area with access to several popular trails. The mile long **Windows Trail** leads to the north and south windows (first three-quarters is easy; it's more strenuous if you want to continue to the second window). These arches do, indeed, look like windows of a huge rock house. The first is among the easiest arches to reach in the park and you shouldn't miss the opportunity to climb up into the arch and sit beneath its shade, look out and contemplate the amazing scene before you. Also in this area is another almost mile long trail, this one to beautiful **Double Arch**. The trail is sandy in some places.

Now return by car to the main road and continue to the right. Stop briefly for the big-picture view at awesome **Panorama Point** before coming to another junction. Turn to the right for the two-mile ride to the end of the spur and the **Delicate Arch Viewpoint**. Delicate Arch has an opening of 35 feet and is one of the most beautiful of all the arches in the park. From this vantage point it is clearly visible although, because of the distance, it appears quite small. Binoculars are helpful. If you want to get to the arch on foot you can do so via the **Delicate Arch Trail** that starts on the spur about halfway back to the main road. The trail is three miles round trip and has an altitude gain of almost 500 feet. Between that and the fact that there is no protection from the sun, it isn't one of the easier trails. The rewards, especially in the late afternoon or early evening sunlight, justify the effort for those who are fit enough.

Upon returning to the main road turn once again to the right. Two nearby overlooks, the **Salt Valley Overlook** and the **Fiery Furnace Viewpoint** are top-notch. The Fiery Furnace is an area of large rocks whose color is unusually intense. Several miles further up the road is a trailhead that leads to **Sand Dunes Arch** and **Broken Arch**. The first is only a little more than a quarter of a mile and the latter is over a mile. However, both are easy. The trail to Sand Dunes goes through the sand. The only problem is that the sand can become quite hot during the summer. Be sure you're wearing sturdy shoes and avoid the temptation to go barefoot. A little further up the road is **Skyline Arch** which can be seen closer up via a half mile trail over some rocks.

The road ends at the **Devil's Garden** an area that contains many of the most spectacular arches. Unfortunately, all of the trails here are rather long and mostly difficult. On the positive side is the fact that one of the best arches, **Landscape Arch**, can be reached by the easiest and shortest (1-1/2 miles) trails in the Devil's Garden. Landscape Arch stretches for a little more than 300 feet across and is more than a hundred feet high, making it one of the largest arches in the world. In some places the arch is only six feet thick.

After completing all of these wonders it's time to head back along the main road and leave Arches. You can make a quick cursory visit in about just under three hours but I suggest that you allow at least a half day (a full day is better) to get out and do some more exploring. If you are going to be exploring the back country and via some of the unpaved roads in Arches you'll need more than a day for your visit. Be sure to inquire at the visitor center as to conditions before setting out and make certain that you carry plenty of drinking water with you.

General Information: Tel. 435/259-8161 or write, Superintendent, Arches National Park, PO Box 907, Moab UT 84532. Visitor Center is open daily 7:30am to 6:30pm from March through October and from 8:00am to 4:30pm the rest of the year. Admission is by 7-day permit costing $10 or annual permit for $25 to those not holding a valid national park service passport. The admission pass is also good at Canyonlands National Park. During the winter months the weather is quite comfortable and snow can be seen on nearby mountain peaks.

CANYONLANDS NATIONAL PARK & DEAD HORSE POINT STATE PARK

Arches is spectacular but so is Canyonlands. So nearby geographically but far apart geologically, **Canyonlands National Park** is surely going to be one of the most memorable sights you've ever had the good fortune to gaze out upon. An amazing panorama of thousand foot deep canyons, high mesas with towering vertical red walls and almost countless unusual rock formations all await you. The Green and Colorado rivers are the primary forces that have shaped Canyonlands and the two rivers converge within its confines in a series of rapids, including the wild **Cataract Canyon**. The rivers divide the park into three distinct sections, each one different from a geologic point of view and physically separate from one another as well.

If seen from high in the sky Canyonlands would look almost like three pieces of a giant jigsaw puzzle that have been matched up by the solver but not yet put together–the spaces between the pieces are the river filled canyons and the pieces themselves the high ground of the three sections. The sections, known as districts, are the Island in the Sky, The Maze, and The Needles. The first is the easiest to reach and travel around in and, hence, the most heavily visited. There are good roads and easy hikes in Canyonlands, especially in the Island in the Sky, but much of Canyonlands is wild back country and is among the most rugged in the nation. That makes it a delight for the adventurer, too.

The three districts of the park are not connected by road and even the adventure traveler cannot readily get from one to another. Each section has to be visited separately. The Maze isn't particularly near anything and we'll take a brief look at it on our way out of the Green River area. Both the Island in the Sky and The Needles are close to Moab, but in different directions. You can visit The Needles on a day trip from Moab but I'll have you going there at the end of the southeast loop as you return to Moab. For now, then, we'll concentrate solely on the **Island in the Sky**.

The entrance to the Island is located about 30 miles from Moab via US 191 north to the junction of UT 313. The latter road is the entry way into the park and is a wonderfully scenic drive that turns and climbs through a colorful canyon of red walls. Once you reach the top you're on the Island in the Sky and will come upon the park's main visitor center in about a mile. Continuing past the visitor center you'll immediately reach the **Shafer Canyon Overlook**, a beautiful vista of a deep red canyon. You'll see a dirt road that leads into the canyon where some early mining took place. The **Shafer Trail Road** can be taken into the canyon itself. This four-wheel, high clearance vehicle road is quite challenging and should only be attempted by the experienced dirt road and mountain driver. Opposite the overlook is the beginning of the **Neck Spring Nature Trail**, the easiest in Canyonlands. It isn't nearly as scenic as most of the others but does acquaint you with some of the flora in what appears at first to be a rather desolate landscape.

A little more than five miles further down the main park road you will come to a junction in the road. Both directions off the junction are dead

---

DESERT VARNISH

*Throughout the canyon country and even in many other parts of Utah and the southwest you will see dark streaks on canyon walls and rock faces that almost seem as if they were painted on by ancient Native Americans. But this is naturally occurring **Desert Varnish**, which is a mixture of airborne dust and clay left from evaporating water. Showing up in a multitude of colors and patterns that are often quite beautiful and amazing, it is even more surprising to learn that desert varnish is actually alive! A combination of bacteria and fungi are literally cemented to the sandstone. The colors are dependent upon the minerals in the mix. If it is rich in iron then the varnish will be either red or rust colored. If there is ample manganese then it is black or, if you're lucky, a beautiful iridescent shade of blue-black. Look for desert varnish during your travels. It isn't hard to find.*

ends so it doesn't matter which way you go but let's start to the right. Take the road to its end, a distance of another five miles. This is the parking area for the trailhead to **Upheaval Dome**. The trail covers about a mile over rocks and is quite uneven but not overly difficult. It is believed by geologists that the 1,500 foot dome was once a huge salt cavern. Although it's called a dome it looks more like a crater and is one of the oddest features in the park. On the way back on this portion of the road you can make brief stops at the **Holeman Spring Canyon Overlook** and the **Green River Overlook**. The second, and more spectacular view, is reached by a short unpaved spur road. From the desolate viewpoint is a magnificent vista of the Green River canyon as well as many other smaller canyons, mountains and odd formations that look almost as if they're giant pieces of furniture in some mammoth creature's living room.

At the junction with the main road continue straight on the other spur. This portion of the road stretches for about six miles. En route you'll want to stop at the **Candlestick Tower Overlook** where the scenic attraction is adequately described by its name, the **Buck Canyon Overlook** and the colorful spectacle of the **Orange Cliffs Overlook**. The exact color of these formations will depend upon the lighting and they may not appear orange when you see them. But regardless of the time and color, it is an out-of-this-world sight.

The road ends at the **Grand View Point Overlook**. From here you will look out on an endless panorama of canyon after canyon. Actually, it isn't that many canyons but appears that way because of the turning of the Colorado River. Beyond the flat mesa, which houses the deep gorges, are colorful mountain peaks. You cannot see the river bottom from this vantage point, only the tops of the canyons. Because of the vast size you can't tell how deep they are and in some ways it doesn't look that big when you concentrate on just one small area. But the attraction of Grand View, and it is one of those places that will keep you riveted to the spot, is the overwhelming immensity of the canyon country that lies beneath you. Once you can drag yourself away it's just a matter of retracing the main road and following UT 313 out of the park. You should allow a minimum of two hours to explore Islands in the Sky but the more adventurous will have no trouble spending a full day.

If you're looking for a more difficult auto route, in addition to the aforementioned Shafer Canyon Road, then get information at the Visitor Center about conditions on **White Rim Road** which follows the course of the rivers creating the Island in the Sky on a level beneath the mesa top. It's a really wild ride!

General Information: Tel. 435/259-7164, or write Superintendent, Canyonlands National Park, 2282 SW Resource Blvd., Moab, UT 84532. The visitor center is open from 8:00am until 6:00pm daily during the summer season *and has varying hours at other times. The weather is suitable for a visit at any time of the year. The heat in summer makes it important to carry water. Admission is by $10 permit good for seven days or $20 annual permit for those people not holding a valid park service passport. There is camping in the Island in the Sky and picnic tables but no food or lodging services.*

Now that you're leaving Canyonlands National Park and you think that you've finally "seen it all," you're in for a smaller but no less spectacular surprise. A few miles after the park exit follow the signed side road for the ten minute ride to **Dead Horse Point State Park**, surely the most gorgeous sight in the outstanding Utah state park system. There is a visitor center that explains the history and geology of the area as well as overlooks and short trails behind the center and a mile or so down the road at the Dead Horse Point Overlook. The park's name is based upon an actual event. A group of wild mustangs was herded into the area because of its natural corral like environment. Contrary to the expectations of the cowboys who herded the horses, the poor animals died of thirst. That is ironic because they were in view of the Colorado River.

And what a view it is. While this park certainly cannot compete with Canyonlands, Bryce or Zion in size, diversity of terrain or in unusual formations, the panorama from **Dead Horse Point Overlook** may well be the single most beautiful vista in Utah and the half hour or so you spend in the park will be among the best decisions you ever made. You'll be standing 2,000 feet above the Colorado River and watch as it slowly flows through the canyon in a series of graceful turns. The mesas between several bends in the river are only about half the height of your vantage point, giving you a bird's eye view of canyons like nowhere else. Many pinnacles and buttes are also visible, and the changing display of colors depending upon the sunlight conditions is fantastic. *Tel. 435/259-2614. Visitor Center open daily from 8:00am until 6:00pm (to 5:00pm from the middle of September to around mid-May). There is a $4 daily vehicle use charge.*

Upon exiting Dead Horse Point State Park you'll return to UT 313 and either make your way back to Moab for the night or continue on with the southwest loop in the direction of Green River.

Since it's almost certain that you'll be spending at least one night in Moab you might want to consider taking a pleasant evening boat ride on the Colorado River. **Canyonlands By Night** offers flat-bottom boat trips suitable even for the most cowardly traveler. It travels along a calm section of the river adjoining scenic highway UT 128. Spotlights illuminate the cliffs and the narration tells about the geology and human history of the region. The lighting isn't powerful enough to make this a substitute for daytime touring but the experience is an interesting one. Similar boat rides are also given during the day. Boats leave from the north side of the

Colorado River bridge on US 191. *Tel. 800/3949978 or 435/259-5261. Call for time schedules, fare information and reservations.*

ROLLIN' ON THE RIVER

River running in Utah's canyon lands is among the best places for this activity anywhere in the United States and is extremely popular. What makes it even more appealing to visitors is that many parts of this remote region can only be seen from the river. Several portions of Canyonlands National Park, for example, can only be seen in this manner. You've already learned that the Colorado and Green Rivers meet in Canyonlands. Both rivers, along with the nearby Dolores, are the places to take to the river in Utah.

Some of you, no doubt, will not be to thrilled to hear that river-borne transportation is the only way to see some of the best scenery because white-water and you don't mix. No problem. Not all of the river running of canyon country is wild. Calm water float trips lasting from a couple of hours to several days can be had on long stretches of the Green River and there are even some short calm sections along the Colorado. The latter even has nighttime calm water trips. On the other hand, if white water appeals to you then you can certainly find it at its wildest on both the Green and Colorado. One section of the Colorado through Westwater Canyon features 1,000 foot high cliffs and no less than eleven rapids. Wow!

A long list of river operators of both types along with some details about the trips can be found in the Sports & Recreation section of this chapter.

GREEN RIVER & GOBLIN VALLEY

Proceed north from Moab on US 191 to the junction of I-70 and then travel west on the Interstate for two exits (get off at #162) at the town of Green River. Despite its Interstate location, Green River sits astride the spectacular scenery that envelops the river of the same name. To the north is wild and remote **Gray Canyon** and to the south the river twists endlessly into Canyonlands. River trips in both directions are offered (see *Sports & Recreation*). Unpaved but two-wheel drive accessible roads also lead in both directions. Inquire locally for further information.

The main attraction within the town itself is the **John Wesley Powell River History Museum**. The large and attractive museum documents the explorations of Powell as well as the early history of the region. An exhibit on river running includes a river runners "Hall of Fame" and is also of interest. The museum features automated figures, maps and dioramas as well as a continuous showing of a 20-minute multi-media presentation. The gift shop has a good selection of unique souvenirs. *Tel. 435/564-3427. Operating hours are daily from 8:00am to 8:00pm, April through October and 8:00am to 5:00pm the remainder of the year. It is closed on New Year's Day, Thanksgiving and Christmas. The admission is $2 for adults, $1 for students with identification. There's also a $5 family rate.*

A number of scenic points of interest are located along or near to I-70 in the vicinity of Green River. The first is the **Crystal Geyser**, located about eight miles from town via the south frontage road of I-70 and then on a gravel road for about five miles. This isn't a naturally occurring geyser like in Yellowstone. It was the result of a petroleum test well in 1936 hitting a section of the Green River. It erupts three or four times a day and lasts about seven minutes each time. The water may reach heights of up to 60 feet and sometimes higher. The Crystal Geyser is unusual in that it is a cold-water geyser. Unfortunately, eruption times are unpredictable.

Two other sights are just off of I-70 to the west of town. The **Black Dragon Pictograph** is reached by a dirt road just past mile marker 145 (it isn't a regular exit) and then for about 1-1/2 miles following several washes. You have to cross a couple of the usually dry washes, which may present a problem for regular automobiles. The winged dragon is the most outstanding of several ancient paintings found on the rocks in this area. Part of the second attraction is much easier to reach and is known as the **San Rafael Swell**. The swell is a large uplift in the earth's surface located 19 miles west of Green River. The area contains beautiful sandstone formations and canyons covering more than 2,000 square miles.

You can see quite a few features of the swell from along I-70 between exits 147 and 114. Adventure travelers can make use of a network of back country and often primitive routes both north and south of the Interstate highway for a full day exploration. In order to navigate through the confusing maze of "roads" you should obtain a large-scale area map from the BLM in Green River beforehand. For everyone else, how far west you go to see the swell and the accompanying **San Rafael Reef** depends upon how much time you have. You can turn around and head back either at Exit 129 or 114 or skip them altogether if you want to stick to the main touring route.

At Exit 147 of I-70 is the beginning of UT 24. This road is the gateway for several routes into **The Maze** district of Canyonlands National Park. Perhaps the "easiest" way into this rugged region are a couple of unpaved roads that lead to, respectively, **Horseshoe Canyon** and **Hans Flat**. Beyond each are more primitive roads that interconnect and lead to two points from where you will be able to see a panorama of The Maze.

Panorama Point Overlook and **Maze Overlook** are the destinations for those with high clearance 4-wheel drive vehicles. Regardless of whether you're going to be attempting to get to The Maze, follow UT 24 from the Interstate for 23 miles to Temple Mountain Road. Then go 12 miles (the last seven being unpaved but easily negotiable in a regular car) to the unusual **Goblin Valley State Park**. The park contains literally thousands of eroded sandstone formations in an endless variety of shapes and sizes. Most are fairly small and frequently look like goblins, gnomes or other weird creatures, hence the name of the park. While the majority have a grayish color there are enough other colors to even make it look kind of pretty in a weird sort of way. Children will be delighted by the shapes. You can see the goblins from the parking area at the end of the road or you can take some more time to venture out and walk among them. If the goblins say anything to you it probably means you've been out in the sun too long. *Tel. 435/564-3633. Open at all times. There is a $3 vehicle use charge. Picnicking. Facilities are limited.*

Then return to UT 24 and continue on your journey through this sparsely settled area. The only town of significance (if you can call it that) is Hanksville, which lies about half-way between Goblin Valley and the next destination, the spectacular Capitol Reef National Park.

CAPITOL REEF NATIONAL PARK

The park's name is derived from the reef-like cliffs that stretch for miles through this remote section of the state. They're topped in many places by white sandstone that does look a bit like the United States capitol building. Capitol Reef is part of an immense geologic formation called the **Waterpocket Fold**. The fold stretches for some hundred miles and, to geologists, shows much of the building process of the earth including uplifting, folding, and eroding. The erosion process has left large "pockets" in the sandstone that can hold rainwater.

Capitol Reef has been known for some time and was a national monument. It was only designated a national park relatively recently, not for lack of wonderful scenery but because of its remote location. This splendid treasure of nature is lightly visited compared to most national parks, even many in Utah, and makes a wonderful way to get closer to nature. That can be done the easy way, via the park's two main roads, or by hiking the many trails. UT 24 runs from east to west through the central section of the park while the 25-mile long Scenic Drive provides access to even more sights.

Coming in from the east, UT 24 parallels the **Fremont River**, an important factor in the early settlements in this area. Pleasant scenery gives way to the massive **Capitol Dome** formation on the north side of the

4-WHEELING IT IN CANYON COUNTRY

Just as popular as river running as a means of getting to out of the way places in canyon country is a jaunt via a four-wheel drive vehicle along primitive roads or even no roads. Few places in the world are as suited to this type of adventure exploration as is southeastern Utah. There aren't as many formalized backways as in the southwest but for some that means the wild nature of the adventure is even better. You can get detailed four wheel drive trail guides in Moab or from the Bureau of Land Management offices. Rentals are available in Moab if you aren't driving your own 4-wheeler or you can go on guided tours if you don't think you can handle the driving (or if you're afraid of getting lost in the wilderness). Rental agencies and tour operators are listed in the Sports & Recreation section but for now here's a brief rundown on some of the more popular four wheel drive trails in the region.

***Chicken Corners Trail:** 22 miles, one way. Descends to the Colorado River west of Moab and follows the bends in the waterway to a point opposite Dead Horse Point.*

***Gemini Bridge Trail:** 14 miles connecting US 191 between I-70 and Moab and UT 313.*

***Monitor & Merrimac Buttes Trail:** 15 miles through colorful canyons and mesa lands in the Islands in the Sky district of Canyonlands.*

***Poison Spider Mesa Trail:** 16 miles along a mesa on the north side of the Colorado River west of Moab. Has great mountain views.*

***Potash Scenic Byway:** This 34 mile round-trip via UT 279 can be attempted in good weather without 4-wheel drive and thus may not really qualify for listing here. However, it's not your ordinary Sunday drive. It follows the Colorado River from three miles north of Moab on US 191. There are several pullouts along this spectacular drive that will provide views of towering cliffs, petroglyphs, arches and other wonders.*

*In addition to the above, excellent four-wheel and off-road opportunities exist in the **Abajo Mountains** area of the southeast reached from either Blanding or Monticello.*

river and then you'll reach an area where trails run parallel to the road and river. Here you'll find remains from an early Mormon farming community as well as petroglyphs created by ancient Native American groups. There are even orchards and groves where you can pick fruit. Soon after you'll reach the visitor center at the junction of Scenic Drive. After stopping to view the exhibits continue west on UT 24 almost to the park's western boundary. Right along the north side of the road are some of the most impressive rock formations in Capitol Reef.

The Castle, **Chimney Rock** and **Twin Rocks** are among the best and there are pullouts for each. The castle perched high on the ridge and containing hundreds of tall fracture columns that look like turrets is a most awesome sight. But even more inspiring than the individual formations is the massiveness of the Reef and its layers of different colors. It's not hard to imagine that thousands of workers scaled these gigantic cliffs and performed the greatest paint job in the history of the world! Nature, however, has done it for us and the result is miraculous and beautiful. On the south side of the road is a short spur (about a half-mile) that leads to **Panorama Point** from which a short walk up a rocky trail takes you to an overlook of the **Goosenecks**. Here you can see a colorful twisting canyon created by the Sulphur Creek. A trail from Panorama Point in the opposite direction leads to **Sunset Point** and its great view of cliffs and domes. The combined trails are well under a mile and are not difficult.

Once you've taken in all the sights in this section of the park return to the junction of **Scenic Drive** and turn right. This paved road parallels a portion of the reef and, besides the marvelous scenery, provides access to a number of excellent trails. At the end of the paved portion of the road is the interesting looking **Egyptian Temple** rock formation. A short unpaved side road leads into **Capitol Gorge** and ends at **The Tanks**, one of the formations that gives the Waterpocket Fold its name. You can also leave your car at the end of the pavement and walk the mile through the sheer color-filled walls of the gorge. From The Tanks there's a two-mile trail to the base of the **Golden Throne**, which has magnificent views. The trail is steep and difficult.

Other trails along the Scenic Drive include the **Grand Wash** (2-1/4 miles, mostly level) and more canyon scenery as well as the three-mile and strenuous **Frying Pan Trail** that follows the ridge of Capitol Reef. Maps and brochures at the visitor center will list additional hiking possibilities. You can also continue south past the end of Scenic Drive on the difficult but passable Pleasant Creek Road and, if you have a four-wheel drive high clearance vehicle, further still on the South Draw Road. Both continue along the Waterpocket Fold past the seemingly endless colorful cliffs of the reef.

A visit to Capitol Reef will require a minimum of two hours just to do the main drives and a few short trails. The longer trails or a drive further along the Waterpocket Fold and back can take anywhere from a few hours to a whole day. *General Information: Tel. 435/425-3791, or write Superintendent, Capitol Reef National Park, PO Box 17, Torrey, UT 84775. The visitor center is open daily from 8:00am until 7:00pm from Memorial Day through Labor Day and until 4:30pm at other times. It is closed on Christmas. Admission is by $4 permit for each vehicle to those not holding a valid park service passport.*

The park has a campground and picnic tables but there is no food or lodging service and limited ranger activities.

When you're ready to depart from Capitol Reef return to UT 24 and head west, retracing your route as far as Hanksville. (As was mentioned in the preceding chapter, Capitol Reef lies at the edge of the southeast region and is only a couple of miles from the southwest regional loop. So, this is the ideal place to link up or combine portions of the two regions.) At Hanksville get on UT 95 in a southerly direction. Be sure that you have a full tank of gas before leaving Hanksville–it's the last "civilization" for some time.

MORE CANYONS & NATURAL BRIDGES

UT 95 stretches for almost a hundred miles from Hanksville to Natural Bridges National Monument (and continues for a time past there to Blanding). It is one of the most scenic highways in the state, traversing one of the most remote regions in the United States. There are few towns or services. So remote is the area that there was no highway here at all until 1976. Because of the year of its completion the road is sometimes called the **Bicentennial Highway**. Along the way you'll pass through magnificent sandstone gorges that are especially beautiful in the vicinity of the Colorado River which UT 95 crosses near the southern end of **Cataract Canyon**.

At the junction of UT 275 take that road for six miles into **Natural Bridges National Monument**. I hope you remember the lesson on the difference between natural bridges and arches because you won't find arches here. What you will find, however, is perhaps the only place in the

AN ALTERNATE WAY TO RAINBOW BRIDGE

*Boat trips to **Rainbow Bridge National Monument** are most frequently taken from Page, Arizona as was described in Chapter 12 (and you should refer to it for contact information). However, you can do the same from the Bullfrog Marina. Take UT 276 from UT 95 to reach it. If you're coming from Hanksville UT 276 leaves UT 95 26 miles south of Hanksville and goes for 46 miles to the marina. If you're coming the other way, leave UT 95 seven miles north of the cutoff for Natural Bridges National Monument and take UT 276 for 42 miles to Hall's Crossing. At that point a ferry will take you to the other side of the Colorado River and Bullfrog Marina. Although the portion of UT 95 between the two points where it intersects UT 276 is highly scenic, you can save a substantial amount of mileage if you complete the loop of UT 276 rather than returning to UT 95 the opposite way you came to the marina.*

world where three natural bridges of great size are located in such close proximity. The bridges are situated in two winding canyons called **White** and **Armstrong Canyons**. The bridges were well known to the Anasazi but were first "discovered" by white men in 1883. The Monument has a nine mile long loop road that has parking areas fronting short walks to overlooks of each of the three bridges. There are also more difficult trails that descend to the base of each bridge as well as a trail that is as long as the road and connects all of the bridges.

The three bridges all have Hopi Indian names and are among the most beautiful examples of this landform to be found anywhere. **Sipapu** is considered to be the second largest bridge in the world and is 268 feet long, 31 feet wide and 220 feet high. It is 53 feet thick. **Kachina** is 204 feet long and 44 feet wide. It is, however, 93 feet thick and is, therefore, among the most massive of all natural bridges. The **Owachomo** bridge is the oldest of the trio and is 180 feet long and 27 feet wide. Because it is only nine feet thick geologists consider it to be a mature bridge that is in its final stages of existence before the forces of gravity causes it to come crashing down into the canyon floor. This event will take place "soon" in geologic terms but may not occur for a hundred years or more.

The Monument has a small visitor center. Of interest near the center is a solar array that provides electric power for Natural Bridges National Monument. Allow about one hour for your visit but more if you intend to hike down to one or more of the bridges. *Tel. 435/692-1234. Visitor Center open daily from 8:00am to 6:00pm except from October through April when it is open from 9:00am until 4:30pm. Per car admission is $6 to those not holding a valid park service passport.*

SAN JUAN CORNER & MONUMENT VALLEY

Return to UT 95 and continue on it for two miles to the junction of UT 261. You are now in the extreme southeastern corner of the state, an area of many beautiful sights as well as the part of Utah with the most extensive remains of ancient Native American civilizations. It is also the section of the state with the greatest Indian population as it contains part of the vast Navajo Indian Reservation. Most of the reservation is in Arizona and some is in New Mexico. Seeing the sights of this area requires passing through a few miles of the same road no matter how you arrange it but I'll route it in such a way as to keep it to a minimum.

Stay on UT 95 to begin with. This section of the road and UT 261 to be done shortly are referred to as the **Trail of the Ancients** because of all the important sites connected with the Anasazi and other early Native American groups. Along the approximately 20 miles of UT 95 that you'll be traveling on are five attractions, some of which are simple to reach and some that are difficult. The first is **Salvation Knoll**, so called because an 1879 pioneer expedition was hopelessly lost. But a scouting party climbed this hill and was able to figure out where they were and where they were going. The **Mule Canyon Ruin** is located by a rest stop on UT 95 and you can see the remains of a kiva, tower and surface pueblos that are more than 700 years old. **Cave Towers** are located via a short hike near mileage marker 103 at the beginning of Mule Canyon. Seven Pueblo towers, three of which sit on the canyon's rim, are visible. They are about 900 years old and not in good condition. Therefore, don't touch or climb on the ruins.

You can also get to the towers via an unpaved road passable to four-wheel drive vehicles. **Comb Ridge**, located about three miles past the Cave Towers, is an eroded ridge that extends for more than eighty miles into Arizona. It used to present a major impediment to travel in the area. The last point of interest is the **Butler Wash Indian Ruins**, which are off of a signed parking area along the highway. The one-mile trail to the ruins is somewhat difficult, as it requires negotiating some slick rock and several washes. You can see all of these places in a couple of hours. Then return on UT 95 in the opposite direction to UT 261 and turn south.

During the 23 miles that you'll first travel on UT 261 you'll pass through the **Grand Gulch Primitive Area**. There are many pictographs and petroglyphs in this region but most require extremely long and difficult hikes to reach. If you're interested contact the BLM office in Monticello for information and maps, *Tel. 435/587-2141*. An unpaved road to the right will take you four miles to the **Muley Point Overlook**. From this point you'll be able to see all the way to Monument Valley and Navajo Mountain. The road to the overlook is graded but should only be attempted in dry weather. The overlook itself is at the edge of a precipitous and high cliff. There are no railings so if you're prone to vertigo or scared of heights, exercise caution.

Upon returning to UT 261 and continuing south you'll soon have to make a decision. A signed cutoff for another unpaved road leads to the magnificent **Valley of the Gods**. This loop road can be done by regular cars although high clearance is advisable. The area is a miniature version of more famous nearby Monument Valley. Among the large colorful rock formations on this 17-mile scenic drive are **Seven Sailors**, **Southern Lady** and the **Rooster**. Should you do this route the road ends at US 163 which you'll take south. Otherwise, continue on UT 261. Near the point where UT 261 and US 163 converge is a short side road (UT 316) leading to the incredible **Goosenecks State Park**. The park is small but has a gigantic sized view–you stand at the edge of a rim and look down into the 1,500-foot deep canyon and see the double-s curve of the San Juan River. The turns are so severe that the river flows for more than six miles in an area that measure under a mile as a straight line. Sometimes boaters can be seen on the river, mere specks in this huge and beautiful landscape. Continuing south on US 163 you'll soon come to the small hamlet of **Mexican Hat**. The town gets its name from a nearby boulder that resembles a sombrero. It is 60 feet wide and stands gracefully balanced on a 200-foot high cliff. It's hard to see from town. The best view of it is near the end of the road through the Valley of the Gods.

About 25 miles south of Mexican Hat via US 163 is the Arizona border. Just north of the border on the Utah side is the entrance to **Monument Valley Navajo Tribal Park**. Most of the monument lies within Arizona, but what the heck. We won't quibble as to who should lay claim to this wonderful piece of real estate. It is a region of gorgeous orange-to-red colored rock formations dating back about 160 million years. Monument Valley has been made famous throughout the world because dozens of movies, television programs and commercials have been filmed here.

Large buttes, mesas and canyons all vie for your attention along with unusual free-standing rock formations. Some of them can best be described by simply stating their names–**The Mittens**, **Elephant Butte**, the **Three Sisters**, **Totem Pole** and the **Thumb**, for example. Several of these sandstone monoliths rise to a height of more than a thousand feet above the valley.

A few miles into the valley is a visitor center where you can obtain information and arrange for guided tours in four wheel drive vehicles that penetrate less frequented areas of the park. You can also drive your own car, even the family sedan, along the 17-mile long **Valley Drive**, which passes most of the major formations at 11 marked stops. The road is not paved but isn't that difficult unless it has been raining. Allow at least ninety minutes to take the basic ride through Monument Valley. *Tel. 435/727-3353. The tribal park is open daily from 7:00am until 7:00pm, May through September, and from 8:00am to 5:00pm the remainder of the year. It may be closed during severe weather. It is closed on New Year's, Thanksgiving and Christmas. The admission price is $2.50 for persons over 8 years of age and $1 for seniors. Prices for guided tours vary depending upon length. Inquire at the visitor center.*

Now retrace your route north on US 163 and continue until the road ends at the junction of US 191 near Bluff, a distance of about 40 miles from Monument Valley. The town lies near several large sandstone formations and cliffs. Some people like to climb along the cliffs by **Sand Island** because there are numerous examples of rock art. Especially notable are the **Kokopelli** figures, a hump-backed flute playing figure that is a recurring theme in the region's Native American culture.

TO THE FOUR CORNERS

*As mentioned in the beginning of this book, the **Four Corners** is the only place in the United States where four states adjoin. Utah, Arizona, Colorado and New Mexico are the four states and much of the surrounding area is referred to as the Four Corners region. The point at which they all meet is quite unremarkable. There's a large diagram engraved on the paved ground with the symbols of all the states. Around the perimeter Native Americans set up shop each day and sell their wares to the many tourists. Visitors like to take a picture of their companions standing or otherwise contorted to be in all four states at one time.*

*The only road that goes to the Four Corners point runs from Arizona into Colorado. The best way to get there is via a loop that starts just before Bluff and ends immediately after it. Take US 191 south to US 160 and then go east on that road. The Four Corners is right on US 160. Then continue into Colorado and turn left on CO 41. At the Utah border it becomes UT 262. At Montezuma Creek travel west on UT 163 back to US 191 and the southeast loop. The total distance is 115 miles (or 110 more than you would do if you skipped it altogether). I strongly doubt whether this is worth it. However, if you want to make more of a trip out of it you can take an additional side excursion from Aneth along UT 262 to one of the scattered units of the **Hovenweep National Monument**. Hovenweep preserves some ruins of an ancient Indian culture that built impressive towers of rock. Most of the Monument lies across the Colorado state line. Access to all units is fairly difficult and the ruins aren't in that great shape. However, if you're interested you can call the monument headquarters for further information, Tel. 970/529-4461.*

Approximately 22 miles north of Bluff is the town of Blanding. In town is the **Dinosaur Museum**, *754 S. 200 West.* There is a chronological exhibit that includes, among other things, a fossilized tree, dinosaur skeletons and a meteorite that weighs more than 350 pounds. Also of interest is a display of movie posters that shows how Hollywood has depicted dinosaurs. *Tel. 435/678-3454. The museum is open daily except Sunday from 9:00am until 5:00pm. It is closed from mid-October to mid-April. Admission is $2 for adults and $1 for seniors and children ages 3 through 12.*

On the north side of town is the **Edge of the Cedars State Park**. Within the park is the site of a pre-Columbian era Pueblo ruin as well as a regional archaeological museum. The ruin site is on a ridge atop Westwater Canyon and consists of a half dozen residential and ceremonial structures of the Anasazi dating from the period around 750 AD. The museum's collection of Anasazi pottery is outstanding. *Tel. 435/678-2238. The park and museum is open daily from 9:00am until 6:00pm (until 5:00pm mid-September to mid-May). It is closed on state holidays. There is a $5 daily vehicle use fee.*

THE NEEDLES & RETURN TO MOAB

You have two choices when you set out from Blanding. The easy way is to take US 191 north for about 20 miles to Monticello, largest community in this part of the state. If you're looking for some adventure, however, the scenic **Abajo Mountains (Blue Mountains)** can be traversed by a number of roads through the southern unit of the Manti-La Sal National Forest. Roads range from paved to gravel to dirt. Some are easy and some are difficult. There is even some off-roading possible in this area for the real rough terrain enthusiast. Although the views of the Abajos from US 191 are pretty, the only way to really appreciate them is by exploring some of the back roads.

The mountains are of interest to geologists because they are only one of three ranges in the United States that are of the rare *laccolithic* type. For all of you non-earth science majors, laccolithic refers to mountains that formed underneath thousands of feet of rock and did not push through to the surface through faulting, eruption or other process. Rather, they slowly became exposed over millions of years as the rock above them eroded. There are only two other laccolithic ranges in the country and both are, you guessed it, also in Utah. They are the Henry and previously visited La Sal Mountains. While the drive on US 191 to Monticello will take under a half-hour, exploring in the Abajo region can take anywhere from an extra hour or two to a full day.

Monticello itself is also a good place to gas up the car and get a bite to eat. There isn't much of interest within the town. Another 14 miles north on US 191 from town will bring you to the junction of UT 211. This road, the **Squaw Flats Scenic Byway**, is incredibly scenic and travels west for 48 miles to **The Needles District** of Canyonlands National Park. The road is paved all the way.

The part of the Needles section that can be visited by car is much smaller than the Island in the Sky District. Easily accessible is the visitor center and a not too difficult twisting roadway with several spurs leads to numerous outstanding overlooks. Of most interest are **Big Spring Canyon Overlook** and the **Wooden Shoe Overlook**. The Needles contains a fascinating array of unusual rock formations including the many tall sandstone spires that give the section its name. There are also arches and many other shapes to be seen, all in the usual array of colors. The paved road gives way to a series of much more difficult back roads requiring four wheel drive. There are also many challenging trails that wind their way among some of the formations. Information on trails and unpaved roads is available at the visitor center. Allow a minimum of four hours to visit The Needles District including the drive to and from US 191. *General information applicable to The Needles is the same as for the Island in the Sky. See above for details.*

Either on the way into or out of The Needles you can stop along UT 211 at the **Newspaper Rock State Historic Monument** located about a dozen miles west of US 191. Located near Indian Creek Canyon, the rock is a large cliff containing a mural like collection of petroglyphs and pictographs from three different Native American tribes. *The site is open at all times and there is no admission fee.*

There is one other opportunity to see The Needles District, either if you didn't have enough in the previously discussed visit or if you didn't have time to do it. About eight miles north of UT 211 off of US 191 is a paved side road that leads 21 miles to **The Needles Overlook**. From this vantage point you'll have an excellent panorama of The Needles and its many strange formations as well as other districts of Canyonlands. Including the round trip from US 191 you can make this side excursion in under 90 minutes.

Continuing north on US 191 you'll soon come to the last sight before returning to Moab. **Wilson Arch** is located just a few feet off the highway and is probably most notable as being the largest natural arch that lies along a major through roadway. After Arches National Park and so many other wonderful sights it may be a little on the anti-climatic side but, if you're following my suggested route, it will have the distinction of being the last arch you see during your visit through southeast Utah. It's under a half-hour drive from Wilson Arch back to Moab.

NIGHTLIFE & ENTERTAINMENT

Rather than leave you with the impression that I left it out by accident, I'll describe the nightlife in the southeast in two words. Forget it! Sit out under a clear sky and enjoy a relaxing evening. Or try the evening boat ride on the Colorado River that was previously described.

SPORTS & RECREATION

Bicycling

Just as in the southwest region, the southeast's uncrowded roads and many national parks afford the biker with some of the most wonderful places to ride. In addition to these (especially the roads in Canyonlands and Arches) the following trails are particularly noteworthy:

- **Abajo Mountains,** *Monticello.* The Blue Mountain Loop is 53 miles long.
- **Kokopelli's Trail,** *Moab.* Extends for 128 miles all the way to Colorado but you can concentrate on sections closer to Moab.
- **Slickrock Trail,** *Moab.* 11 miles.
- **Taylor Flat Loop,** *Moab.* 10 miles.
- **Trail of the Ancients,** *Blanding.* The entire route is 105 miles long but you can do smaller sections.
- **White Rim Trail,** *Canyonlands.* 96-mile long route.

Rental locations and outfitters in the southwest include:
- **Dreamrides,** *Moab. Tel. 888/MOAB UTAH.* Tours.
- **Kaibab Mountain Bike Tours,** *391 S. Main, Moab. Tel. 800/451-1133.* Tours.
- **Nichols Expeditions,** *497 N. Main, Moab. Tel. 800/648-8488.* Tours.
- **Poison Spider Bicycles,** *497 N. Main, Moab. Tel. 800/635-1792.* Rentals.
- **Rim Cyclery,** *94 West 1st North, Moab. Tel. 435/259-5333.* Rentals.
- **Western Spirit Cycling,** *478 Mill Creek Drive, Moab. Tel. 800/845-2453.* Tours.

Boating

Pleasure boating of the non-river running type is not easily found in the southwest, an arid region except for a few outstanding wild rivers. There are relatively calm portions of the Green and Colorado Rivers that can be explored (access from Moab and Green River) but the best place to go out on the water is on the waters of the Colorado northeast of Lake Powell in the Glen Canyon National Recreation Area. The **Bullfrog Basin Marina** and the **Hall's Crossing Marina** are both accessible via UT 276.

Fishing

Other than the Glen Canyon National Recreation area, the **Green River State Park,** *Green River, Tel. 435/564-3633,* is one of the better places to fish in the southwest. There's also some fishing available in the streams of the Manti-La Sal National Forest. One section is south of Moab and another is west of Monticello.

Golf

- **Blue Mountain Meadows,** *241 E. Circle Drive, Monticello. Tel. 435/587-2468.* 9 holes.
- **Moab Golf Course,** *2705 S. East Bench Road, Moab. Tel. 435/259-6488.* 18 holes.

Hiking & Backpacking

Arches, Canyonlands and Capitol Reef National Parks are among the best places to hike in southeast Utah. Other excellent sites can be found along the San Rafael Swell (on BLM lands) and in the extreme southeastern corner of the state in San Juan County. Various BLM facilities have great backcountry hiking. Consult a BLM office for further information, maps and permits where required.

Horseback Riding

- **Ed Black's Monument Valley Trail Rides**, *Mexican Hat. Tel. 800/551-4039*
- **Cowboy Trails**, *Moab. Tel. 435/259-8053*
- **Navajo Country Guided Trail Rides**, *Monument Valley. Tel. 435/727-3210*
- **Outlaw Trails**, *Hanksville. Tel. 435/542 3421*

Hunting

Deer and elk can be hunted in the La Sal and Bookcliff Mountains. Contact the Utah Division of Wildlife for licensing information.

Off Road, ATV's & Four Wheel Drive Vehicles

Refer to the sidebar, "Four-Wheeling it in Canyon Country," for information on some of the more popular off road routes in this region. Listed below are a number of off-road guide services and rental locations:

- **Bennet Tours**, *Monument Valley. Tel. 435/727-3283*. Tours.
- **Farabee Adventures**, *83 S. Main, Moab. Tel. 800/806-5337*. Rentals and tours.
- **Fred's Adventure Tours**, *Mexican Hat. Tel. 435/739-4294*. Tours.
- **Goulding's Lodge**, *Monument Valley. Tel. 435/727-3231*. Tours.
- **Lin Ottinger Tours**, *600 N. Main, Moab. Tel. 435/259-7312*. Tours.
- **Mike Young Rentals**, *Monticello. Tel. 435/587-2258*. Rentals.
- **Needles Outpost**, *Monticello. Tel. 435/979-4007*. Rentals.
- **Slickrock 4x4 Rentals**, *284 N. Main, Moab. Tel. 888/259-5337*. Rentals.

Rafting

- **Adrift Adventures Canyonlands**, *Moab. Tel. 800/874-4483*. Half, full and multi-day trips (up to 8 days) on Green River and Cataract Canyon of the Colorado River. Float trips also available.
- **Adventure River Expeditions**, *Moab. Tel. 800/331–3324*. Half, full and multi-day trips (up to 11 days) on the Green River and Cataract and Westwater Canyons of the Colorado River. Float trips also available.
- **Canyon Voyages**, *Moab. Tel. 800/733-6007*. Half, full and multi-day trips (up to 4 days) on the Green and Dolores Rivers and Westwater

Canyon of the Colorado River. Float trips also available.

- **Moab Rafting Company,** *Moab. Tel. 800-RIO MOAB.* Half, full and multi-day trips (up to 6 days) on the Green River and Cataract and Westwater Canyons of the Colorado River.
- **Navtec Expeditions,** *Moab. Tel. 800/833-1278.* Half, full and multi-day trips (up to 7 days) on the Green and Delores Rivers and Cataract and Westwater Canyons of the Colorado River.
- **Sheri Griffith Expeditions,** *Moab. Tel. 800/322-2439.* Full and multi-day (up to 6 days) on the Green and Dolores Rivers and Cataract and Westwater Canyons of the Colorado River. Float trips also available.
- **Tag-A-Long Expeditions,** *Moab. Tel. 800/453-3292.* Half, full and multi-day trips (up to 6 days) on the Green River and Cataract and Westwater Canyons of the Colorado River.
- **Wild River Expeditions,** *Bluff. Tel. 800/422-7654.* Full and multi-day trips (up to 16 days) on the San Juan River.

Most operators also offer combination tours on the longer trips that combine rafting with other forms of sightseeing. In addition to rafting many offer river trips on canoes or kayaks or rafts where the passengers do the paddling. Adrift Adventures, Navtec and Tag-A-Long also have jet boat trips. Besides the"local" operators, many rafting companies are headquartered in Salt Lake City or elsewhere and arrange multiple-day vacations that include rafting and other activities. If you're interested in one of these more comprehensive type trips (usually originating other than in the southeast touring region) then you should contact **Colorado River & Trail Expeditions,** *Tel. 800/253-7328;* **Moki Mac River Expeditions,** *Tel. 800/284-7280;* **Western River Expeditions,** *Tel. 800/453-7450* or **World Wide River Expeditions,** *Tel. 800/231-2769.*

Reservations are generally required for *all* river trips as are deposits. Fares vary greatly depending upon length of the trip. Minimum age restrictions apply depending upon the nature of the trip. Some are as low as four years but most are between six and eight while some are as high as 12 years. Inquire before you book if you're traveling with children.

Swimming

In Moab, try **Moab Swimming Center,** *181 W. 400 North, Tel. 435/ 259-8226*

Tennis

In Moab, try **Grand County Middle School,** *217 E. Center. Open to public when school is not in session.*

SHOPPING

No big malls and no big stores. This is small-town America at its smallest. Most visitors don't come here to shop and the locals seem to be cognizant of that. So don't plan on spending much time looking for that special gift or item for your home. There are numerous gift shops featuring southwestern and Native American crafts in Moab and in communities in the Four Corners region of San Juan County (Blanding, Bluff, Mexican Hat and Monticello).

Among the best in this genre are **Goulding's Trading Post** located at the entrance to Monument Valley; the gift shop inside the **Hole N' The Rock** home south of Moab; **Purple Sage Trading Post**, *South Main* in Blanding; **Blue Mountain Trading Post** in Bluff; and the **Multi Agency Visitors Center**, *117 S. Main* in Monticello.

PRACTICAL INFORMATION

Airport
   Moab: *US Highway 191 (18 miles north of town), Tel. 435/259-7421*

Bus Depot
   Green River: *525 E. Main, Tel. 435/564-3421*

Hospital
   Moab: *Allen Memorial Hospital, 719 W. 400 North, Tel. 435/259-7191*
   Monticello: *San Juan Hospital, 364 W. 1st North, Tel. 435/435/587-2116*

Hotel Hot Line: *None specifically for this region. See the statewide listings under Accommodations in Chapter 6.*

Police (non-emergency)
   Green River: *Tel. 435/564-8111*
   Moab: *Tel. 435/259-8938*
   Monticello: *Tel. 435/587-2273*

Taxi
   Moab: *The Taxi, Tel. 435/259-TAXI*

Tourist Office/Visitors Bureau
   Blanding: *Tel. 435/678-2539*
   Green River: *885 E. Main Street, Tel. 435/564-3526*
   Moab: *Main and Center Streets, Tel. 435/259-8825 or 800/635-6622*
   Monticello: *117 S. Main Street, Tel. 435/587-3235 or 800/574-4386*

Train Station
   Green River: *250 South Broadway*

14. NORTHEAST UTAH: DINOSAUR COUNTRY

While **Dinosaur Country** may not quite be like the movie *Jurassic Park*, it is a notable reason for coming into this part of the state. Paleontologists salivate at the thought of this region, because there is no other place on earth that contains a greater collection of fossil evidence of the prehistoric beasts than right here. The pleasures and educational opportunities for the non-scientist are almost as great. It's something that both adults and children can enjoy equally, even if it is for different reasons. Whether you encounter your dinosaurs in the natural state of **Dinosaur National Monument** or in one of the northeast's great natural history museums, there's much to see and learn.

It would be unfair to characterize the northeast as just one big dinosaur quarry. It's definitely much more than that. The fantastic scenery that by now you've come to equate with Utah is here, too. While a lot of it doesn't take the same unusual form and colors of southern Utah, the sights in and around the **Flaming Gorge National Recreation Area** are simply gorgeous. So is the mountain scenery in the **High Uintas**. A big portion of the latter is a primitive wilderness area that especially appeals to the more adventurous traveler. Outdoor recreation opportunities for all levels are as prevalent in the northeast as they are throughout Utah.

Although there are several good sized towns in the northeast such as **Price** and **Vernal**, the region is generally sparsely populated and parts of it are as remote as you can get and still be in the contiguous United States. That, too, is part of its unique appeal.

ARRIVALS & DEPARTURES

Except for the Amtrak station in Helper (there's once-a-day service to Salt Lake City or points east), there isn't much in the way of scheduled public transportation to the northeast region. Several towns, including Duchesne, Price and Vernal do have Greyhound bus service. Because parts of this region are relatively close to Salt Lake City, you should plan to arrive there and make your way to the northeast. Travelers coming directly to northeast Utah from other parts of the country can reach it from a number of directions.

Coming from the east or west via I-80 you can take US 191 south from Rock Springs, Wyoming and begin seeing the northeast from the end of my suggested routing. US 40 comes in from Colorado near Vernal. Other travelers from the east can take I-70 to either US 191 at Green River and drive north to the loop at Price or exit from I-70 at Salina and take US 89 north to the loop at Manti. The latter two connections from the I-70 corridor can also be hook-up points for those of you doing the southeast or southwest regional loops.

ORIENTATION

If you would take a moment to refer back to the *Utah Touring Regions* map you'll see that the northeast region has an odd shape. The curved western edge borders on the heavy population center of the northwest region. To be more precise, the population lies on the other side of the Wasatch Mountain Range. Because of a lack of roads in the extreme north and eastern sections of this region, your trip through the northeast won't exactly be a loop. Some doubling back will be required unless you want to return to Salt Lake City via Wyoming (there will be a sidebar about that option later on).

The most important route within the northeast will be US 40 which runs from east to west across the approximate center of the region. US 191 is the primary north-south highway although a good portion of it is contiguous with US 40. US 6 & 89 are two other important roads in the southern section. All in all there are few roads, important or otherwise, so getting lost shouldn't be a strong likelihood even if you usually can't find your way out of the supermarket.

GETTING AROUND

The sparse public transportation that can be relied on to get to the northeast is even more limited as a means of getting from one point in the region to another. A car is the only answer. Organized tours that concentrate on the northeast are difficult if not impossible to find. A good travel agent might be able to put together a reasonable FIT tour but don't count on it.

HAPPY DINOSAUR HUNTING

*As any hunter knows, you can't go after the wildlife unless you have the proper license. Dinosaurs are no exception. If that makes sense to you then you'd better do a quick reality check. But, the tourism officials of northeast Utah do take their dinosaurs very seriously. And they do issue a Dinosaur Hunting License! The **Dinosaurland Travel Board** has put together a humorous and official looking permit (supposedly issued by the U.S. Reptile Control Commission) which allows the holder to bag one adult male Tyrannosaurus Rex, one Diplodocus Giganticus weighing more than 5,000 pounds, two male Stegosauruses and up to four Pterodactyls (but no babies).*

Children will surely want one to show to their friends and adults returning from vacation are almost certain to bring it in to the office to show their co-workers. You can pick one up free of charge at just about any tourist attraction in Dinosaurland. By some chance if you don't encounter one on your travels then just give the tourism folks a call and ask for it.

WHERE TO STAY
DUCHESNE
Inexpensive

RIO DAMIAN MOTEL, *23 W. Main Street. Tel. 435/738-5332 18 Rooms. Rates: $75 during the summer and $50 at all other times. American Express, Discover, MasterCard and VISA accepted. Located in the center of town.*

Considering that Duchesne is one of the larger communities in the sparsely populated northeast, Duchesne has almost nothing to offer in the way of good accommodations. Among the several motels the Rio Damian is about the best as it is clean and comfortable and certainly affordable for even the most conservative travel budget. The interesting gift shop is probably the inn's highlight. Restaurants are located within a short distance.

FLAMING GORGE NATIONAL RECREATION AREA
Moderate

FLAMING GORGE LODGE, *US Highway 191, Greendale. Tel. 435/889-3733; Fax 435/889-3788. 45 Rooms. Rates: $50-125. American Express, Discover, MasterCard and VISA accepted. Located along the main highway about 3 miles south of the Flaming Gorge Dam.*

A focal point for recreational activities and services in the Flaming Gorge National Recreation Area, the lodge offers fishing guides, mountain bike rentals and a host of other outdoor options. As such, it's a good base for those who plan to take in the great outdoors for a few days. The wide range of prices reflects differences in facilities more than season. Units range from small to large and from plain and basic to fairly attractive. Rates are only slightly higher during the summer months. The restaurant on the premises, although nothing extra special, is one of the better eating places along the south side of the recreation area.

RED CANYON LODGE, *790 Red Canyon Road, Dutch John. Tel. 435/ 889-3759; Fax 435/889-3759. 20 Rooms. Rates: $45-115. American Express, Discover, MasterCard and VISA accepted. Located 24 miles south of Manila on UT Highway 44.*

This is an attractive and rustic looking resort facility that has cabin accommodations ranging from rather basic to almost luxury standards. The great variation in the size of the cabins as well as the nature of the furnishings explains the rather large variation in the rates. The A-frame main building contains a good restaurant, gift shop and services desk that can arrange for activities in the Recreation Area. The lodge has its own lake for fishing as well as a pond strictly for the children to fish in. Horseback riding is also available.

PRICE
Inexpensive

BEST WESTERN CARRIAGE HOUSE, *590 E. Main Street. Tel. 435/ 637-5660; Fax 435/637-5660. Toll free reservations 800/528-1234. 41 Rooms. Rates: $45-65 including Continental breakfast. Major credit cards accepted. Located in town along the main street via US 6 to Exit 243.*

Having been completely renovated in the early part of 1996, the Best Western Carriage House can boast quite attractive and spacious guest rooms inside a pretty white colonial style exterior. About a third of the rooms are "family units" that have a separate sitting area. Some rooms have a microwave oven and refrigerator. For recreation there are indoor and outdoor whirlpools. Restaurants are located nearby.

GREENWELL INN, *655 E. Main Street. Tel. 435/637-3520; Fax 435/ 637-4858. Toll free reservations 800/666-3520. 125 Rooms. Rates: $52 including Continental breakfast. Major credit cards accepted. Located in town along the main street via US 6 to Exit 243.*

Another recently renovated property, the Greenwell also boasts very nice and comfortable rooms. There are plenty of recreational opportunities including a swimming pool, spa, well equipped exercise room, basketball court and horseshoes area. Also on the premises are a restaurant and lounge.

ROOSEVELT

Inexpensive

BEST WESTERN INN, *East Highway 40. Tel. 435/722-4644; Fax 435/ 722-0179. Toll free reservations 800/528-1234. 40 Rooms. Rates: $49-79. Most major credit cards accepted. Located six blocks east of downtown Roosevelt via US 40.*

The Inn has an attractive rustic looking exterior and better than average rooms, especially considering the price. Some rooms have refrigerators. There's a heated outdoor swimming pool as well as an indoor spa and exercise facility. JB's Restaurant is adjacent and offers tasty family style dinners at reasonable rates. A convenience store is also located on the premises. Guests receive a complimentary newspaper each morning.

FRONTIER MOTEL, *75 S. 200 East. Tel. 435/722-2201; Fax 435/722-2212. Toll free reservations 800/248-1014. 54 Rooms. Rates: $41-53. Most major credit cards accepted. Located along US 40.*

While not up to the level of the Best Western Inn, the Frontier is the second best place to stay in Roosevelt and offers clean and comfortable accommodations. There's a swimming pool and hot tub. The Frontier Grill is a more than satisfactory restaurant.

VERNAL

Moderate

BEST WESTERN ANTLERS, *423 W. Main Street. Tel. 435/789-1202; Fax 435/789-4979. Toll free reservations 800/528-1234. 43 Rooms. Rates: High season (May through September): $85-100; Low season (October through April): $60-80. Major credit cards accepted. Located west of downtown on US Highway 40.*

Higher priced than most places in this region (because of Vernal's proximity to Dinosaur National Monument), the Best Western Antlers may well be the fanciest looking place in town although it certainly isn't the best buy. You will get decent accommodations, however, and groups of up to six can stay in one of the dozen or so family units. There's a hot tub, kiddy pool, exercise room and playground so both grown-ups and children will find something to amuse themselves with after check-in. A restaurant is located adjacent to the property.

WESTON PLAZA HOTEL, *1684 W. Highway 40. Tel. 435/789-9550; Fax 789-4574. 102 Rooms. Rates: $64. Most major credit cards accepted. Located a couple of miles west of the town center on the main highway.*

More in the way of basic accommodations is on tap at the Weston Plaza, one of the bigger places in town. Some rooms have kitchen facilities. The only recreation is a swimming pool. A decent family restaurant is located on the premises.

Inexpensive

SPLIT MOUNTAIN MOTEL, *1015 E. Highway 40. Tel. 435/789-9020; Fax 435/789-9023. 40 Rooms. Rates: $42-54. Major credit cards accepted. Located a half-mile east of town on US Highway 40.*

During the height of the touring season Vernal's accommodations can fill up so you might have to downgrade a notch and that'll bring you to the Split Mountain Motel which has clean and comfortable rooms and nothing more. Some rooms have a microwave oven and refrigerator.

CAMPING & RV SITES

National Parks and other federal lands: Dinosaur National Monument has several campgrounds. Contact the monument superintendent's office for information. The largest selection of public campgrounds are located in the Ashley National Forest's High Uinta area and in the Flaming Gorge National Recreation Area, especially in the Dutch John vicinity. Call *Tel. 800/280-2267* for information and reservations. The Bureau of Land Management has many camping sites scattered throughout the northeast. Contact the Vernal District office for information, *Tel. 435/789-1362.*

State Parks: Starvation (Duchesne), Red Fleet and Steinaker (Vernal) State Parks all offer camping. The number for reservations is *Tel. 800/322-3770.*

For **commercial camping** and **RV sites**, try:
- **Classic RV Park**, *145 S. 500 East, Roosevelt. Tel. 435/722-2294*
- **Dinosaur Village RV Campground**, *7700 East Highway 40, Jensen. Tel. 435/789-5552*
- **Fossil Valley RV Park**, *999 W. Highway 40, Vernal. Tel. 435/789-6450*
- **Mount Haven RV Park**, *130 N. Main, Manila. Tel. 435/723-7615*
- **Western Heritage RV Park**, *271 S. 500 East, Vernal. Tel. 435/781-1347*

WHERE TO EAT
DUCHESNE

Moderate

COWAN'S CAFE, *57 East Main. Tel. 435/738-5609. Discover, MasterCard and VISA accepted. Breakfast, lunch and dinner served daily.*

This is, unfortunately, another one of those towns where people who consider great food to be an important part of their trip will likely be unhappy. Cowan's is popular with the locals due to it's friendly staff and fairly diverse selection of decent food. You have to eat so this might as well be the place to do so in Duchesne.

FLAMING GORGE NATIONAL RECREATION AREA
Moderate

FLAMING GORGE CAFE, *Junction of Utah Highways 43 & 44, Manila. Tel. 435/784-3531. MasterCard and VISA accepted. Breakfast, lunch and dinner served daily.*

It's hard to find a really good restaurant in these parts, but the Flaming Gorge Cafe will do in a pinch. The menu has something for just about everyone, including some traditional American favorites, Italian and Mexican. You can even find some German and Chinese dishes. The chef is apparently a jack of all trades but, alas, master of none. It's simply decent food at an affordable price.

PRICE
Moderate

THE KING'S TABLE, *11 W. Main Street. Tel. 435/636-0728. Most major credit cards accepted. Lunch and dinner served nightly except Sunday.*

In a city of mostly fast food restaurants and a few family style places that are unremarkable, the King's Table is a better than average steak and seafood restaurant that offers very good food in an attractive setting at reasonable prices. The service is good. Cocktail service.

RICARDO'S, *655 E. Main Street. Tel. 435/637-2020. Most major credit cards accepted. Dinner served nightly.*

A casual family dining spot featuring very good Mexican cuisine that is authentic and extremely well prepared. The decor is attractive and the service is better than average. Cocktail service.

ROOSEVELT
Moderate

JB'S RESTAURANT, *East Highway 40 in the Best Western Inn. Tel. 435/722-4644. Most major credit cards accepted. Breakfast, lunch and dinner served daily.*

Simple standard American fare in adequate sized portions at an affordable price. No more and no less. Unfortunately, that's about the best you can get in Roosevelt, which certainly isn't the homeland of gourmet dining. Children's menu.

VERNAL
Expensive

CURRY MANOR, *189 S. Vernal Avenue. Tel. 435/789-2289. Most major credit cards accepted. Dinner served Tuesday through Saturday. Reservations are suggested.*

This is the finest restaurant in Vernal and provides an unusually satisfying dining experience. It's located in a large two-story home on a quiet street just off the main part of town. The historic house is on the National Register of Historic Places. The service is excellent.

The chef prepares a variety of American and Continental dishes with some flair. The appetizers are especially good but you'll find that each course offers something special right up to the rich desserts. Some entrees are priced in the moderate range.

Moderate
CRACK'D POT RESTAURANT & LOUNGE, *1089 E. Highway 40, Tel. 435/781-0133. Most major credit cards accepted. Lunch and dinner served daily except Sunday.*

While the Curry Manor is fine dining and is best suited to adult tastes, the Crack'd Pot is a good choice in Vernal for family dining. The menu includes varied selections of well-prepared beef dishes along with Mexican, pasta and seafood items. Check out the daily special, which always represents a good value. The separate lounge is a private club where temporary memberships can be purchased. In addition to drinks you can play darts and pool or enjoy a variety of sports programming on their big screen TV's. There's also a nice gift shop on the premises.

7-11 RANCH RESTAURANT, *77 E. Main Street. Tel. 435/789-1170. Discover, MasterCard and VISA accepted. Breakfast, lunch and dinner served daily except Sunday.*

Long hours make this a good place to drop in for any meal of the day. It certainly isn't fancy but it's comfortable and casual and the service is friendly and efficient. Dinner is a pleasant family affair with such dishes as roasted chicken and barbecued beef ribs being the staples. On Saturday evenings the 7-11 offers an excellent chuckwagon buffet. Children's menu. Gift shop on the premises.

SEEING THE SIGHTS
SOUTH ALONG THE WASATCH FRONT
& THE WASATCH PLATEAU

Our northeast journey juxtaposes nicely with the excursion south from Salt Lake City by beginning at Spanish Fork. That town is located along I-15 about eight miles south of Provo. The walls of the Wasatch seem like an impenetrable barrier to the east but US 89 south will bring you easily through it as you rise to the **Wasatch Plateau**. In Fairview, a 45-mile drive from Spanish Fork, is the **Fairview Museum of History and Art**, *85 N. 100 East*. The museum houses an interesting collection of Native American and pioneer era artifacts as well as old farming equipment. Best among the collection are the thousands of miniature wood carvings. *Tel. 435/427-9216. The museum is open daily from 10:00am until 6:00pm except* *for Sunday when it opens at 2:00pm. There is no admission charge but donations are requested.*

The town of Manti is situated about 35 miles south of Fairview along US 89. There isn't enough there to warrant a special trip unless it is the month of July and you're going to attend the annual **Mormon Pageant**. This historical play that tells the history of the Mormons is a blockbuster event. With a cast of a thousand, the story unfolds on the grounds of Manti's Mormon Temple, a most beautiful setting. The temple is perched on a hillside and is itself visible for miles around.

For those not going to the pageant (or upon returning from it) follow UT 31 from Fairview as it traverses the Wasatch Plateau and a section of the Manti-La Sal National Forest. The 48-mile long road from Fairview to Huntington is called the **Huntington Canyon Scenic Byway** and it varies in elevation from about 5,000 feet to almost 10,000 feet above sea level as it travels through subalpine forest and meadows. Several pretty mountain lakes can be seen along the way and there are a number of side roads that lead to some of the better fishing areas in Utah. **Huntington Beach Reservoir State Park**, located at the end of the byway, is a major recreation area. At Huntington and the junction of UT 10, take the road south for six miles into Castle Dale.

This quaint little town of 2,000 people isn't far from the southeast's San Rafael Reef region and parts of it can be seen in the distance. You can also see the rock spires of the Castle Valley. Within the town are two small but mildly interesting museums that together can be seen in about an hour. The **Pioneer Museum**, *161 E. 100 North*, documents local history from the late 1800's through the early part of the 20th century and has a recreation of a schoolroom and several pioneer era businesses. *Tel. 435/ 381-5154. Open weekdays from 10:00am until 4:00pm and on Saturday from noon to 4:00pm. It is closed on holidays. Donations are appreciated.* The **Museum of San Rafael**, *96 N. 100 East*, has a collection of mounted animals depicted in their natural surroundings. A number of artifacts that were found in the caves and rock ledges of the surrounding countryside are also on display. *Tel. 435/381-5252. Operating hours are the same as the Pioneer Museum. Donations.*

Now travel north back on UT 10 past Huntington to the cutoff for UT 155. Five miles to the right is Cleveland, gateway to the **Cleveland Lloyd Dinosaur Quarry**. The quarry site is about 20 miles from town by gravel roads but it isn't overly difficult so long as the weather has been dry. For dinosaur enthusiasts it's definitely worth the effort to get there. In prehistoric times the quarry area was a muddy lake that attracted both dinosaurs and their predators. Many were trapped in the mud. Thus was set the scene for today. More than 12,000 bones have been recovered from over 70 different species. Although the quarry has provided plenty of specimens for museums throughout the world, there are still many on display right here at the visitor center. You can also walk through the quarry itself and along a nice nature trail. Allow about 2-1/2 hours for the drive to and from Cleveland and visiting the site. *Tel. 435/637 5060. Open daily from 10:00am until 5:00pm during the period Memorial Day through Labor Day. From Easter weekend through Memorial Day it is only open on Saturday and Sunday. There is no admission charge.*

Upon finishing your visit to the quarry return to UT 10 and continue north for the short drive to Price.

PRICE

With almost 10,000 people Price is the metropolis of the northeast. The **College of Eastern Utah Prehistoric Museum**, *155 E. Main Street*, is housed in a large modern building and contains a lot more than you might think from the name. Of course, this being dinosaur country the term "prehistoric" conjures up visions of *T-rex* and you will find several complete dinosaur skeletons in the Hall of Dinosaurs as well as a Mammoth from the later Columbian era. But the museum devotes most of its space to Fremont Indians, who lived in the area about 900 years ago. You may recall something about them from the southwest region's Fremont Indian State Park. Among the many artifacts are clay pottery. Exhibits depict what Fremont village life would have been like. Minerals and fossils from the surrounding region are also on display. Allow at least half an hour to tour the museum. *Tel. 435/637-5060. Museum hours are daily from 9:00am until 6:00pm from April to September and daily except Sunday from 9:00am until 5:00pm the remainder of the year. Donations are requested.*

About 11 miles north of Price via US 6/191 is the town of Helper. The community grew as a facility of the old Denver & Rio Grande Railroad. Because of the difficult ascent up to nearby Soldier Summit, extra locomotives were required to "help" pull trains. The **Western Mining & Railroad Museum**, *296 S. Main Street*, chronicles the railroad and mining days of Helper and the surrounding region through photographs, mining tools and other equipment. There is also a large display of art work commissioned during the Great Depression by the WPA. Outdoor sections of the museum display larger coal mining equipment and a railroad caboose. *Tel. 435/472-3009. Museum hours are daily except Sunday from 10:00am until 6:00pm from May through September. During the rest of the year it is open Tuesday through Saturday from noon to 5:00pm. Donations are requested.*

North of Helper US 6 and 191 split up. Take US 191 north for the 45-mile ride into Duchesne via the **Indian Canyon Scenic Byway**. Although

NINE MILE CANYON

US 191 isn't the only way from Price to Duchesne. While the alternative route of 100 miles is only about 40 miles longer than via US 191, it can take a half day or more to do. About three-fourths of the route is unpaved although it can be done without four-wheel drive in good weather. Take US 6/191 for 7-1/2 miles west of Price to Wellington and look for the Back Country Byway sign. The road travels along Soldier Creek, rises up to higher than 7,000 feet at the West Tavaputs Plateau and then goes through spectacular Nine Mile Canyon. You'll now travel north along the Wells Draw before ending near Myton. It's then a short jaunt westward on US 40 to Duchesne. There are absolutely no services along the way so you should eat and fill up the car with gas before venturing out from Price (or Duchesne if traveling in the reverse direction).

That's the route but what will you see? Plenty. Besides the buff colored badlands cliffs and the plateau, Nine Mile Canyon has been called the "world's longest art gallery." Beautiful sandstone cliffs extend along the entire canyon and have been home to various Native American groups for centuries. They have left their legacy chiseled into the stone and painted with natural pigments in red, white, gold, green and black. The road from Wellington to Myton covers a portion of Nine Mile Canyon but a part of it extends for a few more miles east at Gate Canyon. Altogether there are about a dozen major areas of petroglyphs with the Cottonwood Panel and the Balloon Man being among the best. The canyon also has the remains of settlements from the pioneer era. Wildlife such as deer and elk are frequently to be seen.

Price and Duchesne (pronounced **doo-shane)** are almost at the same altitude (5,567 and 5,515 feet, respectively) the road through Indian Canyon isn't flat at all. It rises to a maximum elevation of 9,100 feet at Indian Creek Pass before descending once again. The scenery of the Ashley National Forest, the distant Book Cliff rock formations and the Uintah & Ouray Indian Reservation along the way is just fine but not all that unusual for Utah.

DUCHESNE & THE HIGH UINTAS

Duchesne itself has little of interest to visitors except that it is the gateway to the beautiful scenery and recreational opportunities of Utah's **High Uintas**. These mountains stretch from east to west for about 80 miles and cover portions of the Wasatch-Cache and Ashley National Forests as well as the Uintah and Ouray Indian Reservation. Within the national forests is the High Uintas Primitive Area where no roads exist and only the most adventurous hikers will be found. Elevations in this region are almost entirely in excess of 9,000 feet and there are several peaks exceeding 13,000 feet. Utah's highest mountain, **Kings Peak**, soars to 13.528 feet. The main attraction is the relative solitude of the area. In addition to hiking and camping, horseback riding, ATV travel, fishing, hunting and boating are all popular. Some facilities and operators are listed in the *Sports & Recreation* section.

There is a fairly good network of paved roads north of Duchesne that provide access to some of the recreational facilities. Once in the national forests, though, most roads are unpaved and some are quite difficult. Scenic **Rock Creek Canyon** can be reached without trouble. Take UT 87 north from Duchesne for 14 miles and then follow 2100 West to Mountain Home. Turn west on Forest Road 134 and follow it for 13 miles to the canyon. The heavily forested canyon contains many trails that can be done on foot, horseback or by bicycle. If you want recreation closer to Duchesne then visit **Starvation State Park**, which is located on US 40 just east of town.

From Duchesne travel east on US 40 (the road is also US 191 north) through Roosevelt and Fort Duchesne, which is the headquarters of the Uintah and Ouray Indian Reservation, on into Vernal. The total distance is about 60 miles and the road is good all the way.

VERNAL & DINOSAUR NATIONAL MONUMENT

If the northeast is dinosaur country than Vernal is the heart of the dinosaur. There are a few important points of interest in town before we get on to the main event out at the National Monument. Vernal's premier attraction is one of the best natural history museum facilities to be found anywhere. The **Utah Field House of Natural History**, *235 E. Main Street* is a unit of the Utah state park system and has, in addition to the usual exhibits of skeletons, fossils, minerals and Native American artifacts, a huge outdoor area called the "Dinosaur Gardens."

The gardens have been landscaped to show how this area of the world would have appeared about 65 to 150 million years ago. There are lakes and waterfalls and, of course, a spooky swamp. Along the pathways are life-size and ferocious looking replicas of 18 animals from that period, most of which are dinosaurs. Give yourself at least an hour to fully explore the museum and gardens. *Tel. 435/789-3799. Operating hours are daily from 8:00am through 9:00pm during June through August and from 9:00am to 5:00pm the remainder of the year. Closed on most state holidays. The admission is $2 per person in addition to a $5 daily vehicle use charge.*

Nearby at *300 E. 200 South* is the **Western Heritage Museum**, which contains lots of artifacts from the old west and mounted animal specimens. The collection of Fremont Indian objects is one of the better ones in Utah. *Tel. 435/789-7399. The museum is open daily except Sunday from 9:00am to 6:00pm. From after Labor Day through Memorial Day weekend it closes an hour earlier. Closed on New Year's Day, Thanksgiving and Christmas. There is no admission charge.*

During the summer Vernal celebrates its western heritage in two ways. The first takes place from late May through August in the **Outlaw Trail Theater** located at the Western Park Amphitheater, *302 East 200 South.* In this attractive venue one or more different outdoor "dramas" are performed. Common themes are Butch Cassidy and the Wild Bunch or other outlaw groups, lawmen, frontier women and pioneers. The plays are lively affairs put on by the Uintah Arts Council. *Tel. 800/477-5558. Both reserved and general admission seating is available. Performances are nightly except Sunday at 8:30pm with pre-show entertainment beginning a half-hour earlier. Reserved tickets are $8 for adults, $7 for seniors and $6 for students up to age 17. All general admission seats (located in the upper section of the amphitheater) are $6.* The other popular western event is the **Dinosaur Roundup Rodeo**, which has been taking place now for fifty years. It is Utah's largest rodeo and is generally held following the Independence Day holiday for about a week. *Call Tel. 800/421-9635 for information.*

A couple of other minor attractions in town are the **Daughters of Utah Pioneer Museum**, *500 West 200 South* and the **Ladies of the Whitehouse Doll Collection** located in the Uintah County Library building, *Main between 100 & 200 East.* The former has pictures and artifacts that depict area history dating back to the mid-19th century while the latter has a beautiful doll for each American First Lady in an authentic reproduction of her Inaugural Ball gown. I bet your little girl would love to see that! *The museum is open Monday through Saturday from 10:00am to 6:00pm, June through Labor Day. Donations are appreciated. The free library exhibit is open daily except Sunday all year from 9:00am to 5:00pm. It is closed on state holidays. Free admission.*

You may also want to take a quick look at the 1919 **Bank of Vernal** located on Main Street. It's not the building itself that's so interesting as the way it was constructed. Vernal was an expensive place to deliver things to at the turn of the century because freight charges were so high. So the frugal bankers to be shipped all of the bricks via parcel post. Only seven at a time could be sent that way because of weight limitations imposed by the post office.

HELLO, BUTCH CASSIDY

If you travel throughout the northeastern and mid-Atlantic states it seems that nearly every historic house claims that George Washington slept there. Well, in Utah it seems that every place was visited by the notorious outlaw, Butch Cassidy and his Wild Bunch gang. I can't verify all of these claims but the gang definitely did hide out in the rugged country surrounding Vernal. Butch was born Robert LeRoy Parker and was of Mormon parents. Certainly the Mormon Church isn't proud to announce his religious affiliation.

His first nefarious act was done in Colorado although the gang roamed throughout the mountain west. Train robberies were the specialties of Butch and the Wild Bunch. Cassidy, along with his girlfriend and the Sundance Kid eventually were feeling too much heat from the authorities and fled to South America where they were supposedly killed in a shootout. There are those, however, who insist that the shootout either never happened or that they escaped with their lives. No one knows for sure, it seems, but many people in and around Vernal like to think that their "Robin Hood" escaped. Either way, his friendly ghost still permeates the rugged canyons around Vernal.

From Vernal take US 40 east for 13 miles to the town of Jensen and then UT 149 north for about six miles to the **Dinosaur National Monument**. As early as the late 19th century it was known that the Uintah Basin was a large source of dinosaur bones and fossils. In 1909 an archaeologist from the Carnegie Museum discovered what was to prove to be the largest deposit of Jurassic period dinosaur bones in the world. That quarry formed the basis for Dinosaur National Monument. While many bones have been removed to museums throughout the world, visitors can still see about 2,000 bones that lie in an exposed sandstone cliff and are visible through a glass wall in the Dinosaur Quarry Visitor Center. Allow about an hour to see this portion of the Monument. During the peak summer travel season visitors are transported via shuttle bus from the parking area to the visitor center. At other times you can drive all the way to the center.

The monument's 325 square miles contain much more than what I just described. The larger portion of the monument lies in Colorado and is completely different than the Utah quarry section. While dinosaur history is "the" attraction on the Utah side, the Colorado side features beautiful canyon scenery and white water rafting on the Green and Yampa rivers. Several overlooks provide great views along the 31-mile long scenic road from the town of Dinosaur, Colorado to the Harper's Corner. Details are available at the visitor center back in Utah since this side trip in another state requires at least a half-day and is beyond the scope of this book. However, if you're interested just follow US 40 about 21 miles further east from Jensen to the town of Dinosaur and the beginning of the Harpers Corner Scenic Road.

For information, Tel. 435/789-2115 (or 970/374-3000 for the Colorado section visitor center). The quarry center is open daily from 8:00am until 7:00pm from Memorial Day weekend through Labor Day and until 4:30pm the remainder of the year. It is closed on New Year's Day, Thanksgiving and Christmas. Admission is by $10 per vehicle permit (good for both Utah and Colorado sections) to those not holding a valid park service passport.

DRIVE THROUGH THE AGES

Once you're through with Dinosaur National Monument, work your way back to Vernal and proceed north on US 191. Designated as the **Wildlife Through the Ages Scenic Byway** but often going by the shorter name of Drive Through the Ages, this route covers more than a billion years of the earth's history. More than 20 different geologic formations can be seen along the easy drive and signs at each of the many pullouts explain exactly what you are seeing. That includes the wildlife that is found today as well as in former times. The drive technically extends for 70 miles via US 191 from Vernal to the junction of UT 44 and then on the latter road to the town of Manila on the Wyoming border. However, that second section is within or along the southern edge of The Flaming Gorge National Recreation Area and will be described in the section that follows.

You can pick up a brochure in Vernal that will list all of the stops along the drive. The 35-mile stretch from Vernal to UT 44 has an abundance of beautiful scenery including the reservoir in **Steinaker State Park** and the **Red Fleet State Park**. The latter is backed by three towering red sandstone cliffs that resemble old sailing ships and makes for a great photo stop. Both parks were heavily populated dinosaur areas in ages gone by. Some dinosaur tracks are still visible at the latter park. You should give yourself about 90 minutes to complete this portion of the drive because you will want to stop at many of the informative signs.

FLAMING GORGE NATIONAL RECREATION AREA

The beautiful **Flaming Gorge National Recreation Area** is a vast region that extends well into Wyoming and surrounds the 91-mile long Flaming Gorge Lake. The recreation area provides some of Utah's best fishing and boating opportunities for the sports enthusiast (see the *Sports & Recreation* section for further information) but its scenic attraction is

DINO'S DETOURS

*Dino the Dinosaur (my alter ego when traveling through Dinosaur Country) has a couple of side trips out of Vernal that you might be interested in if you're looking for a little more adventure. The first is the **Red Cloud/ Dry Fork Scenic Backway**. It begins 14 miles north of Vernal on US 191 and travels through pretty groves of aspen trees and Lodgepole pine forests. There are excellent views of the High Uintas as well as oddly shaped sandstone cliffs and remnants of early settlements. You can also find Indian rock art in the Dry Fork Canyon. The 45-mile long route has paved and gravel portions and is only open during the summer months. It ends at US 40 just a couple of miles west of Vernal. Figure on about two hours for the round-trip.*

*The second route is known as the **Jones Hole Scenic Backway** and starts four miles east of Vernal. The road ascends more than 2,500 feet to the top of the **Diamond Mountain Plateau**. It ends along the Green River at the **Jones Hole National Fish Hatchery** after you make a thrilling descent into a steep walled narrow canyon that is highlighted by wonderfully colorful cliffs. You might also see deer and elk. The hatchery raises trout in both indoor and outdoor pools. Trout leave the hatchery via a stream that goes through a hole in the canyon wall (thus the name of the hatchery) and travels about 3-1/2 miles to the Green River. There's a hiking trail that follows the course of the stream to the river. Tel. 435/789-4481. Hatchery open daily from 7:00am until 3:30pm and admission is free. The drive to Jones Hole covers 40 miles each way so you should allow about three hours for this side trip without the hike to the river.*

equally important if not even more so. Just about every point within the area can be considered as highly scenic but the most interesting formations and best sights lie on the Utah side of the border. That, then, is what we'll now explore, first traveling north along US 191 before doubling back to UT 44 and taking that road all the way to the town of Manila via UT 44.

Along US 191 is the **Flaming Gorge Dam**, located about where the Green River intersects with Flaming Gorge Lake. The 500-foot high concrete arch dam offers self-guiding tours of the powerhouse during the off season and guided tours during the summer. The site affords excellent views of the rocky canyon that encloses the deep blue waters of the lake. Another good lake view is from the Cedar Springs Marina off of US 191 a mile south of the dam. *Tel. 435/885-3135 for times. There is no admission charge.* Coming back south on US 191 about a mile before you reach UT 44 is the **Swett Ranch National Historic Site**. Several ranches were built in this remote region after the Homesteading Act of 1862. The ranch depicts agrarian life in the early 20th century. *Open Thursday through Monday from Memorial Day to Labor Day only. There is no admission charge.*

A little further down the road is a cutoff to the right leading into **Red Canyon**, perhaps the most beautiful part of the Recreation Area. The overlook located behind the visitor center provides a breathtaking panorama from its 1,400-foot high perch above vividly colored Red Canyon and the Flaming Gorge Lake. Upon returning to UT 44 and traveling further along the southern boundary of Flaming Gorge, you will be driving along the forested slopes of the Ashley National Forest.

Soon you'll come to another spur road leading to the right. This unpaved but short route will take you to the **Dowd Mountain Overlook**, which gazes out upon a stunning vista of canyon and lake. Soon after is the cutoff for the paved **Sheep Creek Geological Loop**. This 13-mile long loop (beginning and ending at UT 44) contains dramatic rock spires and a section of the interesting Uinta Fault. During the summer you can take an optional drive off of the Sheep Creek Loop to Spirit Lake. This road is unpaved and four wheel drive is helpful.

Allow about a half-day to tour Flaming Gorge. That time is exclusive of any recreational activities that you may want to partake in. The national recreation area has extensive facilities and services including lodging, dining, camping, marinas and both land and water sports facilities, and more than a hundred miles of hiking trails. *Tel. 435/784-3445. There are visitor centers that can provide you with detailed maps and information located just off of US 191 and in Red Canyon. US 191 visitor center open daily from 8:00am until 6:00pm, Memorial Day through Labor Day. It closes an hour earlier during the spring and fall. During the winter the hours are 10:00am to 4:00pm. Red Canyon center open daily from 9:00am to 5:00pm from Memorial Day to Labor Day only. There is no fee for entering the Recreation area.*

THE WYOMING CONNECTION

Rather than seeing a lot of the same scenery on the way back to Salt Lake City you can take one of two routes through **Wyoming** *and save some mileage at the same time. From Manila you can follow UT 43 to where it crosses into Wyoming and becomes Wyoming highway 414. That road will take you to I-80 where a westbound drive will quickly bring you to Salt Lake City. This saves about 40 miles over the route within Utah. Or you could proceed north from Manila on Wyoming highway 530 to I-80. While this option only saves you around 20 miles it has the advantage that it continues along the west side of the Wyoming portion of the Flaming Gorge National Recreation area. In other words, the scenery is better.*

THE WAY BACK

Returning to Salt Lake City from the Flaming Gorge area requires quite a bit of doubling back on the same roads unless you want to travel by way of Wyoming. To return within Utah take US 191 and 191/40 until Duchesne. Where the two highways diverge stay on US 40. That will take you all the way back to Salt Lake City.

NIGHTLIFE & ENTERTAINMENT/SHOPPING

We've been going downhill in these categories since leaving Salt Lake City and you'll hit rock bottom now in the northeast. Believe it or not, this isn't meant to be a knock. Quite simply put you don't come to this part of the world to shop or paint the town red. If that's your idea of a vacation, then you should really plan on going elsewhere.

The entertainment category does have some things in Vernal. Shows at the **Outlaw Trail Theater** and the **Dinosaur Roundup Rodeo** were described in the *Seeing the Sights* section. The shopping is limited mainly to a few gift shops although the selection isn't as wide as in the southwest or even the southeast. Again, Vernal has the most. A couple of places you might want to take a look at are the handcrafted items available at the **Simple Treasures Boutique**, *120 E. Main*, and the nearby **Gift Emporium**, *73 W. Main*.

SPORTS & RECREATION

Bicycling

Dinosaur National Monument and the Flaming Gorge National Recreation Area are the most popular areas for biking in the northeast. Nine-Mile Canyon and some of the scenic backways around Vernal are also good choices. For the experienced mountain biker the High Uintas are heaven on earth but due to the altitude and rough terrain it isn't recommended for the novice.

Dinosaur Expeditions, *540 E. Main, Vernal, Tel. 800/247-6197* offers guided bicycle trips through Dinosaur Country. Rentals are available from **Altitude Cycle**, *510 E. Main, Vernal, Tel. 435/781-2595*.

Boating

The Flaming Gorge National Recreation Area is the primary venue for boating of all types in the northeast although some of the larger mountain lakes are also possibilities. The two largest marinas in the former are the **Cedar Springs Marina** in Dutch John and the **Lucerne Valley Marina** in Manila.

Additional boating opportunities are as follows:
• **Big Sand Lake State Park**, *14 miles northeast of Duchesne*
• **Red Fleet State Park**, *10 miles north of Vernal*

• **Starvation State Park**, *Duchesne*
• **Steinaker State Park**, *Vernal*

Fishing

The state parks listed above under boating also provide some of Utah's best fishing. The mountain streams of the High Uintas are also excellent places for fishing. The Ashley National Forest includes much of the latter. The Flaming Gorge National Recreation Area has no fewer than 15 different locations for fishing. Inquire at any Recreation Area visitor center for further information.

Some of the fishing outfitters in the northeast are:
• **Altamount Flyfishers**, *Altamont. Tel. 435/454-3737*
• **Conquest Expeditions**, *Manila. Tel. 435/784-3370*
• **Flaming Gorge Lodge Guide Service**, *Dutch John. Tel. 435/889-3773*
• **Triangle G Fishing Service**, *Manila. Tel. 435/784-3265*
• **Trout Creek Flies**, *Dutch John. Tel. 435/889-3735*
• **Willow Springs Outfitters**, *Manila. Tel. 435/784-3481*

Golf

• **Carbon Country Club**, *US Highway 6 between Price & Helper. Tel. 435/637-2388.* 18 holes.
• **Dinaland Golf Course**, *675 S. 2000 East, Vernal. Tel. 435/781-1428.* 18 holes.
• **Roosevelt Golf Course**, *1155 Clubhouse Drive, Roosevelt. Tel. 435/722-9644.* 18 holes.

Hiking & Backpacking

For many hikers in Utah the Uinta Mountains are the premier location to hike. Although the scenery may not be as unusual as in the southern part of the state, it's still quite beautiful and the temperatures are considerably milder. Uinta Canyon, Lake Fork, Swift Creek, and West and East Granddaddy Lakes are popular hiking areas. Trail maps are available in Duchesne and Roosevelt. Trail lengths range from a few miles to adventures requiring several days. The **High Line Trail** runs through the middle of the High Uintas Wilderness and connects with dozens of other trails that cross the region.

Dinosaur National Monument and the Flaming Gorge National Recreation Area both provide excellent hiking opportunities as well. Maps are available at the Visitor Centers of each facility.

Horseback Riding

Once again the High Uintas are the northeast's leader in recreational pursuits. There are many trails suited to horseback riders of all levels

throughout the Ashley National Forest. Some horseback riding can also be done in the Flaming Gorge National Recreation Area. Following is a list of some trail outfitters and places where you can rent horses.
• **Cassidy Trails,** *Jensen.* Tel. *800/230-4868.* Trail rides.
• **Piute Creek Outfitters**, *Marion.* Tel. *800/225-0218.* Trail rides and overnight trips.
• **Red Canyon Lodge**, *Manila.* Tel. *435/889-3759.* Trail rides and rentals.

Hunting
The High Uintas and the Ashley National Forest are probably the best hunting areas in all of Utah. Both small and big game can be found. The communities of Duchesne, Roosevelt and Altamount are the main gateways. Private hunting preserves (membership required but can be arranged on a temporary basis) are a good way to go. Among the better known preserves are the **Ouray Valley Hunting Preserve**, *Randlett*, Tel. *435/722-2009;* and the **Pleasant Valley Hunting Preserve**, *Myton, Tel. 435/646-3194.*

There are also numerous hunting outfitters. A partial list follows:
• **Cassidy Trails**, *Jensen.* Tel. *800/230-HUNT*
• **JL Ranch Outfitters & Guides**, *Whiterocks.* Tel. *435/353-4049*
• **Rocky Meadows Adventures**, *Bluebell.* Tel. *435/454-3176*
• **Uinta Range Guide Service**, *Roosevelt.* Tel. *435/722-2225*

A final way to do some hunting in the northeast is to stay at one of several guest ranches that have guided services as part of their daily routine. See the final chapter for further information.

Off Road, ATV's & Four Wheel Drive Vehicles
The Ashley National Forest and Uinta Mountains have many areas suitable for off-roading. Access to the best areas is via UT 87 and Forest Road 119 from Roosevelt. Nine Mile Canyon in the southern part of the region also has some excellent routes for both four-wheel and all terrain vehicles.

Rafting
• **Adrift Adventures Dinosaur,** *Jensen.* Tel. *800/824-0150.* One day on the Green River through Split Mountain Gorge or 2-5 day wilderness white water adventures on the Green and Yampa Rivers.
• **Hatch river Expeditions**, *Vernal.* Tel. *800/342-8243.* One to six days in length on the Green and Yampa Rivers.

Swimming

Mustang Ridge and **Lucerne Valley**, both in the Flaming Gorge National Recreation Area, are the most popular swimming holes in the region. Red Fleet, Starvation and Steinaker State Parks also have swimming, as do several areas in the Ashley National Forest. For the latter you should make inquiry with the National Forest area offices in Roosevelt, *Tel. 435/722-5018,* or Duchesne, *Tel. 435/738-2482.*

PRACTICAL INFORMATION

Bus Depot
    Duchesne, *432 West Main, Tel. 435/738-5961*
    Price, *277 N. Carbonville Road, Tel. 435/637-3457*
    Roosevelt, *23 S. 200 East, Tel. 435/789-0404*

Hospital
    Roosevelt: *Duchesne County Hospital, 250 W. 300 North, Tel. 435/722-4691*
    Vernal: *Ashley Valley Medical Center, 200 West 100 North, Tel. 435/789-3342*

Hotel Hot Line: *none specifically for this region. See the statewide listing under Accommodations in Chapter 6.*

Police (non-emergency)
    Duchesne: *Tel. 435/738-2424*
    Roosevelt: *Tel. 435/722-2210*
    Vernal: *Tel. 435/789-5835*

Tourist Office/Visitors Bureau
    Price: *90 N. 100 East, Tel. 435/637-3009 or 800/842-0789*
    Roosevelt: *48 S. 200 East, Tel. 435/722-4598*
    Vernal: *25 E. Main Street, Tel. 435/789-6932 or 800/477-5558*

15. GUEST RANCH VACATIONS

So you didn't think of Utah when it came to planning a dude ranch vacation? Don't feel bad. Most people, including myself, categorize Utah quite differently from Arizona or Colorado. It's natural to think of it as being different from those "cowboy" states. But the fact is that Utah has a surprisingly large selection of **guest ranches**. Most will allow a stay of a day or two if you don't want a long ranch stay or simply don't have the time.

When planning a guest ranch vacation you have to keep in mind that there are two basic types of ranches. The first type is similar to resorts that are off the beaten track and a whole lot less fancy. The emphasis is on horseback riding and other forms of outdoor recreation. The other type is the working ranch–and those of you who are looking for that real *City Slickers* kind of adventure may be more pleased with the satisfaction that comes with taking part in a real cattle drive or other ranch chores. Either way a ranch vacation can be a great escape all by itself or combined with sightseeing and other more usual travel activities.

Utah's guest ranches are located throughout the state but the largest number of them by far will be found in the remote northeastern mountain area. More important, however, is the nature of these ranches. If I can be permitted to bring up ranches in Arizona and Colorado again for a few moments, you'll learn that Utah's ranches are, more often than not, a whole lot different than their sophisticated neighbors. While the types of accommodations at ranches in the former states can range from simple and rustic to luxury, most are at least on a par with a decent resort. Many of Utah's ranches will be made to sound fancier then they are if you were to refer to them as "rustic." In fact, a lot are about as simple as you can get from an accommodations and dining perspective. This isn't meant to discourage you.

On the contrary, I would have to say that Utah's ranches, basic as they are, are a much truer reflection of what it was like in the "old" days and may well be exactly what you are looking for. The important point is that you should be informed beforehand about what you're getting into. If you have any questions about whether this might be "roughing it" more than you anticipated, call the ranch and ask as many questions as you have–it beats checking in for a week and winding up being miserable.

Another unusual thing about Utah's ranches (at least a significant number of them) is that the price is not all-inclusive. The price for a ranch often includes all meals, riding and other activities. There is little, if any, additional cost. Check the listings below carefully because you will find that not all of them operate this way at all–it's more of an "a la carte" type selection. This, again, isn't necessarily bad. It doesn't mean that you'll be paying more in total. It can actually save you some money since you'll only be paying for the things you want to do. Regardless of whether it's a one-price-for-all scheme or separate fees for different activities, you'll definitely find that the rates for guest ranches in Utah are significantly less than in Colorado or Arizona.

The majority of guest ranches requires a deposit (usually by check) and often insists on cash, travelers check or certified check payment for the remainder of your bill. Some do accept credit cards but it is wise to discuss payment requirements and methods at the time you book your reservation to avoid any problems.

BOULDER MOUNTAIN RANCH, *Hell's Backbone Road, Boulder. Tel. 435/335-7480; Fax 435/335-7480. Rates: vary depending upon nature of experience selected (up to $850 for five days). Located in Salt Gulch, approximately 7 miles east of Boulder via Utah 12 and then 3-1/2 miles north.*

A working cattle ranch set in the midst of a breathtaking and verdant valley close to the famous red rocks of southern Utah, Boulder Mountain offers guests the option to choose between an adventure vacation or a relaxing one. Horseback riding is available for all levels of experience through stunning landscapes. Overnight horseback trips range from two through five days. The latter travels along the Great Western Trail from the ranch all the way to Bryce Canyon and includes outdoor Dutch oven dinners. Visitors to Boulder Mountain can also take part in real cattle drives with rides to different areas each day of your stay.

Among the leisure activities available are hiking and swimming, visits to nearby National Parks and fishing in the ranch's own well stocked creek for trout. Wildlife viewing is also a popular pastime be it by foot or horseback. The ranch also has an exercise room.

Accommodations are varied. The central lodge with its pine log and open beam construction, huge stone fireplace and panoramic views from the wrap around deck is a wonderfully rustic facility that has several rooms. Some have private facilities while others are bunk style. There are also several cabins with private bath and shower. The largest cabin can accommodate up to six people. Guests can also choose to camp out in either tents or their own vans.

CEDAR CANYON GUEST RANCH, *5410 Cedaredge Lane, Blanding. Tel. 435/459-4888. Rates: $65 per person per day plus additional charge for optional dinner. Located about 7 miles north of Blanding via Blue Mountain Road.*

Situated close to some of the ancient Anasazi sites of the southeast, this guest ranch occupies a beautiful stretch of Cedar Canyon surrounded by rocky cliffs and great views of the Blue Mountain and Recapture Reservoir. Horseback riding is the most popular activity but hiking, fishing, wildlife viewing and day trips to some of the surrounding points of interest are also excellent ways to pass the time of day.

Such folksy forms of entertainment as line dancing and western crafts are also offered in addition to a recreation room, croquet and volleyball courts. The Cedar Canyon Guest Ranch has special week-long programs for children where each is matched to an appropriate sized horse, which is then placed in their care for the week under close supervision.

The accommodations at Cedar Canyon are authentic western bunkhouse style (semi-private bathroom facilities only). Food service is similarly western and simple. Evening cookouts with toasted marshmallows from the campfire are a hallmark of any visit to the ranch.

CEDAR TRAIL RANCH, *Route 3, Roosevelt. Tel. 888/852-6706. Rates: From $65 to $250 per day depending upon the type of accommodations. Located on County Route 3 to the north of Roosevelt. Obtain traveling directions at the time you book reservations.*

In a secluded location in the High Uintas, the Cedar Trail Ranch is perfect for those who really want to get away from it all. It's a small ranch in terms of the number of guests that can be accommodated but has plenty of space to wander around. Or you can just relax at the main house where the staff is warm and friendly. Guests have the option of doing their own cooking since all of the units have full cooking facilities or you may choose to have some or all of your meals prepared for you.

In addition to the usual horseback riding there is a swimming pond, canoes for rafting, game lawn, basketball court and room for RV's to be stored (no hook-ups available). A popular optional activity is a covered wagon ride or (when the snowfall is sufficient) a dog sled ride.

LA SAL MOUNTAIN GUEST RANCH, *Highway 46, La Sal. Tel. 435/ 686-2223 or 888/870-1088. Rates: $70 for up to two adults and $20 for each additional adult. All ranch activities are at additional cost. Located approximately 32 miles southeast of Moab via US 191 and then Utah Highway 46.*

Previously the Home Ranch and now under new management, the La Sal Mountain Guest Ranch is in a majestic setting at an altitude of more than 7,000 feet. It is a working cattle ranch and most guests come for that experience. However, guests have the option to do as little or as much as they want during cattle drives or other ranch operations. The ranch provides facilities for croquet, volleyball and horseshoes but many visitors like to take a day or more to explore the surrounding areas including several national parks. Fishing, mountain biking, jeep rides and hiking are all extremely popular and the ranch staff will be happy to help you make arrangements for any or all of them.

The Lodge offers a number of individual guest rooms or you can opt for homes with two, three or four bedrooms including full kitchen. Meal plans are available for those who don't want to cook. Some of the cabin homes date from the 19th century and are filled with authentic antique western furnishings and hand quilted spreads. A couple of rooms in the main house have shared baths but the majority of units have full private facilities. All meals are served in the main house.

NINE MILE RANCH, *Wellington. Tel. 435/637-2572. Rates: $55-70 per night with additional charges for activities. Located in 9 Mile Canyon about 25 miles east of Wellington.*

In scenic Nine Mile Canyon, the ranch offers a variety of activities but horseback riding is the first priority for most guests. Wranglers Don and Jean Gressmen will ensure that all of your needs are attended to regardless of your previous riding skills. Horseback rides range from under an hour to half-day, full day or overnight trips. There are also two-hour lessons on working with horses. (Prices for horseback riding range from $5 to $100 depending upon the length).

Room accommodation rates include breakfast but Dutch oven dinners can also be arranged. Among the facilities at Nine Mile Ranch are camping, a country store with snacks and gifts, picnic park pavilion, hayrides, hiking and mountain biking. Guided tours of the ancient Indian writings found in the canyon can also be arranged either in your own car or one supplied by the ranch. Guest cabins are one of three styles–Cowboy, Victorian or Indian. All are attractive in a rustic sort of way. There are also family room facilities.

ROCK CREEK RANCH, *Mountain Home. Tel. 435/454-3332. Rates: $49-79 plus extra charge for most activities. Located approximately 22 miles from Mountain Home via a paved road into the High Uintah Primitive Area.*

As soon as you reach the tree lined entrance to the Rock Creek Ranch with its old time hanging sign you'll realize that you're in a very special place. Amid the majestic mountains and unspoiled surroundings of the Uintah wilderness, the Rock Creek Ranch offers a getaway where you can go horseback riding, fly fish in crystal clear creeks or even go big game hunting. While families are welcome the nature of the activities at Rock Creek is probably better for grown-ups than at some of the previous listings. The lodge is nestled in a grove of lodgepole pine and is about as secluded as you can get. The accommodations are "frontier" style, consisting of authentic rustic cabins. The main lodge building is where you'll be served home cooked-meals or stop in for a refreshing ice cream cone.

The three main activities at Rock Creek are fishing, horseback riding and hunting. As far as the latter is concerned you're in good hands with the Rock Creek Ranch Guide Service. Pack-trips can be arranged. The United States Forest Service allows the Ranch to operate in wilderness areas under a special use permit.

U-BAR WILDERNESS RANCH, *Little Park. Tel. 435/645-7256 (Park City office) or 800/303-7256 within Utah. Rates: $64-109 per day for cabin accommodations; additional charges for meal and activity plans. Located literally at the end of the road that leads north from Roosevelt through Neola on the Ute Indian Reservation.*

Like the preceding facility, the U-Bar Ranch has a special permit from the Forest Service to conduct hunting and exploratory pack trips into the High Uinta Wilderness, an area of almost a half million acres that includes Utah's highest mountain peak and is one of the most significant wilderness regions in the country. Elk, black bear and moose are the most commonly found big game and cutthroat trout is the most popular fish for anglers to seek out. The U-Bar, however, is far more than just hunting and fishing, although it was originally established as a fishing ranch way back in 1933. All of the ranch vacation options are available, including horseback trips.

The accommodations are all cabins ranging from those with a double bed to two double beds and all the way up to the largest cabin, which can sleep as many as ten people. They're quite rustic and on the simple side. Bath facilities are shared. The rates indicated above can be discounted ten percent for those who stay four nights or longer. All meals are served family style. Adult prices range from $8 for breakfast or lunch only to $14 for dinner and $25 for all three meals.

INDEX